THE ORDER OF TERROR

Wolfgang Sofsky

THE ORDER OF TERROR: THE CONCENTRATION CAMP

Translated by William Templer

PRINCETON UNIVERSITY PRESS   PRINCETON, NEW JERSEY

Library of Congress Cataloging-in-Publication Data

Sofsky, Wolfgang.
[Ordnung des Terrors. English.]
The order of terror : The concentration camp / Wolfgang Sofsky :
translated by William Templer.
p.   cm.
Includes bibliographical references.
ISBN 0-691-04354-X (cl : alk. paper)
1. Concentration camps—Germany—History.   2. World War, 1939–
1945—Concentration camps—Germany.   3. Concentration camps—
Psychological aspects.   4. Nationalsozialistische Deutsche Arbeiter–Partei.
Schutzstaffel—History.   I. Title.
DD256.5.S5813   1996
940.54′7243—dc20   96-19212 CIP

The publication of this work has been subsidized by Inter Nationes, Bonn

This book has been composed in Times Roman

Princeton University Press books are printed on acid-free paper and meet
the guidelines for permanence and durability of the Committee on Production
Guidelines for Book Longevity of the Council on Library Resources

Printed in the United States of America

10 9 8 7 6 5 4 3 2 1

It happened,
therefore it can happen again. . . .
It can happen everywhere.
(Primo Levi, *The Drowned and the Saved*)

Contents

Tables and Figures _____

Tables

Figures

Acknowledgments

I WISH TO THANK the many friends, colleagues, and students with whom I have had the opportunity over a number of years to discuss the problems treated here. Their stimulating comments and probing questions have contributed to the sharpening of my thinking on these topics. In particular, I owe a debt of gratitude to Horst Kern, Walter Euchner, Iring Fetscher, Hans Joas, and Bernd Weisbrod for their detailed remarks and critical suggestions. Rainer W. Hoffmann read an earlier version and made helpful comments and suggestions. Michael R. Heydenburg's remarks contained many valuable pointers. Martin Kronauer, Michael Neumann, and Rainer Paris followed the progress of my work on the manuscript with friendly interest and, in numerous fruitful discussions, helped me overcome various obstacles. Fred Lönker was, as always, a trusted companion and an attentive reader.

I would like to extend special thanks to the Department of Sociology at Göttingen University for generously allowing me ample time to do research and complete the manuscript. The study was accepted by the Division of Social Sciences at Göttingen University as a habilitation thesis in the spring of 1992, and was slightly altered for publication in its German original edition by S. Fischer Verlag in 1993.

The English-language edition is a faithful rendering of the German original and contains some added bibliographical references and minor changes. I am very grateful to William Templer for his accurate and insightful translation, and for preparing the glossary.

Part I

INTRODUCTION

1

Entry

MARCH 22, 1933. The first prisoners arrive in Dachau.[1] The abandoned powder factory looks dreary and depressing: more than twenty flat stone buildings, half-dilapidated, dot the grounds. The only structure that appears usable is the former administration building. It has just been fenced in with a triple barrier of barbed wire. Down in the basement, the police officers, newly arrived for work the evening before, prepare a list, recording the names of the inmates. There is no set uniform for the prisoners. The procedure is orderly: no hitches, no shouting, no one is mistreated. No one thinks of shaving the heads of the newcomers. That evening, the first meal is distributed: tea, bread, a chunk of liverwurst for every inmate. In the rush of the moment, that is all the food that can be put together. Afterward, the prisoners are led upstairs to makeshift sleeping quarters on the first floor. Because there are no cots and there is no straw, they have to bed down on the concrete floor. The thin blanket each prisoner is given from police stocks is meager protection against the cold.

The next day, the prisoners search through the empty buildings and factory halls, rummaging for material. From scattered boards they piece together the first beds. A joiner is given permission to set up a workshop. The inmates fend for themselves; they make do. No one is forced to work against his or her will. But there are few tools, and there is not enough barbed wire to close off the grounds. The hoes and spades that are gradually amassed are kept in a storeroom administered by an inmate together with a camp official. Surveillance is correct and proper. Guards and prisoners converse; they even discuss the political situation. Some inmates are slipped cigarettes on the sly; rations are adequate and tasty. Prisoners get the same meals as the security personnel.

But this lasts only for a few days. One night, the sleeping inmates are awakened by the thud of marching feet, the clang of weapons. An SS unit, militiamen in brown shirts and black caps, has formed up in front of the administration building. Its commander gives the men a pep talk that terrifies the prisoners:

> Comrades of the SS! You all know what the Führer has called upon us to do. We haven't come here to treat those swine inside like human beings. In our eyes, they're not like us, they're something second-class. For years, they've been able to pursue their criminal devices. But now we've got the power. If these swine had taken over,

they'd have made sure our heads rolled in the dust. So we too know no sentimentality. Any man in our ranks who can't stand the sight of blood doesn't belong here, he should get out. The more of these bastards we shoot, the fewer we'll have to feed.[2]

Twelve years later, on the afternoon of April 29, 1945, three jeeps of the Forty-second Rainbow Division, United States Army, roll through the southern entrance into the camp enclosure. In order to open the gate to the prisoners' barracks, a soldier must shove aside the body of a prisoner who was shot the night before in an attempt to get out to meet the Americans. The rattle of machine-gun fire sounds from the watchtowers. On the north side of the camp, a Forty-fifth Infantry Division patrol is still locked in battle with the last of the SS. But the huge expanse of the *Appellplatz* (roll-call square), the camp yard, stands empty. The main street of the camp is also deserted. Among the soldiers is a journalist, Marguerite Higgins. Her report appears a few days later in the *New York Herald Tribune*:

> But the minute the two of us entered, a jangled barrage of "Are you Americans?" in about sixteen languages came from the barracks 200 yards from the gate. An affirmative nod caused pandemonium.
>
> Tattered, emaciated men, weeping, yelling and shouting "Long live America!" swept toward the gate in a mob. Those who could not walk limped or crawled. . . . I happened to be the first through the gate, and the first person to rush up to me turned out to be a Polish Catholic priest, a deputy of August Cardinal Hlond, Primate of Poland, who was not a little startled to discover that the helmeted, uniformed, begoggled individual he had so heartily embraced was not a man. In the excitement, which was not the least dampened by the German artillery and the sounds of battle in the northern part of the camp, some of the prisoners died trying to pass through the electrically charged barbed wire. Some who got out after the wires were decharged joined in the battle, when some ill-advised S.S. men holding out in a tower fired upon them. The prisoners charged toward the tower and threw all six S.S. men out the window. After an hour and a half of cheering, the crowd, which would virtually mob each soldier that dared to venture into the excited milling group, was calmed down enough to make possible a tour of the camp.
>
> The barracks at Dachau, like those at Buchenwald, had the stench of death and sickness. But at Dachau there were six barracks like the infamous No. 61 at Buchenwald, where the starving and dying lay virtually on top of each other in quarters where 1200 men occupied a space intended for 200. The dead—400 died of sickness yesterday—lay on concrete walks outside the quarters and others were being carried out as the reporters went through.
>
> The mark of starvation was on all the emaciated corpses. Many of the living were so frail it seemed impossible they could still be holding on to life. The crematorium and torture chambers lay outside the prisoner inclosures. Situated in a wood close by was a new building that had been built by prisoners under Nazi guards. Inside, in the two rooms used as torture chambers, an estimated 1,200 bodies were piled. In the

crematorium itself were hooks on which the S.S. men hung their victims when they wished to flog them or to use any of the other torture instruments. Symbolic of the S.S. was a mural the S.S. men themselves had painted on the wall. It showed a headless man in uniform with the S.S. insigne on the collar. The man was astride a huge inflated pig into which he was digging his spurs. . . . Below the camp were cattle cars in which prisoners from Buchenwald had been transported to Dachau. Hundreds of dead were still in the cars due to the fact that prisoners in the camp had rejected S.S. orders to remove them. It was mainly the men from these cattle cars that the S.S. leaders had shot before making their escape. Among those who had been left for dead in the cattle cars was one man still alive who managed to lift himself from the heap of corpses on which he lay.[3]

The liberators found thirty-three thousand inmates still alive in Dachau—a third of them Polish, thousands of them Russian, French, Yugoslav, Italian. Prisoners from thirty-four nations, and about a thousand Germans. In their zebra-striped rags, the survivors looked like creatures from another planet. Liberation had arrived, yet the dying was far from over. During the following month, another 2,226 inmates would perish from exhaustion or typhoid fever. Civilians would loot the nearby SS supply depot, oblivious to the procession of death nearby. Children on bicycles would ride past the corpses, their handlebars slung with clothing picked up along the way.

It began as terror against political adversaries, and it ended with the death of millions. In the beginning, vengeance raged: the lust for revenge of a regime that had just gained power, bent on suppressing any who had stood in its way. But after its opponents had been eliminated, a new species of absolute power was unleashed that shattered all previous conceptions of despotism or dictatorial brutality: systematic destruction by means of violence, starvation, and labor—the businesslike annihilation of human beings. In the span of twelve years, the concentration camp metamorphosed from a locus of terror into a universe of horror.

Some survivors reported on the camps and their ordeal immediately after liberation, others only after decades had elapsed. The justice authorities amassed a large corpus of documents, affidavits, and testimony. But trials were late in coming and few in number. Some of the verdicts smack of astounding leniency, although they also attest to the discomfort felt by the judges, their perplexity in applying juridical norms to the exceptional "emergency" conditions of the camps. Educators, officially charged with the task of "mastering the past," have tried laboriously to impart a kind of historical conscience to the generations born later—as if the mass death were a morality play from which coming generations might learn a lesson. Historiographers have been able to establish sequences of events and interconnections, and have documented the history of several camps. In recent years, younger researchers in local history have been combing the archives, collecting oral testimony from witnesses of the time, and unearthing evidence of the many unknown camps that existed back then in the neighborhoods—just around the corner, across the street or down the block. Yet although numerous facts are now familiar, our understanding lags behind. The reality of the camps appears to burst the bounds of imagination, the precincts of conceivability. It still triggers diverse forms of defense meant to exculpate conscience, to extinguish memory.

When it comes to defensive maneuvers, people are far from finicky. The spectrum ranges from bald denial of the camps to comparisons that downplay their gravity to intellectually more subtle techniques of reinterpretation and rationalization. Much energy is expended on defensive parrying; the snarl of diverse methods employed is often difficult to disentangle. Thus, the very existence of the death camps is still categorically denied by some. Then there is "everyday revisionism," a grim accountancy that tallies up a balance sheet of atrocities: Auschwitz set against Dresden, Dachau weighed against Katyn or the "special camps" of the Soviet occupiers, genocide on one side of the scales and the expulsion of the German population on the other—the obscene numbers game of a fallacious arithmetic that seeks to defuse the past, to dispose of it by balancing the ledger. There are those who claim they knew nothing, although the regime had instrumentalized the concentration camps, using them to intimidate the German people. Many who fervidly celebrated the regime looked idly on as their neighbors suddenly vanished. When a column of prisoners was marched through town, onlookers stood watching—indifferent, maybe frightened, perhaps even gloating. This gives rise to a double denial: a disavowal today of what the watchers had even then already refused to acknowledge.

When that method fails, people take refuge in euphemism. Many Germans (and not only Germans) are quite willing to incorporate the title of an American television series into their vocabulary in order to be able to delete the term "genocide." In the meanwhile, the word "holocaust" has been drained of meaning, reduced to a token that permits rapid concord, sparing one the need to confront the facts. In the language of the Hebrew psalms, however, "holocaust" signifies a "complete burnt offering."[4] It designates the ritual martyrdom that Jews took upon themselves because they refused to renounce their faith. The expression thus forges a link, totally inadmissible, between the genocidal murder of the Jews and the fate of Jewish martyrs, although the Jews were not murdered because they had refused to renounce their religious convictions, but simply because they were Jews. By distortion of the term's core meaning, the impression is generated that the mass murder of the Jews had some deeper religious import—as if the victims had, in a sense, offered themselves up for the slaughter.

Another example of such discursive disburdenment is the redesignation of the numerous concentration camps that existed on German soil, the external work Kommandos (*Außenkommandos*) of the main camps. The list of such camps reads like a directory of Central European place-names. Yet abruptly, conveniently, they have been retermed "work camps" (*Arbeitslager*) or "external stations" (*Außenstationen*). These concentration camps were located right next door, along busy transportation arteries, in the nearby municipal forest preserves, in requisitioned school buildings, or on the grounds of private firms. Now that regional researchers, often underfunded, have uncovered evidence of many a forgotten local camp, concerned city fathers want to have the public believe that these camps were not such a terrible thing after all. A truly fastidious distinction is made between the supposedly innocuous "work camps" inside Germany and the "death camps" (*Todeslager*) in the distant East—a basic difference that no one had contested. Yet talk of such "work camps" masks the truth: that labor itself also led to death; that the exhausted and emaciated inmates who toiled in such camps were removed and sent back to die in a main camp or a so-called *Sterbelager* ("camp for dying"); that there were gas chambers in Germany as well. Such discursive maneuvering attempts to block out the crimes from the field of vision; it tries to exterritorialize their reality.

It is merely the other side of the coin when public discourse turns evasive and noncommittal, such as in the clichés of hollow Sunday speeches, droning on about tragic guilt and entanglement, forgiveness and reconciliation—though nothing can actually be reconciled. We perpetrators, children and grandchildren of perpetrators, we do not bear any grudge against the victims. . . . Some invoke the notion of incomprehensible forces of fate that swept over the Germans, speaking of crimes committed "in the name of Germany"—as though there were no flesh-and-blood culprits, no oppressors who could be searched out, found, and arrested. Others speak about "crimes against humanity," as if the tormenters' only failing was their lack of humanity. There is a veritable inflationary boom in the spread of expressions such as the "unjust regime," "contempt for the human being," the acceptance of "full responsibility"—again, as if all the regime had done was to treat people with "contempt." As though someone could assume "full responsibility" for the consequences of mass murder. . . . The ideology of disburdenment, of "safe disposal" (*Entsorgung*), has penetrated public discourse, leeching the lexicon. It diminishes the significance of facts and takes flight into sanctimonious moralizing, although no form of traditional religious or political morality can adequately grapple with the enormity of the atrocity.

If discursive obfuscation does not achieve the desired effect, defensive maneuvering changes to defiance and self-pity: we have made enough amends, given enough compensation; we have paid our debts, our dues. Depending on the political climate, there are also official statements asserting that the whole matter is finally finished and laid to rest; a new national consciousness is proclaimed. There is the pious claim that necessary lessons have been learned from history. But the very choice of words proves the opposite. Shame gives rise to rage, and that rage is turned against the victims. Now it is the perpetrators and the generations of their innocent descendants who supposedly suffer under the barrage of accusations from the victims. Conversely, the critical opposition is preoccupied with scrupulously avoiding any charge of collective guilt. This is not a question of some banal confusion between collective guilt and historical responsibility for the consequences of actions. Naturally, not all Germans were criminals or trusting supporters of the regime. Yet neither were they the helpless victims of some mode of satanic seduction. They were not guileless, unsuspecting children who had no idea of what was happening. Just as there is no collective guilt, there can be no collective innocence. Admittedly, knowledge of events was less widespread than the victors assumed. But it was far more pervasive than many Germans were willing to admit. The active accomplices numbered in the tens of thousands, the accessories in the millions. Complaints about repression and the call to confront and "work through the past" have long since become hackneyed. Experience suggests that one cannot seriously expect Germans now to have feelings of shame, or any insight into the connections among commission, omission, and toleration.

The patterns of defense are replayed in curious variations within the discourse of the scholarly community. The crude balance sheet commonly tallied up at the local bar, evil against evil, is replaced by questionable comparisons and abstruse causal chains meant to relativize the extent of the German crimes. Critical discourse all too quickly seeks to evade the issue by detouring to weighty questions in the history of philosophy or social theory. Why waste effort analyzing the realities of camp existence? Instead, scholars dwell on the typological features of fascism, thus avoiding the essence of the Nazi regime: organized terror and genocide. All too quickly, researchers turn to the question of *how* all this could have happened, without having tried to comprehend in detail *what* in fact occurred. Such tactics of evasion are convenient: they let you tarry in the antechamber of the problem. In another approach, analytical interest is focused on the presumed authoritarian dispositions and biases of the culprits—a perspective that is scandalous in the way it downplays the importance of social factors, affording no insight into the processes of violence and organized terror. One can thus skirt the unpleasant truths that humans can be cruel without feeling resentment, and that to reduce prejudice is not to guarantee that it will never arise again.

But can the concentration camp—where power, bureaucratized, was organized in its most extreme form—ever be made comprehensible through scientific methods? Can it ever be described and grasped in this way? In order for us to enter into sociological analysis, several preliminary observations seem unavoidable. Any attempt to engage in a theoretically guided investigation runs up against two reservations: the topos of the basic incomprehensibility of the camps and the notion of singularity, the incomparability of that welter of crimes subsumed under the name of Auschwitz. Both theses are familiar in political debates; their defensive function remains transparent. They serve to justify a barrier erected to block perception: if something is labeled incomprehensible, one can avoid having to perceive its horror in all its details. Yet such remarks take on a different weight if they come from survivors. They warn the generations born later to be vigilant: they should not thoughtlessly equate the suffering and dying of the victims with familiar conceptions. This counsel is admonitory, not a defensive ploy.

If the caveat of incomprehensibility is interpreted in a theoretical sense, then any cultural science seeking to understand what is alien or unique would be destined to fail right from the start. Counterposed to this is the epistemic axiom that all human action and suffering are in principle interpretable, although understanding the "other" may be more difficult in some cases than in others. Since the camps were a product of human action, they are amenable to analysis and rational comprehension. This does not imply that events and their consequences can be easily traced back to the motives, intentions, or decisions of individual culprits. Once the camps were established, a configuration of power evolved whose dynamic was neither planned nor predictable. The present study attempts to reconstruct the practices, structures, and processes of this power. It does not seek to discover any historical meaning in the events, and it refrains from philosophical speculations. Instead, the camp is examined as a specific form of society, albeit one lying at the margins of sociality. Part of the essence of absolute power is that it shifts arbitrarily between sociation and dissociation, between the total formation (*Formierung*) and complete dissolution of society. This sociological approach has as little in common with psychological empathy as it does with the narrating of a story or the construction of historical finality.[5] Analysis focuses on the typology of social (con)figurations and processes. Herein lies its limit, and its opportunity.

However, the topos of incomprehensibility has, first and foremost, a moral meaning. Manifestly, the customary moral criteria geared to the actions of individuals break down in the face of collective crime. In describing such crime in terms of responsibility or "criminal energy," individual psychopathology or ideological blindness necessarily leads to a banalization of the concrete deeds. There is an unbridgeable gap between the perpetrators and their actions. The organized crime was monstrous—not the perpetrators. Yet this should not mislead the analyst into orienting the investigation toward the genesis of political and macrosocial structures. The alternative to criminology or psychology is not a general theory of society. Between the two poles lies the true and distinctive field for the analysis of power: the organization of the camp, and the situated actions and suffering within it.

Just as the interpretive recourse to individual intentions and plans is blinkered and inadequate, little light is shed by the functional perspective: it degrades the perpetrators, debasing them into the attendants of a terror machine running seemingly by itself. The camp system functioned because the murderers actually took on their roles; they were only too willing to carry out the work of terror. They exploited the opportunities offered by the absolute power to kill, and expanded its scope.[6] Social relations exist only in the regular behavior of individuals interacting, organizations only in the actions of their personnel. Collective crimes, in the final analysis, are individual crimes in a collective.[7] The tactic of emphasizing historical constellations and social functions is misconceived. It misses what is precisely the distinctive feature of the concentration camp: absolute power that has broken free, fundamentally and totally, from the familiar forms of social power. Functional analysis aspires to grasp only the external history of the system; the explorations here begin their probe one stage deeper. They do not examine social history, but focus on relations within the camps and on the situations of absolute power.

The topos of incomprehensibility takes on greater importance insofar as it relates to the experience of the victims, their burden of suffering and death. Eli Wiesel describes the burden thus:

> Those who have not lived through the experience will never know; those who have will never tell; not really, but completely. The past belongs to the dead, and the survivor does not recognize himself in the images and ideas which presumably depict him. Auschwitz means death, total absolute death—of man and of all people, of language and imagination, of time and spirit. . . . The survivor knows. He and no one else. And so he is obsessed by guilt and helplessness. . . . At first the testimony of survivors inspired awe and humility. At first, the question was treated with a sort of sacred reverence. It was considered taboo, reserved exclusively for the initiated. But popularization and exploitation soon followed. . . . As the subject became popularized, so it ceased to be sacrosanct, or rather was stripped of its misery. People lost their awe. The Holocaust became a literary "free for all," the no-man's land for modern writing. Now everyone got into the act. Novelists made free use of it in their work, scholars used it to prove their theories.[8]

What Wiesel describes is the banalization of this catastrophe in human history, the disenchantment of a taboo, a sacrilege. Modern science has always tried to contribute to the disenchantment of the world, its *Entzauberung*. The illumination of mysteries is part of its fundamental agenda. Certainly, a sociological study can contribute little to an appropriate manner of remembrance (if there is any such "proper" mode). Nor can one expect it to provide any "ultimate" reasons. The camp is quite unsuitable as an experimental arena for testing sociological hypotheses. On the contrary: the concentration camp demolished the central concepts of civilization, the ideals of reason, progress, freedom, and understanding. It also made obsolete the very concepts with which we attempt to render society intelligible: social action and reciprocity, work and power. The ideal of an abiding society, which is covertly intrinsic to both everyday thought and sociological reasoning, has been shattered, its foundations razed.

The question of the singularity of the German crimes has recently emerged as a hotly debated political issue, although there has been no painstaking analysis of the nexus between moral significance and historical uniqueness. This is not the place to review the arguments in that debate.[9] Yet one cannot help noticing a certain reciprocity in the claims and countercharges. To be too quick to compare Auschwitz with other atrocities—the British concentration camps during the Boer War, the genocide in Armenia at the hands of the Turks, the atrocities in Uganda and Cambodia, Vorkuta and Kolyma—is to open oneself up to the suspicion of revisionism decked out in the trappings of science. Such revisionism not only wishes to exculpate, but presumably also violates elementary rules of historical comparison. On the other hand, those who insist on the singularity of Auschwitz can be suspected of wishing to diminish the importance of those other crimes, of not wanting to perceive them in their full and atrocious magnitude. The very act of comparison is regarded as necessary for one's moral and political integrity.

Yet to call an event "incomparable" presupposes that one has already compared it with other events and come to the conclusion that it is radically different. It is only proper to assert incomparability after it has been established by comparison.[10] However, comparisons are totally ill suited as a means for exculpation. In moral judgment, there is no moral arithmetic, no tu quoque. Murderers who justify their actions by arguing that there are other murderers do nothing to lessen their responsibility. Even if one can see structural similarities among German, Soviet, and Chinese camps—a comparison both meaningful and necessary[11]—this does not change the moral facts one iota. The crime remains the same. Injustice can only be judged from within itself; it cannot be lessened or mitigated by comparison.[12] The Germans and their accomplices cannot be exonerated of their guilt for Auschwitz.

For the most part, the present analysis does not engage in synchronic and diachronic comparisons. It does not aim at general validity, but tries to achieve interpretive depth. Nonetheless, an investigation that attempts to ascertain the typical structures of absolute power can contribute to further analyses of organized terror on a comparative basis. It provides serviceable analytical categories for making valid comparisons. Yet what was singular about the camps can certainly be spelled out here in advance. The mass murder and massacre of strangers, social outsiders, political adversaries, enemies in war, and ethnic minorities have been recurrent features throughout human history. But the concentration camp—the locus of organized terror and extermination—is an invention of the twentieth century. In its organizational structures and methods, in the indiscriminate selection of its victims and their destruction by starvation and work, it is not a German specialty.[13] What remains historically unique and unparalleled is the state-initiated and industrially organized mass annihilation of Jews and Gypsies by the Germans. The *unicum* lies less in the procedures of murder practiced than in genocide having been carried out with the aid of an experienced bureaucratic administration, a civil service for extermination. The setting up of death factories, to which an entire people, from infants to the aged, was transported over thousands of kilometers to be obliterated without a trace and "exploited as raw material" was not just a new mode of murder; it represented a climactic high point in the negative history of social power and modern organization.

Fundamental to any sociological analysis is the distinction between the concentration camps and the extermination camps. Like the "euthanasia institutions" in the Reich, the "death factories" of Chelmno, Belzec, Sobibór, and Treblinka were not concentration camps. Bureaucratically, they constituted separate facilities. Their sole purpose was the destruction of the Jews. The SS kept only as many alive there as were necessary for the smooth functioning of the machinery of death. All others were shot at mass graves immediately after arrival, or lured into the gas chambers. Here, there was no inmate society that persisted over a certain time. The few work squads that existed can only be compared with the *Sonderkommandos* (special units of corpse workers), whose job was to keep the death factories in Auschwitz running. By contrast, in the concentration camps inmates were registered by name, given numbers, assigned quarters, and usually deployed as laborers. They were almost totally isolated from the outside world, compelled to eke out an existence bereft of all rights, living in extreme misery and deprivation. Hundreds of thousands were killed in every manner imaginable: by shooting, gassing, torture, starvation, or work. Auschwitz and Majdanek occupied a kind of intermediary position within the spectrum of terror in that they were simultaneously concentration and extermination camps. The "selection" at the ramp in Auschwitz was the historical hinge where the genocide of the Jews was linked with the organization of the concentration camps. In contrast with the death factories, which were kept strictly secret, the concentration camps were multifunctional facilities. They served as places for incarceration, production, and execution, as training centers for the SS Death's Head units (*Totenkopfverbände*), and as instruments of social terror.

The concentration camps formed only a subsegment within the National Socialist camp system. Based on figures ascertained to date, there were fifty-nine early concentration camps; during the war, there were twenty-three main camps (*Stammlager*), along with about thirteen hundred subcamps of differing size. In addition, the SS and other Nazi authorities set up many other camps and camplike incarceration facilities: thousands of camps for foreign forced laborers, "labor-education camps" (*Arbeitserziehungslager*), camps for criminal prisoners, POWs, and civilians, camps for adults and for children. There were "transit camps" (*Durchgangslager*) and "collection camps" (*Sammel-*

lager), some five hundred forced ghettos, and more than nine hundred forced-labor camps for Jews in occupied Eastern Europe.[14] The establishment of camps in which inmates were deprived of their liberty, compelled to work at slave labor, and subjected to arbitrary terror was central to the National Socialist apparatus of power.[15] The concentration camps lay at the very center of this network of terror.

The present study does not investigate the social history of the German concentration camp system and of the murder of the Jews.[16] Rather, it analyzes the concentration camp as a distinctive system of power. It proceeds from the thesis that in the camps, a social form of power crystallized that was essentially different from the familiar types of power and domination. Absolute power should not be confused either with asymmetrical relations of exchange or with punitive power. Nor should it be confused with modern disciplinary power or with relations of domination founded on obedience. It is not based on exploitation, sanction, or legitimacy, but rather on terror, organization, and excessive violence. The focus of the following study is on the processes typical of this power, the structuring of space, time, and sociality in the camps, and the excessive and organized intensification of the power to kill.

How can we grasp the way this power functioned? How can it be described? If one focuses on the functional change the camps underwent, it is impossible to move beyond an external view. As important as social history may be for the question of why the camps were originally set up, it is of little use for the analysis of this system of power. That approach adds little or nothing to our knowledge about the structures of absolute power and their effects on the microcosm of everyday life in the camps. By contrast, if one foregrounds the psychology of the perpetrators and their victims, social reality is reduced to the motivations and experiences of the individuals involved. The processes of sociation and dissociation, organization and violence, are thus overlooked.[17] In order to penetrate to an internal view of the *univers concentrationnaire*, the present study adheres to three general rules:

1. The social reality of the camp cannot be equated with the aims and objectives planned (or proclaimed) by the top organizational echelon of the SS. The camp system was a focus of differing (and at times opposed) interests, an object for dispute and negotiation, a bone of contention between numerous offices and agencies. As in any social system, organization here was not a means to an end, but a dynamic field of action.[18] The self-preservation of the system, the processes of power and terror, often had little if anything to do with the plans of the terror managers. To speculate about a teleological explanation is to confuse the intentions of a group with the structures that crystallize in a social field. The social world of the camp was not a rational system with an unambiguous, purposeful orientation. Rather, its everyday round was shaped by dependencies and antagonisms among beneficiaries, personnel, auxiliaries, and victims. Consequently, any analysis of this configuration of power must

try methodologically to achieve a double perspective, in order to capture both the strategies of power and the reactions and powerlessness of the victims.

2. Within society, the concentration camp was a closed universe. Nowhere is the theory of the closed social system more pertinent than in the case of the concentration camp. Its boundaries could not be crossed; its inmates were isolated and locked into a world of terror in which the camp personnel enjoyed a free hand. It is true that the camp was integrated into a mesh of administrative offices and economic beneficiaries. Its internal social structure was linked to stereotypes found in the surrounding social milieu. The camp system was unable to stand free of the turbulence of the historical events raging beyond its precincts. But these apertures in the system remained radically limited. They involved only the organizational structure and spatial distribution of the camps, the mobility of the transports, and limited, functional changes in labor-deployment practices. For the inmates, there was only one direction. After the initial phase in which the camp system was consolidated, no one, aside from a few escapees and released prisoners, ever came out again. For them, the camp was a colony of terror at the far extremity of the social world.

3. Organized terror takes place in situations of action and suffering. Ultimately, even absolute power targets the social situations in which human beings live and function. Here, it breaks their resistance, herds them together, shreds social ties; it dissolves action; it devastates life. Any investigation of the camps is shortsighted and flawed if it fails to include the power that micrologically pervades the structures of space and time, sociality and identity. For that reason, a methodological close-up on the typical situations of the world of the concentration camp is indispensable. Consequently, the present study not only employs a battery of concepts drawn from the general sociology of power, but also is indebted to work on the analysis of social situations.

The aim of the investigation is a "thick description" of the universe of power in the concentration camp.[19] In methodological terms, thick descriptions are analyses of meaning. They do not provide protocols of events but rather interpretations of actions and situations; not reports, but explications of structures and processes. Thick descriptions present a reading of the meaning of what has happened. They are interpretive and microscopic, not deductive and generalizing. Their quality criterion is neither the stringency of a deductive theory nor the presumably correct mapping of a model. Thick description succeeds to the extent that it expands the understanding of a strange and alien world. At first glance, this approach differs from the exercise of strict historiography, narrative or structural in orientation, by virtue of its greater freedom of discretion. Yet it obeys the equally exacting criteria of the sociological analysis of structures and situations.

In order to craft a thick sociological description, the studies here use historiographic investigations and documentation. In particular, they make use of inmate reports and testimony. Files of the camp administrations and documents from the Nuremberg trials have also been tapped. Of special value in this connection are texts that already contain thick descriptions. Naturally, these materials give rise to a number of questions regarding the nature of primary sources.[20] The presentation reflects the way in which given authors experienced the camps and tried to make sense of them for themselves. As a rule, these interpretations are not falsifications after the fact, but are readings that had already crystallized during the period of incarceration. Even if numerous reports are inaccurate when it comes to dates and numbers, that defect is amply offset by their graphic description of typical situations. A spot check indicates that a relatively small number of reports from various camps is enough to arrive at a typifying description. Despite all local and temporal differences, the standardization of terror and the monotony of everyday life in the camps are also reflected in the reports.

Especially instructive are those texts either based on additional research by the authors or that offer a detailed description patterned along the lines of a literary form of discourse. The *littérature de témoignage* is a specific genre that combines the microscopic description of everyday life with theoretical reflection. It provides a point of entry into the world of meaning of the prisoners—one that historiographic presentations cannot give. This is probably because a literary mode of narration also describes various events that would be considered self-evident (and not worth commenting on) in nonliterary reports. The concentration camp had its everyday routine as well, its "normalcy"—a dimension that many reports, favoring the presentation of special or unusual events, do not treat. For the grist of a literary text, however, almost everything becomes noteworthy, describable—even the supposedly most insignificant detail. *Post festum*, despite the ordinariness of many events in the camp, nothing could again be taken for granted.

The perspective of the political prisoners predominates in the reports. They formed the nucleus of resistance. Most of the prisoners able to describe their camp experiences in written form emerged from their ranks. Among the inmates, the privileged prisoners were an exiguous minority; but among the survivors, they composed the majority. This limitation of the sources is only partially offset by the reports of Jewish or foreign prisoners. They too were generally classified as political prisoners; as a rule, however, they did not belong to the upper class of the camp, a stratum dominated and marked by the German prisoners. The existence of these texts is itself a significant piece of data that reflects actual relations in the camps. The history of the concentration camps could only have been written by those "who . . . never followed them to the bottom. Those who did so did not return, or their capacity for observation was paralyzed by suffering and incomprehension."[21]

2

Absolute Power

ABSOLUTE POWER is a power structure sui generis.[1] The concentration camp cannot be integrated into the history of despotism, slavery, or modern discipline. Organized terror cannot be mapped onto a continuum of domination. The differences are not gradual, staggered along a cline of coercion, but fundamental. To describe the power system operative in the concentration camps using the customary conceptions of social power is a category mistake. This historical and anthropological rupture in the history of power calls for a radical shift in the theoretical point of departure. Even a cursory look at other forms of power reveals essential differences.

In despotism, one individual directs all according to his or her own arbitrary will and caprice, unencumbered by bonds to law or considerations of justice. Each one is afraid of everyone else. Tyranny is a desert of bondage. It knows neither social classes nor hierarchies. Except for the auxiliary troops of the despot, it lacks any middle-level authority that might structure the field between the sovereign and the serially structured mass. Despotism atomizes society; it levels all differences until equality is total: the equality of universal powerlessness. Terror is meant to intimidate, to crush resistance, to spread fear. It comes to an end when the last opponent has been eliminated and the peace of the grave holds dominion. Violence, however, remains an instrument of suppression, a means to an end. Once that end has been reached and the regime's power consolidated, despotisms make do with arbitrary, lawless rule, shifting pragmatically among punishment, incentive, and reward.

Social rule is characterized by an abiding willingness to obey, to submit. Subservient subjects make the command the maxim of their actions. They follow it because it is an order. They obey because they wish to and they accept subordination because they have a certain interest in obedient compliance.[2] Stable rule can rest assured that those dominated put their own interests aside, even considering them to a certain extent unjustified, and do so quite apart from the concrete content of any specific order. Obedience is a general willingness always to do what is demanded. The motives for this "coerced voluntariness" may change. They can be rooted in obtuse habituation or be based on an insight into the threat of potential disadvantages, on affective ties to authority or the belief in the legitimacy of the social order. But obedience is always a social act. Social reciprocity is preserved. Unlike tyranny, social domination does not transform society into a serially ordered mass; rather, it holds society together by the glue of coordinated obeisance. It itself creates and consolidates social bonds.

Punitive power wishes to realize its goals and interests against reluctance and resistance. It defines alternative paths of action and imposes sanctions if a person does not decide to follow the prescribed direction. It steers action by the threat of penalties, and by obligating itself to enact such penalties if need be.[3] This has nothing in common with arbitrary terror. Punitive power is precisely the opposite. It guides the social future, letting individuals know what they can expect. If one submits, there is no penalty; if one is recalcitrant, one must fear the consequences. Punitive power guides action by the instrument of fear, but always leaves open the door to obedience. It operates with deterrence, not terror. It coerces a person's will in the desired direction, but does not seek to break that will. It directs action, but does not destroy it.

Disciplinary power remolds human beings by subjecting them to constant control.[4] It has no need to make an example of someone to serve as a warning to others. Instead, it employs an extensive repertoire of subtle techniques of power that block the emergence of any kind of resistance. Unceasingly, it supervises spatiality, organizes temporal sequences, documents deviations, and inculcates normality. It examines progress, ordering it hierarchially, ultimately arranging disciplined individuals into smoothly functioning social machines. Total institutions are the parade grounds of disciplinary power, but that power's goal is the totally disciplined individual who obeys schematically, beyond conscious awareness. Discipline is a power, devoid of a center, that has lodged in the brain of the obedient. It requires neither arbitrariness nor violence. It is a silent power that has become *habitus* (attitudinal disposition), without chains of iron and steel, without barbed wire.

Absolute power as realized in the concentration camp differs from all this. Here, power does not shed its shackles until after all opponents have long since been vanquished. It does not forgo violence, but liberates it from all inhibitions and impediments, intensifying it by organization. Where the terror of tyranny ends, it begins. Absolute power is not bent on achieving blind obedience or discipline, but desires to generate a universe of total uncertainty, one in which submissiveness is no shield against even worse outcomes. It forces its victims together into an aggregate, a mass; it stirs up differences and erects a social structure marked by extreme contrasts. It uses various procedures for total control—not for the development of individual self-discipline, but as instruments of quotidian harassment, of daily cruelty. Terror dissolves the link between transgression and punitive sanction. It requires neither occasions nor reasons, and has no interest in obligating itself by threat. Absolute power goes on a rampage whenever it so desires. It does not wish to limit freedom, but to destroy it. It does not seek to guide action, but to demolish it. It drains human beings, depleting them by labor both useful and senseless. It sets economic goals from which it then breaks free. It liberates itself from ideological convictions after first having organized camp society in accordance with its ideological model of social classes. Even killing, that final reference point of all power, is not sufficient. Absolute power transforms the universal structures of human relatedness to the world: space and time, social relations, the connection with work, the relation to the self. It seizes on various elements and methods of traditional forms of power, combining and intensifying them, while casting off their instrumentality. In this way, it becomes a form of power of a distinctive, singular kind.[5] In order to interpret the concentration camp as a specifically new type of modern power, it is necessary to take a more detailed look at the most salient characteristic features of absolute power.

First, absolute power is organized power. It relies for support not just on a monopoly of military means of violence, but on a stable framework of social structures. The sources of camp power were terror and organization, not legitimacy or habit. It locked individuals into a spatial system of zones and grids, shaping their movements. It steered social time, erected a social structure, and organized work, violence, and killing. The camp displayed the classic features of formal organization: hierarchy of command, division of labor, standardized sequences of service and schedule, codes of discipline for personnel and inmates, and a high degree of bureaucratic record keeping. Like any larger organization, the concentration camp needed a specialized staff for administration and surveillance. The tasks were performed by the camp SS and also "self-administered" by the inmates. The advantages in power that accrue to formal organization are familiar. Such organization provides constancy, discipline, predictability, rationalization of work, and social control. Above all, formalization vitiates the need for high standards in the recruitment of personnel. Without forfeiting effectiveness, the organization can make do with quite mediocre individuals.

Nonetheless, the organization of the concentration camp should not be equated with that of military units or bureaucratic civil agencies. The SS was an organized "movement," a party-affiliated formation regarded by the top echelon as the motor of expansion and terror. A rigid bureaucracy would only have stood in its way. Formalization did not achieve the degree of objectivity of a traditional administrative apparatus, in which set rules are binding on all. The SS bureaucracy was permeated by corruption and protection, rivalries and comradeship. One should not underestimate the extent of the delegation of power, local autonomy, and spontaneous improvisation. From its members, the SS demanded individual initiative, not blind obedience, flexible "operations," not orders followed to the letter; it was faithful to the principle that competence is won by those who act. Independence and personal allegiance, along with correct accounting, were always demanded of its members, right down to the lowest levels of personnel. This diminished power by calculation, but intensified it via uncertainty and disorder by design. Personalized organization unleashed the impulse of arbitrariness on which terror is predicated. The

SS issued an impenetrable thicket of rules and regulations that no inmate could ever follow in their entirety, and which could be employed by the guard personnel arbitrarily. The formal rules did not limit power, hedging it in, but rather provided the freedom of terror with an institutional underpinning.

Second, absolute power is the absolute power to label. It upends the relationship between class and social classification, turning it on its head. By defining a taxonomy of categories into which every prisoner was pigeonholed, it created a social structure that regulated the distribution of goods, privileges, and prestige. This practical schematism absorbed social stereotypes, radicalizing them in the process; it ordered the social field, heightening social, political, national, and racial differences among the inmates. The use of the class hierarchy was a strategy of graded discrimination, persecution, and annihilation. The ultimate value in this pecking order was the worth a person's life was accorded. That value sign was sewn to an individual's clothing, visible for all to see, a stigmatic patch.

The system of identification badges had immediate material effects. It was decisive in determining who was allowed to exercise power as a prisoner-functionary, who was granted temporary protection, who was exposed to ruinous, ravaging labor, what rations a prisoner received. Labeling was a procedure that aided distribution. It regulated the distribution of misery, the dissemination of wretchedness. Thus, a prisoner society arose marked by variable distances between the classes, a differentiated, sharply stratified system, with extreme contrasts between bottom and top, and minimal transitions between levels. With the aid of categories, power implemented its model of society. It branded its victims with stigmata, guiding the prisoners' behavior by its stamp.

Third, absolute power is graduated power. It sets up a cleverly devised system of collaboration by turning some victims into accomplices, outfitting the functionary elite with substantial authority. One of the pillars holding up the camp system was an auxiliary force of *Kapos* (prisoner-functionaries who supervised prisoner work squads, or *Kommandos*) and "scribes" (*Schreiber*, record-keepers) who helped maintain everyday routines and relieved the burden on the SS personnel. Through their agency, absolute power became omnipresent. It filled almost every cranny, every niche in the camp. Without that delegation of power, the system of discipline and surveillance would quickly have collapsed. The attendant rivalry for positions in supervision, administration, and supply provided the SS with a welcome opportunity to play the various factions among the prisoners' elite off against one another, keeping them dependent. However, the typical prisoner was at the mercy of a dual authority: the members of the SS, who hardly ever appeared in the camp, and the prisoner-functionaries (*Funktionshäftlinge*), who were always around, a ubiquitous presence.

Delegation of power plugs the gaps in power and condenses control. Yet simultaneously, it creates certain free spaces, pockets of latitude. In order to gain active accomplices, the SS had to put up with developments it could not keep track of, taking them into the bargain. It had to concede opportunities for action that could be used by a minority of uncorruptible functionaries to the advantage of their fellow prisoners and to save lives. The delegation of power punctured the line dividing the SS from the prisoner elite. As a consequence of corruption, individual SS members became dependent on their confederates among the prisoners. Nonetheless, the camp regime did not forfeit any of its surfeit of power. Gradation of power does not diminish absolute power; it enhances it. The pressure of annihilation made the prisoner-functionaries into accomplices of the system. Terror became for them a means of self-preservation. They were thus faced with an unresolvable dilemma. In order to avoid being hurled back into misery or lynched by their fellow prisoners, these inmates had to proffer their services to the center of power. On the other hand, assistance was impossible without first becoming an accessory. Even if the accomplices wished to protect their comrades, they had to become representatives of the regime, rejecting numerous requests from fellow prisoners for help, implementing the requisite discipline even by violence if necessary.

Fourth, absolute power sheds the ideological constraints of legitimation. Power would not be absolute if it had to justify itself. To be sure, the SS leadership was also pursuing goals motivated by race ideology when it set up the camps: the incarceration of all social outsiders, the destruction of the Jews and everyone the regime defined as "superfluous." However, equally important for the SS were goals that sprung chiefly from an interest in the maintenance and augmentation of power: the suppression of political opponents, the elimination of potential resistance, the intimidation of the population and dissemination of terror in the occupied territories. The rationale for police security, the prophylactic expansion of the camp system in the event of war, the locating of camps on or near factory grounds, the search for conscripted workers—all these had little to do with ideology.

In any case, to link what was actually happening inside the system—the motivational structure propelling the perpetrators and the dynamics of excessive power—to *ideology* is unconvincing. Ideologies serve to legitimate. They are intended to coach the subjected toward voluntary subservience—an objective that was pointless and unnecessary in the camps. In addition, legitimations persuade those in power, if they should be plagued by any doubts, that their actions are correct. But all this was irrelevant in the camps. The camp SS was anything but an ideologically schooled unit. None of the commandants viewed the concentration camp primarily in terms of a historical mission. They were careerists, technocrats, corrupt criminals, assiduous subordinates. Some of the thugs may have been incited to commit atrocities on the spur of a malicious harangue. But most of the camp personnel were neither racist fanatics nor sadistic monsters. They used the opportunity to land themselves secure positions, gain social recognition, or avoid being sent to the front. During the war, thousands of soldiers deemed unfit for combat were put in the *Waffen-SS* (elite military units of the SS); *Volksdeutsche* (ethnic Germans) from the East or foreigners were recruited into the SS ranks who were unable to grasp its ideology simply because they spoke hardly a word of German. It is difficult to demonstrate that the SS guards and warders were imbued with the elite consciousness propagated by the SS leadership. Moreover, the everyday routine in the concentration camps was not determined by what the camp leadership occasionally proclaimed as an ideological goal. A different set of qualities was required: allegiance to duty, a knack for organization and getting things done, a sense of comradeship—and the readiness to use violence.[6]

Absolute power is self-based; not a means to an end, but an end in itself. Power that must legitimate itself is a weak mode of power. The conventional view of power is that it must always seek legitimation as a kind of shield. But organized terror was enough for the camp regime. It is totally mistaken to apply the yardstick of legitimation to the organization of the concentration camp. And it is a grave methodological error to project the substantial need for interpretation back into the era: to assume that the culprits had the same problems of explanation in flagrante delicto that they had later on in the dock before a tribunal. To whom would they have had to legitimate their actions? Many atrocities were committed quite matter-of-factly, even casually. Terror does not need to justify itself. Its basis is fear, an anxiety that it unceasingly generates. It is its own objective, self-contained. It proves itself by the act of its own exercise. And it remains effective by constant intensification, by self-exponentiation. Absolute power does not obey the pattern of purposeful, result-oriented action. It is purposeless; not poiesis, but negative praxis. Ideology here is not just superfluous, but obstructive. It ties power to certain aims, degrading it to a mere instrument. Terror that allowed itself to be guided by aims and purposes would be calculable. It would no longer be terror. To take recourse in ideology is a false interpretation *post festum*, nourished by the mistaken belief that there always has to be an intellectual reason, that everything has some historical meaning.

Fifth, absolute power transforms the significance of human labor. Labor in the camp should not be confused with forced labor. In forced labor, coercion is an instrument of work, but labor in the camp was a means of oppression, an instrument of terror. It was meant to humiliate, to torment, to break the power of the inmates to resist, to drain and destroy them. Anyone who employs forced laborers or slaves has a certain interest in preserving their physical strength. They are fed, clothed, and housed so as to be able to regain their strength, to husband their energy. By contrast, labor in the camp sapped the life energy of the prisoners totally, irretrievably. The economy of the concentration camps was an economy of waste, the squandering of human labor power. Personnel there had little interest in the reproduction of that power, despite contrary instructions during the phase of the total war economy. The prisoners did not work in order to produce. They labored in order to die.

Undeniably, camp labor also met economic goals. Prisoners had to construct the camps and maintain them by internal effort. Building materials were extracted from the stone quarries; on the moors, barren land was cultivated. The prisoners labored for SS firms, for countless private companies, and for the armaments projects of the interministerial *Sonderstäbe* ("special staffs"). There were orders to maintain the labor power of the inmates in order to transform the camps into economical slave-labor camps. I do not intend to dispute these facts. But the goal of economic effectiveness was not seriously pursued until the final phase of the war, after all the reserve armies of foreign forced laborers had been exhausted. That shift ultimately foundered on the praxis of terror common in the camps. The working and living conditions of the inmates contradicted any notion of economic rationality. There was no need to worry about the preservation of a prisoner's labor power. Right from the start, the objective relation of labor was dominated by the relation of power. Absolute power is always able to abandon any rationale of economic utility and devalue human labor power. Its economic universe differs fundamentally from that of capitalist rationality and efficiency. It is an economy of strain, harassment, sovereign waste, drudgery, grind, and torture. Absolute power strips labor of its productiveness, liberating its destructive properties. Terror does not aim at exploitation but at ruination, the process of suffering, destruction for its own sake. Emaciation, depletion of strength, death—that is the victory of power over human beings.

Sixth, absolute power is total. It cancels the deadly symmetry of absolute violence: the ability of each to kill the other. In the state of nature, the power of one person to kill ends where the power of the next begins. Even slaves can reverse the violence perpetrated against them by their masters, directing it against those masters—or against themselves. For that reason, complete power over life and death is always incomplete.[7] This is attested by the most radical forms of resistance, namely assassination and martyrdom. The assassin reestablishes the equality of the power to kill by proving that the master is mortal. Martyrs take their own deaths upon themselves, demonstrating that no one can force them to remain alive and complaisantly accept subjugation. But absolute power abrogates this antinomy of complete power. Assassinations were virtually impossible in the camps. There simply were no means and no weapons; there was insufficient physical strength. Individual acts of counterviolence would not have changed anything; moreover, they would have triggered extreme mass reprisals.[8]

Martyrdom was just as rare. The only groups that could, with a certain justification, properly be labeled martyrs were the dedicated political resistance fighters and the Jehovah's Witnesses. The latter, persecuted for their conscientious objection to military service, were adamant in their determination not to renounce their basic beliefs. Among the other categories of prisoners, none could have saved themselves by disavowal, renouncing some specific conviction or other. People were not incarcerated and killed on account of their religious beliefs, but because they had been stigmatized as superfluous. Even suicide, that ultimate and final act of self-determination, was systematically denied to the prisoners. It is true that there were repeated instances of suicide in the camps, but the attempt to kill oneself was punished by draconian measures. Whoever tried to reach the electrically charged death fence was shot or taken into custody. That prisoner then had more to fear than mere death. Absolute power cannot brook suicide. The decision to take one's own life is an offense, an insult it cannot permit.

Seventh, the most direct form of absolute power is sheer violence. It demonstrates its overwhelming might by manifest violence. Absolute power in action does not issue threats; it injures, maims, and kills. In no way is violence a sign of weakness. Power in the camps was not a system of rule that ultimately used violence after all other means had proved ineffective—as a last resort. Systems of rule generally are quite frugal in the way they employ violence, since it creates disorder and threatens the consent of the subjugated. In this regard, absolute power is fundamentally different. Violence and cruelty are the essence of its terror. In this way, it demonstrates the permanent vulnerability of the subjugated, and its own complete power of destruction over human life.

The camp was a laboratory of violence. Absolute power in action liberates a perpetrator from all inhibitions; cruelty comes unhinged. Virtually anything can be ventured, repeated, intensified, or halted, without reference to norms or goals. Absolute freedom is imbued here with a barbaric ingenuity. Its paradigms are not public execution, the calculated torture of interrogation, or the regulated punishment of transgressions; rather, its models are terror punishment, excess, and massacre. The motives for violence in the camps were manifold. Many deeds were perpetrated on the basis of a momentary mood or lark, a sense of boredom, during a contest, or because a person wanted to pocket a few cigarettes as a reward. Side by side with sadistic aggression stand habitual tormenting, indifferent killing, collective massacre under the influence of alcohol, or killing under specific orders. However, in the case of excessive violence, another factor is decisive. Excess is not a punishment, not an instrument of punitive power. In any event, it seeks grounds and reasons after the fact. But excess provides the perpetrator with a distinctive sense of self-esteem. It vaults all internal and external barriers. By making the victim into a defenseless body and ultimately into a nonreactive object, the culprits gain the certainty that they are capable of anything, any outrage. Excess is an act of uninhibited self-expansion,[9] one that simultaneously extinguishes sociality. Cruelty wishes from its victims nothing further.[10] In the execution of violence, the perpetrator loses interest in time. This accounts for the rapid averting of attention after the deed. Absolute power in action does not aim at subjugation. All it wishes to achieve is fear and terror for its own sake; all it seeks to demonstrate is how it can obliterate the human being as a personal and social being.

The end point of violence is killing. Killing is the total victory over the other. It is the emblem of absolute superiority. Violence cannot be further intensified beyond this terminus. Death is frequently the final, albeit cryptic reference point of permanent domination. However, the power to kill and the powerless fear of death were not latent determinants of the social relations in the camp. Killing was ever-present, predominant in the camp's everyday round, supreme. It was no exception; it was rank normality, routine. The power to kill turned prisoner society into a provisional society.

Eighth, absolute power engenders absolute powerlessness. Most prisoners lived in constant fear of death. None could be certain of surviving until the next day. The unquestioned idealization of one's own continued existence, on which all action is based, was shattered. It was uncertain whether action still had any effect, whether conformity and obedience actually helped prolong one's life. Absolute power turns every situation into one of life or death. It can foil any plan of action. The continuity of internal time-consciousness is fractured; past and future are radically devalued. The prisoner existed in an eternal yet irregularly pulsating present, an endless duration that was constantly interrupted by sudden attacks and incursions. In this world of terror, a single day was longer than a week.

As a consequence of the pressure to annihilate, there was a merciless struggle in the camp for sheer survival. Misery does not weld people together; it rends the fabric of reciprocity. The dominant social structure of powerlessness is the serially ordered and coerced mass. In that mass, every person is one too many. Although there were harsh penalties, one prisoner stole the last crumb of bread from the next. On the black market, prisoners bartered their last belongings in exchange for food, at the mercy of the profiteers who controlled prices. Inmates "sold themselves" into service to "prominent" prisoners, fulfilling their every wish in order to benefit somehow from their advantages. Whoever could still muster some modicum of strength was constantly involved in "organizing" something: a piece of cardboard for protection from the cold, or a chunk of wood that could be burned down to charcoal to treat the unrelenting diarrhea that sprung from the hunger ravaging one's bowels. In extreme distress, almost everything can be used somehow. Self-preservation demanded ceaseless activity, caution, and unscrupulousness. Mutual emergency assistance, acts of solidarity, and personal contacts had to be wrenched laboriously from the serial isolation forced on the prisoners. The society of the concentration camp was not a social community. Absolute power hurls humans into a social state of nature, a Hobbesian universe of theft and bribery, mistrust and animosity, the struggle of all against all.

In the face of the absolute power to kill, sheer survival is already an act of resistance. What would be considered secondary adjustment in total institutions was a naked struggle for survival in the camps.[11] This also included those acts of resistance aimed directly at the camp regime: the organizing of escapes, the provision of information, the puncturing of isolation, sabotage at work. But resistance ran up against a critical boundary. Absolute power destroys the causal nexus between action and survival. The ultimate fate of prisoners did not depend on their own actions. Only a minute fraction managed to escape. The others survived only because the Gestapo released them or the liberators arrived in time.[12] Absolute power gives the lie to the familiar notion that a human being's survival lies in his own hands.

Ninth, absolute power eradicates the line of demarcation between life and death.[13] Before their deaths, persons were destroyed gradually, step by step. The production of "living skeletons" is one of the genuine inventions of the concentration camp. Persons were starved, emaciated, left to the merciless rage of epidemics. Many died not as a result of direct physical violence, but because of systematic infliction of misery. This indirect annihilation did not kill immediately; it allowed death time. Power created an intermediate sphere, a state of misery and sickness between life and death. In this limbo, the perpetrators could find countless victims when they desired to act. The mass dying transformed the camp into a field of the dead. But even when all the prisoners perished within the course of a year, new transports assured the preservation of the power system of the camp. Their ranks were replenished.

The leading figure in the cast of mass dying was the *Muselmann* ("Moslem"; Auschwitz jargon for the "walking dead"), the human being in the process of dissolution. He or she symbolizes the anthropological transformation of a human being under the conditions of camp existence. No longer capable of anything but mechanical reactions, the *Muselmann* was trapped in a state of mental agony and social abandonment. The physical, bodily unity of the person disintegrated; intellect, spirit, and consciousness succumbed to a kind of inner sclerosis. The soul self-destructed, collapsing into total apathy and torpor. The person lost all ability to act. Although a victim of hunger and misery, the *Muselmann* was despised by the other inmates, kicked and beaten, ultimately left to his or her own devices, or killed. In this way, survivors protected themselves from the menacing visage of their own fate. Before physical expiration, the *Muselmann* died a death that was social.

Finally, absolute power aims at its own aggrandizement. It operates under the compulsion of totality. Its end is not reached until there are no longer any exceptions. If it abandoned this objective, it would relinquish itself. Power is total when it can multiply the numbers of its victims, killing indiscriminately. Killing succors power. Power perpetuates itself by means of the victims off of which it lives. Its excesses generate the need for ever-greater excesses. Each dead corpse enhances the power over the survivors. By contrast, however, the survivors constitute an affront to all-pervading power. It is no accident that there were especially cruel excesses in the wake of unsuccessful attempts at killing. Power's hatred is directed against anyone who survives after the others have been killed. The complete subjects of power are those it has eradicated.[14] It cannot, on principle, tolerate any survivors whatsoever. The greatest proof of power is the mass grave, the camp as a field of the dead. However, total power here cancels itself. Death is the absolute antisocial fact. For that reason, the absolute power to kill can never become total. In order to escape this dilemma, it constantly searches out new victims, defining new groups of opponents. Everyone is on terror's proscription list—extended to its logical conclusion, all of humankind.

Mass murder demands organization. Absolute power exceeds the threshold of excess and starvation at the point at which it transforms killing into work. Repeated killing is not a deed, a single act, but an activity with all the distinguishing features of work: a task done methodically, according to plan, over time, oriented to a goal, marked by bureaucratic efficiency and routine. Killing was centralized spatially, coordinated and standardized in its sequencing; it was functionally divided into segments, and technologically based to a limited extent. The victims of the killing stations in the concentration camps and "death factories" were nothing but an anonymous series. They were killed row by row. "Industrial" genocide, the factorylike annihilation of the Jews, transformed human beings into "material," "raw material" that was "exploited," and whose residua were disposed of without a trace.[15] The system of absolute power reached its apogee in the death factories of Auschwitz and Treblinka.

The concept of absolute power provides a guide for the sociological investigation of the concentration camp. The chapters below analyze in detail the domains of this power and the structures over which it assumes control. After a brief overview in chapter 3 tracing the history of the German concentration camp system, part 2 deals initially with the ordering of space and time. Absolute power defines social zones; it distributes persons in space and guides their movements (chapter 4). It erects a controlled space with insurmountable boundaries (chapter 5) and with sites of extreme density (chapter 6). In the daily round of camp routine, it establishes a social standard time, yet it extends and interrupts this time arbitrarily (chapter 7). Absolute power is not content merely with the creation of a system of social time. It penetrates into internal time-consciousness, disrupting the relationships among past, present, and future. By this skewing of time, it destroys identity, one's relationship with oneself (chapter 8).

Part 3 focuses on the social structures that power engenders and on which it relies for support. The social field of the concentration camp is divided into three domains: the world of the personnel (chapter 9), the aristocracy among the prisoners (chapters 11 and 12), and the mass society of inmates, with its system of classes and categories (chapters 10 and 13). Each of these regions had its typical social forms that must be looked at separately. The forms of association range from the personalized organization of the SS and the graduated protection of the functional elite to illegal relations of exchange and barter, serially structured massification, and total dissociation. The system of terror altered the various states of the social world; it guided and penetrated them, crushing their aggregation at the first signs of counterpower.

Part 4 addresses work in the concentration camp, focusing initially on the question of whether prisoner labor can legitimately be viewed as slave labor (chapter 14). Although many offices and enterprises profited from the labor of the prisoners (chapter 15), work was determined by a relation of power that fundamentally transmuted the character of human labor. Absolute power reigns in the work situation (chapter 16), intensifying the burden of labor to the level of an extreme annihilatory pressure. It destroys the purposeful structure of activities, transforming work into a means of constant torment and gradual destruction.

Part 5 explores the indirect annihilation of human beings by the systematic infliction of misery (chapters 17 and 18), and the forms of violence and killing that are unleashed by absolute power. The camp regime turned sanctions into brutal terror punishment (chapter 19), intensifying violence to the level of excessive cruelty (chapter 20). In the end, it magnified its lethal power by means of organization, imbuing that power with permanence in the enterprise of selection (chapter 21) and the death factories (chapter 22). Although initiated from the outside, the factorylike mass annihilation was in keeping with the internal dynamics of a system of power and terror bent on its own totalistic fulfillment.

3

On the History of the Concentration Camps

THE ORGANIZATIONAL HISTORY of the German concentration camps began in an atmosphere marked by improvisation, rivalry, arbitrary decisions, and revenge.[1] On the night of February 27, 1933, the Reichstag was set ablaze; the following day, the Emergency Decree for the Protection of the Nation and State abrogated the rights to freedom enshrined in the Weimar constitution. This created the legal basis for putting political opponents behind bars for longer periods. The secret police and their auxiliaries in the SA (*Sturmabteilung*, the elite paramilitary "storm trooper" units of the Nazi Party) and SS were empowered to order *Schutzhaft* (protective custody) without a court decision. Even before the burning of the Reichstag, the police in Prussia had taken an oath to uphold National Socialist principles of struggle, and the paramilitary Nazi units had been granted police authority. During initial raids on the night of the conflagration, numerous communist functionaries and parliamentary representatives were arrested. On March 23, the so-called Enabling Act (*Ermächtigungsgesetz*) made the civil state of emergency a permanent fixture; two days later, the police and the SA occupied forty-six trade union office buildings; on April 1, the first nationwide boycott was instituted against Jews. On April 7, the regime removed undesirable officials from the civil service by passing the Civil Service Law (*Berufsbeamtengesetz*); two weeks later, "non-Aryan" doctors were denied permission to practice in hospitals. On May 2, the unions were dissolved. On May 10, books were set afire on pyres in university towns. On June 22, the SPD (Social Democratic Party) was banned; other political parties were disbanded under coercion at the end of the month. After members of the left opposition were hauled in, the wave of arrests now extended to members of the bourgeois center: clerical workers, civil servants, and journalists. In May, the number of those arrested dropped, only to crest again during the summer. On July 31, at least 26,789 persons were in protective custody in the Reich; of these, 14,906 were in Prussia, 4,152 in Bavaria, and 4,500 in Saxony.

In the wake of the political consolidation of the regime, arrests declined once again in the following months. In November 1933, some 11,000 were incarcerated in Prussian concentration camps. In the spring of 1934, after a large-scale Christmas amnesty, there were just under 5,000 in the camps; by the beginning of August, their numbers had dropped to 1,243. There was a similar development in Bavaria. In December 1933, there were 3,855 prisoners registered in protective custody; ten months later, that figure had declined by more than half, to some 1,700. Between February 1933 and August 1934, some 50,000 individuals were remanded to protective custody in the two states for varying periods of time; some 3,000 were not released again.

The establishment of the first concentration camp was not centrally guided by the new government in Berlin; it came about on the initiative of subordinate offices and local party groups. Most camps were under the authority of state agencies, the political police, the state ministries of the interior, or the administrative heads of various government districts (*Regierungspräsidenten*). Prison facilities had been set up by local party leaders; these remained totally shielded from any state supervision. Many prisoners were not even brought to the overcrowded jails of the justice system by units of the SA and the SS; they were initially confined in the jail facilities, meeting halls, basements, or indoor riding rings of those groups. Later, the prisoners were transferred to newly comandeered quarters. Improvised terror in these provisional jails, although it was generally only of short duration, anticipated later developments. These were sites for beating and torture pure and simple, settings for vengeance against actual or presumed opponents of the regime. The party groups also enjoyed appreciable influence in the camps under the supervision of the civil administration or the regular police. The groups were often in close cooperation with government offices, which increasingly were staffed by party members. Where, due to administrative rivalries, that did not immediately come to pass, the SA and the SS largely retained the local right of disposal over the prisoners. As the official auxiliary police, they provided the supervisory and guard personnel in most of the state concentration camps.

In Bavaria, there was no competition between provisional SA camps and the offices of the interior and justice ministries.[2] From its inception, the camp at Dachau (twelve miles northwest of Munich) was under state supervision. On March 9, Reichsführer-SS, Heinrich Himmler had advanced to the post of police commissioner of Munich. On April 1, he was appointed commander of the Bavarian political police, which was separated from the police bureaucracy as a special ministerial agency. This provided the basic outlines of the model for the later fusion of the secret police and the SS. Himmler was in charge of both the police admissions office and the guard units in Dachau, the first camp under exclusive SS supervision. Equipped with this control, Himmler could parry attempts by the Bavarian justice authorities to intrude, and could also block efforts by the Reich governor in Bavaria further to limit the numbers of detainees in protective custody. Between June 1933 and November 1934, the number of Dachau inmates fluctuated between twenty-seven hundred and seventeen hundred. Despite the lack of a proper infrastructure, the camp had been designated as a central facility to house all detainees in protective custody in Bavaria.

A similar move toward centralization in Prussia proved abortive, initially because of the rivalry between administrative offices. The state interior ministry took over camp administration, and in mid-March made plans for a central camp complex to house ten thousand prisoners in the Emsland, the rather remote area west of Bremen between the Ems River and the Dutch border. Inmates were to be deployed as laborers to drain the nearby moors.[3] In order to curb the local power of the SA and the SS, the Prussian interior minister, on October 14, granted formal recognition as state facilities for protective custody to the Papenburg, Sonnenburg, Lichtenburg, and Brandenburg camps and also to the political departments in the Brauweiler Institute near Cologne and the Provincial Workhouse at Moringen (north of Göttingen), which were linked to the Gestapo (*Geheime Staatspolizei*, the secret state police). However, the power to decide on the admission of detainees lay not with the interior ministry, but with the Gestapo. It had been separated from the general administration as an independent prosecuting agency and placed under the personal supervision of Hermann Göring, the Prussian chief minister. Attempts by the interior ministry to set up an administrative structure headed by a director foundered because of opposition by SS guard units. Thus, rivalry between competing agencies prevented the uniform planning of the camp system. The SA camps were gradually disbanded; at the same time, however, protective custody was removed from ministerial supervision and made the exclusive domain of the Gestapo and the local SS units. On April 20, 1934, Himmler assumed control of the political police in Prussia. The SA no longer had any camps of its own; its guard personnel were under the control of the justice administration. Now the SS could set about revamping the system of concentration camps.

Although the number of prisoners was steadily declining and they still could have been transferred to the regular justice system, Himmler (whose plans were always approved by the Führer) ordered the Dachau commandant Theodor Eicke in May 1934 to begin reorganizing and expanding the camp system. This foreshadowed a fundamental functional change in the concentration camps. Instead of a temporary instrument of repression necessary for the consolidation of the new regime, these camps were now to be permanent facilities for the preventive detention of anyone whom those in power might define as opponents. Eicke replaced commandants, and he withdrew the guard units from the general SS, combining them into barracked guard formations. At the same time, he dissolved the remaining prison facilities and concentrated the prisoners in a small number of camps. In the early summer of 1935, the inspector of concentration camps and commander of SS guard units (*Inspekteur der Konzentrationslager und Führer der SS-Wachverbände*) was in charge of six camps with approximately thirty-five hundred prisoners: along with Dachau, the Esterwegen, Lichtenburg, Sachsenburg, and Moringen camps, as well as the Columbia House in Berlin-Tempelhof. Beginning in 1935, the new super-

visory agency, the *KZ-Inspektion* (concentration camp directorate), was initially located in the Gestapo offices in Berlin. In August 1938, Eicke's staff
was relocated to Oranienburg, not far from Sachsenhausen, a camp set up in
1936. The *Inspektion* remained there until 1945.

This office was relatively small.[4] In 1935, its staff numbered eight SS members and five police officers. One year later, some thirty positions were approved for the leadership staff of the Death's Head units. Nonetheless, the
KZ-Inspektion enjoyed a basically free hand in its decisions. The organizational principle of dual and personal subordination, typical of the SS bureaucracy, favored protected privilege and promoted independent concentrations
of power; those in the *KZ-Inspektion* were able to act with a high degree of
independent initiative and make decisions not bound by rules. As camp inspector, Eicke belonged to Heydrich's secret state police; as head of the
Death's Head units, he was responsible solely to the central office of the SS.
State and party functions were united in one man. As soon as one supervisory
authority attempted to control affairs, Eicke was able to fall back on the other
side of his dual competency. In cases of conflict, he brought all his bundled
authority to bear, or circumvented the offices above him, turning directly to
Himmler. Despite this, his position was controversial. The concentration
camps remained an object of debate and contention in the organizational field.[5]
Now it was no longer the justice authorities or the SA who disputed the right
of the camp SS to exercise full control. The SS administrative office headed by
Oswald Pohl, as well as the later SS personnel office and the surgeon-general
SS, all had the opportunity to influence the activities of Eicke's inspection
agency. Moreover, relations between the *Inspektion* and Heydrich's Gestapo
were apparently also tense. The Gestapo decided on the admission and release
of prisoners, and maintained a Political Department in each and every camp as
a Gestapo base. Many members of the camp SS viewed that department with
nothing but mistrust. Externally, vis-à-vis the authorities, they closed ranks
and demonstrated unity as soon as the interests of the SS were involved. Internally, however, there was a welter of personal rivalries, not only between
Heydrich and Eicke, but also between the camp commandants and local officers of the Gestapo or the criminal police.

Along with the establishment of a central bureaucracy, the reorganization of
the SS camps was one of Eicke's principal tasks. The consolidation during the
years 1934 through 1936 led to the formalization of the camp administration
and to a certain standardization in the detention system. A pattern of distribution of tasks and competencies had already crystallized. That pattern was to
remain in place until the end of the war. The sentry and escort service was
separated from the administration, and the bureaucracy was structured according to a uniform scheme.[6] This formal structure stabilized the framework of
positions. The organization of the concentration camp was rendered independent of any changes in personnel and their initiatives. Consolidation thus

meant not only the concentration of prisoners under a unified leadership, but also the institutionalization of the camp as a social system.

In keeping with this was the internal standardization of camp operations according to the "Dachau model."[7] Dachau at this time was not merely an important practical training center for the camp SS, where the careers of many SS leaders began, men who would carry the *habitus* of the "Eicke school" to other camps. Dachau was more: it served as the paragon for the reorganization of the entire system of concentration camps. The model encompassed four components: classification of the prisoners; labor as an instrument of terroristic detention; a graduated system of penalties that could be imposed officially as well as informally; and military law for grave offenses such as mutiny or attempted escape (although it also served as a cover for spontaneous and concealed killings). Eicke introduced the 1933 regulations governing guard service in other camps as well; these regulations essentially remained in force until the end of the war. The disciplinary and penal codes for the prisoner camps were altered in order to curtail the arbitrary decisions of the commandants, yet no limits were set on mistreatment and cruel harassment. The rules established terror as a principle, at the same time opening the door to arbitrary caprice. They indicated to the guard personnel the scope and latitude of what was permissible. The Dachau model was more than a catalog of codified, standard rules and regulations; it was a paradigm for the everyday practice of terror, which the camp personnel was able to carry out according to its own experience, habits, and whim.

Until 1936, preventive detention was primarily a way to abet the internal consolidation of the regime. The Gestapo engaged in a policy of arrest aimed at frightening and intimidating the population—a strategy of deterrence. In every locality, a few individuals suddenly disappeared; most returned after a certain period of time, depressed and frightened. This gave rise to a climate of paralyzing fear. What snippets of information people heard about the camps sufficed to suppress opposition. Often, legends of horror circulated that surpassed even the stark reality of the camps. The concentration camps, far from being a well-kept state secret, were publicly known institutions. The release of a relatively high number of persons from custody was a shrewd way to consolidate further the grip of the regime.

All this changed fundamentally in 1936. The SS began with the planning and construction of new concentration camps. Year by year, sites of absolute power were established that would continue in operation until the war's end: Sachsenhausen (in the town of Oranienburg, north of Berlin) in 1936, Buchenwald (outside Weimar) in 1937, Flossenbürg (between Weiden and the Czech border in northeastern Bavaria) in 1938. Immediately after the invasion and *Anschluß* (annexation) of Austria in 1938, the Mauthausen camp was set up near Linz; in 1939, the women's camp of Ravensbrück was established (fifty miles north of Berlin). The only camp from the first phase that still existed was

Dachau; all the others had been disbanded. Prisoners from Esterwegen (in Emsland) and the Columbia House were transferred to Sachsenhausen, Sachsenburg prisoners were sent to Buchenwald, and the women from Lichtenburg were relocated to Ravensbrück. After consolidation and contraction, the system was readied for the next phase of expansion. The new barracks camps were to be made available for the heightened security measures anticipated in the event of war; they were to have an expandable absorption capacity, and contribute to the four-year plan by deploying inmates as laborers in SS enterprises. Now, the location of the camps was not determined by the availability of prisons, workhouses, fortified palaces, or castellated monasteries; rather, the decisive factors were production facilities for building materials, granite quarries, and tile and brick factories.

Although the political opposition had long since been eliminated, a development arose with the establishment of the new camps that gradually extended terror to encompass more groups. A new category was added to that of the political adversary: the *Volksschädling* (pest harmful to the people). The camps changed from a locus of political repression into an instrument for racial-ethnic (*völkisch*) social policy, a dumping ground to which the SS dragged all those it considered noxious or superfluous.[8] Preventive detention was redefined as an unlimited "substitute penalty" that could be imposed on anyone the police labeled a social outsider. Already in 1934, there were some 350 "work-shy" prisoners in Dachau; in 1935, Lichtenburg had 325 "homosexuals" in detention, while 476 "professional criminals" were confined in the Esterwegen camp. These categories of prisoners were to gain even more importance in the subsequent period. On June 17, 1936, Himmler took over the criminal police. One year later, with the setting up of the central Reich Office of the Criminal Police, the organizational basis had been created for new waves of persecution. In March 1937, some two thousand "professional and habitual criminals" and "dangerous sexual offenders" were taken into preventive custody; these persons were already listed in specially prepared files. At year's end, the circle of individuals targeted for detention was expanded to include social outsiders. Local labor offices and Gestapo head offices were ordered to take the initiative in recording the particulars of "work-shy" and "asocial" persons (*Asoziale*) and recommending them for detention. This collective category included beggars, "vagrants," "ruffians," those suffering from venereal disease, prostitutes, homosexuals, alcoholics, "psychopaths," "traffic offenders," "fault-finders," and Gypsies—in short, anyone and everyone who had fallen out of favor with some authority or with an informer in the neighborhood. The first "Operation against Asocial Elements" (*Asozialen-Aktion*) in April 1938 led to the arrest of some fifteen hundred persons. In June, Heydrich ordered every district office of the criminal police to send at least two hundred able-bodied men as well as all Jews with previous convictions to the Buchenwald camp. Camps were no longer being set up because prisoners could not be accommodated elsewhere. On the contrary: persons were taken into custody in order to fill the waiting camps and secure laborers for the SS factories. At the beginning of 1937, the total population of the camps was seventy-five hundred prisoners; by October 1938, it had more than tripled, to twenty-four thousand. The forced recruitment of workers was cited as a reason for the mounting search, along with the need to create social order in the folk community (*Volksgemeinschaft*). However, the makeup of the prisoner population in the camps shifted. Political prisoners were now in the minority. Until the middle of the war, some two-thirds of all non-Jewish German prisoners were in the catchall category *Asoziale*.

Several thousand more political prisoners were incarcerated in the wake of the occupation of Austria and the Sudetenland. After the Crystal Night (*Reichskristallnacht*) pogrom of November 9–10, 1938, the SS rounded up some thirty-six hundred Jews and sent them to the camps, which were totally unprepared for such large numbers of detainees.[9] The Jews were plundered there, jammed together in special sections, and left without medical care, adequate clothing, or food. Although most were released after a short time, this mass arrest can arguably be classified as the first annihilation operation. The number of deaths in the severely overcrowded emergency quarters reached several hundred over a period of two months; this was a scale previously unknown among camp detainees. Many were murdered; others succumbed to the constant torment, agony, and strain. Yet that contradicted the official aim of the operation. These arrests had been conceived as a means of exortion. Those Jews who pledged to emigrate and signed an agreement regarding the "Aryanization" of their assets were generally released after several weeks. In the spring and summer of 1939, the number of prisoners declined once again. In the wake of the pogrom, there had temporarily been as many as 60,000 inmates in the camps; at the end of August 1939, the camp population had declined to approximately 21,400.

The outbreak of the war led to a radical caesura. It did not change the principles of organization, but it altered the functions of the camps and the structure of prisoner society. Detention was intensified, food rations were reduced, everyday routine was rendered more strict, time for roll call was extended at the expense of free time. In the first winter of the war, death rates soared, reaching previously unknown levels, and the camps filled with foreign prisoners from the occupied countries. The further the German troops advanced, the smaller the percentage of German prisoners in the camps. During the war, they constituted only 5 to 10 percent of the total prisoner population. Most of the foreign prisoners were from Poland and the Soviet Union, where they were seized and taken to the camps directly after occupation. The waves of arrests in northern and western Europe were initially limited to isolated reprisal operations against "saboteurs" and resistance fighters. These also included prisoners taken in so-called *Nacht-und-Nebel* ("night and fog") operations.[10] In September 1941, Hitler ordered the seizure of any persons considered "suspicious"; they were to be brought across the border into the Reich and then made to vanish into the "night and fog" without a trace. Most were interned in the camps at Natzweiler (in Alsace) and Groß-Rosen (in Silesia). Despite the indiscriminate raids and searches in western Europe, summary arrest was initially restricted to the occupied territories with Slavic populations. Here, the more important factor was the racist population policy, which outweighed that of suppression of the opposition.

The internationalization of prisoner society increased internal social differentiation, leading to profound contrasts between the various national groups. German prisoners rose in the social pecking order, and accounted for the majority of functionaries in prisoner self-administration. At the bottom of the heap were the "non-Aryan" categories: along with the Jews, principally Poles and Russians. The number of prisoners surged, quickly reaching the level of the winter of 1938, and stabilized at some 60,000; by August 1942, the figures had risen again, nearly doubling, to approximately 115,000.[11] Overcrowding became a permanent feature. The concentration camp changed into a mass society; annihilatory pressures mounted rapidly, though the tempo and scope differed in the individual camps. This is reflected in figures for new admissions and deaths in several main camps (see table 1).[12]

The batching of new prisoners varied from camp to camp. At the end of June 1939, Buchenwald had 5,523 prisoners; by the end of the year, that figure had more than doubled with the admission of 2,500 Jews from Austria, the transfer of 2,200 prisoners from Dachau, and the admission of 2,098 Poles. However, the new admissions were largely offset by the numerous deaths and transfers, so the camp population leveled out at the end of 1942 at below 10,000. In Sachsenhausen, some 6,500 were confined at the outbreak of the war. Shortly thereafter, in September 1939, 900 Polish and stateless Jews from the Berlin area were taken to the camp; at the beginning of November, 500 Poles were interned. At the end of that month, 1,200 Czech students were added, and approximately 17,000 persons, mainly Polish nationals, were admitted as inmates in the period from March to September 1940. Despite the high number of new inmates, the camp population here too stabilized at the level of roughly 10,000 prisoners. That was because of the high mortality rate as well as the transfer of large numbers of Poles to Flossenbürg, Dachau, Neuengamme (in the Bergedorf section of southeastern Hamburg), and Groß-Rosen.

Mauthausen began to expand a year later, but at a faster pace. The camp population did not rise significantly until March 1940, with the transfer of the first Polish prisoners from Buchenwald. About eight thousand Poles were incarcerated in Mauthausen that year, augmented from 1940 to 1942 by some seventy-eight hundred Republican Spanish prisoners. Although the mortality figures the first year resembled those in Sachsenhausen, the annihilatory pressure in subsequent years at Mauthausen far exceeded that in any other main

TABLE 1

New Admissions and Deaths in Four Camps, 1937–1945

	Buchenwald		Sachsenhausen		Mauthausen		Dachau	
	Adm.	Deaths	Adm.	Deaths	Adm.	Deaths	Adm.	Deaths
1937	2,912	48	750	38	—	—	2,015	69
1938	20,122	771	8,300	229	1,080*	36	18,681	370
1939	9,553	1,235	9,144	819	2,800*	445	3,932	300
1940	2,525	1,772	18,925	3,892	11,000*	3,846	22,675	1,515
1941	5,890	1,522	8,662	1,816	20,000*	8,114	6,153	2,576
1942	14,111	2,898	16,590	4,968	20,387*	14,293	12,572	2,470
1943	42,177	3,516	20,031	3,807	21,028	8,481	19,358	1,100
1944	97,866	8,644	50,560	2,347	65,645	14,766	78,635	4,794
1945	43,823	13,056	54,794	15,000*	24,793	52,814*	30,958	15,384

* Estimated figures

camp. Along with Auschwitz and Majdanek, Mauthausen and the neighboring camp, Gusen, were the centers for mass annihilation within the concentration camp system. Dachau went through a special trajectory of development. From September 1939 to March 1940, the camp was closed, and most inmates were transferred to Buchenwald, Mauthausen, and Flossenbürg. After return transfers, the camp population at the end of March was less than three thousand; it rose rapidly once more to some ten thousand by the end of that year, thus again rivaling the size of Sachsenhausen.

The soaring numbers of prisoners led to overcrowding in the old camps, which originally had been planned to house only five thousand inmates each. Therefore, the SS set up additional camps in 1940 to absorb the influx of prisoners from the occupied countries. In June 1940, the first Polish prisoners were admitted to the old military barracks at Auschwitz. Initially, Auschwitz had only been planned as a quarantine and transit camp to handle some ten thousand inmates. By mid-1941, however, more than seventeen thousand had been registered. In March of that year, work commenced on the construction of the largest camp complex at Birkenau, three kilometers from Auschwitz; it eventually had 250 barracks, and temporarily housed more than a hundred thousand inmates. The SS had the death factories built close by; these were put into operation in the first half of 1943.

In addition, Neuengamme, which had been functioning as a satellite of Sachsenhausen since 1938, was upgraded in 1940 to a separate concentration camp. The plan was to concentrate prisoners from northern and western Europe there. Two months later, in August 1940, the Groß-Rosen camp was set up in Lower Silesia; initially it was also a satellite of Sachsenhausen, but it became a separate, full-fledged camp on May 1, 1941. That was also the date of the establishment of Natzweiler in Alsace, where many of those seized in *Nacht-und-Nebel* operations were interned. In January 1942, Stutthof (near Danzig) was added to the list of concentration camps; it had been in operation since 1939 as a camp for civilian prisoners. One year later, the SS established Herzogenbusch in the Netherlands;[13] its inmates included people in preventive detention, prisoners of the German police in custody awaiting trial, and Dutch Jews. After a short stay, most were deported via Westerbork to Sobibór and Auschwitz.

Until 1939, the concentration camp system served primarily to eliminate political opponents, isolate social outsiders, and terrorize the population. Labor deployment was of secondary importance; it tended to be used more as a means than as an end of imprisonment. In the subsequent period, little changed in this regard at the local level. However, economic considerations became ever more important in the thinking in the top echelon of the SS leadership. The decisive factor in selecting the location for the camps at Natzweiler and Groß-Rosen, as earlier in the case of Mauthausen and Flossenbürg, was the proximity of a granite stone quarry. In the spring of 1941, I.G. Farben began with the construction of a Buna plant in Auschwitz. Initially, the main camp, seven kilometers away, furnished a pool of laborers, until the Monowitz camp was opened in 1942 directly at the construction site in order to shorten the route to work. The SS tried to gain complete control over the entire production cycle for goods vital to the war effort, though that policy met opposition from private industry and Speer's Armaments Ministry.[14] After several rounds of negotiations, an agreement was reached in the summer of 1942 not to transfer skilled workers from industrial firms to the camps, but rather to hire out prisoners to private firms and set up external camps near the armaments plants. The model for this mode of cooperation was the Buna camp at Monowitz. This local differentiation in the concentration camp system did not take hold on a larger scale until 1943.

During the early phase of the war, a second functional shift spread more rapidly: the transition from terroristic arrest and confinement to execution and mass annihilation. The concentration camp was transformed into a place of execution, first for individual "war saboteurs" and criminal prisoners the police wished to dispose of without trial, and then for registered prisoners as well. Finally, in the fall of 1941, that came to include thousands of Soviet prisoners of war who, after the invasion of the Soviet Union, had been captured and incarcerated in segregated sections of the camps.[15] The mass killing of POWs marked a new stage of power in the history of the camps. Not only were the prisoners systematically starved; new procedures for killing were also devised. In Buchenwald, some eighty-five hundred POWs were killed serially by a single shot to the nape of the neck (*Genickschuß*) in a facility specially constructed for the purpose. In Sachsenhausen, some thirteen thousand were killed in a similar fashion. In Auschwitz, the first experiments were conducted in September 1941 on a group of six hundred POWs using the poison gas Zyklon B. A bit later, execution orders were eased once again in order to pursue another tack: working the prisoners to death in the stone quarries. Not until the end of 1942 did the top echelon shift completely to deploying prisoners as forced laborers, dissolving the segregated camp sections and integrating the few survivors into the normal routines of camp life (and death).

The numbers of the dead surged, not only as a result of the executions, but particularly due to the cycle of "indirect" mass annihilation. Food rations for the prisoners deteriorated rapidly. The chronic hunger in the camps led to physical exhaustion, aggravating susceptibility to infections. This reduced performance and led to ever more brutal mistreatment; that in turn acted further to diminish an individual's labor power and chances for survival. The willful infliction of misery and violence were intermeshed. The SS murdered in order to come to grips with overcrowding in the camps and create room for new able-bodied prisoners, yet the latter were soon caught up in the same lethal cycle of emaciation, disease, exhausting labor, and violence.

From 1942 on, the second half of the war was marked by several parallel developments: the mass annihilation of European Jewry, labor deployment in the arms industry and in the construction projects of the special staffs for rocket and aircraft production, the establishment of hundreds of *Außenlager* (external subcamps), and the rapid rise in the number of prisoners. At the start of the war, the total inmate population was still some 24,000.[16] In 1941, that had surged to approximately 60,000; in August 1942, the figure reached 115,000, climbing to more than 200,000 in May 1943. In August 1944, the number of prisoners reached 524,268;[17] by January 1945, it had swelled once again, to 714,211, including 202,764 women.[18] In order to fill the camps with fit laborers, the SS initially fell back on prisoners in the clutches of the justice system. In mid-September 1942, Himmler and Thierack, the Reich minister of justice, reached an agreement that all imprisoned "security detainees," Jews, Gypsies, Russians, Ukrainians, Poles with sentences of more than three years, and Czechs and Germans serving sentences of more than eight years should be interned in the camps—for the expressly stated purpose of "extermination by work" (*Vernichtung durch Arbeit*).[19] Of the 12,658 prisoners from the justice system transferred during the winter of 1942–43 to the camps, primarily to Gusen, 5,953 (more than 47 percent) had perished by the following April.[20] However, in the eyes of the SS, by far the largest reservoir was the millions of foreign civilian workers in the Reich, especially Poles and Russians.[21] Any of these "foreign workers" (*Fremdarbeiter*) who caught the attention of the authorities was no longer handed over to the justice system, but was sent by the Gestapo to a labor-education camp or transported directly to a concentration camp. In this way, tens of thousands of Polish and Russian conscripted foreign laborers were sent every month to the camps. They were no longer registered in separate files; their numbers were only reported to the admissions office (the

RSHA—*Reichssicherheitshauptamt*, the Reich Security Main Office) as a global figure. Once this reservoir was exhausted, Hitler gave permission in April 1944 for an exception to the program of genocide, allowing some 100,000 Jews to be brought into the Reich from the East to work in armaments production and bunker construction.[22] Thus, for example, some 108,000 were selected from the 458,000 Hungarian Jews in Auschwitz, and then transported in contingents of 500 persons each to work as laborers in the Reich.[23] Under pressure of a labor shortage, the regime deviated for a short time from the policy of mass annihilation.

The measures of annihilation directed against the Jews had already reached their most radical stage in the winter of 1941–42. In occupied Poland, the Jews were initially herded into forced ghettos, where intentional selections were subsequently carried out.[24] Those fit to work were systematically destroyed by means of labor, terror, and enforced misery in the newly established "forced-labor camps" (*Zwangsarbeitslager*); the others were deported immediately to the death camps. In December 1941, mobile extermination vans, using engine exhaust gases, began functioning in Chelmno (the first extermination camp, between Lodz and Posen in the so-called Warthegau); in the spring and summer of 1942, construction was begun on the death factories of Operation Reinhard: Belzec, Sobibór, and Treblinka. These killing facilities were not under the direction of the *Inspektion*, but were controlled by the local SS leadership of Lublin District in the *Generalgouvernement*, the largest administrative unit of occupied Poland. By contrast, the Baltic camp complexes in Riga-Kaiserswald, Vaivara, and Kaunas were under the administration of the *Inspektion*; they were set up in the summer and fall of 1943 for the internment of able-bodied Jews who had not been exterminated in the ghetto liquidation operations in Riga, Daugavpils, Vilna, and Kaunas.[25] Only the camp at Riga housed non-Jewish prisoners as well: some four hundred "Aryan" inmates with German citizenship, along with a small number of Poles. Moreover, seven hundred political prisoners from Estonia were interned in the facility at Klooga, a subcamp of Vaivara, along with eight hundred Soviet POWs. All other prisoners were Jewish; they either perished because of harsh labor and poor conditions or were shot after being selected. Only some twenty-five hundred inmates out of the total inmate population of fifty thousand in these camps survived to the end of the war. Auschwitz and Majdanek were also under the supervision of the Oranienburg *Inspektion*. Here, the policy of genocide intersected with the program of labor deployment. That policy's historic focus was the notorious "ramp" at Birkenau, where most incoming transports were subjected to the filter of selection, and the SS sorted Jewish workers according to the camps' momentary needs and absorption capacity. Prisoners selected were admitted to the camp; they were then worked to death. Despite the labor shortages, genocide clearly had priority, although this meant the loss of millions of Jewish workers.

The conversion of the concentration camp system to meet the needs of labor deployment was carried out primarily by a new agency of the SS, set up in 1942. On February 1, 1942, all SS matters pertaining to administration, economy, and construction were gathered together in a new office, the WVHA—the *Wirtschafts- und Verwaltungshauptamt* (Economic and Administrative Main Office), run by the previous head of SS administration, Oswald Pohl.[26] With a bureaucracy of fifteen hundred to seventeen hundred persons, the WVHA formed the counterweight within the SS to the RSHA, the central prosecuting authority of the criminal police and the Gestapo. Along with responsibility for troop administration and supplies for the units of the Waffen-SS, this office for SS industrial and commercial interests encompassed three branches (*Amtsgruppen*): "Construction" (C), "Economic Enterprises" (W), and, from March 5, 1942 on, *Amtsgruppe* D, the *KZ-Inspektion* located in Oranienburg. Pohl was thus entrusted with the central leadership of the camps and the task of removing the system from the grasp of the Armaments Ministry and Fritz Sauckel, the GBA—*Generalbevollmächtigter für den Arbeitseinsatz* (plenipotentiary for labor deployment). Using the most brutal methods, Sauckel had been recruiting civilian *Ostarbeiter* (Eastern workers) in the Soviet Union. The aim of integrating the camps into the economic central office for SS enterprises was not only to economize; it also had a strategic intention: to make sure the camps stayed within the sphere of power of the SS. Despite formal subordination to the WVHA, the *Inspektion der Konzentrationslager*, under Richard Glücks, Eicke's successor, continued to be a relatively independent agency.

The internal organizational structure of Branch D was largely in keeping with the tried and tested division of labor in the camps. The Central Office DI dealt with basic questions pertaining to the treatment of prisoners, in conjunction with the admissions agency, the RSHA. Office DII handled labor deployment: DIII supervised medical services. DIV was in charge of material equipment for the camps; de facto, however, it had only coordinating functions, because Branch C was responsible for all construction operations within the WVHA, while Office BII oversaw the provision of uniforms for the guard personnel and prisoners. Each office head had immediate authority to issue orders in his specific area of competence. Thus, the organizational principle of dual subordination was also operative in the case of the camp administrations. The labor-deployment leaders, camp doctors, and administrative heads received their orders both from the local SS command post and from the relevant central office. The local headquarters had no monopoly on command authority; orders from above could be sent directly from the special offices in the WVHA to the camps, bypassing the local SS headquarters.[27] The more important labor deployment became, the greater was the influence that accrued to Office DII. This office handled negotiations with the firms and the Armaments Ministry, deciding on the selection of workers and the establishment of new camps. In this way, Maurer, for many years a close associate of Pohl and the head of Office DII, was able to become the actual inspector of concentration camps—in contrast with Richard Glücks, who was nominally in charge of *Inspektion*.[28]

The policy of labor deployment opened up the camp system to external beneficiaries, interministerial special staffs, and a host of private munitions firms.[29] Yet it should be borne in mind that the concentration camps were not integrated into the total war economy until rather late, and then only with various misgivings. Although the top leadership echelon had touted the utility of labor deployment as early as the end of 1941, it was not until 1943 and 1944 that hundreds of satellite camps were set up: the drastically deteriorating military situation left no other option. The turbulence and exigencies of the final phase of the war were what sparked the dramatic expansion of the system—not the policies of the *Inspektion*. In December 1942, there were only 82 external work Kommandos (*Außenkommandos*); 29 of these were in Dachau alone. A year later, the total had climbed to 196. Most of the satellite camps were not set up until 1944; in June of that year, there were 341, and by January 1945, there were 13 main camps with a total of 662 *Außenkommandos*.[30] This local differentiation undermined the principle of the closed, single, self-contained camp. The concentration camp was transmuted into an enterprise for hiring out laborers. The main camps now formed the center of an organizational unit with numerous branches and external satellites. However, labor deployment in this framework brought no lessening of the threat of annihilation for the prisoners. Their work was not slave labor, but terror labor (*Terrorarbeit*),[31] performed under the most miserable and harrowing conditions. Even if labor had not been planned and engineered everywhere as a means of annihilation, it nonetheless became a major cause of death.

The final period coincided with the advance of the Allied armies and the dissolution of the concentration camp system. In July 1944, Majdanek was the first large camp to be vacated. In the preceding months, transports with thousands of prisoners had left Majdanek for Groß-Rosen, Ravensbrück, Bergen-Belsen, and Auschwitz. The final contingent of 1,000 prisoners set off on foot to Auschwitz; six days later, only 698 arrived at their destination.[32] From August 1944 to January 1945, Auschwitz also was dissolved in stages. Some 65,000 prisoners were freighted off in transports to the Reich; during the week of January 17–23, 1945, the remaining 60,000 were herded onto the roads leading west. Thousands perished during these forced marches. Many were shot dead; others, too feeble, collapsed and froze to death in the snow. Of the 800 prisoners who set out from the subcamp Janinagrube, 600 died on the eighteen-day trek to Groß-Rosen. On January 18, a column of 3,000 prisoners set out from Birkenau; at the end of March, 280 of them arrived at their destination, Geppersdorf near Görlitz. Some 29,000 Jews were evacuated by ship and train from Danzig and Stutthof, but only 3,000 survived to reach Ravensbrück and Sachsenhausen.[33]

The deeper the Allies penetrated, the more rapidly the network of the camps crumbled. In this process of dissolution, prisoners were caught up in a maelstrom, driven ever more quickly from camp to camp. The intention was that no prisoner should fall into the hands of the liberators. Down to very last minute, prisoners were deployed on construction projects "vital to the war effort": building railroad embankments, repairing bridges, digging bunkers, or erecting tank barriers. The harried columns were marched back and forth from camp to camp. A few examples: in Neuselz on the Oder, a contingent of 1,000 Jewish women set off on foot on January 26; after forty-two days on the road, 200 of them reached Flossenbürg in eastern Bavaria. Eight days later, the survivors were herded onto a train to Bergen-Belsen. On April 15, a last prisoner train was sent from Neuengamme via Nuremberg to Ebensee on Lake Traun in the Austrian Salzkammergut. That same day, 17,000 women from Ravensbrück and 40,000 men from Sachsenhausen were herded off on a march heading west. In Brandenburg, thousands died of exhaustion or were massacred by their guards. On April 15, British troops liberated Bergen-Belsen, where they found 10,000 unburied corpses rotting in the spring air. On May 5, a United States armored unit reached Mauthausen; the following day, Ebensee was the last camp to be liberated.[34]

It is impossible to determine precisely how many died in the camps and on the death marches. Camp records, insofar as they exist, were not kept according to uniform rules, and they exhibit numerous gaps.[35] SS figures on monthly mortality served as an official indicator of living conditions in a camp. However, they must be evaluated as "political statistics," manipulated totals with which local SS headquarters wished to present themselves in as favorable a light as possible to the central authority.[36] If there was an order to reduce mortality rates, the camp command posts tried to pass on sick and exhausted prisoners from one camp to another by transport. In this way, figures for the dead could be reduced at the point of dispatch; the transports were often not even registered at their destination. Prisoners died en route or were killed immediately after arrival, and thus disappeared, unrecorded. The central administration operated in a similar manner. If it appeared to be convenient to present a low number of dead to a superior office, only the cases of "natural death" were counted. If, on the other hand, there was an order instructing the camps to maintain labor power, all deaths were tallied, so as to document and underscore the catastrophic living conditions responsible for their difficulty in maintaining the desired level of labor. Within the concentration camp system, the accountancy of death was an instrument for death's manipulation; in the hierarchy of bureaucratic offices and channels, such bookkeeping served as a tactical means of proof.

TABLE 2

Admissions and Deaths in Selected Camps, 1933–1945

		Admissions	Deaths
Camp			
Dachau	(1933–45)	206,206	31,591
Buchenwald	(1937–45)	238,979	56,545
Mauthausen	(1938–45)	197,464	102,795
Neuengamme	(1938–45)	106,000	55,000
Flossenbürg	(1938–45)	96,217	28,374
Groß-Rosen	(1940–45)	120,000	40,000
Auschwitz	(1940–45)	400,000	261,000
Majdanek	(1941–45)	250,000	200,000
Dora-Mittelbau	(1943–45)	60,000	20,000
Bergen-Belsen	(1943–45)	125,000	50,000
Concentration Camp System	(1933–45)	(1,650,000)	(1,100,000)
Extermination Camp			
Chelmno	(1941–43)		225,000
Belzec	(1942–43)		600,000
Sobibór	(1942–43)		250,000
Treblinka	(1942–43)		974,000
Auschwitz	(1941–44)		1,100,000

Table 2 can nonetheless provide a picture of the annihilatory pressure in the various camps. It includes only those camp complexes for which there are relatively reliable figures, or at least plausible estimates based on the present state of research.[37] Even if one assumes a large margin of error, proceeding on the basis of a highly restrictive assessment of these statistics, it is evident that approximately two-thirds of the prisoners in the concentration camps did not survive. If the more than three million Jewish victims in the death factories of Operation Reinhard, Chelmno, and Auschwitz-Birkenau, who were liquidated immediately after arrival, are added to these figures, the total rises to far more than four million persons who perished in the concentration and extermination camps.

Part II

SPACE AND TIME

4

Zones and Camp Plans

> We're separated from each other by barbed wire.
> The Germans evidently have a very special affection
> for barbed wire. Wherever you go, barbed wire.
> But you gotta give credit where credit's due: the
> quality's good, stainless steel. Densely covered
> with long barbs. Barbed wire horizontally, barbed
> wire vertically.[1]

EVERY POWER OF any duration organizes space and time. These constructs are not marginal conditions of social existence, but forms that allow reciprocity. Temporal and spatial orders guide social action and relations. Absolute power exploits this. It transforms natural space into a space of social coercion, barricading all exits, marking out the areas for control. The concentration camp is a system of rigorous surveillance, a receptacle for violence. The interrelation of human beings and space has been abrogated, discontinued. The possibility for prisoners to appropriate space for themselves has shrunk to virtually nil. Absolute power destroys space as a domain for acting and living. It packs people together, ordering them to and fro, hounding them back and forth. The individual is no longer the centerpoint of his or her world, but only an object in space.

Sealing persons off from the outside world is merely the simplest procedure pursued by power. Social control demands an internal structuring of space. It extends not only to boundaries, paths, and assembly grounds, but also to the social relations operative there.[2] In order to channel contacts, camp space was divided into social and functional areas, zones of surveillance and visibility. Bodies were distributed in space and condensed into collectives; the time, tempo, and direction of movement were permeated with coercion, saturated with force. This was accompanied by an unshakable localization of events. Absolute power chains action to spatial facts, to stations and passages. It defines backstage sites of violence, scenes of triumph where absolute power itself goes onstage. Terror leaves its imprint on space, transforming it into a medium of itself. The ordering of coercive space is not merely a material fact; at the same time, it generates social and symbolic significations. Consequently, an analysis of space must provide more than mere topography: it must explore social functions, trace human movements, and endeavor to render the symbolic meaning of the sites in space intelligible.

The earliest camps did not yet have the typical spatial order that characterized later barracks camps. During the first few weeks of arrests, the SA and the SS placed their victims in improvised detention facilities where the authorities were able to take vengeance unhindered by the justice system.[3] In Oranienburg, an empty brewery was occupied, in Dachau a half-dilapidated powder factory was used; in Prettin an der Elbe, they comandeered Lichtenburg Castle, which until 1928 had been used as a prison. The Werden and Sonnenburg camps were also set up in former jails. In Brauweiler, the prisoners were locked up in a workhouse; in Bremen, they were herded onto an old ship; in Breitenau near Kassel, they were interned in an old monastery. Women were brought to the provincial workhouse in Moringen and to Gotteszell near Schwäbisch Gmünd (east of Stuttgart), a women's prison on the grounds of a monastery. At Kislau in Baden, a castle surrounded by water served as a detention facility; in Ulm, the Oberer Kuhberg fort, an abandoned and overgrown fortress with dank underground casemates, was used. It was unimportant whether these sites were suitable for confining human beings. With an infallible sense for the aura of a place, the henchmen occupied old monuments of total institutionalization: workhouses, jails, fortified castles, monasteries. These were structures that had sprung from the secular process of discipline. Meter-thick walls and fortified towers, long passageways and low arches, cells and iron gratings—the architecture itself was a sign of repression, force, and violence.

In contrast with the earliest camp, the barracks complexes had no past. The geography of the modern concentration camp was not the product of historical development; it was the result of an ideal plan that paid no heed to historical or natural conditions. Buildings or localities that stood in the way were converted to new purposes or eliminated; the forest was cut down, swamps were filled in with sand, narrow valley hollows and steep mountain slopes were terraced. The site was cleared, a tabula rasa for erecting the camp according to strict design. Power occupied space and transformed it totally. Not only did the modernization of the concentration camp system from 1936 on expand the functions of the camps; it also rationalized the ordering of space. Now the external visage of the camp was determined not by heavy fortified walls, but perimeter fences; not cells, but housing blocks; not roofed rooms, but open expanses. Activities were functionally dissociated; sites of work, accommodations, and places of execution were rendered spatially separate. The camp enclosure was "zoned," divided into regions. A typical geography is evident in blueprints for the camps, which provided a clear summation of districts and fields.

A concentration camp was not just a collection of wooden barracks.[4] Depending on its stage of completion, its perimeters included workshops, factory halls, and agricultural enterprises, a heating plant and a fire-extinguishing pond, barracks and offices, a brothel and a movie house, mess halls, an infirmary and dispensaries, a jail and a crematorium. Fully finished, it was a complete settlement with a network of streets and a railroad siding—a town for personnel and prisoners housing thousands, at times tens of thousands, of people. In its modern standard form, the camp was a self-contained, built-up area with facilities similar to the infrastructure of a town.

The center of power was located in the administrative area. The offices of the camp commandant, the Political Department, and the administrative department were in close proximity to the prisoner camp, but just outside the barbed-wire perimeter. Every office of the *KZ-Inspektion* had its branch in this administrative zone. It served as the local representative of the central bureaucracy. A leafy, wooded area was set aside for the living quarters of the SS officers. In Dachau, these were located on the *Straße der SS* outside the camp; in Buchenwald, the SS residential complex was on *Eicke-Straße* on the sunny southern exposure of the Ettersberg, an idyllic spot with wooden houses graced by low saddle roofs, equipped with central heating, each with a garden, garage, and patio. In Natzweiler, the commandant's villa, complete with swimming pool, was located on the path that led from the camp to the gas chamber, five hundred meters away. Although the officers lived in green and attractive surroundings, the guard personnel were housed in barracks. The hierarchy of ranks also determined the structuring of zones. Dachau, Buchenwald, Sachsenhausen—and Mauthausen and Auschwitz later on as well—were simultaneously militia garrisons for the Death's Head units. The Sachsenhausen garrison had ten multistoried stone barracks, and forty-five made of wood; in Buchenwald, there were sometimes six thousand persons housed in eighteen large barracks. In Auschwitz, the buildings of the Polish tobacco monopoly served as troop quarters. As in any military barracks, the guard units also had their own infrastructure: a mess hall and an infirmary complex, an armory, garages, shooting ranges, a sports field, and a dog kennel for the patrols.

During the day, the "large cordon" (*Große Postenkette*) enclosed the entire area of the camp. The prisoner camp was virtually empty, and after the Kommandos had been marched off, the watchtowers were left unmanned. Inside the barbed-wire perimeter, the infirmary complex, kitchen, laundry, and stockroom were the only sites where there were still prisoners. All the other inmates were temporarily dispersed across the entire domain of the SS. Some were deployed in the workshops, which sometimes were grouped into an "industrial area": shops for carpentry, metalworking, plumbing, and shoemaking. The factories and shops of the private firms and the SS, the stone quarries, brickyard, and textile and wood factories were located a bit further away. Camp space was divided up according to work zones as well as residential areas. Work operations linked with supplying essentials for the prisoners were situated near the barracks camp; supralocal production was at a separate factory location.

The zoning of areas separated personnel and prisoners. The SS enclosure was similar to a garrison to which the prisoners had access only during working hours. Access was limited in the other direction as well. As a rule, administrative staffers and guards did not enter the prisoner camp. At night, the "small cordon" (*Kleine Postenkette*) occupied only the watchtowers, and patrolled the perimeter. The only persons other than the prisoners inside the barbed-wire area were the staff that ran the camp, the SS rapport leader (*Rapport-führer*), and the block leaders; they had direct contact with the inmates. Spatial zoning thus guaranteed that there would be social distance, and a spatialized contrast, between personnel and prisoners.

Behind the barbed wire, another world commenced. It too had a typical spatial structure, reminiscent less of a modern garrison than of the geometric grid of early military camps.[5] Nothing here was irregular; nothing eluded visible control. The barracks of the prisoner camp, constructed mainly of thin wooden boards, with an occasional barracks of stone, were surrounded by a perimeter fence—in Dachau there were 15 acres, in Sachsenhausen 18, in Buchenwald about 40, in Birkenau an enormous expanse of 420 acres. It was a uniform, homogeneous settlement. In contrast with the spacious and un-crowded SS domain, the dominant principle here was visibility and concentration. In Sachsenhausen, the 44 acres were covered with seventy-eight barracks, of which fifty-six were for prisoners. Originally planned to accommodate six thousand inmates, Sachsenhausen generally had a population of between ten and fifteen thousand, rising to about thirty-five thousand in the final months of the war. The blocks were arranged in a fanlike configuration in a semicircle around the *Appellplatz*, which had a radius of about a hundred meters. The camp as a whole was similar to an isosceles triangle: at the base, the semicircle of the parade ground, then the blocks in four concentric rings, and at the apex the nursery and pigpen.

In general, the SS opted for a rectangle, not a triangle, as the basic form. In Dachau, the model camp, an area measuring two hundred fifty by eight hundred meters was marked out; bunkers and working quarters were located on one side, with the roll-call square in front. The latter could easily accommodate 40,000 persons. Then came thirty-four blocks arranged in two rows, separated by the camp street. The barracks were numbered in series, with uneven numbers on the right side, even on the left. Here too, the original plan had been to house only 5,000 prisoners, but from 1940 on, there were never fewer than 12,000 inmates; Dachau had more than 32,000 when it was liberated in 1945. If a single rectangle did not suffice, one simply arranged several in a neat series.[6] Majdanek, which would later reach a population of 250,000 POWs and prisoners, consisted of six separate fields, each surrounded by barbed wire and with a death zone, its own entrance gate, *Appellplatz*, gallows, kitchen barracks and toilet barracks, medical complex, and twenty-two blocks. In August 1943, up to 1,000 inmates were crammed into blocks originally planned for 550 persons each. Jews for whom no other place could be found were locked up in the area for coal storage together with the coal. This field system permitted the self-contained transfer and separation of individual groups. The women, initially placed in Field V, were transferred to Field I, and then (except for three blocks) shipped off to Auschwitz and Ravensbrück. Field IV contained hostages under the control of the regular police; Field III housed political prisoners from the Generalgouvernement, local farmers, and Jews from the ghettos of Warsaw and Bialystok. Each field was a camp within a camp.

The largest example of the field system was in Birkenau. The construction plan of August 15, 1942, envisaged four sections over a surface area measuring 720 by 2,340 meters. However, only two sections were completed: BI to the left of the camp street, and BII to the right. BIII, which the inmates nicknamed "Mexico," was never finished. In the summer of 1944, this section served as a "depot camp" for Hungarian Jewish women who were compelled to wait there, without registration numbers, either to be transferred to the women's camp or to pass through selection for the gas chambers. Next to the four crematoria, the supply camp known as "Kanada" was built, containing thirty barracks, filled to the rafters with possessions taken from the victims who had been gassed. Sections BI and BII, in turn, were subdivided into several sectors surrounded by barbed-wire fencing. BIa and BIb, the women's camp, contained sixty-two brick housing blocks, along with ten blocks for washing facilities and toilets; in August 1944, the prisoner population there peaked at 39,234 women. BIIa, with its sixteen stables, served as a quarantine camp for an average of 4,000 to 6,000 men. BIIb was the "family camp" for those deported from Theresienstadt; BIIc was the "depot camp" for transports from Hungary; BIId was the camp for able-bodied men; BIIe the camp for Gypsy families. BIIf took in the sick: it was a special field with twenty-five hundred places in beds and common bunks, insufficiently equipped and always overcrowded. Sectors BIIb through BIIe all had the same layout and equipment: a kitchen with four blocks for washing and latrines, plus thirty-two stables, arranged in two staggered rows, one behind the other. This was the purest form of the functional zoning of the camp. In these sectors, there were no work quarters, just housing blocks and toilets. They were mass-housing complexes. The area at Birkenau had been divided into sectors as though with a ruler, each filled to the last corner and crevice, a geometrically plotted, gigantic camp space to accommodate human beings—and, over in "Kanada," to store the possessions of the dead.

In order to structure and divide the sectors, the SS employed the grid system as an additional instrument of power. Zoning separates functions and collectives, but does not guarantee order in the regions created. The problem of organization the guards faced was quite complicated: limited camp space had to be optimally used and properly secured. Thousands of persons had to be clearly sorted out; new arrivals had to be placed in quarters smoothly and efficiently; movements in the sectors had to be coordinated. So what was done? A regular rectangle was marked out, divided in the center by a camp street; the latter intersected at right angles with side streets. This created a grid of small rectangles, a series of land parcels; on each of these plots, a block was erected. Meeting places or open areas were superfluous, except for the *Appellplatz* for the daily counting of the camp population, the human inventory. Each block was given a number, its own guard personnel, and its own furnishings. They all looked alike; it was a standardized, uniform settlement for a serially ordered mass.

In prison, the predominant law is that of individual isolation. In the concentration camp, the principle that holds sway is that of the condensed and segmented mass. Space was divided not into small cells, but into fields and blocks. The inmates were guarded as compact units. The guards feared nothing more than prisoners massed together in large collectives, in groups that eluded their grasp. Nonetheless, instead of inmates being dispersed, they were jammed so densely together that personal space for action was virtually eradicated. Cellular structure combats dangerous individuality by obstructing social contact. By densification, the mass-housing block destroyed the latitude for movement. The cell breaks prisoners, subjugating them by abandonment. The camp throttled them by overcrowding them in the ceaseless, suffocating presence of others.

The right-angled order had several advantages for the SS. Space could be filled totally, down to the corners and crevices; there were no curves, arches, or blind spots. It was easy to survey the grounds visually; the watchtowers at each corner had a field of vision and fire of ninety degrees. Each boundary line allowed for a dual check. A short glance along the barbed wire or into the streets sufficed to determine immediately whether anyone was approaching the boundary or out in the open without permission. No single individuals were allowed to use the straight paths—only squads of prisoners and guards. Finally, the grid system permitted the schematic expansion of camp space. All that was necessary was to lengthen the main streets and side streets and extend the numbering. The system of fields could be expanded indefinitely as long as there were no natural obstacles to block it.

Camp space was an addition of fields and plots, a geometric summation. One sector resembled another, each block a carbon copy of the next. The serial structure of the social mass was in keeping with this seriality of space. But this was merely one physical aspect of camp society; the grid system was only a general ordering schema. The social map of the camp differed; it was by no means isomorphic with that grid. Social differences, functions, and taboos also shaped and determined social space. Where freedom of movement is a privilege bitterly fought for, housing indicates rank and is a mark of social

status. Thus, the stone blocks near the *Appellplatz* were reserved for prominent prisoner-functionaries; the number of prisoners housed there was largely
in keeping with the specified norm. Here, each person had his or her own bunk
and locker. Only those belonging to the top rungs of prisoner society, its upper
class, were admitted to these facilities. The underclasses were banished to the
camp slums, overcrowded mass-housing blocks lacking adequate hygienic facilities, and without room for the individual.

Not all barracks served as housing quarters. Along with the kitchen and the
provision room, the stockroom and the laundry, and the bathing and disinfection block, there were special areas separated by barbed wire: the so-called
Revier, which was the infirmary complex with isolation blocks for those with
dangerous epidemic or infectious diseases and laboratories for SS doctors; the
quarantine area for new arrivals; the camp jail; blocks for the *Strafkompanie*
(punishment company); and the special sections for Soviet POWs and for Jewish prisoners. After analytic dissection, inner zoning brings land parcels together once again, regulating movement. The only persons with access to the
hospital were those permitted to go there by the SS medics and the *Revier*
Kapos. In this way, Jewish prisoners were excluded for a long time from receiving medical care. No one ever reemerged from the isolation blocks and
quarantine areas. Contact between the sexes was virtually impossible, as was
any assistance for the prisoners in the special fields. Inner zoning was an
instrument used to regulate death. The quarantine areas and special sections
were centers for the systematic infliction of misery.[8] There were no hygienic
facilities, beds, or cots whatsoever in the tents and stables; medical care was
minimal, rations reduced. Thus, within the prisoner camp, there were separate
regions of mass dying where the SS pursued a willful policy of death by starvation. These regions were nothing other than extermination camps within the
concentration camp.

For killing, absolute power withdrew from view. Violent excesses could
erupt anywhere, but for the business of torture and execution, the SS preferred
special sites where it could pursue its dark craft without onlookers. Among
such select spots were the old familiar institutions of disciplinary power: the
camp jail, the residential blocks of the *Strafkompanie*, the infirmary for those
with dangerous infectious diseases, and the experimental blocks of the hospital. Prisoners were not punished or healed there; they were tormented and
murdered. Not without reason, the inmates tried to avoid these areas. Only few
had any idea what was really happening in the back rooms of the hospital block
and in the prison cells. But many knew that to be sent to the bunker or the
isolation barracks was tantamount to a certain death sentence.

The sites of mass extermination outside the prison camp were also zones
of death: the gravel pits, firing ranges, killing stations, and crematoria. These
were places for massacre, sites for methodical killing. The facility for killing
prisoners by a shot administered to the nape of the neck in Buchenwald,

the *Genickschußanlage*, was located next to the riding hall outside the barbed-wire perimeter; in Sachsenhausen, the SS set up a combined liquidation facility close to the crematorium, "Station Z," after the last letter in the alphabet. Station Z included a *Genickschußanlage*, a shooting pit, a gas chamber, and a multiple gallows with block and tackle. The structures had been kept low intentionally so as to block visibility and prevent anyone from looking in over the wall. The first provisional gas chambers in Birkenau were outside the camp, set up in former farmhouses. But the modern crematoria were built in close proximity to the camp. They were surrounded by barbed-wire fences and shielded from view by barriers of willow trees. Flower beds lent the facilities an innocuous air. The zones of death were disguised areas beyond the round of everyday camp routine. No one had access to them except the Sonderkommandos—the corpse carriers and oven stokers. The zone of death was taboo, a place of mystery where the power to kill could unfold unhindered.

Zoning separated guards from prisoners and marked out the territories of the various categories of prisoners. It structured space by social rank, in the SS area and in the prisoner camp. In that way, it heightened the confrontation between personnel and inmates, and steered contacts within prisoner society. It distributed actions and segregated the housing blocks from the regions of work and death. Space was transformed into a serially and functionally structured arena for supervision. Although the prisoners were subjected to total control, power was able to withdraw, to secrete itself in isolated spots and taboo zones. Absolute power carves social space into zones of survival, dying, and killing. Along with detailed control, a long-standing characteristic feature of disciplinary power, it bifurcates society into those fit to work and those who are superfluous. Whoever was granted a temporary reprieve was housed in normal barracks; the others were systematically starved to death in special areas of the camp, or murdered immediately. For the old mode of disciplinary power, space was a means of conditioning, disciplining, and observing. For absolute power, space is an instrument of social discrimination and death.

5

Boundary and Gate

> Characteristic for the situation of the prisoner con-
> fronted with death was that only very few chose to
> "run to the wire," as the expression went. I.e., to com-
> mit suicide by coming into contact with the barbed
> wire charged with high voltage. The wire itself was a
> good thing, quite certain—but perhaps one might be
> caught beforehand in the attempt to approach it,
> and then be thrown into the bunker, a death more
> difficult, and more painful.[1]

SEVERAL BOUNDARIES separated the camp from the outside world. Because
prisoners were not incarcerated in individual cells, but confined within geometric fields, the security problem was shifted to the external boundary lines.
The SS required extensive, mobile barriers to prevent escape, smuggling, and
mass breakouts. It thus transformed the boundary into an insurmountable par-
tition, a dangerous, taboo barrier that none dared approach. Only after space
was sealed off totally, hermetically, did the camp become that closed locus
where absolute power could unfold freely, unhampered by limits.

Sealing off the camp served several functions. First, it marked out a domain
of power that none inside could leave, and into which none outside could peer.
Although prisoners were occasionally released, and news about the inner
camps was repeatedly leaked to the outside, the boundary line shielded the
camp from the outside world, transforming it into a secret site of crime. Generally, one of the most effective methods of terror is to make individuals disappear, to imprison them behind impenetrable walls. The boundary transmuted
the camp into a visible but secluded and silenced place of terror in the midst of
society. The prisoner was forever removed from the protective sight of the
public domain. Once in its clutches, power could do with him or her what it
wanted. The boundary liberated force from all inhibitions. It unhinged violence. Every atrocity, any perverse experiment was now permitted. License
was total. Behind the sealed barrier, power extricated itself from the constraints of civilization. The closed boundary was indispensable for the delimi-
tation of absolute power.

There was a further function: the isolation of space was the precondition for
the social autarky of the camp. Behind the boundary, a total society sprang into

being, with a class structure of its own and a system for the distribution of goods. All domains of life were united in a single place. From their admission to their death, the inmates were caught in the machinery of this total institution. The camp became an isolated and exclusive province of meaning devoid of an external horizon; all efforts had to be concentrated on sheer survival. The surrounding world lost sense; gradually it disappeared beyond the barbed barrier, faded from view and memory.

One boundary line to close off the camp did not suffice for the SS. It usually combined several material obstacles with diverse technical precautions. In addition, it made sure the boundary was guarded by patrols and sentries, because there can be no absolute reliance on mere physical barriers. A boundary generally separates two regions while linking them at the same time. It does not become impermeable until human surveillance fashions a final barrier, a blockage that turns any approach to the boundary into a lethal risk.

Because of a lack of material, several weeks passed in Dachau before the prisoners were closed in by barbed wire.[2] Beginning in the summer of 1933, the camp island already resembled a bulwark. In front of the wire fence, charged with high-voltage current at night, there was a low, slatted fence that marked out the "neutral zone." Whoever entered it was shot down without warning. Directly behind it ran a concrete wall three meters high that surrounded the entire area of the camp. Patrols moved in the area between the wall and the internal fence; these patrols maintained eye contact with the two sentries posted on each of the four watchtowers. Machine guns were pointed at the camp from all directions. Searchlights illuminated the grounds at night. Every corner could be lit up brightly and brought under fire at will. In the beginning, the patrols had to drive away strangers and the curious, but this was a problem that soon took care of itself. After modernization, the entire area was surrounded by a high wall and encircled during the day by the *Große Postenkette*. Patrols with dogs scoured the areas in between. The prisoner camp was enclosed by a moat; then came the concrete wall with the wire fence and watchtowers, a path for the nightly patrols, and a double row of electrified barbed wire. Finally, there was the death strip, covered with white gravel to make any shadow readily visible at night.

With minor variations, these precautions were found in all the camps. Sometimes the SS decided to do without the costly concrete barrier, and instead built small wire gates into the fences or placed "knife-rests" (barriers of barbed wire and timber) in the death strips. In small satellite camps, a simple fence without an electrical charge often sufficed, since the group was easy to keep under surveillance. With this barrier system, the camp was secured against attempted escapes as well as mass breakouts. The small cordon guarded the mechanical barriers at night; during the day, the large cordon formed a human chain around the camp enclosure. The guards opened fire on any prisoner who ventured across this line or approached within a few steps of them. Despite the mechanical barriers, it was only possible to close off the boundary by employing a considerable number of guards. Attempts to reduce personnel costs by using bloodhounds or additional technical devices proved abortive.[3] Only human vigilance can seal a boundary hermetically.

The camp boundary line was a focus of antagonism between the prisoners and the personnel. The presence of the guards was a constant threat. Their orders were to punish any violation of the boundary. From the start, since the introduction of the first disciplinary code in Dachau,[4] the death penalty hung over the head of anyone who smuggled secret messages out of the camp, sent signals by light, or aided others in escape attempts. It was strictly forbidden to stay in the neutral zone expect for purposes of work. To fiddle about with the wire fence in any way was considered sabotage, and was punished by death. Whoever stepped out onto the death strip intentionally or by mistake was shot without warning. Attempted escapes were punishable by arrest and hanging. Those executions were public on the *Appellplatz*, and served as a warning to one and all. The boundary was a taboo whose violation was mercilessly punished. This taboo was supported by the regulations for the guard units. Warning shots were strictly forbidden; violent assaults among prisoners were to be broken up only by the use of firearms. A guard who violated this rule risked immediate dismissal. He was obligated to punish by killing and received a reward for this: cigarettes, money, special leave, or an official citation. That he was ready to pull the trigger at any slight provocation was by no means because of his unbridled lust for blood. There were normative regulations he simply had to carry out. But these rules also provided a convenient pretext for arbitrary acts of killing. To "shoot a prisoner attempting to flee" was always permissible, even if he had not tried to escape.[5] The guards thus invented a deadly game.[6] They provoked an "attempted escape" by taking a prisoner's cap and tossing it into the death strip or across the line of posted sentries. The unsuspecting prisoner was then ordered to go and get his or her cap, on the double; otherwise, its loss would be reported as "sabotaging one's clothing." Whoever did not know the game and actually tried to recover the hat was gunned down. Sometimes a guard devised a plan with an accomplice who lay in wait until the victim stepped into the forbidden zone. The next time, the roles were switched, so that each guard could earn himself a bounty.

The boundary was an untouchable taboo, its violation an affront to absolute power. This also applied to acts of suicide, when prisoners threw themselves onto the high-voltage wire fence. As a matter of principle, the SS could have nothing against suicide: the more prisoners there were who did away with themselves, the less the SS had to kill. But an unsuccessful suicide attempt was punished by draconian penalties: beating on the whipping post or solitary confinement in the bunker, from which few ever reemerged alive. This sanction had multiple meanings. First, it was meant to deter others from imitating the act, and to prevent the short-circuiting of the fence, which had to be recharged after a suicide. In addition, in an actual escape attempt, the sanction was designed to defend the boundary taboo. The delinquent prisoner was also punished for having failed in the attempt at suicide. Above all, however, the punishment was targeted at this final act of attempted self-determination.[7] Suicide was a final act of human will. It took place at a locus that ranked among the most supreme signs of absolute power, the inviolate camp perimeter. Suicides insulted power by their martyrdom, robbing it of the decision over their own deaths. And they carried out this decision precisely at the spatial point where power believed it had finally vanquished freedom.

Very few prisoners escaped from the camps.[8] Sachsenhausen reported the first three escapes in 1942; the next year, no one escaped. In 1944, 96 managed to flee, and in the first months of 1945, 288 absconded to freedom. In Dachau, there were 338 attempted escapes recorded for the period from March 11, 1943, to January 18, 1945. In Mauthausen, only 30 escapes were reported over the four-year span from 1938 to 1942; in 1943, there were 44; in 1944, 226 escapes were documented, followed in early 1945 by 339, though only 31 of these were from the heavily fortified base camp. Of the 639 prisoners who escaped Mauthausen, at least 165 were recaptured. According to incomplete statistics, eight escapes were registered for the entire Auschwitz complex in 1940–41; that figure jumped to 120 in 1942, and the Gestapo managed to recapture 65. Of the 310 reported escapees from Auschwitz for 1943, 156 were seized; of the 209 documented for 1944, 42 were recaptured. The number of attempted escapes rose as the war wore on. Chances for success mounted with the establishment of satellite camps, whose boundaries were less heavily fortified. By contrast, the main camps resembled regular fortresses. A successful escape always required extensive organization and collective assistance. One had to arrange a counterfeit pass, a bicycle or car from a military garage, food, and a sketched map of the environs. Now and then, a guard or civilian worker could be bribed. Of paramount importance, however, was an address to which one could go, a safe hideout where one could lie low and wait out the search. If resistance groups were operating in the area, the escapee was usually taken in quickly and helped. Frequently, however, the local population formed an additional barrier around the camp. Inside the territory of the Reich, Jews, Poles, and Russians, who made the boldest attempts at escape, always had to expect that they might be reported by German civilians. Jews who had managed to escape from Auschwitz were delivered into the hands of the Gestapo by Polish anti-Semites. The boundaries of the camp did not end at the physical barrier and the barbed wire.

Because escape was virtually hopeless, the only breach of the boundary was generally achieved by smuggling goods and information. The camp space was sealed off not only by physical barriers, the threat of death, and collaborators, but also by a mental wall. The policy of terror, and that of forgetting,[9] included strict postal censorship, the prohibition of private conversations with civilian workers, and a total ban on writing for certain categories of prisoners.[10] Soviet citizens, almost all Jews, prisoners seized during *Nacht-und-Nebel* operations, Italians, Greeks, and (in 1944–45) all those whose homelands had been liberated by the Allies were not allowed to write to relatives. Others were granted permission, generally block by block, once or twice a month, in accordance with printed instructions, and only in German. Inmates were allowed to receive two postcards or letters a month, as well as remittances of money; starting in September 1941, they were permitted packages with clothing. Beginning in October 1942, food packages were also allowed, though these were often confiscated or pilfered by the SS. Using these official avenues, it was possible to transmit clandestine information via hidden letters concealed in the packages and secret symbols scribbled on the postcards. Otherwise, all that remained were secret channels using intermediaries who had greater freedom of movement in the camp, trustworthy Kapos, corruptible SS militiamen, or civilians.[11] That procedure was risky and expensive. The prisoner had to pay for sworn silence and to take an accessory into his or her confidence. Like escape, smuggling often required some sort of conspiratorial assistance. The prisoner paid for violating the boundary, and had to place himself or herself in the hands of an intermediary whose reliability could only be determined after the fact. In this way, the boundary also contributed indirectly to social differentiation in prisoner society. Whoever had some belongings could pay for smuggled goods. A prisoner who chanced upon a civilian worker in the same Kommando willing to assist was in a position to gain access to goods that increased the chances of survival in the camp. But those who had nothing, never received a package, had no external contacts on the job, and were not protected by any prisoner-functionary had no chance to break through the isolation of the pervasive misery and deprivation.

The only exit from the prisoner camp was through the gate. It formed a narrow sluice in the boundary through which newcomers were herded into the camp, a checkpoint at which Kommandos were counted and searched each day. The gate marked the transition between two zones. Ahead of it stretched the domain of the SS; behind it lay the barracks settlement of the prisoners. At the same time, it symbolized the code of terror. It did not open up a path to freedom, but marked its end.

The specific architecture of the camp gate was completely in accordance with the overall camp system. It was a simple, unadorned building made of bricks or wooden beams, expedient, practical, one or two stories high. There was a passageway running through the middle, along with two symmetrical side wings; these were punctured by short bands of windows or hatches covered by metal grilles. In its simple, stark regularity, it resembled the depressing entrance gates of many factories, military barracks, or customs stations. But it was a building that burned itself into the mind, leaving an unforgettable impression. The gatehouse was situated at an angle to the access road. Unlike the walls and fences that enclosed an open area, the gate blocked the road, closing it off. From a distance, it looked like a compact latch, at its center a stocky, squat tower, barely higher than a third story. Passing through the entrance, one went under the tower of the main sentry guard. The platform for the guards was surrounded by a wooden balustrade; searchlights, flanked by loudspeakers, stared down at the *Appellplatz*. The apex of the small pyramid-shaped roof was topped by a clock and a flag. In a normal complex, the gatehouse would hardly have attracted any attention; in the camp, however, it towered over all other structures.

This gatehouse type was realized in a pure form in Dachau, Buchenwald, Sachsenhausen, Gusen, and Niederhagen. This pattern of central tower and side wings was also used in Birkenau, though with expanded dimensions. The main gate was meant not only for vehicles and columns of marching prisoners; it also accommodated the deportation trains. From mid-May 1944, they ended their journey inside the camp. The whistle of the locomotives at the gate announced to the Sonderkommando in the crematoria that a new transport had arrived. In the camps set up during the course of the war, it is possible to discern a certain simplification of the type and a reduction of the elements. In Natzweiler, a double wooden frame some five meters high was deemed sufficient; this structure framed the two gate wings, made of slats, wire cables, and barbed wire. In Stutthof, the gate was constructed of heavy and light boards; on the left side, a wooden stairway led up to the guards' platform that surrounded the entrance. The unity of gate and tower had been preserved, but the construction had been pared down to a skeletal wooden frame. The subcamps, often on the grounds of private companies, had nothing but gates the height of the fences, fashioned of steel pipes and wire netting, with movable barriers in front and sentry houses. The gate in Mauthausen was an exception; it resembled a fortress. The gate was flanked by two mighty towers whose roofs extended outward. This fortress gate doubled the effect of security and control.

City walls exude a feeling of unity and security. They safeguard the residents from foreign intruders and attacks. By contrast, knife-rests and electrified barbed wire transformed the camp town into a sealed-off archipelago. These boundaries were clear, unmistakable, and insurmountable. They did not protect inhabitants from external dangers; rather, they shielded the camp powers from internal uprisings. The town gate is a hinge between inside and outside, between the enclosed space of the settlement and the surrounding countryside. It is the point where two worlds meet. Internal and external worlds, openness and closure, freedom and its lack—these are the symbolic oppositions that the gate marks and mediates. The camp gate was totally different: even if the gate stood open and the barrier was lifted, there was no way out. Whoever marched out in the morning with the Kommando always returned, alive or dead. The camp gate was not a sign of linkage, an interface between inner and outer, but a sign of final and irreversible inclusion. However, because it could be opened, because it constantly held out the elusive promise of egress, its closure had an even more stifling, depressive effect.

The inscriptions over the gate entrance did not deceive people about the camp's true meaning. In Sachsenhausen, new arrivals read the words "Protective Custody Camp" (*Schutzhaftlager*) instead of "Concentration Camp" emblazoned on the front of the camp, a juridical pacification in angular Gothic lettering. On the outside wall of Buchenwald appeared the words "My Country—Right or Wrong," a totally meaningless slogan for the international prisoner society inside. The motto at Dachau, "Arbeit macht frei" (Work Is Liberty), is well known; it was also used elsewhere, a hollow, cynical promise from the tradition of the work society. No prisoner was ever released because of hard work and good performance. The slogan hung over the gate in Buchenwald was "Jedem das Seine" (To Each His Own), the old motto of respect for variety and natural inequality, and of the equal right of all to that difference. The camp transmuted its meaning into the very opposite. All who did not conform to total social homogeneity were banished behind an insurmountable boundary where only one form of equality existed—that of those slated to die.

The gate was more than just a symbolic locus: it was also a social site, a place of service, a prominent point of control, an arena of harassment and torment.[12] The newcomers, after having been chased through the entrance under a hail of blows, were often left to wait at the gatehouse, standing rigid in rows of five, facing the wall of the side wing or the adjoining wall, their hats or caps in hand. Whoever moved, stamped a foot, or whispered something to a fellow inmate was immediately shouted at, struck, or beaten. The guards at the gate and the block leader on duty were able to keep a casual eye on the column. Thus, the prisoners were kept standing there in uncertainty, sometimes for hours, in all kinds of weather: motionless, a block of human pillars, while the hands of the clock above their heads moved slowly and the guards at the gate hung around, shuffling, inactive. Now and then a *Blockführer* (block leader) approached, examining the successive rows, scrutinizing the first prisoner in line, then the second. Finally he would stop, legs apart, before some prisoner to ask, with a grin, the reason the prisoner had been sent to the camp. If the answer satisfied him, he went on to question the next; if it did not, he taught his victim a terse lesson, delivering a barrage of punches to the body and head. And if he chanced to stumble upon a Jew, his rage intensified into a tirade of hate; pummeling the prisoner, he attacked with blows from his whip, kicking and beating the prisoner until he or she collapsed. The new arrivals at the gate were a welcome target for the excesses of violence.

Just as the boundary served as a locus for execution, the gate was used by the SS as a public site for torment. In Mauthausen, the new arrivals who had been set apart as unfit for work were lined up, half-naked, after disinfection and a shower, in front of the "wailing wall" next to the gatehouse. During the summer, the guards would wait until the exhausted prisoners collapsed in the searing heat; in the winter, they poured cold water over them several times until they had finally frozen into pillars of ice. In many camps, those who committed minor transgressions were punished by having to stand at the gate. While the Kommandos filed out, the offenders were brought to the gate in the early morning and forced to stand there, rigid and motionless, the entire day—a *Stehkommando*. Soon, some began to sway like drunks, and leaned their heads against the wall; others were forced to squat, their hands clasped behind their necks in a "Saxon salute." If a guard came by, these prisoners summoned up the last bit of strength in an effort to stand at attention. Otherwise they would be kicked, or prisoners' heads might be pounded against the stone wall until their noses were broken. Standing at the gate was a static mode of torture without technical aids, a torment of silence; the prisoners formed a public statuary in stasis, at a site dominated by the flow of people coming and going.

The statics of torment stood in stark contrast to the gate as a place of passage. However, in the vicinity of the camp gate, a natural, civil way of walking was hardly possible. The new arrivals were chased through in double time; the Kommandos were marched out in military formation, accompanied by the camp band, one unit after another, in rows of five. But many were too exhausted to follow the orders of the Kapos. Tired, they limped forward, dragging their bodies toward the gate, although a difficult test awaited them there. The Kapo ran on ahead and reported the strength of his unit. Then he shouted "Hats off! Eyes right!" as his unit filed past. Mechanically, the shaven heads snapped to the left, saluting the rapport leader, who counted the rows with his assistants. The prisoners on the outside of the column might expect blows and a kick from a boot if they caught a guard's attention in any way— even for an infraction as minor as that their extended fingers were not properly touching their trouser seams, according to camp regulation. In the large camps, there were several thousand prisoners who marched through the gate in this way day after day, morning and evening. They had to show that gate their respect, saluting it as though it were the sacrosanct site of power. The gate was a control station, a checkpoint where one could read the tempo of the day, the beat of camp routine. The marching column, that macabre parade of debilitated, footsore prisoners, symbolizes the highest degree of order of collective movement. It is a monotonously regulated juxtaposition, a uniform, parallel forward motion in which each prisoner has a place; any glance to the side is strictly forbidden, and all perform the same gesture on command. The gate was the stage on which the powerlessness and humiliation of the entire prisoner society could be seen. That society was transmuted into a defenseless series in movement, demonstrating its deference to absolute power with a collective gesture.

There was another strict set of rules for the individual prisoner who had to pass through the gate during the day to accomplish some appointed task. On the path leading through the gate, or in the sentry booth in front of it, there was often a window at which the block leader sat on duty, recording in the rapport book each person who passed through. To assist him, a second block leader was situated at the gate; armed with a truncheon, he stopped all the passersby and directed them to the window. At a distance of at least three meters from the gate guard, the prisoners had to stop abruptly, snap smartly to attention, tear their caps from their heads, shout out their numbers, and report where they were coming from and where they were headed. This was a tricky task, especially for the foreigners. No one was allowed to pass without a good reason. The entry in the rapport book listed each and every movement; the file guaranteed order and completeness.

Located in the side wing of the gatehouse behind the sentry room were the offices of the camp leader, the rapport leader, and the *Arbeitseinsatzführer*, the SS noncom responsible for organizing prisoner labor. A microphone was set up in one room; orders and announcements read out there reached every nook and corner of the camp. The loudspeakers for the roll-call square were mounted above the gate path; smaller loudspeakers were located in the blocks and the workshops. Day and night, a steady, penetrant stream of sound could be directed across the entire enclosure of the camp. Sometimes a speech by the Führer was broadcast, and radio music sometimes blared on Sunday afternoons. The all-penetrating acoustic barrage went hand in hand with complete and total visibility. The searchlights at the gate illuminated the huge *Appellplatz* after dark, transforming night into blinking day. A broad panorama of the camp could be seen from the tower where the two guards were posted. The machine gun was loaded, its safety on, set for automatic fire. The box of hand grenades lay ready next to it, at hand if needed. The unobstructed field of vision from the gate tower was simultaneously a free field of fire.

The gate was a locus with multiple meanings and functions. Far from being a mere passageway, a hinge between the inside and outside, it represented absolute power. It served as a station during the ceremony of admission and a place of public torment. It was a customs checkpoint, a site for control, a place of bureaucratic registration. This was power's arch of triumph. In its mottoes, the keepers had documented their cynical philosophy. Its clock, the only one in the camp, dictated time. Loudspeakers, searchlights, and weapons assured total surveillance, total threat. The rapport book recorded every passage to and fro. The gate was the symbol of the camp, its architectonic emblem. In marching past, the columns of prisoners saluted the gate, not the rapport leader. The contrasts at this locus were radical: a ban on speaking for those waiting below; above, the blaring metallic voice of the loudspeakers. Here, a prohibition on movement and the lockstep of the ordered march; there, the lolling guards. On one side, prisoners staring rigidly at the wall; on the other, the open panorama from the guard tower. Here, humiliation and collective subjugation; there, power and triumph. The gatehouse was a simple, functional structure, architecturally hardly worth an extra glance. Yet as a social locus it was the symbol of camp power, its squat monument.

6

The Block

I do not know who my neighbour is; I am not even sure that it is always the same person because I have never seen his face except for a few seconds amidst the uproar of reveille, so that I know his back and feet much better than his face. He does not work in my Kommando and only comes into the bunk at curfew time; he wraps himself in the blanket, pushes me aside with a blow from his bony hips, turns his back on me and at once begins to snore. Back against back, I struggle to regain a reasonable area of the straw mattress: with the base of my back I exercise a progressive pressure against his back; then I turn around and try to push with my knees; I take hold of his ankles and try to place them a little further over so as not to have his feet next to my face. But it is all in vain: he is much heavier than me and seems turned to stone in his sleep. So I adapt myself to lie like this, forced into immobility, half-lying on the wooden edge. Nevertheless I am so tired and stunned that I, too, soon fall asleep, and I seem to be sleeping on the tracks of a railroad.[1]

ABSOLUTE POWER compresses space, destroying the territories of the person. Prisoners were only confined individually when they were sent to the detention cells in the bunkers; in the wooden barracks and stables that were on the plots of the grid, hundreds were crowded together. The camp regime sliced prisoner society into segments and distributed the inmates to the various blocks, jamming them into the narrowest spaces. There they had to remain penned in from the end of the evening roll call until morning roll call. Their living quarters were a site of social control, a place of constriction, compression, and social inequality, of anonymity and misery.

A change in quarters because of transfer or transport could mean a fundamental alteration in living conditions.[2] To be transferred to an unfinished sub-camp generally meant not only heavy menial labor by day but nights spent in improvised emergency dwellings.[3] In Hannover-Misburg, a satellite of the Neuengamme camp, prisoners were initially bedded down in army tents before being requartered in stables. For a population of seven hundred inmates, there was a single provisional washing facility, and one latrine with six seats. In

Drütte near Salzgitter, the prisoners were confined in converted locker and supply rooms beneath the overhead roadway of an ironworks. Each block was about forty meters long, with one entrance and barred windows. From March 1943 to mid-1944, some six hundred persons were squeezed together in each of the filthy, unheated blocks; the number later rose to seven hundred. In Echterdingen, an airport hangar served as mass quarters; it was a large, drafty hall fifteen meters high, and its warm-air blower was defective. During the first few weeks, prisoners in Gandersheim were housed in a former church that had later been used as a barn. In Porta Westfalica, some fourteen hundred prisoners were billeted in the hall of a hotel, 25 × 15 meters. Its windows had been covered with metal shutters and protective grilles; the center of the hall was set off from the rest by special pillars and used as a clearing for roll call. The walls were lined with four-tiered bunks, two prisoners to a single bed.

The conditions in Dora-Mittelbau, opened in the late summer of 1943 as a subcamp of Buchenwald,[4] were particularly catastrophic. Thousands were housed there, month after month, in four subterranean tunnels of the Kohnstein massif. Wooden floors were first laid at a height of 3 meters in the tunnels (each 11.5 meters across) to form a horizontal surface of 120 × 10 meters. Four-tiered bunk beds were then set up on this floor. Each tunnel had a sleeping capacity of about a thousand. Sleeping was by shifts, a "hot bed" system. When one shift left for work, the other occupied the just-vacated beds. The water-supply system for washing and drinking was totally inadequate; the cool air, dank and stuffy, accelerated the spread of tuberculosis. In the beginning, prisoners were brought outside for fresh air every day; later on, this was done only once a week. Not until the summer of 1944 were the last prisoners transferred from the tunnel accommodations to the nearby barracks camp.

As a rule, there were two basic types of blocks in the fully developed main camps and numerous satellites.[5] The standard barracks was about 50 meters long and 8 meters wide, and was divided into two wings. Each wing had a dayroom measuring 9 × 6 meters, furnished with tables, benches, stools, lockers, and a stove for heating. Doors led from the hall to the washroom, toilet, and broom cupboard. The dormitory was 12 × 8 meters, and contained two- or three-tiered iron bunk beds or wooden frames. Two woolen blankets and a sack of straw were standard issue for each bed. The facility was planned to accommodate some 150 prisoners, but that norm was adhered to only in the blocks reserved for the "Prominents." From 1939 on, most of the blocks were overcrowded. Generally, two prisoners had to share a single bunk, a berth eighty centimeters across. In periods of extreme overcrowding, the dayroom and dormitory were cleared out, and the sacks of straw that served as mattresses were placed on the bare floor. In this way, more than 400 prisoners could be confined to a single block.

Army stables were also used as mass housing; their prefabricated sections were quickly assembled and dismantled. These drafty barracks made of thin wooden boards and cardboard roofs were used strictly as housing blocks, and had no sanitary facilities. Latrine buckets stood in a corner near the exit. The stalls contained three-tiered wooden bunks; these were 2 meters high, and measured 280 × 185 centimeters; they were meant to sleep fifteen prisoners each. In fact, as many as 1,000 persons were bedded down in these stables; depending on size, they had originally been planned to house 250 to 400. Instead of fifteen, some forty prisoners were packed into a single bunk, frequently in "sardine formation," the head of one at the feet of the next. Although many inmates suffered from diarrhea, they were not allowed to leave the block to go to the latrine hut at night. The doors remained locked, and the narrow hatches were insufficient for ventilation. The straw sacks were filthy and infested with vermin.

Although they all were subject to the cramped space, stench, and filth in the blocks, inmates were not all equal. Space was a privilege. Housing quarters indicated a prisoner's value and status. Social differences determined the assignment of space, and its apportionment in turn determined the degree of social mixing and differentiation. Heterogeneity is an effective strategy of power. It stirs up rivalries and impedes solidarity. But an equally effective strategy is to separate the categories, aggravating social antagonisms by overcrowding. Even when prisoners were housed according to Kommando and nationality, the assignments were in keeping with the predetermined hierarchy of classes, the given pecking order. The spatial order of the quarters was an incorporated class order. The camp pariahs—Jews, Soviet POWs, and Slavs—were placed in the dilapidated wooden barracks or tents, and new arrivals, confined in the quarantine blocks, were compelled to vegetate in the most wretched conditions. The greatest mixing was in the blocks of the camp "middle classes," though one nationality often predominated in a given block. The Prominent blocks were reserved for the camp aristocracy: the German and Austrian Kapos, clerks, and general factotums of the SS. They alone had the privilege of single beds and their own lockers. The straw sacks and blankets were covered with a grey-blue checkered sheet. The Prominents were allowed to wash regularly, and to change their linen and underwear.[6] The block was the special preserve of a group where each person had his or her own place. In the slum barracks, by contrast, space for individual movement was kept to a minimum. When prisoners were sitting or sleeping, the spaces between them were limited to a few centimeters at most.

The distribution of space in the blocks was also determined by social differences. Although the normal prisoner had to fight for the smallest bit of elbow room, the block personnel had a special closed-off and reserved corner where they had their beds and private lockers. Frequently, the *Blockältesten* (block chiefs) and *Stubendienste* (assistants) expanded their own territory at the expense of the prisoners. They occupied the entire dayroom and restricted the others to the dormitory. Only where the prisoner-functionaries tried to create order by way of authority were they satisfied with a separate corner and no more.[7] This was a privilege granted even in the stables and provisional emergency quarters of the external subcamps. While the other inmates had to lie on paper sacks of straw, naked boards, or the bare clay floor, and had to eat perched on the planks of their pallets, the prisoner-functionaries always had their own territory, a table and chairs, their own bed linen, and several blankets each. A territory is an invariant area appropriated and marked out by an individual or group and then defended from incursion, encroachment, or attack.[8] In the blocks of the concentration camp, only the prisoner-functionaries had a secured territory at their disposal. This group had the power to occupy certain spaces; it had sufficient room to deposit belongings and demonstrate its superior position.[9] The social contrast was manifest more in the fact of its existence than in the size of the territory—that is, whether or not an individual had his or her own lebensraum.

The block was a space for surveillance. Only if the prisoner-functionaries considered themselves part of the rank-and-file prison population and were able to act as a buffer against incursions could the housing block serve as an island in the swirling stream of the camp, a place of retreat after work. The control policy pursued by the prisoner-functionaries determined whether the block became a social niche for the inmates. Everything depended on their ability to maintain order by group pressure and forceful action so as to avoid being harassed by the SS. The larger the camps became, the more the living quarters deteriorated, growing ever filthier and more vermin infested. The bigger the camp, the more the SS limited itself to sporadic spot checks and arbitrary actions. But everyday life was determined by the block personnel. Together with the SS block leaders, the prisoner-functionaries were the bosses in the block. Their task was to implement the prescribed rules, but they had considerable latitude. Many took the role of local custodians of camp power. They preserved their privileges by behaving as if the SS itself were acting when they did. They exercised the power delegated to them in an excessive manner, turning their blocks into their own special dominions.

There were ample occasions for terror penalties and harassment. The official block code regulated even the smallest detail. The rules stated that prisoners had to sleep dressed only in their shirts. Whoever was caught wearing other articles of clothing under the thin blanket—because he or she felt cold or was afraid of being robbed—was beaten severely. As long as each prisoner had his or her own locker, every object had to be in its assigned place: towels, bowls, clothing. Surprise checks kept the prisoners under constant pressure. Sometimes the inmates were greeted by chaos when, exhausted, they returned from work: during the day, the SS had maliciously overturned all the cabinets, strewing the floor with their possessions. The SS created disorder so as to be able to intervene—in the name of order. There had to be strict, fastidious order and cleanliness everywhere—inside in the barracks, outside on the surrounding paths. Tables were polished, cabinets dusted, floors scrubbed, washrooms hosed down, toilets cleaned. The pathways around the block were flattened by a roller or swept clean; weeds and grass were removed from the flower beds.

A special source of hazing and harassment was the regulations for making the beds (*Bettenbau*).[10] Every morning, during block inspection, the straw sack mattresses had to be pulled taut as a board. The edges had to form a ninety-degree angle; the pillows had to be smoothed down into wrinkleless cubes. Checkered sheeting had to be aligned precisely—not just on a single bed, but for the whole row of beds. Some SS inspectors checked the beds with rulers and levels. After reveille, however, the prisoners had little time or space to "build" their beds properly. Those who slept in the upper bunks were told to hurry up by those underneath, or cursed out if they stepped on the lower straw mattresses. The block chief intervened immediately if a bed was not in perfect alignment. The faster one finished, the better one's chances to grab a place up front in the line for the washroom, at the toilets, and in the crush of inmates waiting for breakfast to be distributed. Whoever could not manage to make the bed had to ask others for help—or hire a "bed specialist," whose services were paid for with bread, soup, or money. The fear of punishment was compounded by the social pressure from fellow prisoners. If a single bed violated the norm, all were threatened with a collective penalty, such as "sports" (penal exercises) or a slash in the amount of allotted food. Thus, each prisoner had an interest in making sure the other inmates did not become conspicuous in some way and disturb block order. Terror was superimposed on the block like a mold, shaping relations between the inmates. Power took control and spread through space, without the SS having to intervene. Even when everything looked acceptable, there was always a speck of dust on the locker, a wrinkle in the last bed at the end of the corridor.

The practices of block order are reminiscent of the rules and regulations of military discipline. Such harassment is not an uncommon practice in military barracks. Indeed, prisoners with military experience had a decided practical advantage when it came to adjusting to the rigors of camp life. Nonetheless, the camp powers were only secondarily concerned with drill, discipline, and conditioning. In military organizations, hazing and humiliation are an intermediate phase during which raw recruits are processed into obedient soldiers full of esprit de corps. But for absolute power, abasement is an end in itself. The rules of spatial order made terror a permanent fixture. They were designed in such a way that it was impossible to obey them completely. A high degree of organizational skill and joint coordination was necessary to arrange the beds, clothing, and shoes according to regulation, to obey the morning's hygienic rules, to distribute and eat the breakfast rations—and all this in the short span from reveille to the morning roll call. That was a task that could only be successfully accomplished by a relatively homogeneous group of block residents with a low level of spatial compression. Overcrowding and social mixture provided opportunities for the exercise of power in the camp. They generated so much disorder that there were always occasions for encroachment, intrusion, and attack. Discipline and order render terror redundant. By contrast, disorder provides pretexts for intervention. Absolute power has an interest in chaos, which is why it repeatedly (re)creates chaos itself via the rules for spatial order.

Spatial crowding had an immediate impact on the relations of the prisoner with others, and with himself or herself. Block society was predicated on coercion. Few could choose with whom they shared a bunk and straw—unless they had good connections with the *Schreibstube* (the orderly room or prisoners' camp office) or block personnel. Coercion did not mean merely being compressed with others in the narrowest space. Inmates had no influence whatsoever regarding the people with whom they were incarcerated; this was also an element of coercion. Physical density alone is generally not the determinant factor in whether people feel cramped.[11] Social relations in space are no less salient. Homogeneous groups, bound together by familiarity, social similarity, or common convictions, are more likely to be able to transmute density into a sense of community—either by internal group pressure or by a shared attitude toward external threat. In anonymous and serial mass formations, however, dissociative tendencies are intensified with the slightest degree of crowding. Although mutual aid and group discipline were possible in blocks with a homogeneous population, there was a constant struggle of all against all in the mass barracks, a struggle for the elementary spatial prerequisites for survival. Prisoners were forced to jostle for a place at the washbasin or over the latrine,[12] a place to sit down when eating or near a warm stove, room to move around in the bunk, a piece of blanket. Once territories are eliminated, norms of distance destroyed, and avenues of escape blocked, territoriality intensifies. Action loses its reciprocal character. The norms of spatial reciprocity, mutual recognition of territories, stalls, and intimate zones are abrogated; personal space is deleted.[13] The more densely people are boxed together, the more powerful is the struggle for a modicum of distance, and the more virulent mutual aggression becomes.

Crowding also shifts the sensual foundations of social contact. The senses of eye and ear, those main organs of social interaction, forfeit significance to the more proximal senses of touch, heat, and smell. One prisoner pushed aside the next, shoved and jostled; he pressed his sharp knees into his bedmate's body when sleeping, and irritated him with foul odors and excretions. The territories of the self—even the exterior wrappings of clothing and skin, which otherwise serve to protect the body—were constantly under threat.[14] There were constant infringements, intrusions, and encroachments, not only because of noise, obtrusiveness, or theft, but as a result of the sheer shortage of space. Even if all had behaved considerately and had developed a set of shared rules about distance, a proxemic code, the maintenance of distance was totally impossible; territorial violation was unavoidable. Those who slept on the top berths enjoyed a small advantage, as did inmates who had wooden chests at the head of their straw mattresses.[15] Like the territory for possessions, the zone of intimacy was also endangered. Personal space normally varies between groups and cultures. However, the dire lack of space in the camp reduced these differences below the brute minimum. Feelings of shame became pointless when prisoners were constrained to push and shove for a spot at the toilet pail, or when an inmate had grown so weak that he was no longer able to make his way over the obstacles in the dark central corridor, and consequently relieved himself on the spot where he was lying.

A special irritation was forced motionlessness. The nights on the wooden bunk or the floor, when all lay on one side facing in the same direction, heads on contorted arms, only allowed to turn over en masse on command, were part of the torment of daily camp life. Crowding generated an oppressive isolation. If an inmate wanted to keep a spot, he or she simply could not afford to move, because the next prisoner would spread out immediately. Push the prisoner in front a few centimeters away, and the one to your rear involuntarily would move in closer. People were incarcerated in a cell composed of human bodies, a living cubicle. The presence of the others overwhelmed the self. Each prisoner lay alone, for himself or herself, in the midst of the mass—powerless to protest, to pull back, to move. The only way out was sleep. It was not the violence of the supervisors that demolished one's space for movement—it was the bodies of one's fellows. Although jammed together in a constricted capsule, this mass was devoid of any internal links or unity. Nowhere is the forlornness of the individual greater than in an atomized, densely packed mass, where each is eager to grab the place and space of the other. Thus it was that prisoners often felt a certain sense of relief in the morning as they watched the dead being carried out of the block: they, the survivors, had gained a bit of vacated space. One person's death meant extra room for the others.[16]

The ordering of space is a preferred technology of absolute power. By manipulating space, it spares itself the need for permanent violence. It saturates space, forcing people into a situation without exit. In the camps, it zoned the terrain, marking out the sectors and girding the camp with insurmountable fortifications. It channeled movements, compressing bodies into a constricted mass. Zoning and segmentation, collective seclusion and constant boundary control, regulated locomotion and motionlessness, the granting of special privileges, crowding—these were the strategic methods for the ordering of space. Power stretched from the boundaries, extending into the microspace of the bunk pallet. It began with the regionalization of sectors and ended in the minuscule intervals remaining in the prisoners' block. It asserted its hegemony over camp social space and personal, individual space. The destruction of human beings commenced with this organization of camp space. But this was not the only structure that supported the camp regime of power. Another was the camp's social time, and the time of the prisoners.

7

Camp Time

Filled with its hourly harassments, a small span of
time, like a day, seemed to last an eternity. A larger
length of time though, such as a week, with its monotonous daily round, appeared to fly by incredibly fast.
And my fellow prisoners always concurred whenever
I said: "In the camp, a day lasts longer than a week!"[1]

SPATIAL ORDER determines sites and localizes events; temporal order marks
ruptures and generates sequences. Space is structured in terms of distances
and extensions; time is structured according to intervals, periods, duration.
Spatial control distributes bodies, guiding their movements; temporal control
jackets action into recurrent sequences. Social time is an objective, imposed
standard time of organization, but power can arbitrarily expand, slow down,
or accelerate it. Camp time was more than the external compulsion characteristic of all social time.[2] Camp power permeated inner time-consciousness,
sundering the internal band that laces together memory, expectation, and hope.
Absolute power far surpasses the familiar forms of organized temporal control.
It is not satisfied simply with the synchronization and coordination of events.
It destroys the continuity of inner time and severs the ties between past and
future, locking people into an eternal present. Far from being satisfied with
controlling human bodies, it seizes hold of biographical time and the motions
of the mind.

The planning of time is one of the proven tools of social power.[3] Scheduling
fixes obligatory chains of events and determines change and duration; it generates repetitions and habits. Schedules mark beginning points, end points,
phases, transitions, linear sequences or cyclic returns. Schedules are programs
of succession. They prescribe when something should be done; they define
times for action and pauses, directing future events into predetermined paths.
Through them, action becomes predictable and amenable to social integration.
The fuller the schedule, the less time that remains for unplanned incidents,
deviations, the wasting of time. The more dense the temporal grid, the more
intensive the use of time. Planning determines the smallest moment; it knows
only maximum rapidity, precision, effectiveness. Schedules guarantee effectiveness and provide a criterion for its monitoring. In its factorylike organiza-

tional form, the camp resembles other disciplinary institutions that gain stability by regimenting everyday temporal sequences.[4]

But absolute power has only a limited interest in a rigid institutionalization of time. It regularly departs from the standardized time tracks it has instituted.[5] As in any formal system, the regulation of time is an effective technology of power; on the other hand, however, order binds the regime, endangering its sovereignty. With a rigid time structure, terror would abrogate itself. Its intrusions and attacks would be predictable; the victims could take countermeasures; power would degenerate into a mere means for order. Nothing of the kind existed in the concentration camp. Terror alternates between planning and disorder, between regulation and assault. It installs a temporal order that assures a minimal degree of organization, but builds phases of acceleration and hesitation into that time path. By reserving for itself the choice of deviations and special times, power secures its rule over time. The temporal law of absolute power is not calculability, but the free variation of tempo, the shift between duration and abrupt suddenness, hectic rush and waiting, rest and shock. The camp's standard time was deceptive. Within the external framework of cyclical repetition, time pulsated irregularly.[6] Consequently, no prisoner was able to devise long-term plans for action. Whatever inmates decided to do could always be foiled, thwarted, or nipped in the bud.

Camp time did not evolve. It is true that the organization had a history: it was established, built up, expanded; personnel were replaced with a certain regularity. There were displacements in function, local traditions, and habits of suppression. There were watershed events: the first public execution, the outbreak of an epidemic, putting a specific workshop into operation. And there was a gradual, ultimately headlong deterioration in material conditions. Nonetheless, the time system of the camp was not one of development. Its function was not to create discipline, to inculcate abilities, or to reinforce set activities. Penalties were not meant to improve or educate the penalized. It is a fundamental mistake to confuse the temporal structure in the camp with the time that predominates in modern disciplinary institutions.[7] Camp time was not goal oriented. It lacked the gradation of internal elements, the increasing series, the constancy of accumulation. The temporal law of terror combines cyclical recurrence with endless duration and suddenness or abruptness. Despite changing historical circumstances, this temporal law governed the course of daily routine right to the end.

The course of the dense day obeyed a recurrent schema.[8] The prisoners were awakened at 4:00 or 4:30 A.M. by clanging bells, whistles, or sirens; in the winter, this reveille was generally one hour later.[9] Prisoners who did not get up immediately were beaten from their beds by the block personnel. In a hectic rush, beds had to be made, the block cleaned, clothing put on, breakfast distributed, and a visit paid to the latrine. Inmates had half an hour, or at most forty-five minutes, from the crack of reveille until they formed up for the morning roll call. Although the prisoners were still by themselves in the blocks, this first phase of the day was full of shouting, forced hurry, feverish frenzy. The principal task was to leave the block in a neat and orderly condition, and for all to appear outside for inspection. Whoever dallied was punished by beating, or shoved along by fellow prisoners. Even before the SS made its appearance, the day commenced with a brutal, frenetic scramble.

This rush was followed by a period of waiting. The prisoners marched out by block onto the *Appellplatz* and waited there for the SS to appear. The block personnel counted the inmates and reported the results to those on duty in the prisoner orderly room. They in turn passed the total on to the SS rapport leader. The SS block leaders double-checked the results, running through another count so that the reporting officer could compare the two totals. In order to make sure the final tally was correct, the prisoners in the sick bay and those who had died during the night also had to be counted. This double bureaucratic procedure should hardly have required more than half an hour, given the experienced and well-rehearsed chain of reporting. But the process was often delayed or interrupted by violence. Despite the fixed time for morning roll call, the SS was often late. Illuminated by searchlights, the columns had to wait in the first light of dawn in every conceivable type of weather until the camp lords took the stage. Their entrance was a carefully calculated show of power.[10] To leave thousands waiting is always a demonstration of total power. And time was something the camp masters had plenty of. Inmates did not march off to their places of work until it was light. Consequently, morning roll call in the winter months could drag on for more than ninety minutes, until the command was given over the loudspeakers for the prisoners to form up into Kommandos. The accommodation of working hours to daylight was the only concession the camp regime made to natural time.

After roll call, the prisoners ran to the assembly points for their Kommandos. For several minutes, there was pandemonium on the broad square. The roll-call formation dissolved, transforming itself into a turbulent mass, until the throng had regrouped into work columns. To an outside eye, this short period of transition looked like chaotic confusion. Each prisoner ran as fast as possible to his or her preassigned spot; the crush and jostling was not a circulating motion. In no case could one afford to be late. Latecomers always had to expect that they would be beaten by the Kapos. Those who still had not been assigned to a unit and tried to join one were chased away immediately. The Kommandos fell in and formed up, were counted, and marched off, one after the next, to the camp gate. Striding in step, they performed the obligatory ritual of salute while marching past, and were then taken over by SS guards, who escorted them to work. By this time, it was about 6:00 A.M. (or in the winter, an hour later). Within the span of just under two hours, the camp society had changed its social aggregation several times: first the tumult in the blocks, then the long wait standing in block units at roll call, then the mad rush of the throng, and finally the controlled marching exit of the Kommandos.

The march was also an occasion for mistreatment. Kapos and SS prodded the hobbling prisoners to march in double time, or ordered them to sing.[11] If the singing faltered or a prisoner lagged behind, there was a hail of blows and kicks.[12] The march was anything but a regular, ordered, carefully measured movement. Only those at the head of the column were able to move at an approximately even pace. There were constant disruptions at its center and its end. Those on the outside were threatened by possible blows from the guards; some could not keep up with the tempo, fell behind, and had to make up for the distance by performing a double-time march. Only when the guards happened to be in a jovial mood did they leave the prisoners to themselves. Yet then too, a prisoner had to be careful not to become conspicuous by talking too loud, having an improper look on his or her face, stumbling, or limping. The journey to work was the longest stretch of space that the prisoner had to cross in the camp enclosure. Inside the perimeter of the large cordon, it was generally only a few hundred meters, but numerous places of work were several kilometers away.[13] If they were wearing rough wooden clogs, that was sheer torture. The shoes chafed the skin, cutting open bloody wounds; they caused infections and swelling.[14] One's feet turned to lead. But despite this, no prisoner could afford to be last. For that reason, many preferred to go barefoot or in rags wrapped around their feet, even when they had to plod ankle-deep through swamps.

The frenetic pace continued at work. At times, the order was given to execute all movements in double time—an order obeyed only when the work site was under constant surveillance. For the prisoner, "putting on the brakes" was the supreme dictate. Work tempo was reduced to a minimum as soon as the guards or Kapo were out of sight. When the superior returned, prisoners did their utmost to appear as if they were working at a brisk pace. Since most of the tasks were not mechanized and not bound to the individual time specific to technical devices, working time was pure social time. It was possible to protract it into a continuum, and interrupt it by terror. The regimen of prodding could only be eluded by those clever enough to arrange a leisurely special task, go somewhere the long way round, or join a group being led to the latrine. Vigilance and rest breaks on the job were important for survival. Time seemed to last forever. The only way to diminish the annihilatory pressure of work was to husband one's energies.

There was only one official pause planned during work: the noon break. When the Kommandos returned to the camp at noon, the time it took to go from work to the camp and back was subtracted from this allotted break, as was the time for the noon roll-call count, so only a few minutes remained for eating one's soup. But this noon break was also full of forced hustle and harassment. In the crowd thronging and jostling around the soup pails and tin bowls, some hapless prisoners ended up with nothing to eat at all. This time pressure was not diminished until the decision was made to forgo a noon roll call and deliver lunch directly to the work sites. Of course, the reason for this was not to lengthen the break but to extend working hours. Instead of one hour, the noon respite was now only thirty minutes. There was no further break until work was finished for the day; in winter, that was at dusk; in summer, around 5:00 or 6:00 P.M. Thus, the effective work time in the winter was some eight to nine hours; in the summer months, it was about eleven hours. Out in the satellite camps, where activity was organized in shifts, working time even stretched to twelve hours.[15]

Working time was merciless in duration. No prisoner, aside from a few of those belonging to the Prominents, was allowed to wear a watch. Only the personnel knew precisely how much time had passed. Out in the open, prisoners could only have a rough estimate of time's passage, gauged by the position of the sun. Along with the ruptures in the measurement of time, numerous activities also lacked set, limited objectives. Action was distended into continuous activity without any meaningful end.[16] Digging a large ditch, carrying away a pile of stones, and dragging railway dumping cars up a hill are activities that offer little opportunity for structuring time, for segmenting it by setting up intermediate objectives. Movements run on in a pure, nonstop stream; action is unalleviated by transition and devoid of intermediate stage markers. The only countermeasure is the individual construction of phases and stretches. If a person knew that it took him about ten minutes to transport something, he could calculate from the number of times he traversed the stretch how much time had elapsed, and how many more times he would have to go through that same motion. Duration was divided into equal intervals, though these passed with differing speed.[17] This internal countertime did not abrogate the nightmare of timeless duration, but it diminished its horror, bolstering the feeling that one had gotten through a certain stretch of time, that one had survived another span.

Objective duration and subjective countertime were repeatedly punctured by moments of acute danger. Work time was always terror time. Excesses, mistreatment, and maliciously induced accidents were possible anywhere, at all times. People labored under a constant pall of anxiety. The exact point when violence would erupt was hard to predict. Attacks usually occurred abruptly, without announcement or forewarning. Although the worst could always be expected, violence erupted suddenly. For a brief, shattered moment, the brusqueness of the attack burst time's continuity. The more surprising the violence, the more lightning-fast a guard rushed over to seize a prisoner, the greater was the victims' powerlessness, the deeper their horror and dismay. For this, however, time requires a duration that it instantaneously interrupts and then immediately restores. More than a mere means of abuse, endless time is also the temporal background of terror. Suddenness, the temporal mode of terroristic incursion, requires continuity for contrast. Yet these events do not structure duration; they only interrupt it. They do not give time a direction, but reduce it to a critical instant. The temporal structure of the situation of immediate violence is always occasional.[18] It knows no before and after, only absolute presence. It divides time into now and not-now. The momentary situation has one sole theme: mortal danger. Terror destroys the flow of time. In its wake, it leaves its victims powerless, uncertain, full of tormenting fear of the next attack to come. Thus, time at work was endless and point-focused, continuous and disrupted, an aimless state punctuated by moments of extreme danger.

After work, the morning rhythm was repeated in the opposite direction. To a certain extent, the time of the day's beginning ran backward, a film in reverse. The Kommandos were counted; the bodies of the dead were heaved onto wheelbarrows or hauled back to the camp on the shoulders of their comrades. Although most were totally exhausted and thirsty and many were injured or footsore, the prisoners were often forced to march back at a shuffling double-time pace. At the gate, the same salute ritual as in the morning awaited them. The external Kommandos who had contact with civilians were searched for tobacco, money, or food. Despite the long workday they had put in, the prisoners were not allowed to go back to the barracks for the evening meal. After entering the camp, there was a renewed time of terror: the evening roll call.

Like every mass assembly, evening roll call was held for one ostensible purpose: a bureaucratic check on numbers. This procedure could have been completed in less than an hour, despite the changes during the day—the transports, new arrivals, changes in work units, cases of illness, prisoner deaths. But evening roll call was far more than just a technical administrative affair. It constituted the high-water mark of the daily tide of power. Prisoner society was fully assembled down to the last person; thousands stood in rigid formation, confronted by a handful of SS men to whom they were compelled to show respect. Even the dead and dying had to be present for roll call.[19] They were laid on the ground next to their respective block formations. The fact that the dead could not be brought to the morgue until after roll call was not just a question of record keeping, of quantitative completeness. All the prisoners were meant to witness time's ravages: just how many victims the day had claimed. And they were supposed to see that they too were doomed to die. Those who collapsed during roll call were placed right next to the dead. Although far outnumbering their guards, the prisoners were forced to watch the spectacle of dying. They could do nothing. They were merely a collective body, a conglomerate bereft of internal unity. The evening roll call staged the lethal contrast between the powerless mass and absolute sovereignty.

The triumph of power was manifest not only in the faces of the dead, but also in the movements of the living. Power permeated the collective body down to the smallest, most minute gesture. The masters of the camp stood before the assembled mass, legs spread, knees straight, bodies bent slightly forward, tapping their whips casually against the leather of their boots. Their eyes glided over the mass of prisoners; their voices, amplified over the loudspeakers, reached the farthest corners of the assembly ground. A few guards roamed through the formations, on the lookout for any irregularity. There was always something: a foot that extended a few centimeters over the line, a missing cap, eyes not looking rigidly straight ahead. Only those in the very middle of the formation and covered by the others could relax their posture a bit, or even try to catnap. Since the mass formation was one single collective body, the slightest deviation was noticed immediately. Any hesitation or clumsiness exposed the individual. Counting was completed in no time; on command the prisoners all came to a halt and stood in the same position, or tore their caps from their heads. The roll call often lasted for several hours, but power scanned this period with the microtime of the most minute gesture. Absolute power binds individuals together into a mass, shaping its structures. It synchronizes the collective anatomy, whose movements can be measured in mere fractions of a second.

Unlike other inspections, the evening roll call did not have any time limit. After work, the roll call could be extended at will. Every minute it lasted meant a minute less for the prisoners; it was subtracted from their time for eating, relaxation, and sleep. Its prolongation was a temporal sanction, a mode of punishment that used time itself as a means. If a single prisoner was missing among the many thousands, a lengthy procedure was initiated. Each number was called; interpreters read the foreign names in all languages represented in the camp. If an attempted escape was suspected, search parties were sent out. The large cordon was not disbanded until the roll call had been terminated. Usually, however, there had not been a genuine escape. Some prisoner, exhausted, had curled up in a hidden corner and fallen asleep where he or she lay—a sewer pipe, the pigpen, or under the floor of a barracks. If the prisoner was sniffed out, he or she was battered bloody and dragged out into the *Appellplatz* yard by the Kapos and the SS, and then either beaten to death or hanged as a "fugitive." During the search, all the others had to remain standing. The quicker the SS ferreted out the missing prisoner, the shorter the roll-call time for the others. The collective sanction of time pitted the massed society against the individual. Everyone had an interest in hoping that that none was absent or had attempted escape.

In the large main camps, the normal evening roll call usually lasted one and a half to two hours; in the event of a public punishment or execution, it went on a bit longer. However, the punitive roll call was occasionally extended into a roll call of extermination, dragging on into the night. During cold winter nights, the SS left the prisoners standing until they froze by the dozens or had collapsed in exhaustion.[20] Like the newcomers at the gate, the entire camp population was exposed to the torment of standing. Murder was committed here without truncheons or firearms. The SS used an everyday procedure in order to kill—because absolute power always has time, it can take its time. While the prisoners had to endure the stationary ordeal, the guards could replace one another, taking breaks to get something at the canteen. But for the victims, every minute the roll call was prolonged meant hunger, exhaustion, sickness, and death.

For the remainder of the day, the prisoners were largely left to themselves. The prisoner personnel distributed the evening rations in the blocks. Some repaired their clothing or cleaned their shoes. The sick stood in line, pushing and shoving in front of the medical block. In a corner of the barracks or a transfer area in the camp enclosure, prisoners bartered or exchanged goods. Some walked back and forth in the camp lanes between the blocks, or visited friends in other barracks. Yet even in this brief period of "free time," prisoners were not secure from possible attack and harassment. Although for most SS personnel their duties for the day finished with the end of roll call, several block leaders would show up unexpectedly now and again and take malicious pleasure in checking the lockers, chasing the prisoners eating dinner under the tables, or hounding them into an endurance run around the barracks. These incursions had nothing to do with some sort of spot check. Their only purpose lay in making anxiety ceaseless, rendering terror omnipresent, reducing the time left over for uncontrolled contact. Even if nothing happened for a limited time, one could always expect power to strike, like a "bolt of lightning." And there might be surprise swoops at night as well. After the final whistle at 8:30 or 8:45, it was forbidden to leave the block; lights out started at 9:00 P.M. However, one could never rule out the possibility that a few drunken SS officers might, in the middle of the night, decide at whim to force the prisoners to run barefoot through the mud or snow.

The sequence from waking to lights out was repeated day after day. This cyclical time was interrupted only by Sundays. If Sunday afternoon had not entailed a half day off from work, the prisoners would have had no way to establish that a week had ended. The regular recurrence bent time into a circular movement. The cycle of social forms accorded with this rhythm: the hectic commotion in the barracks, the long waiting in the roll-call formation, the huddled hubbub of re-formation, the columns marching out, the Kommando, the marching column returning, the standing mass at evening roll call; finally, the informal barter and trade, the contacts during "free time." The circular sequence of association ran parallel to the circuit of camp time. Naturally, de facto, no day was ever like another. There were no carbon copies. The weather might be more favorable one morning, or there would be unexpected second

helpings at dinner. But the recurrent rhythm of feverish commotion and waiting, duration and abruptness, gradually ravaged one's sense of time. The future
contracted, withered, and closed up, as did the past. There was no beginning,
and no prospect of an end. Increasingly, differences became immaterial.[21]
Camp time, to be sure, had a standard form, but the time norms provided terror
only with an armature. Absolute power is not subject to time. Rather, it manipulates time by expansion and acceleration, sudden incursions and attacks, and
the torment of duration. This multiple time destroyed the security that cyclical
time structures otherwise guarantee. The camp forced its inmates into an eternal present, a constancy of uncertainty and horror.

8

Prisoner's Time

> They placed us in a line to tattoo the number. Some
> fainted, others screamed. Now it was my turn. I knew
> that these pains were nothing in comparison with
> what awaited us. A female prisoner from the Political
> Department, with a very low number, wearing a red
> triangle without a "P" (ethnic German), grabbed my
> hand and began to tattoo the next number: 55 908. It
> seemed she wasn't actually pricking my arm, she was
> jabbing me in the heart. From that moment on, I
> ceased to be a human being. I stopped feeling, think-
> ing. I no longer had a name, an address. I was prisoner
> no. 55 908. And that same moment, with every jab of
> the needle, a piece of my life dropped away.[1]

CONTROL OVER social time is only one element of the total overpowering of
the human being. Absolute power does not merely seek to control the external
time of bodies, their movements, postures, and positions. It aspires to remold
or eradicate any form of individual time: the time for action, for the spirit, for
the soul. Just as it varies social time, accelerating and retarding it in order to
cage a human being in an eternal present, it obtrudes into identity, penetrating
one's mental and practical relation to oneself. It permeates the biographical
time of the individual; it wipes out memory; it frustrates plans for action. Its
final goal is not attained until personality and the time in which to act have
been destroyed, and time-consciousness has been extinguished. It is useful to
examine the specific practices used by this destructive power in devastating
personal time.

Confinement began with a shock. On their arrival in the camps, newcomers
were subjected to a processing procedure that devalued their past instantaneously.[2] As in many total institutions, the new arrivals had to undergo a rite of
passage that sundered them from their biographies, programming them to become camp inmates.[3] A cleverly devised sequence of humiliation, violence,
and mutilation forced prisoners into a situation from which they emerged profoundly transformed. Prisoners were not only changed; they became different
individuals. The ritual affected the prisoners' social identity, and more: it was
designed to engineer the collapse of their personal and moral integrity. It de-

molished their sense of successive identity and its continuity—the feeling of being the same persons as they were yesterday.

Rites of passage generally occur in three stages.[4] Separation procedures remove people from their accustomed surroundings, casting them into an ambiguous threshold state characterized by submissiveness and silence, sexlessness and lack of possessions, anonymity and absence of social status. After this, aggregation ceremonies commence; the ritual object is accepted into the new world and the new group. Separation, marginalization, and reaggregation form a general pattern of social and biographical transition. Although the sequencing was occasionally varied and the stations were shifted around, this pattern also underlay admission to the camps. Structurally, it did not differ from civilian rites of passage—indeed, not even in the practices of violence and humiliation involved.[5] The salient difference was in the pattern's effects and functions. The admission ceremony did not mark either a shift in social status or a temporary reversal—it was a permanent degradation, a fundamental transformation of personal and social existence. The prisoners did not receive any new roles to compensate for the loss of their earlier roles. To be a prisoner was not a social role, but a mode of existence at the very nadir of human society. Violence and mutilation were not elements of some temporary threshold condition; they were signs of the beginning of constant mortal danger. The ritual did not assure the continuity of time; rather, it was a radical rupture. It did not regulate biographical transition; it destroyed the cohesion of personal history.

What stations did admission move through? How was the transformation of the person effected? On their way to the camp, many were already tormented by hunger, thirst, and beatings. Some prisoners were tortured even before being confined to jail, or during interrogations. Nonetheless, most came to the camp totally unprepared for what awaited them. On their arrival, they were initially left in uncertainty for a limited time until the reception committee chose to act. This debilitating wait allowed the supervisory personnel time to prepare the procedures of admission. The new arrivals were beaten and insulted; they were pelted with stones, drenched with buckets of water, hounded to and fro; they were forced to do knee bends, or literally to run the gauntlet. Whoever protested the mistreatment or tried to spring to the aid of an injured comrade was beaten mercilessly. Spontaneous assistance was converted directly into harm for the victim and anyone attempting to help. Even before the beginning of the official ritual, the prisoners were forced to experience their total defenselessness. In a basic sense, to be powerless means to be stripped of the ability to act and exposed to physical overpowering.[6] The first bit of violence, the first blow shatters one's basic faith in the inviolability of the body, demolishing the expectation of possible assistance in distress. By its destruction of these fundamental certainties of everyday life, violence prepared human beings, like biological specimens, to be objects of initiation.

The initial shock was followed by direct frontal attacks on the self. People were forced to disrobe and to surrender all their belongings. This dispossession was, at the same time, a mutilation of the person, a despoilment. Not only were prisoners divested of their clothing—they were stripped of all the small personal and private things that were part of the material outfitting of their inner identities. The theft of all their possessions was a material and symbolic loss. The victims were dispossessed not only of what belonged to them, but of what was part of them. Then the naked prisoners were left to wait again, or herded to the barber. The women frequently were compelled to file on past the SS men and Kapos in a parade of shame, greeted by laughter and obscene mockery from the onlookers. The physical transformation began at the barber's. All the hair on a prisoner's head, face, and body was first shaven; then the closely shaven areas were scrubbed with dirty rags that had been soaked in disinfectant. Along with the hygienic purpose of epidemic prevention, this procedure had an obvious symbolic significance. The new arrivals were to be made visibly alike, degraded to their naked bodies, stripped of all signs of vitality and individuality. Exposed in this way, they were harried into the showers, where they were subjected to a torrent of either scorching hot or freezing cold water. In the midst of the ritual threshold phase, they were naked, without possessions, defenseless victims of metamorphosis.

After the symbolic mutilation and denudation, their aggregation into prisoner society began with the distribution of camp uniforms. The men were each given old and worn overalls, often filthy and vermin infested, one pair of underwear, a shirt and cap, wooden clogs instead of shoes—and, if they were lucky, a pair of socks. The women were each issued a striped blue-grey cotton dress, a shirt, one pair of panties, a slip, and long stockings. Distribution was generally indiscriminate; shoes, jackets, dresses, and trousers did not fit; the rags disfigured the person. But they were uniform. They rendered all identical, specimens of a single species. Differences in external appearance were completely leveled and erased. The prisoners were hardly able to recognize themselves. Yet because all looked the same, each became the image of everyone else.

In the final act of the admission procedure, the newcomers were deprived of their last vestiges of individuality. At registration in the office, each prisoner was assigned a number.[7] To be dispossessed of one's own name is among the most far-reaching and profound mutilations of the self. It documents the termination of one's previous life history. Now the individual was nothing but a cipher among thousands of others, an anonymous case. The number made each person identifiable, but it was not a qualitative criterion of identity; it was a quantitative sign, a dot in an endless series. The number signified the metamorphosis of the individual into an element of the mass, the transformation of personal society into the serial society of the nameless.

There was violence and humiliation even during the bureaucratic procedure of registration. In small groups, the new arrivals were jostled to the office, where one after the other they were required to step forward and give their particulars. If a prisoner replied in too low a voice or did not demonstrate the required posture of rigid attention, he or she was mistreated. The admissions procedure, the opening of a file, the classification, and the assignment of the prisoner number were inseparably connected to elements of an interrogation, with insults and violent "lessons" for those who needed to be taught. Once and for all, it was to be burned into the inmate's consciousness that only one attitude was permissible vis-à-vis those in power: subservience. The bureaucratic act was a test of obedience, a first trial run of the transformation of the individual into an object of power bereft of will. Whoever did not pass this test was punished, immediately and visibly.

The admission ceremony shook the prisoners to the very foundations of their being. It signified their death as members of civil society, stripping them of names and pasts, possessions and dignity, and external appearance. It flung them into a state of total defenselessness, demolishing the fundamental presupposition of human existence: the idealization of the continuity of the familiar world, the unquestioned past certainties—such as how one should behave to avoid any injury to the physical self, and that one could expect assistance in times of distress. Not surprisingly, this procedure was experienced by the victims as a paralyzing shock. The ritual regulated the transition from the civilian world into the universe of the concentration camp. But it was not gradual; it erupted precipitously, upending the person, tearing the very ground away from under his or her feet. Prisoner's time began when the prisoner was abruptly overwhelmed; it was a rape of the person.

The admission formalities were generally completed with the assignment of sleeping quarters. However, there was a substantial expansion of the entire procedure during the war. As epidemics raged in many camps, the SS set up separate quarantine blocks where the new arrivals were held, isolated and segregated, for two to three weeks before they were integrated into the normal camp routine.[8] This measure was designed to prevent the spread of infectious diseases; it also entailed an extension of the period of integration, accompanied by intensified annihilatory pressure. The provisional living quarters were appallingly overcrowded and extremely filthy, and mortality rates there were higher than in other sections of the camp. The prisoners were either deployed at exceptionally exhausting tasks or tormented the entire day with roll-call inspections that dragged on for hours, physical exercises, and diverse harassments. The weak and elderly were sorted out and slaughtered; the others were finally transferred to other barracks in the main camp or a satellite. Thus, the extension of the period for integration was a deliberate measure of selection and annihilation. In order to limit overcrowding, the SS instituted an organizational buffer; it manipulated mortality by exposing those who had the least camp experience to the most stressful conditions, right from the start.

After the shock of admission, the prisoners had little time to adjust to camp conditions. It is mistaken to posit a process of secondary socialization or a phased "career" in the case of the concentration camps.[9] The camp was not an institution that incorporated periods of trial and adjustment. The usual alteration between demands made and lessons learned, between expectation and role taking, did not take place. The prisoners were not supposed to acquire any new skills or attitudes. From the first minute, they were exposed to an extreme situation to which they had to react immediately. Just as organizational time did not evolve, prisoner's time was not one of gradual adjustment. The prisoner had no time for learning. Terror, omnipresent, demanded presence of mind right from the first moment. For that reason, there was an experiential rule of thumb among the inmates: whoever survived the first three days had a chance to make it to the end of a month; whoever remained alive for the first three weeks had a chance to survive a year. And whoever could survive three months would survive the next three years. Thus, the first precondition for survival was immediately to cast aside any earlier experiences, pretenses, and convictions that stood in its way.

The reshaping of time-consciousness was the result of the reciprocal intensification of terror, defensive reaction, and protective maneuvering. Self-preservation demanded an immediate and fundamental re-formation of mental and spiritual activities. The only defense against the overwhelming power of the situation was to change the meanings of time fundamentally, even at the cost of a near-total obliteration of the temporal horizon. It was not only the external conditions of prisoner existence that were responsible for the destruction of personal time; the psychological and social strategies of survival also had a hand in this demolition. Absolute power extends its reach so far that it forces human beings to engage in the destruction of their own time. This is evident from a detailed examination of the time structure of the camp situation and the time strategies of the prisoners.

The first temporal feature of prisoners' existence was the indefinite duration of confinement. Although the speeches and diatribes the SS leaders sometimes gave during the reception ceremony left no doubt about the fate of the prisoners,[10] many new inmates initially clung to the illusion that their confinement would be limited. They expected to be held in the camp for a few weeks or months at most. Many had no idea whatsoever why they had been arrested, and harbored the hope that their cases would be cleared up quickly, and that they would soon be allowed to return to their families. But the rarer the releases became and the more the pressure of annihilation in the camps intensified during the war, the more quickly this illusion was shattered. The prisoners had to recognize that they were incarcerated indefinitely; the prospect of ever emerging from the camp alive was infinitesimal. Existence in the camp was a "provisional existence without final date."[11] The orientation toward a future end was fundamentally undermined. This loss of futurity constituted a deep cleft in the consciousness of existence. The inmates were not only uncertain when their period of confinement would end; they did not know whether they would survive the incarceration, whether sticking it out had any meaning whatsoever. Devaluation of the future means that human existence forfeits its character as a project, a plan. One's life plans lose their teleological orientation; existence becomes merely temporary, an interim arrangement, on call.

The second temporal feature of prisoners' existence was the omnipresence of death.[12] From the war's outbreak, if not before, death lurked everywhere in the camps: at work, on the streets and paths, in the blocks. Any attack by a guard could end in the death of the victim. Hunger and epidemics caused mortality rates to soar. Although death in the camp had many faces, the basic reason for it was only too evident. This was a social fate, not a natural one. Its ultimate cause was the regime of terror in the camp. Only for that reason were prisoners able to accustom themselves to the deaths of the others, while simultaneously keeping alive a hope for their own survival. Where death is an unstoppable natural process, without exception, one's own end is certain. All that remains is resignation or apathy. But where death appears as a consequence of social power, its commissions and omissions, hope for a final way out may still flicker. The fear of violence and death obtrudes, wedging itself in front of despair. It is likely that the consciousness of death in the camps was marked not by death's certainty, but rather by total uncertainty: tormenting anxiety; abrupt changes between hope and desperation, self-preservation and self-abandonment.

Yet absolute power is so overwhelming that social relations appear to have adjusted to an inevitable natural process. The primary frames within which events are classified as social or natural lose their disjunctive salience[13]. Although terror in the camp derived from a social power relation, the victims had only minimal opportunity for controlling the situation. But when survival is no longer in one's own hands, luck and fortuity appear to reign supreme.[14] The happenstance of survival corresponds to the arbitrariness of terror. Despite the daily monotony, the mode of existence of the prisoner was determined by happenings that erupted suddenly, unpredictably. From one day to the next, the SS could aggravate living conditions, pull out individual groups from the better Kommandos, dissolve a block, or impose lethal collective punishments. Absolute power is the power of fate. It operates by attack and surprise, it ambushes existence, it annuls expectations. More is devalued here than the distant future: the immediate horizon of one's current situation is also ravaged. The existence of the prisoner was not merely provisional. At the same time, it was aleatory.

Everyday life in the camp demanded from prisoners a fundamental revamping of their time-consciousness. Because the future was drained of value and temporal continuity was ruptured, it was no longer possible to maintain a composed wait-and-see attitude. There was no basis for trust in a gradual improvement of the situation. Terror shuffles time's order, shifting the present to center stage, extinguishing past and future. The unpredictable dangers required constant vigilance, circumspection, and presence of mind in a specific momentary situation. Neither memory nor expectation was necessary; rapid perception and spontaneous improvisation were vital for survival. Terror reduces the field of human consciousness to the passing moment. Consequently, the third temporal feature of prisoner existence was the absolute primacy of the present, the here and now.

The loss of the future undermines the foundations of action. Terror demolishes the possibility of planning ahead, of orienting oneself in terms of stable circumstances. The victims are not capable of independent action, nor are they in any position to predict the consequences of their actions. The destruction of the possibility for action has immediate consequences for sociality and identity. The basic rules underlying all social interaction have been rescinded: reciprocity of perspectives, the normal forms of action, the retrospective-prospective sense of occurrence, the assumption of continuity.[15] Reciprocal role taking loses its basis if no one is able to pursue plans. Lasting social relations presuppose reactions that can be anticipated, and trust in the future. For that reason, terror has an immediate dissociative impact. Because it eradicates the ability of the person to act, it also eliminates social trust, cooperation, and mutual aid.

One's practical relation to oneself (*Selbstverhältnis*) is in a similar situation.[16] Self-assertion is based on self-confidence, but self-confidence is rooted in the consciousness of one's own abilities, the experience that one's actions have an effect and can influence the future. However, by undermining the ability to act, absolute power simultaneously shakes the very foundations of self-confidence and self-esteem. Self-respect requires recognition by others. A person can only relate to himself or herself by relating simultaneously to others. And one can only relate to others if one can relate to oneself. By acting, human beings show themselves and others who they are. By taking a position vis-à-vis the claims of others, by accepting or rejecting their expectations, people show how they view themselves. If this possibility for social negation is eliminated, there is likewise no possibility for independence and mutual recognition. Since the human self-relation is socially constituted, the destruction of sociality entails a concomitant demolition of identity. The camp did not only kill the moral person. In its final consequences, absolute power is bent on eradicating human personality per se.

Prisoners reacted in diverse ways to the destruction of time. Many lost all hope, ceased taking action, disintegrated, and perished. Others attempted to carve out small pockets of independence and to endure in those niches, biding their time. Those who had weathered painful past experiences with physical deprivation, hunger, or lack of freedom often believed that harrowing times would be followed by more-favorable circumstances. Prisoners with stable political or religious convictions had a reservoir of meaning to tap, one they could counterpose to the inroads of terror. Veteran prisoners focused their interest exclusively on dealing with the necessities of the camp present. Some newcomers were lucky enough to chance upon experienced prisoners, old-timers who assisted them in bridging the initial period. Some were kept alive by their inner bonds to the family; others by their hatred of the guards, or the hope for eventual revenge. Survival depended on diverse factors; generally, several were necessary in order to preserve the energy and will to resist. However, survival always demanded a specific temporal strategy. Self-preservation in the camp inevitably necessitated the preservation and salvaging of time, a restitution of time-consciousness, though that restitution was itself subject to far-reaching deformations.

First, prisoners had to become acclimated to the presence of death. The acceptance of death was the precondition for being able to resist it. As powerful as the pressure of the present was, the only ones who could achieve inner equilibrium were those who girded themselves early on against the perception of mistreatment and murder. There was a practical maxim in the camp: not simply to remain inconspicuous, but also not to notice anything conspicuous.[17] To see too much was life-threatening. Whoever failed to turn away and quickly pass by the site where violence had erupted risked the danger of being attacked. The demands of emotional self-protection were in keeping with this coerced indifference. The conscious perception of the death of others erodes one's own will to survive. It intensifies the fear of death, paralyzing action; it generates rage, indignation, or despair. Thus, only those could elude horror and dread who were adept at overlooking what was horrendous, closing an eye to the dreadful. Only if you became inured, sheathed yourself in emotional armor, walking past the corpses without taking notice, could you avoid psychological collapse. The inner petrification, a process of emotional hardening experienced by many inmates, was essentially the result of this perceptual coat of armor vis-à-vis the suffering and dying of the others. In order to concentrate on the present, the prisoner had to keep a key aspect of that present at bay, regarding death as something normal or commonplace.[18]

Nonetheless, focused attentiveness was indispensable for enduring the abiding present tense of the camp. Although newcomers often clung to the fond illusion that they would soon be released, the veteran prisoners' interest centered on the immediate life in the camp, *hic et nunc*. Their expectations revolved around a concrete, visible improvement in their situation, a toehold for a future in the camp. The consciousness of the possible future was foreshortened here to an elongation of the here and now, a continuation of the present. In any event, longer-term plans can hardly be maintained under the conditions of occasional time. The experienced prisoners were distinguished by their ability to recognize opportunity and seize it immediately; they had little interest in promises and prospects, and tried as much as possible to avoid thinking about tomorrow.[19]

A successful time strategy resembled a tightrope walk. The prisoners had to orient their entire attention to the present situation, yet without allowing themselves to be overcome by the ever-present danger of death. The pressure of persecution devalued past and future, but the prisoners had to dodge the pressure of the present in order to gain that modicum of distance that is indispensable for the maintenance of the ability to act and one's own self-relation. They had to move cautiously through the camp's treacherous terrain, with all their wits about them, simultaneously intensifying their level of stimulus defense. Although plans and hopes were repeatedly dashed, to abandon action and expectation completely meant certain ruin. Inmates who were unable to distance themselves from the present were imprisoned mentally as well as physically. Those who tried to deny the present, migrating internally to another province of temporal meaning, gained momentary distance. Yet they forfeited the practical ability to organize enough food for today and arrange a better job for tomorrow. Thus, the time strategy of many inmates oscillated between defense and adaptation, attentiveness and indifference, preservation and destruction of the internal horizon of time.

This ambivalence left its imprint not only on the relation to the present, but on that to the past as well. The value of memory was mixed and contradictory. To recall one's homeland, school years, or earlier adventures was one way to disengage from the present and temporarily preserve the fiction of biographical continuity. To recount the plots of books or films, sing old songs, or recite poems interrupted the monotony of camp life and was a momentary source of relief and diversion. But prisoners who started to tell about their families after receiving a letter from home often met with the brusque protest of others who did not wish to hear anything that reminded them of their own past. It was one of the unwritten laws of camp comradeship to avoid topics that could evoke sadness, pain, or despair. From the perspective of the camp veteran, it was nothing but a sentimental relapse to go into raptures about former banquets, talk about children, or paint one's eventual return to a former life. Remembrance threatened to weaken inner equilibrium. It made it only too clear to prisoners what their real situation was. All that was permitted were sifted fragments of the past devoid of any emotional value. It was imperative to ward off the past in order to protect oneself from despondency and depression. Thus, the camp was a system of forgetting. The SS insisted that families dissociate themselves from incarcerated relatives. And survival in the camp required that inmates parry the past, draining it of its value. Many followed this compulsion by themselves avoiding the painful backward look to earlier phases of their personal biography, closing the door on reminiscence.

The prisoners' past was not usually brought to life by conscious memory; more often it was reactivated by the catalyst of terror. In a certain sense, individuals were forced to regress to earlier stages of the personality.[20] They were degraded into dependent creatures, their attitudes transposed into a childlike helplessness in which all that was permitted was behavior that had been drilled into their synapses, inculcated by command. The inmates were not supposed to act, but to react automatically; not to reflect or decide, but to obey blindly. They had to perform the most stupid, inane tasks, ask for permission every time they changed location, abide by the norms of cleanliness under the threat of punishment. They were flogged, cursed, insulted, laughed at, and transformed into docile children who were obliged to pay homage to the authority of the guards and prisoner-functionaries. The camp replaced adult action with a condition of infantile dependency. It rolled back personal time, reversing the development of the individual.

When the experimental character of human existence as a project threatens to be extinguished, the future can be imagined only in a deformed manner. Expectation and the planning of action were as fragile as memory was precarious. No prisoner was able to make realistic, medium-range prognoses. The daily terror turned predictions into pure speculation. The only inmates who were able to maintain a certain perspective on the future were those who had succeeded in acquiring a relatively secure position in the hierarchy of prisoner-functionaries or the workshops. Only the small upper class of the camp had any future. The majority of the inmates were in a virtually hopeless situation. A glance forward to the future was indispensable for survival, but this orientation only had a basis for those who had already garnered a protected, privileged place in the camp. For that reason, all that remained for most prisoners were substitute maneuvers. When expectations come to naught and only hope remains, human beings often take refuge in separate provinces of meaning such as religion, ideology, or fantasy. Although the reality content of these reserves for escape differs, they have an equivalent psychological function, serving to help one elude the oppressive burden of the present and maintain at least the fiction of a future.

The most fleeting form of collective fiction about the future is rumor. Rumors are unconfirmed news about upcoming events, unverified information that wanders from mouth to mouth, whose truth is believed until the contrary is proved. Rumors generate a dense reticulation of communication; they spread like wildfire, circulating unregulated and authorless within the social field. The rapid velocity of their propagation is closely linked to the credulity of a group, to its readiness to accept stories being bruited about. Rumors are passed on at face value, unchecked, and thus construct a shared illusion, a collective self-deception about the future. Inmates in the camps were only too susceptible to such tales.[21] The arbitrary quality of terror provided an ideal soil in which rumor could take root. Uncertainty erodes the consciousness of reality, intensifying one's readiness to indulge in escapism. Again and again, the prisoners believed there would be general amnesties on specific key dates; or they believed there would be a quick examination of the reasons for their arrest. Reports made the rounds about improvements in rations, about transports of prisoners sent to better camps, and transfers to less ruinous Kommandos. During the war, rumors repeatedly surfaced about an imminent cease-fire or Germany's imminent defeat. Yet such hearsay reports strengthened social cohesion and the prisoners' power to resist only for a brief moment. When their credibility crumbled, the disappointment was all the greater. Rumors were a welcome antidote to the oppressive, horrendous present. Ultimately, however, they weakened the prisoners' ability to assess reality correctly and confront it with the meager means that remained.

Religious convictions were less frangible.[22] Religions provide interpretive models that allow one to incorporate present events into a framework of expectation and interpret them in the light of a fictive future. The belief in deliverance thanks to divine grace, the healing power of religious practices, prayers and secret sacred services, the prospect for a life to come—all this provided suffering with a meaning, and eased its pain. Faith creates order; it construes luck and contingency as part of the puzzle of divine providence, supporting moral values in the midst of a situation where good and evil seem virtually inextricable. Judaism and Christianity presuppose the existence of evil, countering it with messianic hope or the principles of mercy and compassion. Thus, unwavering faith fortified the individual's will to survive in the camp, and more: it preserved the moral person, extending the horizon of expectation and hope beyond the immediate present. Quite a few prisoners owed their unshakable steadfastness to the strength of their inner faith. Communities of believers held together in the face of the dissociative wedge of terror. And this was true not only of the Jehovah's Witnesses and the isolated clerics in Dachau;[23] groups of Jews, Polish, French, and Dutch Christians also formed a haven of solidarity and resistance.

Political ideologies, especially the communist worldview, had an analogous function. Such ideologies placed the camp within a more comprehensive, embracing world-historical process, so that it was possible to view the present as a surmountable, intermediate phase. Past experiences in organizations and party membership provided the point of departure for internal group solidarity within the camp. Political convictions projected a clear view of who and what was the enemy, providing resistance with a focus and direction. Ideology furnished the basis for social organization. It imbued the death of the individual with a world-historical meaning. No matter how many might perish as martyrs, the just cause would eventually triumph. Compared to religion, political ideology had the advantage that it was more directly linked with reality. It defined a secular future whose shape was also dependent on the opposition generated in the camp, and the hard-won gains of comrades beyond its barriers. Religious orientations provide criteria for morally correct action; by contrast, political convictions offer a yardstick for strategically successful action. As different as the specific content of their beliefs was, religious Jews and Christians and staunch communists had the benefit of a critical resource for survival not available to their nonreligious, nonideological fellow prisoners: belief and trust in the future. They considered themselves to be part of a spiritual-intellectual continuum that could not be called into question by anything—not by the daily violence, not by the mass dying.[24] In this way, they passed beyond their concrete, momentary existence, gaining distance from the presence of terror. Their conviction served to secure the experimental, project-oriented character of human existence and the ability to act. Although the future was a fiction, its consequences were practical and real. It reduced powerlessness, integrated the individual into a group, and bolstered the power to resist. It counterposed a higher temporal plane to the all-powerful time of the camp, salvaging in this way the prisoner's personal time, which had been threatened to its very foundations.

Part III

SOCIAL STRUCTURES

9

The SS Personnel

Four SS members were sentenced by a Munich court—at that time SS courts didn't yet exist—to long terms in prison. These four were brought in full uniform before the entire assembled guard battalion, were personally degraded by Eicke and then dishonorably dismissed from the SS. He tore off their insignias of rank, tabs and SS badges, had them marched past the standing companies of the battalion, and then handed them over to the justice authorities to begin their sentence. Afterward, he took the incident as an occasion to deliver a lengthy lecture to the troops, and a warning. He said he would have preferred putting the four in prisoners' uniforms, and after a beating with truncheons, throwing them in with their comrades behind the barbed wire. But the Reichsführer-SS had not approved. A similar fate awaited anyone who got too involved with the inmates inside the camp. Whether for criminal reasons or because of pity. Both were equally reprehensible. Any trace of pity provided the "enemies of the state" with an exposed spot that they would exploit immediately. Any form of pity with "enemies of the state" was, Eicke stressed, beneath the dignity of an SS man. There was no place for weaklings in these ranks, and they'd be better off disappearing as quickly as possible to a monastery. He could only use men who were resolute, tough as nails. Men who obeyed every order ruthlessly. It was not for nothing that they wore the insignia of the death's head, and always carried a weapon loaded with live ammunition! They were the sole soldiers who stood guard, even in times of peace, facing the enemy day and night, the enemy behind the wire.[1]

THE WORLD OF THE concentration camp was divided into three regions: the society of the prisoners in the mass blocks, that of the elite of prisoner-functionaries, and that of the surveillance and administrative personnel of the SS. These zones formed a complex power configuration bristling with diverse dependencies and rivalries. The social structure of the camp certainly cannot be reduced to two spheres. It is true that a deep boundary line divided personnel from inmates. But in between lay a gray zone of power delegation and collaboration, protection and corruption. Absolute power is a structure that pervades the social field, penetrating other social forms. The center of power privileged a minority, making them into its special band of auxiliaries. Employing the principle of deputization, it transformed victims into accomplices, thus blurring the distinction between personnel and prisoners.[2] However, the majority was classified and forced into a serial mass structure that overlapped with and destroyed other social forms.[3] Mass and power, delegation and classification were the dominant principles determining the social world of the prisoners. But the center of power lay in the hands of a staff that dictated everyday routine in the camp. The personnel made the rules and had unlimited power to kill. It stood guard, imposed punishments, and murdered. Consequently, any analysis of the social network in the camp must begin with the organization and mentality of the camp SS.

In the beginning, camps were controlled by local units of the SA, the general SS, and, in a few instances, by the police. In Dachau, SS units took over guard functions in mid-April 1933. Initially they were still under the direction of the police; from the end of May 1933, they were on their own. The camp leadership changed several times in the Emsland because of wrangling over authority among the police, SS, and SA that dragged on for months.[4] Esterwegen was not finally taken over by the SS until the early summer of 1934, when the Dachau commandant Eicke launched his reorganization of the entire concentration camp system. Half of the 250 SA men joined the SS; the others were absorbed by the justice system and given jobs in the prison camps. Like Dachau, Esterwegen served as a training center. On April 30, 1935, the personnel there was made up of 76 SS members and 279 SS candidates. Of the 778 SS men in Dachau, only 84 were candidates; in Lichtenburg, 91 of the 347 SS members had candidate status.

In order to reduce the influence of the regional SS sector leaders and centralize personnel leadership, the guard formations were separated from the general SS in the autumn of 1934, and assigned to the newly created *KZ-Inspektion*.[5] Until that time, the guard units had been housed in barracks near the camps, but the SS men were paid, trained, and armed as employees of the general SS. The camp commandants were only permitted to use these formations if they had been assigned to sentry duty. As a result of this detachment from the general SS, a separate unit came into being, directly linked with the concentration camp system and personally subordinate to Eicke. Beginning in 1936, the units were officially termed "SS Death's Head Formations" (*SS-Totenkopfverbände*) after their special lapel insignia, introduced in Dachau in 1933, and were organized as "storm battalions." A second stage in centralization was reached in the summer of 1937, when the battalions were regrouped into three Death's Head regiments—Oberbayern, Brandenburg, and Thüringen—and were attached to the three main camps of Dachau, Sachsenhausen, and Buchenwald.

The growth of the Death's Head units did not run parallel with the rise and fluctuations in the number of prisoners. In January 1935, official SS statistics listed 1,987 prisoners; one year later, that number had increased to 2,855.[6] In the spring of 1936, the SS regional sectors were ordered to delegate at least 80 volunteers each. Although the prisoner population in the camps declined, troop strength in July 1936 rose to 3,502. Contrary to Himmler's intentions, however, many of the SS men, especially the officers, were over the desired age. About two-thirds of the camp commandants had served long periods in the Wehrmacht, some of these during World War I, before they joined the NSDAP (National Socialist German Workers' Party) or SS and finally entered Eicke's units. They were already between twenty-five and forty years old when they began their careers in the camps. Yet starting in April 1936, the entire age structure of the guard units changed as more and more young men enlisted in their ranks. Their reasons for joining up were generally quite banal, and had little to do with political ideology. Some saw the expanding Death's Head units as a chance for social advancement to the rank of officer without having to undergo the otherwise obligatory preparatory training. For others, it was a welcome opportunity to gain independence from their parents and earn a modest but secure income. Others were attracted by the prospect of being in a male military community; still others were lured by the image of the snappy black uniform. The mean age of the Death's Head units declined from 23.2 on August 1, 1936 to 20.7 at the end of 1938.[7] For a short time, these guard units were largely a formation of green, inexperienced youths, most under the age of 21.

An expansion in the function of such units had already begun to crystallize at this time, based on plans worked out in 1935. The troops were not only to guard the camps, but would be available as a leadership echelon for a potential police intervention unit in wartime, slated to replace units the regular police had to transfer to the Wehrmacht. During preparations for the attack against Czechoslovakia, Hitler issued an order on August 17, 1938, that all active Death's Head regiments were to be deployed in the framework of the army as police reinforcements in the event of mobilization; the task of guarding the camps would be passed on to older members of the general SS.[8] The Death's Head units were formally part of neither the Wehrmacht nor the police, but were described as "a standing armed unit of the SS for dealing with special policing tasks."[9] In January 1938, the units already numbered 5,371 men; by April, that figure had climbed to 7,847,[10] soaring to 9,172 in December of that same year. In January 1939, SS members born between 1903 and 1913 were called up for exercises lasting three months in the concentration camps. In May 1939, Himmler was authorized by Hitler to bring the units up to a strength exceeding 40,000.[11] Of these, 14,000 were to be the minimum strength for Eicke's guard units, and 25,000 were to be in the category of "police reinforcements," though those reinforcement units were to operate independently of the regular uniformed police (Orpo, or *Ordnungspolizei*). In order to protect these units from the grasp of the Wehrmacht, service with the

Death's Head units was by 1939 officially recognized as military service. Recruitment was mainly among the members of the SA and former members of the SS-VT, the so-called *Verfügungstruppe*, SS military units at the disposal of Hitler or the state. By mid-1939, the Death's Head units had 22,033 men. On August 30, additional reservists were pulled in. Buchenwald, Sachsenhausen, and Mauthausen became assembly points for new regiments; Dachau was shut down for several months and reorganized into a training center for the SS. After the invasion of Poland, Eicke set up the Death's Head Division, which carried out the first measures in a systematic policy of annihilation in areas behind the front.[12] The divisional staff was made up of officers from Eicke's *KZ-Inspektion*; 7,000 men from the Death's Head units formed its backbone. At the beginning of the war, Eicke's office was divided into the Directorate of Concentration Camps (*Inspektion der Konzentrationslager*), now headed by Eicke's former chief of staff Richard Glücks, and the General Directorate of the Reinforced SS Death's Head Regiments (*Generalinspektion der verstärkten SS-Totenkopfstandarten*). In August 1940, the latter was taken over by the command of the Waffen-SS. The concentration camp units were replenished by older reservists from the general SS after the departure of troops to the front, and these men took over the tasks of the guard personnel in the camps.

The organizational history of the Death's Head units is marked by several remarkable developments. Initially it was characterized by a process of increasing autonomy. As the concentration camps were removed from the influence of the justice and interior authorities, the guard units acquired more and more independence, not just vis-à-vis external institutions such as the regular police or the Wehrmacht, but even within the SS itself. They drew a line between themselves and the mass organization of the general SS, the local section leaders, Heydrich's secret police, and the military SS-VT. Himmler's policy of dividing authority and power among various bodies had opened up the possibility for Eicke to set up a military unit that was personally answerable to him, and to train it as he saw fit. However, the more successfully the *KZ-Inspektion* functioned and the stronger the armed units became, the more they came to the notice of the leadership's top echelon. From 1938 on, Himmler now turned that same policy of power splitting against Eicke that he had pursued to Eicke's advantage earlier on. The economic administration of the camps was transferred from the *Inspektion* to the SS Administrative Office (*Verwaltungsamt*) under Oswald Pohl. That office was also able to appoint administrative heads for the camps, bypassing Eicke. At an early juncture, Pohl had responsibility not just for the labor deployment of camp prisoners, but also for the entire array of administrative and economic affairs in the camps. The power of command over the guards was shifted upward and transferred to Hitler's prerogative. Hitler's decree of August 17, 1938, militarized the units and put them on a legal footing; they were placed directly under

Himmler's command as a police reserve. Their deployment was made dependent on task assignments that Hitler reserved for himself, depending on the specific case.

By the time of Eicke's reorganization of the concentration camp system in the summer of 1934, the guard units were already far more than just a camp guard contingent. The strength of the units before the war bore no proportion to the number of prisoners. In Esterwegen, for example, the number of prisoners dropped in 1934 from 600 to 300, but guard-unit strength jumped from about 360 to reach 500 in the summer of 1936. By year's end, there were some 7,500 persons imprisoned in the entire camp system; the strength of guard personnel was 3,365.[13] At the beginning of the war, the prisoner population in the camps had climbed to about 21,400, while the Death's Head regiments numbered 24,000 men. Thus, at least theoretically, at this point there was more than one guard for every prisoner. From the start, the *Totenkopfverbände* had been conceived as a paramilitary formation, not merely a guard unit, although their specific tasks were not spelled out in detail until planning for the war was under way. Along with the SS-VT, the concentration camps contained the germ of the Waffen-SS. The guard service was an integral component of training; its constant confrontation with the "internal enemy" provided a preparatory exercise for its later deployment as a military intervention unit.

However, only a fraction of the units had anything to do with the daily service operations in the camps. At the end of 1937, when there were 4,833 men in the Death's Head units, only 33 of the 216 officers were appointed as commandants or camp leaders. At this point, there were 1,621 stationed in Dachau, 1,617 in Buchenwald, and 1,066 in Sachsenhausen. However, the permanent staff of each of these camps was only about 110 men.[14] In December 1938, total strength amounted to 9,172, yet only 577 SS men belonged to the commandant staffs of the camps. As a rule, the battalions were rotated, serving three-week stints on sentry duty; the rest of their time was set aside for political and military training. Officially, the only persons with access to the area within the barbed wire were members of the commandant staffs, rapport leaders, block leaders, and Kommando leaders. Although personnel shifts between the guard units and the camp staff were not uncommon, the SS garrison was specialized along functional lines. There was a relatively small circle of several hundred SS men who had dominated the camps before the war as core personnel; later, during the expansion of the camp system, they had served as multipliers. This "old guard" was the source for the leadership personnel that staffed the numerous main camps and subcamps established later on in the war.

Until the middle of 1940, the SS Main Office (*Hauptamt*) had responsibility for all armed SS formations. In mid-August, the command of the Waffen-SS was separated from this office and now formed the SS Operations Office (*SS-Führungshauptamt*). Among the elements of the Waffen-SS included in the budget of the Finance Ministry were not only the field units, but the entire organization of the camps. Even after the separation of the Death's Head regiments from the *KZ-Inspektion*, the concentration camps remained part of the Waffen-SS. Transfers of guard personnel were also handled through the command office of the Waffen-SS. Until the early spring of 1942, the directorate operated formally under the designation of Office VI of the Operations Office. But even after being placed under Pohl's WVHA, the Operations Office remained in overall charge of weapons and training for the guard personnel. Both the guard units and members of the commandant staffs wore the uniform of the Waffen-SS.

This bureaucratic interlinkage permitted a smooth exchange of personnel between the field units and the camp formations.[15] Camp personnel was transferred to the front to replace the losses of the *Totenkopf* Division. In 1941, the home administration of the division was set up in Dachau. Wounded soldiers and incompetent troop leaders were seconded to the camps. Transfers in both directions as a form of punishment were not uncommon. The total number of men rotated between the field units and the camps is estimated at some 10,000.[16] With the expansion of the concentration camp system, the ranks of the camp guard also filled with soldiers drawn from the Wehrmacht. In May 1944, Hitler decided to incorporate 10,000 soldiers who had returned from Crimea into the Waffen-SS as guard units.[17] The air force supplied guards on construction projects, and even marine personnel were seconded as guards to satellite camps.[18] The total strength of the guard formations rose from about 15,000 in March 1942 to 37,674 men and 3,508 women in January 1945.[19] If one includes in the calculations, the establishment of the *Totenkopf* Division at the war's beginning and the transfers during the war, even a restrictive estimate suggests that at least 55,000 SS men and women did service in the camps.

By contrast, the internal command and administrative apparatus was relatively compact. With the expansion of the system and the setting up of external satellite subcamps, more guards than staffers were needed. A subcamp of some five hundred prisoners required about fifty guards, but only a handful of block leaders, one rapport leader, and one camp leader. If one takes the peak figure of more than 41,000 members of the camp SS in January 1945 as a basis, and assuming that the permanent staff was roughly 15 percent of the SS personnel stationed at a site, the estimated strength of the permanent staff for all camps toward the end of the war was approximately six thousand persons.[20] This group also included the majority of the "old guard" from the prewar period, who—as specialists in concentration camp terror—had not been transferred to the field units.[21]

In accordance with the "Dachau model," the camp bureaucracy was segmented into specialized task areas. This division of labor, however, was neither the sole nor the decisive determinant of the distribution of power and the behavior of personnel. Formal specialization was only one feature of SS organization. Of equal salience were personal relations and the organizational processes of hierarchy and delegation—both practical and mental standardization. Despite the large amount of record keeping and paperwork, and the high degree of division of labor, the administration of the concentration camps bore little resemblance to the familiar ideal type of a rational bureaucracy. This is often misunderstood when camp terror and mass murder are mistakenly attributed to the functionality and effectiveness of a modern bureaucracy. Undeniably, the SS had a highly specialized administration, but that was interlaced with various arrangements that had little in common with formal organization. Terror requires structures that rescind the rules and power links of formal impersonality. For that reason, an analysis of these special aspects of the camp SS is indispensable for gaining a better picture of the organization of terror and the *habitus* of the camp personnel.

The first salient feature of the camp SS was its military ordering of rank and status. The SS sprang from a gray zone in society, one in which military operations were privatized and the differences between war and peace were blurred. This was the matrix for the ideal of the "political soldier," for whom permanent terroristic struggle against the "internal enemy" had become a way of life. The reorganization of the guard units also entailed a certain degree of militarization. The members wore identical uniforms with insignia; they were armed, drilled, and housed in barracks. Clear subordination relations were created, and there was a hierarchical ordering of ranks. Each had a predetermined place and the prospect of a set career. Members of the militia had to obey superiors, and could in turn issue orders to subordinates. One could consider oneself a soldier, not merely a member of some auxiliary police force or a guard. This status pyramid exercised a certain attraction. It was clear and simple; it was a source of security and support. Hierarchy offers a sense of order. It provides assurances about where one stands and who has something to say. In this way, even the lower ranks acquire an orientation on which they can rely; ranked hierarchies derive their basic legitimacy among their members from this.[22] In contrast with the society of prisoners, which was dominated by terror and uncertainty despite its quasi-military regimentation, the status structure offered SS members a clear, predictable, and thus legitimate order.

While military hierarchies of rank are formal and impersonal, the status hierarchy of the Death's Head units was permeated by personal authority and camaraderie. Comradeship means that people help each other, assuming mutual responsibility; by contrast, camaraderie means that they accommodate each other, each making concessions. Comradeship adheres to general normative rules; camaraderie is purely an internal relation. People cover for each other, hush up misdeeds and mistakes, conceal weaknesses; they cultivate a corps spirit with which the group delimits and defines itself, with which it elevates itself over outsiders. Comradeship is having a friend when in need;

camaraderie is being an accomplice, but solely for the group.[23] It eludes external control; consequently, its moral level tends to be in constant decline. The accomplices orient themselves exclusively in terms of the habits and usages of the group, not in accordance with generally binding criteria. In this way, they liberate one another from justifications and legitimations, opening wide the door to demoralization. Military hierarchies of rank, which simultaneously represent and guarantee a scale of values, are undermined by camaraderie. The fluid of personal cohesion softens discipline. This is the source of the peculiar lenience toward infractions encountered with camaraderie. SS personnel who had been accepted by a narrow circle of *Kameraden* were always able to count on the goodwill of their superiors. As militarily as the camp SS were wont to present themselves, they tended more to resemble a band of conspirators who stuck close together when faced with external checks and controls, even by other SS authorities.

This camaraderie was also promoted in significant measure by the antimilitary spirit that Eicke endeavored to inculcate in the ranks of the camp SS. His personnel policies were guided by a quite open aversion to soldiering and the professional military. For example, he consistently blocked noncommissioned Wehrmacht officers from entering the guard units. Instead, he preferred recruiting young, moldable men in whom he could instill absolute personal obedience and unconditional allegiance. In circulars, he repeatedly criticized the formal military manners that contradicted the esprit of a community united by a shared Weltanschauung.[24] He instructed his men to use the solidarity-laden *Du* (the familiar form of "you") to address each other and even superiors, and abolished the separation between the officers' and the N.C.O. mess. The precept of equality was a fundamental principle for the camp SS: not the respect predicated on the distance of rank, but the camaraderie of like-minded party comrades; not critical obedience, but immediate and unhesitating submissiveness; not soldierly self-control and bravery, but a merciless iron fist against others, and readiness to be deployed for any task. These were the values in which the flogging guard was drilled. Personal ties played an appreciable role here. Whoever violated group morals and failed to demonstrate the requisite brutality ran the risk of being degraded by Eicke or dismissed from the service. By contrast, those who proved their mettle could always rely on Eicke's protection, even when infractions of the rules were involved. On his regular inspection trips, Eicke also sought contact with the lower ranks, though he made sure their immediate superiors were not present.[25] And he set up complaint boxes in all camps—boxes to which he had the only key. Thus, in addition to the path going through official channels, every member of the camp SS had direct access to the central authority figure of the concentration camp system.

The second feature of SS organization was a peculiar linkage of absolute allegiance and far-reaching vertical delegation. Formal hierarchies are based on the principle of regulated obedience. No matter who gives a command, the subordinate must execute it according to the set rules. By contrast, the dominant principle in the SS was absolute loyalty to one's unit leader. The decisive factor was not position in the pyramid and its operative rules, but the person of the leader. The SS member had to obey him absolutely, without questioning the legitimacy or advisability of the order.[26] Whoever refused risked draconian penalties: public disgrace or degrading of rank, reprimands, strict confinement, or even dishonorable discharge. Obedience was synonymous with loyalty. This provided both sides with advantages. Though the superior had sole responsibility, he had ample opportunity for implementing his spontaneous will. The subordinate was obliged to carry out orders promptly, yet this was offset by his being relieved of any need to think about the order. By making the personal will of his superior the guiding principle of his action, he saved himself the burden of having to form his own opinion. This was the basis for the unwavering execution of criminal orders and the effectiveness of terror. Absolute power gains an organizational undergirding if orders are given based on personal, arbitrary will—and are then executed unhesitatingly, without pause for thought. In significant measure, such power rests on the absolute obedience of its executors.

Down to the lowest rungs, every SS superior was supposed to be both a model and a mentor.[27] Formal hierarchy was personified; official authority was alloyed with personal authority. The template valid for the Nazi regime and the SS as a whole also determined the power structures of the camp SS. It consisted of groups and cliques that enjoyed considerable freedom. The reams of paper flowing down from the central office, the many instructions and orders, regulations, public commendations and penalties—all these tend to suggest a lack of homogeneity and discipline in the unit. Actually, the SS had a high degree of local, on-the-spot independence. It was officially forbidden for any *Blockführer* to mistreat the prisoners, but de facto mistreatment was the order of the day. Although there were extremely stiff penalties for shady dealings and corruption, these were quite common in everyday camp life. And though lack of discipline was one of the most serious infractions an SS member could be charged with, the camp SS was anything but a disciplined force. Absolute obedience did not mean mechanical subservience. Just as each superior was supposed to present a personal example, every individual SS member was expected to demonstrate personal initiative. He proved he belonged by doing more than was demanded in a specific instance (an act of supererogation)—by anticipating orders and carrying them out in advance, even before they were given. The rigorous compulsion toward identification, which far exceeded military "blind obedience," intensified terror further. When a subordinate is told that he must demonstrate his social affiliation by personal commitment and engagement, arbitrary action becomes the proof of obedience.[28]

A key reason for the decentralization of power was bound up with a third main feature of camp organization: the combination of a multilinear hierarchical system with a functional division of labor. The camp administration was divided into five departments that were repeatedly beset by conflicts over the sphere of authority.[29] The commandant's office was considered the highest authority in all matters of service and personnel, yet was extremely restricted in its actual powers. The camp Gestapo of Department II had been transferred from its control area and made subordinate to the RSHA, which had exclusive power to decide on admissions and releases. In the camp, the job of the Political Department was to deal with prisoner files and keep statistics, carry out interrogations, process convictions, order executions, and issue death certificates. Gestapo officials were feared both by prisoners and by the camp SS. The department served to assist the RSHA in keeping local tabs on the camp SS. A guard who had been implicated in a corruption scandal could generally count on the superior to whose personal retinue he belonged to back him up. However, he could only expect assistance from officials of the secret police if they also were involved on the sly in secret deals they wished to cover up.[30] Nevertheless, this office was an element external to the system. Its head wore civilian clothes, and it worked more for the regional state police head offices than for the camp. The camp Gestapo office formed a zone of uncertainty that was difficult for the commandant's office to penetrate.

The center of real power lay with Department III, the "protective custody camps" (*Schutzhaftlager*). This department was in charge of internal service operations and labor deployment (*Arbeitseinsatz*). The camp leader functioned as the standing representative of the commandant; directly under him were the rapport leader, the *Arbeitseinsatz* leader, and the block leaders. The rapport leader presided at the daily roll calls, recorded prisoner population numbers, and prepared the reports on punishment and on the amount of rations. The block leaders were the immediate superiors of the prisoners; they had to ensure discipline and cleanliness in the blocks. However, the commandant's office had little control over how they did this, whom they appointed as *Stubendienst*, or when they used violence or showed lenience. Although he usually only held the rank of SS corporal or sergeant, the block leader had several hundred prisoners under his absolute command—in periods of overcrowding, even more than a thousand. In military terms, this was tantamount to a command situation in which a low-ranking noncom had nearly total power over a large force of men, in size somewhere between a company and a regiment.

The *Arbeitseinsatz* leader had a role of special importance. His job was to organize prisoner labor, assemble the Kommandos according to prisoner qualifications, write up the daily work reports, process the offers from private firms, and handle the monthly receipts. Where prisoners had to work, whether they were transferred to satellite camps, and how they were treated on the job were all dependent on his decision. The *Arbeitseinsatz* leader was formally under Department III and the camp commandant, but received his most important orders directly from Office DII in the central *Inspektion*. This meant that a second important area of practical operations had been effectively removed from the control of the commandant's office. In line with the principle of dual subordination, labor administration was in a position to play off one superior office against the other. If the commandant wished to retain a specific group of prisoners in the camp, labor deployment could justify their transfer with an order to that effect from Office DII. Conversely, if a plant manager requested skilled specialists, it could assert the camp's interest in retaining seasoned skilled laborers in the workshops of the camp, and block the transfer.

Material equipment and furnishings for the camp were dealt with by Department IV, which handled administration. It was responsible for the possessions of the prisoners, building maintenance, camp vehicles, food supply, and clothing. Department IV was the economic heart of camp organization. It also was able to act relatively independently. Its power did not consist in violence and discipline, but in a monopoly of the control over material goods in the camp. Since it was located at the fount of all camp wealth, it also was the center of corruption and misappropriation. Many goods never arrived at the camp, but instead landed in some storeroom or were consumed at the eating and drinking orgies of the SS. Department IV decided whether winter clothing and new shoes would be distributed, what supplies the kitchen received, and how block quarters were furnished. It was to blame for hunger and mass misery among the prisoners.

Department V, medical services, also operated with relative independence, and encompassed the doctors, orderlies, and scribes in the *Revier*. By dint of their professional training and social origin, the SS doctors stood apart from the flogging guards in the camp. They were different. As a rule, they did not beat the prisoners; they killed by performing experiments, giving injections, administering gas—or by omission, failing to provide medical assistance when needed.[31] The SS doctors were not only responsible for treatment of sick prisoners, camp hygiene, and epidemic control; they also imposed the serial death penalty during the selection of prisoners unfit for work or otherwise deemed undesirable.[32] The sick bay was a separate area of competence with its own hierarchy and personnel, and not easily controllable by the camp leadership. Disputes were a common occurrence. If the labor administration or camp leader's office wished to be rid of sick prisoners, that led to overcrowding in the sick bay. Camp doctors opposed this because of the associated danger of epidemics. For that reason, many prisoners who were ill were not even admitted, and were sent right back to their blocks. Yet this aggravated the danger of a camp epidemic, which would in turn create serious overcrowding in the *Revier*. On the other hand, the doctors had hardly any leverage they could apply against the regime of the rapport leaders and block leaders to bring about an improvement in hygienic conditions in the camp and maintain the level of fitness of Kommandos at their jobs. Recruitment of orderlies and nurses also posed occasional problems. The labor deployment administration had to give its assent when a prisoner doctor or orderly was transferred from another post and seconded to the sick-bay facility. And for a long time, the Political Department was dead set against deploying Jewish doctors at all in the sick bay, even though there was a perennial shortage of qualified staff in the *Revier*.

As a result of the division of labor and power, each section jealously guarded its own turf. This so-called "departmental egoism" was actually accentuated by the principle of double subordination. The camp Gestapo was answerable to the RSHA, which vied for power with the WVHA. Labor administration (Department III) and camp administration (Department IV), as well as the senior camp doctor, received orders both from the camp commandant's office and the responsible specialized offices for inspection in the WVHA. They all controlled their own "zones of uncertainty," gray areas that could not be completely monitored by the commandant and his staff. On a whole array of key issues within his sphere of command, he was not the master of his own house. On the other hand, the multilinear system had certain advantages. The subsections in departments maintained direct and personal contact with the specialized desks at the *Inspektion* in Oranienburg. This shortened the official channels and enhanced the flexibility of the organization. However, the price for that was a lack of central guidance and direction. Decentralization means that decisions no longer connect at one dominant node in the network; individual offices acquire enormous leeway that they can exploit one against the other, and all against the central office. Thus, the bureaucracy of the concentration camp was anything but monolithic. Simultaneously, the *Inspektion* was close by, yet far away: proximate because of the direct official channel, and distant due to the high degree of autonomy enjoyed by local offices. The commandant's office, though set up as the local central authority, could not monitor all the spheres of camp activity as the camps grew; it was unable to reconcile structurally engendered conflicts and divergent interests. As a result of the independence of the subunits, the system was flexible, but often unpredictable. Formally, it was functionally structured. Actually, however, it was constantly involved with a host of improvisations, corrections, and rivalries.

The deadly effectiveness of camp organization was due more to the high degree of camaraderie, local autonomy, and personal initiative that pervaded its structures than to a smoothly functioning bureaucracy. Agreement was often arrived at by taking a spontaneous vote in a given case. When it came to the spread of terror, this formal subcoordination was anything but dysfunctional. Rather, it generated that ambience of organizational uncertainty and arbitrariness on which terror is predicated. However, the social basis for this was the collective *habitus* of the personnel, along with a certain degree of standardization. Standardization of procedures is always a functional equivalent of centralism. It can offset functional deficits arising from decentralization. If there is a similar round day after day, many decisions become superfluous. And when the personnel form habits and set routines that guarantee regular behavior, constant checks and monitoring are also unnecessary. However, in the case of camp personnel, this was true only to a limited extent. Alongside all the bureaucratic paperwork and regularity, there was a pervasive lack of discipline, compounded by corruption, excessive violence, personal arbitrariness, and caprice. The fourth structural feature of SS organization was a specific interweaving of standardization and deregulation. It programmed action, simultaneously uncoupling terror from constraints.

SS recruitment procedures were characterized by standard rules. In keeping with the ideal of a racial elite, there were strict fitness criteria for the *Totenkopf* units in the first few years, similar to those for the military SS-VT.[33] SS men were supposed to be at least 1.72 meters tall (5 feet, 8 inches), and had to document their "Aryan ancestry"; they had to be healthy and *blutjung* (in the prime of youth)—no older than twenty-three. No candidates could wear eyeglasses, and men from large urban areas were not accepted for regular positions. Intellectual abilities were secondary; the focus was on physical traits, ideological malleability, and the principle of voluntary enlistment. However, all sorts of compromises had to be made regarding these criteria. In the prewar period, many members of the commandant's staff were older than thirty when they commenced their concentration camp service, in contrast with recruits to the guard formations. In any event, at the beginning of the war, the only candidates available to fill the ranks were older men. By 1938, another restriction had been lifted, and candidates who wore glasses were also being accepted; the minimum height was lowered initially to 1.65 meters (5 feet, 5 inches) and then dropped another notch to 1.62 meters (5 feet, 3.8 inches). When the last reservoir of candidates was exhausted, the selection rules were jettisoned completely. Recruiters took anyone they could get: thousands of older soldiers unfit for combat, "ethnic Germans" who hardly knew a word of German, and foreign nationals (mainly Croats, Ukrainians, and Lithuanians). The female guards at the women's camps at Ravensbrück, Birkenau, and Majdanek, who belonged to the "retinue of the Waffen-SS" (*Gefolge der Waffen-SS*) either enlisted voluntarily in the SS, were conscripted for obligatory service by the labor offices, or were recruited in the war factories. Women who were often saddled with the heaviest jobs in the plants were wooed by stories of high pay and easier working conditions in the "reeducation camps."[34] The paths that led to the SS were often fortuitous; applicants were tricked by being given false information, or threatened with being sent to the front if they did not join. In this and other ways, the principle of voluntary enlistment was eroded. It is true that the call-up of members of the general SS at the outbreak of the war involved persons who were already serving under Himmler. But voluntary enlistment in the SS did not mean a person was ready to enlist voluntarily for concentration camp duty. The application of the emergency service decree meant compulsion by the state. The extent of voluntary enlistment among "ethnic Germans," who were under Himmler's control in his capacity as Commissar for the Strengthening of German Ethnic-Racial Culture, was probably even smaller.[35] If one disregards the core group of several hundred seasoned camp functionaries, the camp SS during the war presented a picture that completely contradicted the recruitment ideal. A third-class force, it was neither physically fit nor especially motivated, neither ideologically schooled nor disciplined militarily—a motley crew, anything but an elite.[36]

When the standardization of criteria for membership no longer functions, organizations often turn to methods of mental standardization: training programs, special courses, indoctrination. The purpose is to construct a binding definition of the situation and to channel thinking into a preselected groove. Indoctrination has several functions: it seals off patterns of thinking and belief from alternative interpretations, creating a closed conceptual universe. Images of the enemy instill distance and justify violence, protect one's self-image, and reduce conflicts of conscience. Stereotypes block the perception of the other as an individual, engendering an abstract hatred of anyone different. They provide the cognitive prerequisite for a fantasized "crusader mentality" that negates the humanity of the enemy. The aim of violence now is no longer the subjugation of human beings, but the annihilation of alien creatures who cannot be considered human. The greater the threat appears, the stronger is the need to ward it off, or to find a bolstering confirmation for one's views. Images of the enemy create the fear that is then given vent in violence. Indoctrination liberates the terroristic potential with which the personnel tries to break free from its own anxiety. One source of terror lay in this anxiety among the personnel—their fear of the prisoners, and of transgressing against the loyalty and conformity of the group.

The leadership of the SS greatly valued propaganda. Eicke regularly embellished his instructions and circular orders with ideological teachings. Political-instruction courses were a fixed component in the weekly schedule at the barracks, and in the leadership courses at the Junker academies.[37] However, the underlying intention was not so much to impart knowledge as it was to inculcate and mold an attitude and strengthen identification with the organization. Nonetheless, it would be wrong to overestimate the importance and impact of SS ideology as a guide to action.[38] The content of instructional materials was thin and unsubstantial: expurgated German history coupled with a glorification of "Germanic" culture, sundry legends from the "period of struggle" of the Nazi Party, a few tenets of biological racism, and a list of images of the enemy.[39] The course directors for the *Totenkopf* units, administrators who proved hard to recruit, were all of low rank and had poor qualifications.[40] There was presumably as much "fooling around" and indolence in such classes as in any army. Neither the intellectual content nor the binding nature of these courses can be compared with the rigorous cadre training of communist circles and parties. In order to be accepted as an SS man, the recruit had only to adopt a few slogans and basic concepts such as the Führer principle, "cultivation of the Aryan race" (*Rassenpflege*), or hostility to the church. Standardization in thinking in the ranks was achieved less by direct indoctrination and more by the concrete practice of service and the conformist pressures of camaraderie. Just as the structure of personnel fell far short of the ideal of an elite, the average SS member, especially during the war, was hardly a reflection of the ideal of an ideologically trained follower.

Standardization was a product of everyday action and the formation of habits. Mentality is not a question of ideological conviction, but of practical exercise and social norming. The collective *habitus* was initially strengthened by use of an instrument common to any bureaucracy: procedural paperwork. Putting things down in writing standardizes information and communication, making it accessible to checks and controls. The correct execution of orders, instructions, and rules is readily visible from the written record. Knowledge is uncoupled from the information known to specific individuals and rendered transparent, while information is guided into preprogrammed bureaucratic channels. At the same time, writing things down and keeping records creates a routine, thus enhancing organizational effectiveness. Although there was a widespread antipathy to administrative work within the camp SS, especially among the block leaders, the extent of the paperwork in the concentration camps was formidable. In the blocks, any change had to be carefully recorded in the books; daily work slips had to be filled out for all Kommandos. The *Rapportführer* regularly had to document the complete presence of the prisoner population at roll calls. Each prisoner was recorded in several files, and any transgression had to be reported in writing. Penalties had to be requested in writing, and were granted by the issuance of penalty slips. Service on the commandant's staff primarily entailed office work. Camp commandants spent most of their working days at their desks, where they had to sort through and sign piles of circulars, letters, reports, and countless forms. Dozens of SS personnel were occupied solely with correspondence, putting together reports, and amassing statistics. Hundreds of prisoners worked as clerks in the offices of the SS, the sick bay, and the *Schreibstube*, and in compiling labor statistics in the blocks and Kommandos. Organized terror rests on a substructure of painstakingly exact registration, a pedantic, exhaustive bookkeeping of the most minute changes, the total recording of all events.

In addition to this mania for getting things down in writing was the link between normative programming and practical habit. Standardization by means of social norms defines schematic modes of action for predefined situations. It sets down what should be done—what is permitted, what enjoined. Penalties are established for breaches of norms; special achievements are rewarded by dividends. At the same time, norming creates normalcy. When regulations are regularly followed, habitual patterns of action are generated whose normative basis gradually recedes from the field of attention. What was initially learned by means of order and rule is transformed into discipline. The basis of conformity now is no longer the awareness of normative correctness but the practiced, familiar routine. The more stable the habit, the more solidly founded the validity of the rules. And the more strict the discipline, the more unquestioned is the normative order—indeed, one is no longer even aware of it as such.

The camp leadership issued numerous rules regulating the service of sentry guards and order in the camp. The first standing orders in Dachau for the guards—a code that was then adopted by other camps and remained in force, with small addenda, to the end of the war—regulated the behavior of the guards down to the smallest details.[41] There were rules for the prescribed distance to be maintained from the marching columns and Kommandos, what had to be reported in the case of negligence by prisoners, and the exact phraseology of individual commands. There were also rules about clothing, correct posture,[42] and keeping weapons in proper condition. Suspicious individuals had to be arrested immediately; attempted escapes or attacks by prisoners were to be thwarted on the spot, foiled instantaneously by the use of firearms. It was forbidden to accept packages, to sleep, smoke, or drink alcohol during guard duty, to engage in conversations with prisoners, or to set down one's weapon. In addition, any mistreatment or harassment of prisoners was formally prohibited. The sentries' duty was solely to stand guard and urge prisoners to carry out their assigned tasks; in no case were they to intervene violently.

Though the code of regulations for the guards was thorough and detailed, this does not mean their actual behavior was in accordance with the meticulously prescribed norms. The stringent definition of guard-duty infractions and the regular lectures they were given about how to behave point up that it was necessary to regulate and control the guards. Forbidden exchanges and deals with prisoners and civilians were as much a part of the normal daily round of duty as arbitrary force or total indifference toward the actions and caprice of the Kapos. Since it was impossible to keep a formal check on work sites remote from the camp, guarding was ultimately dependent on the moods of the guards and the arrangements of the various sentries.[43] For the prisoners, this lack of discipline had both advantages and drawbacks. On the one hand, it held out the hope that not all the measures planned at higher levels would actually be carried out in their intended stringency. On the other, the prisoners always had to be braced for the worst. The smallest infraction might be left unpunished by an indifferent, listless guard, yet that very same transgression could be punished by another guard the next day with the ultimate penalty, death. One never knew. Some guards retired into the bushes and left their Kommandos in peace as long as the men appeared to be busy working; others constantly flogged the prisoners and made use of every opportunity to provoke escape attempts and then shoot down the fleeing victims in flagrante delicto. Though the rules were strict in their formulation, on the spot the guards enjoyed substantial leeway. The rules provided occasions of the guards' own choosing for lashing out and engaging in terroristic attacks on the inmates. Those rules defined countless situations in which a guard might intervene: contact with civilians, black marketeering, negligence on the job, leaving one's place of work without permission. Far from restricting terror, the rules gave the guards the absolute power of defining it. The standing orders for guards specified less what was forbidden to them than what license they had.

Only at first glance does the multiplicity of regulations contradict the principle of terror. Only on the surface does normative regulation appear to be the opposite of arbitrary action. Rules are general procedures that are applied in the implementation of social practices; their formulation in explicit instructions is more along the lines of a codifying interpretation than a program for action that has an immediate effect.[44] As elsewhere, practice in the camps preceded codification. Military law invested the modes of action of the personnel with formal validity. Terror was not curbed by the rules; it was systematized, rendered a permanent fixture. Moreover, rules do not simply set limits to action, they also facilitate it. Along with their regulative function, they always have a constitutive role as well. By defining a large number of transgressions and punishable offenses, the code of rules provided personnel with a handle for arbitrary action. The guards had unlimited power over what they defined as negligence, refusal to work, or disorder; these could be responded to by violence or the imposition of "penalties."[45] The code of rules was terror incorporated. It covered virtually all situations of everyday camp life, prescribing every minute detail for the prisoners. As a result, they found themselves in a hopeless situation. If rules encompass everything, it is impossible not to violate some rule or other. Rigorous and total overregulation did not produce order, it spawned disorder. This gave the guards license to act arbitrarily in the name of the rules. Each prohibition, every regulation for the prisoners augmented the freedom of the personnel. Because everything was forbidden to the prisoners, all was permitted for the personnel.

The terror of excessive overregulation was set down in the disciplinary code for the prisoner camp. Although the standing orders for guards were addressed to the personnel, the camp code was directly aimed at the prisoners.[46] It set down in detail where prisoners were allowed to be, the day's routines, the modes of movement, bodily hygiene, the cleaning of clothing and shoes and of the barracks and camp paths, prescribed hair styles, regulations about clothing and dress, the saluting of SS personnel, procedures for reporting to the camp doctor, behavior at work and during roll calls, mail regulations, and rules on shopping in the canteen. Theft and black-market dealings were prohibited, as was negligence in using "state property" that had been issued to them. Every transgression was associated with a graded series of possible penalties. These extended from three days of close confinement, several weeks of penal labor, and assignment to a *Strafkompanie*, to flogging and death in the case of the most serious offenses—mutiny, attempted escape, and sabotage at work. The code was total and all-inclusive; there was no situation without a corresponding regulation. Nothing was left to discretion; everything was guided by some rule. Although the camp code applied to everybody, newcomers were generally given little or no information about the regulations. The camp code was beat into them by truncheon, whip, and fist—or, if they were lucky, taught to them immediately by some thoughtful prisoner-functionaries. By contrast, the rules provided the personnel with guidelines for routine checks and encroachments. They gave guards concrete categories for the application of their power of definition. Although there were officially prescribed penalties, it was in keeping with the spirit of this system for the guards to respond immediately with violence when infractions occurred. Excessive overregulation thus shifted to deregulation, mutating into terror.

The drilling of the guards to be tough and severe, and the pressure of camaraderie, were also key elements. The members of the guard units were likewise inmates of a total institution. They were housed in barracks, uniformed, subject to daily agendas and service schedules, and exposed to a form of training associated with all the humiliations, hazing, and harassment of the barracks yard. Along with the customary military duties of obedience, there were special expectations in the case of SS personnel. They were supposed to evince a certain attitude and bearing, not merely to perform their service according to the rules. They were expected to identify emotionally with the unit and treat the prisoners with unfeeling, merciless severity. The humiliations of the training program generated a slew of frustrations that were later given vent in compensatory violence against the prisoners. The brutality experienced by the SS personnel themselves was passed on to the prisoners under them, multiplied many times. Their fear and powerlessness gave rise to an urge for revenge, deflected onto and vented on the prisoners. The concentration camp had been deliberately constructed as a double total institution. On one side were the inmates of the military formation, who were at the same time the personnel of the prisoner camp; on the other stood the prisoners. Feelings of revenge and hatred among the staff could be redirected toward them. The object displacement of violence was anchored in the structure of the institution. Whatever the trainers and superiors inflicted on the lower SS ranks could in turn be passed on; it could later be vented on the prisoners in multiple and diverse forms. This was a cleverly devised organizational and psychological mechanism that distinguished the camp from other total institutions. Thus, for example, under the direction and tutelage of seasoned thugs, recruits and new arrivals had to pass tests of their courage in using violence. They were required to administer a flogging punishment, or goaded to group violence under the influence of alcohol. Whoever did not participate, expressed reservations, or could not get used to the atmosphere of violence was derided by the others as a spineless weakling. The readiness to use violence was part of the collective *habitus* of the personnel. Camaraderie demanded it from each and every member. Whoever wished to avoid violating group conformity and risking his or her own social place in it had to live up to this expectation—or at least demonstrate the required severity if a superior chanced to appear on the scene.

The compulsion to conform to the group and the constraints of camaraderie, delegation and decentralization of power, local freedom to act, terroristic over-regulation, exoneration from responsibility by means of obedience, the iron tie to authority, the atmosphere of violence, the frustrations of training and guard duty—all these factors helped give rise to a *habitus* among the members of the camp SS that constituted a mortal danger to the prisoners. That same *habitus* also confronted the SS leadership with an array of personnel problems. Although quite conducive for the spread of terror, features such as lack of discipline, brutality, and corruption endangered the units' prestige and ability to function. The SS leaders were indifferent to the suffering of the victims, but not to the morale of their men. Their attention was aroused less by the daily mistreatment of prisoners than by the sadistic excesses of individual tormenters. As a countermeasure, camp brothels were set up, and the task of punishment was delegated to specially selected prisoners. The leadership also transferred certain thugs whose behavior had become intolerable, even for the SS. The innumerable cases of corruption created worse problems. Personal enrichment from storerooms and canteens, shady deals and black marketeering with prisoners, drinking orgies and sexual affairs—all these were scarcely compatible with the elite ideal of the *Totenkopf* units. However, the investigations undertaken by the special commissions, the SS, and the police courts were fiercely opposed by the old camp guard. Accomplices among the prisoners were quickly liquidated, the cliques stuck firmly together, and the top echelon of the WVHA covered for its own people. The upshot was that many proceedings were dismissed with no result, or just petered out, coming to nothing.[47]

The barbarism of the personnel had organizational and social underpinnings. It cannot be attributed to individual intentions or inclinations. It is also misleading to try to account for the atrocities by reference to bureaucratic relations of subordination and obedience, ideals of an elite or ideological fanaticism. Atrocities do not require a deeper underlying ideological meaning or a lengthy reshaping of dispositions. All cruelty needs is a lack of a sense of morality and brutalization by daily routines. The guards flogged, tormented, and killed prisoners—not because they had to, but because they were allowed to, no holds barred. Mechanisms of bureaucratic control had been systematically immobilized, abrogated by decentralization, the overlapping of spheres of authority, local autonomy, and camaraderie. Bureaucracies control the use of violence; they subject all members to set rules, binding power to regulations. This model is inapplicable in the case of camp organization. Each insignificant little *Blockführer* had more power at his disposal than the head of a civilian administration or the commander of an entire army regiment. No officer in the modern military can walk through his men's barracks and choose summarily to drown a recruit on the spot in a latrine. The guards in the camp had every possible freedom—nearly total license. The institution was so constructed that it did not curb power but set it free, transmuting it into absolute terror.

10

Classes and Classifications

We enter the prisoners' dressing room. Stacked on the shelves
are large numbers of uniforms, underclothing and boots. The
prisoners working here appear to be relatively clean; they look
fairly good. Almost all of them have the red triangle. First they
sort us new arrivals into groups. The political prisoners who
are supposed to get the red triangle over in one corner, the work-
shy and asocial prisoners for the black triangle over there.
Jehovah's Witnesses (purple triangle) in one spot, criminals (green
triangle) in another corner, and homosexuals (pink badge), in still
another spot. The Jews are given a second yellow triangle; they
have to combine it with their colored triangle to form a Star of
David. The first thing almost every prisoner working behind the
table asks me is: what is my color. There's some "black" guy
standing next to me. It is very obvious the clothing he gets handed
is worse than mine. At boot distribution, they initially give me a
pair of worn-out shoes. As the prisoner hands them to me, he asks:
"you political"? After I answer "Yeah," he gets me a better pair of
boots. Only we political prisoners are asked whether we brought
along a woollen jacket, or a sweater. Whoever doesn't have one,
is given such an article of clothing. But not for any of the other
categories of prisoners.[1]

THE SOCIETY OF THE concentration camp was a system of glaring differences
and extreme inequality. Although countless prisoners starved in misery, a
small number led a life of veritable luxury. Although many were literally
worked to death, others did not need to work at all. Although most lived in
constant fear of violence, others could torment and murder with impunity.
Social position was not dependent only on a prisoner's will to survive, power
of resistance, and unscrupulousness. The camp was not a porous social field.
Personal resources are only useful if there are opportunities for their use; social
circumstances create the necessary resources for survival. The social structure
distributed goods, power, and privileges, established and destroyed social ties,
and guided life and death. Its final reference point was not, as in civil society,
the opportunities for conducting a normal life; here the bottom line was what
chances one had for limited, temporary survival.

What social facts determined stratification in the concentration camp? The customary criteria of sociological analysis are not directly applicable.[2] No prisoner had control of any means of production; income from labor was paid out in the form of vouchers, but this arrangement was not introduced until late in the war, and then only for a small number of inmates. Education or vocational skills only helped a prisoner land a job in administration, the workshops, or the sick bay. University graduates were often subjected to intensified hounding and harassment. Money is devalued as a general means of exchange if there is nothing to buy; other currencies operate within the framework of a primitive economy where booty is bartered. In the camps, the social strata were determined by the system of categories the SS used to classify prisoners: their power as prisoner-functionaries, by their membership in Kommandos, and by their social and economic contacts with the personnel. How did these factors condition one another? To what extent could they be offset or supplanted?

The system of classifications—the taxonomy of colors, triangles, and insignia— was decisive for the figuration of the social classes.[3] With the reorganization of the camps in 1936, the SS introduced a system of categories with which the various groups of prisoners were then visibly marked. The colored triangles were sewn onto the prisoners' uniforms on the left side of the chest and the right trouser leg. "Criminal" prisoners got a green badge, *Asoziale* a black badge; emigrants received a blue triangle, and Gypsies were first required to wear a brown triangle and later a black one. Political prisoners, as a basic category, were initially unmarked; at the end of 1937, the red triangle was introduced for them. Jews wore the Star of David. Foreigners, who were generally classified as "political," had the beginning letter of their nationality inscribed on the red triangle: "F" for French, "P" for Polish, "S" for Spanish prisoners. Members of the *Strafkompanie* were marked by a special black dot at the apex of the triangle. Those suspected of plotting escape had red-and-white targets on their chests and backs. Prisoners of the *Nacht-und-Nebel* transports were marked by broad red bands; on their backs and both trouser legs was a cross, with the letters "NN" to its right. From these emblems, it was possible to recognize immediately what class a prisoner belonged to and how he or she was pigeonholed and evaluated by the SS.

The category system was more an instrument of power than a means of recognition. Its main function was discrimination and dissociation, not mere bureaucratic classification. The practical schematic arrangement was a guidance system for death. The scale of rank marked the specific distance of the classes of prisoners to the center of absolute power. The further a category was from the SS, the lower was its social position, and the greater was the pressure for annihilation to which it was subjected. The closer a class stood to the rulers, the higher was its social rank, and the greater were its chances for survival. Yet this latent structure of classifications was more complex than the symbolic system of colors. It was based on a total of four hierarchically ordered criteria.

At the apex of the class taxonomy (category I) stood the racial contrast between human beings and *Untermenschen*—subhumans. Members of the Slavic "Eastern peoples" (who at best were assigned lives as helots by racial theory) along with Gypsies and Jews, were not regarded as part of human society. They formed an ambivalent category existing at the very periphery, if not beyond the perimeter, of sociality. Persecution here took on the character of systematic eradication. The racial criterion was predominant. A Jew from Belgium or France who was also classified as a political enemy or criminal was nonetheless primarily a Jew. A Gypsy who wore the black triangle of the German "asocials" and was politically completely innocuous was persecuted because of "genetic inferiority." The Soviet POWs were not merely political and military mortal enemies of the Germans; above all they were Slavic *Untermenschen*. According to the logic of classification, they were doubly threatening: militarily and biologically.

In this category, the non-Jewish Czechs had a special status. In Dachau and Buchenwald, at least a thousand Czech hostages had been incarcerated as "preferential prisoners." The largest contingent, twelve hundred students from Prague and Brünn, were brought to Sachsenhausen in November 1939 after participating in demonstrations against the German occupying power. They were subjected to severe reprisals on admission. However, their situation improved when the SS turned its attention toward more-recent arrivals. When Heydrich took over the *Reichsprotektorat* (Bohemia and Moravia) in the autumn of 1941 and introduced a more stringent occupation policy, the pressure was also cranked up in the camps. In May 1942, after the assassination of Heydrich, they were treated as the Jews and Soviet POWs were. In the final years of the war, however, their status came to resemble that of Germans in the Reich. Despite internal differences, the surviving Czechs formed an active antifascist collective that was regularly supplied with food packages from home. Their level of education and knowledge of German gave them access to lower-level positions as prisoner-functionaries. Czechs worked as translators, clerks, and doctors. Different from Poles or Russians, they were not considered Slavic *Untermenschen* but members of a neighboring people—one that for a time the authorities even wished to "Germanize."

With the outbreak of the war, the concentration camps were transformed into an international society. Consequently, the prisoners were sorted into categories based on nationality. But the geographic and national code (category II) also contained racial aspects. Northern Europeans such as Danes and Norwegians were regarded as "Aryans," and thus were closer to the SS than the French or Spanish. Although most foreigners wore red triangles, the nations were clearly stacked in a hierarchy. In many camps, French prisoners were exposed to increased persecution and harassment. In the pecking order of na-

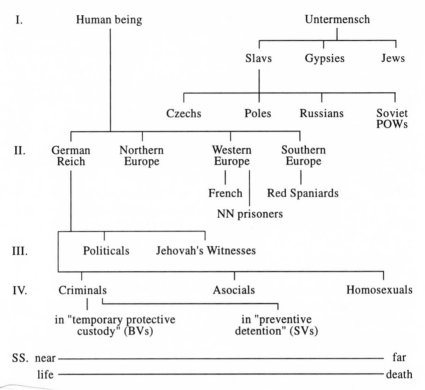

Figure 1. The System of Classifications

tions, they occupied a rung similar to that of the Poles in the hierarchy of races. The only ones treated worse were the Italians.[4] In special categories were the *Nacht-und-Nebel* prisoners (NN) from the occupied countries of western Europe, most of whom were sent to Groß-Rosen and Natzweiler, and the Spanish republican prisoners who had emigrated to France. They were summarily classified as "communists" by the SS, and transferred to Mauthausen or Gusen for liquidation.

The criteria of political hostility (category III) and social deviance (category IV) largely involved German prisoners from the Reich. The foreigners were political enemies by definition; the communists, social democrats, and Jehovah's Witnesses were principally ideological adversaries. The crucial factor here was religious or political worldview—not national or racial origin. Due to their high degree of solidarity, the political prisoners were thought to be especially dangerous, but they contributed to the orderly operation of the camps as a result of their strict discipline. Political prisoners, especially communists, participated in the system of camp power to the extent that the SS set aside posts for them as functionaries in the camp system of self-administration.

They thus were in competition with those in "temporary protective custody" (*befristete Vorbeugehäftlinge*, or BVs) who were termed "professional criminals" in camp jargon; the latter were always given preference by the SS when order was to be established by brutality rather than discipline. On the scale of social deviance, this category was closest to the camp regime. By contrast, the other criminal prisoners, those in "police preventive detention" (*polizeiliche Sicherheitsverwahrte*, or SVs), who were required, beginning in January 1943, to wear green triangles with the apex on top, like pyramids, were largely denied privileges and were deployed at the most physically ruinous tasks—as were the "asocials," who were stigmatized as "work-shy pests injurious to the people" (*arbeitsscheue Volksschädlinge*). At the far end of the scale of deviance were the homosexuals, so-called "175ers" (after section 175 of the former penal code). Although they were politically insignificant, their marginal position was similar to that of the *Untermenschen*. Ideological and political adversaries, insofar as the SS struggled against them, were a part of camp society. They were oppressed, but also feared. However, the marginal groups, such as the "asocials" and homosexuals, were not really perceived as proper adversaries, human beings worth struggling against. They were subhumans: abnormal, noxious, superfluous. For them, the camp power had nothing but scorn, contempt, and death.

The system of classification was not static. As a praxis of social order, it was subject to certain historical changes, although these did not modify its basic structure. Absolute power is always in a position to change the valence of categories, give preference to individual classes, and alter the pressure of persecution, turning the screws here, easing things there. To cite just two examples: initially, the "red Spaniards" incarcerated in Mauthausen were considered just as dangerous as the Soviet POWs because of their military discipline and their experience in the camps of southern France. By the end of 1942, some forty-two hundred of the approximately seventy-five hundred Spanish inmates had been killed in the stone quarries of Gusen. But from the spring of 1943 on, the survivors were suddenly given special preference and transferred to better external subcamps; to a certain extent, this was also because of their resolute resistance to the dominant class of the criminal prisoner-functionaries. They enjoyed considerable respect among their fellow inmates, since their solidarity was not limited to their own category. During the last two years of the war, their mortality rate was lower than that of the other classes of prisoners.

The Jehovah's Witnesses experienced something similar. Although they were only a small group, the SS considered them to be more influential than they actually were. For a long time, they were mercilessly oppressed because of their consistent passive resistance. In order to smash their internal cohesion, the SS split them up and distributed them among various blocks. But this measure was revoked when it became clear that the Jehovah's Witnesses were having success missionizing among their fellow prisoners. However, since their resistance was directed solely against those orders not compatible with their convictions, the SS ultimately switched to a policy of trying to exploit their devotion to duty and their reliability. So the Jehovah's Witnesses began to climb in the pecking order. They were used as general servants in SS households or put to work in small Kommandos where there was a threat that prisoners might escape. In Ravensbrück, they were showcased as "exemplary prisoners," while in Niederhagen, the only camp where they constituted the core population, they were put to work on renovations to the Wewelsburg, which was an SS *Ordensburg* (a training college for the elite).[5]

Shifts in the categories also resulted from the succession of admissions. The SS always paid special attention to the new arrivals. They were the preferred recipients of harassment and mistreatment. As soon as the newcomers had been classified and were being treated as a new underclass, those in the old categories in the social structure moved up a notch. This generated a peculiar social dynamic. Even if there was no absolute improvement in their material conditions, veteran prisoner groups were relatively better off in comparison to the newly arrived. Thus, the "asocials" rose on the ladder at the beginning of the war when the first Poles and Czechs were incarcerated. In Auschwitz, the non-Jewish Poles who had made up the initial transports profited once Soviet POWs and Jews started to be admitted. They even gained access to lower- and middle-level posts, especially in the external satellite camps. When numerous Poles were transferred from Poland to camps in the Reich in April 1943, placed there initially on the very lowest rung, a small number of Jews in Auschwitz were even able to move up and occupy the vacant work positions. However, foreigners and Jews were only allowed to command members of their own groups, never German prisoners. Movements up and down the social ladder were thus in strict accordance with the taxonomic hierarchy. In a camp where the majority of prisoners were Poles, Russians, and Jews, the Poles necessarily advanced up the pyramid; where Germans and western Europeans predominated, they were at the bottom of the class scale. There was no fundamental transformation or abrogation of the classificatory structure.

The system of classification was not the product of social inequality, but rather its most important cause. Absolute power is in a position to construct society according to its model. The political element had priority over the social element in the camp. The power to label was primary; other factors, such as organizational function, work, and prestige were secondary. The classificational scheme was not a reflection of social structure; rather, the latter was an incorporation of power. The categories did not reduce inequality, but rather engendered it. They were general rules of social structure that had been forced on the prisoners. This becomes clear when one examines the functions and effects of the system.

The system of categories acted as a mechanism for differentiation. It created distances, intensified antagonisms and drew lines of social demarcation that none could cross. With few exceptions, a change from one category to another was virtually impossible. Once labeled, the prisoner remained irrevocably pigeonholed. The goal of such taxonomy was not communication but segregation and social separation. Like every categorial differentiation, the color system guided social judgment by intensifying the perception of differences. Persons of the same category seemed more similar to each other than persons of different categories. The imposed class channeled social perception. Every prisoner with a black triangle was now actually considered asocial, work-shy, cowardly, and filthy; every criminal was thought dangerous, brutal, and violent; each Jehovah's Witness was regarded as industrious, neat, and tidy, and uncompromising in his or her religious principles.

It was no different when it came to national antagonisms. For many foreigners, the German prisoners, who were certainly not all political opponents of the Nazi regime, also were members of the enemy nation, even in the camp. Conversely, chauvinism, anti-Semitism, and hatred of the Slavs were rampant among the German prisoners. Spaniards accused the French of neutrality in the civil war and collaboration with the Germans. Czechs criticized them for their appeasement at Munich, and Poles held it against them that the French army had failed properly to defend their country when it was attacked by the Germans. Initially it was hardly noted that many of the French came from the ranks of the Resistance. The Poles, in turn, were regarded by many prisoners as extreme nationalists—an attribution that was in conspicuous agreement with the stereotypes held by many Poles. Among the Poles, there was a pronounced animosity toward not just the Germans and French, but the Russians, Ukrainians, and Jews as well.[6] Nationalistic and anti-Semitic prejudices were not uncommon among the prisoners. The stereotypes often intermeshed, solidifying into a structure that confirmed and reproduced the given classifications.

Although it was forced on the prisoners by the SS, the category system was largely accepted by them. There was resistance to the status of individual classes, but not to the system as a whole. There were several reasons for this. First, the labels used by the SS matched existing stereotypes in the social environment; the camp regime only needed to radicalize them. "Criminal," "asocial," Jew, Pole, and Gypsy were common categories that also shaped social perception in civil society. For that reason, the prisoners attributed criminal, asocial, or solidaristic behavior, almost as a matter of course, to the respective categories. Whoever unexpectedly did not fit this framework was only an exception that confirmed the rule.[7] Second, the rampant repression and international composition of the prisoner population often reduced communication to a series of gestures and rapid exchanges. The badges helped provide a quick orientation as to whom one was dealing with, and who could be trusted. Finally, collective powerlessness furthered the acceptance of the categories. Inferiors frequently ascribe to themselves what is attributed to them by superior powers, and accommodate to what is forced on them.[8] They define each other the way the dominant order defines them. Their logical conformism absorbs the insight that the predominant class order cannot be changed and is inescapable; despite any misjudgment or repression, it is necessary in its unassailable objectivity. Thus, the system of categories became a social reality in the camps, one in which the inmates judged one another in line with the given schemata.

There was no corresponding integration within the classes. The dyadic function of every classification—external separation and internal homogenization—ran up against the multiplicity of social origins and political convictions. Forced affiliation does not create genuine social unity. The sense of cohesion among the Jehovah's Witnesses, Spanish republicans, or Soviet soldiers had its roots in the period prior to incarceration. Among the political prisoners, only the communists constituted a solidaristic core group that occasionally co-opted the members of other parties or foreign Communist Party members. Otherwise it was nothing more than a residual category. Whoever was difficult to pigeonhole was given a red triangle. The category of "asocials," which was the largest group until the outbreak of the war, included hoboes, beggars, Gypsies, pimps, prostitutes, the unemployed, "loafers on the job," individuals who had previous convictions for trespassing, and even former husbands who had been lax in their alimony payments—in other words, anyone who had transgressed in some way or another against the "order of the folk community." Common to all was the fate of discrimination, loss of social status, material distress, and denunciation. Yet this fate was individual; "asociality" was only a summary stigma devoid of social homogeneity.

The principle of arbitrary subsumption applied to a far greater degree in the case of the Jews. The only feature they shared was that they had been branded by the SS as Jews. Their ranks included activists of the political left and right, religious Jews and atheists, merchants and workers, criminals and law-abiding citizens from all walks of life, Belgians, Greeks, Poles, Russians, and Italians. They were not united by a common set of religious practices or political convictions, nor did they come from the same social and national background. The stigma of race allowed no differentiation, and the pressure of annihilation precluded any chance for them to discover some shared uniform identity. Where Jews were confined in mass blocks or in separate sections of camps, conditions were miserable. Their lives were a constant struggle for survival—scrounging for food, clothing, and space.

In addition to mobilizing social prejudices, the system of categories served principally to distribute power and work. It chaneled access to jobs in prisoner self-administration, material privileges, and the Kommandos. The taxonomy determined power, work, and possessions. As a rule, a green or red triangle and

German nationality were necessary preconditions for a post as a functionary; during the war, they also became sufficient conditions. Only where there was a personnel shortage did the SS fall back on "asocials" or people of other nationalities. In addition, administrative service posts required certain bureaucratic or language skills, and a talent for organization—abilities that tended to be found mainly among the political prisoners. Yet this did not alter the situation; such posts were generally delegated only to Germans with green or red triangles.

Frequently, the system of categories was also decisive in the allocation of work. Often, merely belonging to a given category was sufficient reason for such prisoners to be assigned to the worst Kommandos. Entire categories were summarily deployed at hard labor in camp construction and the stone quarries in Gusen and Mauthausen: in 1939, all Gypsies; in 1940, all Jehovah's Witnesses, Poles, and Jews; in 1941–42, the Jews and Soviet soldiers, most Poles, Spaniards, and Czechs; in 1943, all those in "police preventive detention," Yugoslavs, Russians, and Jews.[9] Jews were the only category used for building the Buna Works in Monowitz; Hungarian Jews were the only ones deployed in the underground shafts in Hersbruck and Leitmeritz, the two largest external subcamps of Flossenbürg.[10] In Buchenwald, Poles, Russians, and Jews worked mainly in the murderous labor details assigned to construction and transport projects, in the stone quarry, in the motor pool, or in the latrines.[11] The SS preferred Jehovah's Witnesses as private domestics; on the other hand, they generally recruited artisans for the camp workshops, medical attendants for the sick bay, and clerks from the ranks of the political prisoners. The worse the type of work, the more numerous the prisoners from the lowest classes. Where skills meant nothing and one worker more or less was immaterial, the taxonomy had an immediate impact.

The class system also guided the allocation of housing and the supply of material goods. One's category determined where a prisoner was housed, what clothing he or she was issued, and whether he or she was allowed to receive packages.[12] By determining the staffing of Kommandos, it also decided indirectly on the prisoners' chances of getting extra food. One could scrounge up nothing edible in the stone quarries, gravel pits, brick factories, or construction crews. On the other hand, in the kitchen, stockrooms, and depots, prisoners could get hold of goods they were subsequently able to exchange on the black market. The category system extended its long arm even into the secret distribution system of the prisoners. There it helped a prisoner gain possessions and the power to barter and exchange, generated dependency and *protekcja* (special privileges), affected rank and prestige.

Not until the last two years of the war did the system of categories forfeit some of its centrality. As prisoner labor was made more economic and efficient, individual qualifications took on greater importance. Increasing scarcities and total overcrowding leveled the differences in the middle classes. The

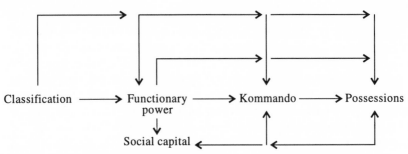

Figure 2. The Ordering of Social Structure.

more the camp changed into a mass society, the more porous the social field became, and the more salient were individual survival abilities. That was particularly true in the case of foreign prisoners who had survived the annihilatory pressures of the initial period, and had become seasoned old-timers in the camps. However, nothing was changed in the array of privileges enjoyed by the German prisoners from the Reich, and nothing altered in the pariah status of the Jews. The endpoints on the scale of evaluation remained the same until the final phase of the war; it was only the national code that lost some of its discriminatory meaning.

To what extent was the forced social order softened and made less severe by the social capital of the prisoners? In the camps, social capital included those resources that came from being part of a group, one's position in a network of "good relations" that formed a basis for the exchange of vital information, goods, and solidaristic assistance.[13] It did not abrogate the dominant power of the classificatory system, but nonetheless it affected the ways in which power, work, and possessions conditioned one another. The schematic model in figure 2 can be used to map the interrelations in the social structure of the camp.

Social capital was the principal weapon against the dissociations of the class system. However, autonomous association in the camp was an illegal form of sociation that had to be wrested from the dominant power of formalism. Autonomy was combated, banished underground, or at best merely tolerated. Officially, all that could formally exist were the relations of the hierarchy and cooperation at work. Other links were constantly threatened by encroachment and attack. Absolute dictatorships have every opportunity to break up and crush coalitions and associations at will. In the camps, this was only offset when prisoners could rely on stable political, military, or national common ground stemming from the period prior to incarceration, and were also able to defend these nuclei of solidarity against the camp regime.

But the most important networks of relations were ultimately guided by the class system. One's category determined proximity to the SS and access to power, and that power helped an individual procure social capital. Dependent beneficiaries clustered around the prisoner-functionaries. Such hangers-on assisted in efforts to obtain goods and influence, and were compensated by being protected against hunger and persecution. Connections with prisoner-functionaries were indispensable if a prisoner wished to traffic with the SS. Conversely, inmates who had personal backing from the SS were in a better position to exercise their own power more extensively and acquire desired goods—even though that practice often was coupled with an erosion of respect from their fellow prisoners, and a loss of the protective veil of anonymity. Service for the SS—whether as an informer, as a fence for pilfered or illegal goods, as a skilled specialist for private assignments, or as a performer at cultural shows—was rewarded with temporary protection.

Over the longer term, group contacts among the prisoners were only of use if they were linked with central power positions. To be transferred to a better Kommando, a prisoner needed the recommendation of an influential Kapo or good connections with those in the orderly room. On occasion, actual or feigned craft, medical, or office skills were enough to merit direct preference from the SS. By landing better positions, prisoners could beef up their social capital. If there was an opportunity at work to organize additional goods, an inmate could consolidate a position in the distribution system. A person who worked in the kitchen could siphon off food and exchange it with the hungry for clothing. A prisoner working in the *Revier* could filch medicines now and then and sell them at a high price. In the cycle of work, possessions, and social capital, those who had already risen in the hierarchy gleaned a chance to climb even further. Those who had were given more; those who had nothing forfeited even that. Solidarity was also of little avail where supplies were below the minimum for survival. Where there is nothing to divide or exchange, social capital lacks the rock-bottom material basis. The internal space of the group was not integrated into the cycle of work, possessions, and power. In other words, social ties and group cohesion were only a resource for survival in the camp when they were linked to the formal structure of order, and that was overdetermined by the system of categories.

Power as a prisoner-functionary, privileged work and possessions brought in social capital. Conversely, it was virtually impossible to obtain food and better assignments without such capital. To acquire such power, however, the social capital of the prisoners was neither a sufficient nor a necessary condition. The ultimate decisive factor here was one's position in the pecking order. Criminal prisoners owed their power as functionaries not to any group cohesion, but to SS *protekcja*. And the "political" prisoners were able to gain ground only where the criminal prisoners had become intolerable to the SS. The power potential of the resistance group ended at the perimeter of the absolute power of the SS dictatorship. Only if the SS kept out of it and left the staffing of posts to the struggle between the various groups of prisoners did group ties gain in salience. In the class struggle between the red and the

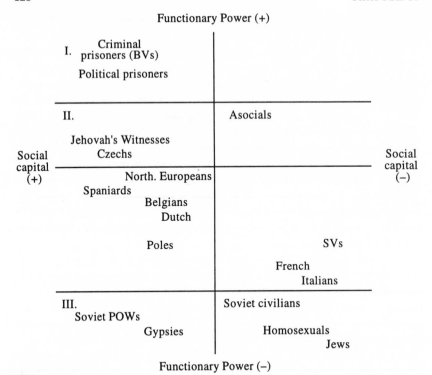

Figure 3. The Social Field

green triangles, connections and close contacts were important prerequisites for protecting power.

If the taxonomic order is linked with the most important formal and informal sources of power, namely the power to assign work and the social capital of the prisoners, the following model emerges for conceptualizing the social field of the concentration camp. Although any model necessarily has to neglect exceptions and simplify the complexity of realities on the ground, this one should provide insight into the hierarchy of the class order and the role of social and national antagonisms.[14] If the entire field is divided into three subfields, it becomes possible to discern where the categories stood in the order of social classes. The apex of prisoner society (category I) was occupied solely by the criminal prisoners (BVs) and the German political prisoners. They were the oldest categories and formed the upper class of the camp prisoner elite. The struggle for positions and privileges was waged among them. The criminal BVs fell back on the SS for support, while the political prisoners relied more on internal solidarity and discipline as well as their reputation among the veteran German prisoners. Nonetheless, the class struggle between the green and the red triangles was a struggle waged internally, inside the upper class.

After the internationalization of the camps, the upper middle class (category II) consisted of the German *Asoziale*, Jehovah's Witnesses, Czechs, and northern Europeans—and, after 1943, the republican Spaniards as well. They owed their positions to long experience in the camps, *protekcja* by the Prominents and the SS, or their particular organizing skills. The lower middle class included the Poles, French, and Italians. The national conflicts among the Poles, Czechs, and French were thus internal, waged within the middle class. By contrast, the two-front struggle of many Poles against Germans, Soviet citizens, and Jews was fought vertically: against the German prisoner-functionaries above, and, in order to establish a clear demarcation, against the underclass of Russians and Jews below. The national and racial antagonism was, at the same time, a defensive struggle against the social downgrading of one's own category.

The transitions to the underclass (category III), the pariahs of the concentration camp system, were fluid. Although the distance from the aristocracy to the middle class was especially glaring, the difference between the middle class and the pariahs often lay in little more than a tiny hunk of bread. Although the lower-middle classes were often protected from direct mass annihilation, the material misery of the lower-middle classes, which had neither internal solidarity nor vertical *protekcja*, was immense. Nonetheless, there was a striking boundary line. The central field became increasingly porous in the wake of the economic use of prisoner labor. Individual advancement was no longer an impossibility. By contrast, there was an immediate and permanent pressure of annihilation at the base of the class hierarchy. Despite mutual aid, powerlessness was virtually total and all-pervasive in the mass blocks and camp sections of the "superfluous"—prisoners helpless in the face of hunger, constant unrelenting reprisals, and mass liquidations.

11

Self-Management and the Gradation of Power

The SS was mainly interested in making sure that everything ran smoothly in the camp, and that they didn't have to bother about anything. We proved to them day after day that we could handle it better without them. We repeatedly let them notice that things got botched up whenever they interfered. I was always so "terribly sorry" when one of their orders had gotten nowhere. The SS had to learn: Just leave it to them, then we'll have our peace and quiet. And they were always concerned about having their peace and quiet. In order to make the best of our situation, we had to exploit every chink the SS left us. We had to approach things psychologically, react fast, make a pretense from time to time of taking the adversary seriously. And bluff when he helped us. We acted as though we had enormous influence, tremendous power. This power was based on deception. Any measly little block leader could have done us in.[1]

ABSOLUTE POWER is a structure, not a possession. The camp leadership organized its regime on a broad base, investing an accessory band of prisoners with considerable powers. The "self-administration" of the prisoners did not diminish power; it augmented it by means of organization and delegation. By making a small number of victims into its accomplices, the regime blurred the boundary between personnel and inmates. At the same time, it reduced the amount of power it expended. Its accomplices relieved the regime of the detailed work of terror; in return, they were given temporary protection from persecution. The power configuration in the concentration camp owed its permanence and strength in particular to this auxiliary force of small satraps, who exercised absolute power over those beneath them. Had it not been for the self-administration and the collaboration of the prisoner-functionaries, discipline and social control would soon have buckled and collapsed.[2]

The system of categories divided society into controllable classes, aggravating the antagonisms among the prisoners. Self-administration defined the prisoner-functionaries' roles and named an elite that kept the others under surveillance, ordering them around. Its organizational principle was not rivalry but deputization and subordination—the gradation of power.[3] Hierarchies prevent solidarity by employing the graduated power of delegation, not by encouraging competition. Though there was a fierce struggle in many camps for posts and privilege, that competition between those with red and green triangles, between political and criminal prisoners, was limited to the upper class and did not involve all strata of prisoner society. For the SS, the rivalry within the elite was only a welcome side effect. The main purpose of the hierarchy was to establish a second camp administration, designed to relieve the burdens on the SS personnel, organize everyday life in the camp, and have the prisoners themselves run their affairs.[4]

Self-administration was the intermediary between SS personnel and prisoner society. Although staffed by inmates, it formed the core of a complex figuration of power. The Kapos, the senior camp prisoners, the block chiefs and room chiefs, the rapport clerks and block clerks were integrated into a network of social relations. First, prisoner-functionaries were obliged to maintain absolute obedience, and were dependent on the *protekcja* of the SS. Second, they had to defend their position against the attacks and intrigues of their rivals. Third, they had to keep their subordinates under supervision and make sure order was maintained. Fourth, they were surrounded by dependent clients, beneficiaries, and cliques. The prisoner-functionary elite stood between guard personnel and inmates; it fought for privileges and sought accessories for support. This structural mesh should be kept in mind when considering the tasks and recruitment of prisoner personnel, their sources of power, and their strategies, positioned as they were between camp leadership and prisoner society.[5]

The sphere of tasks in self-administration was clearly structured; it was a mirror image of the organizational structure of the camp SS. A hierarchy of superiors with the formal power to command and punish had been set up to supervise the prisoners and maintain order. At its apex were one or more senior camp prisoners (*Lagerälteste*) appointed by the SS, generally on a purely arbitrary basis, although occasionally in keeping with suggestions from the dominant group of prisoners. The senior camp prisoners were the responsible representatives of the prisoners vis-à-vis the camp leadership, and simultaneously the highest-placed recipients of orders in the chain. The SS could always rely on them when it wished to take care of some matter through channels. They were ready to be called, and were brought in when problems arose; in turn, they enjoyed considerable leeway in the selection of *Blockälteste*. Their position was characterized by the principle of dual delegation. They had been endowed with powers by those above them, and could exercise these without restriction in dealing with the prisoners. At the same time, they represented the camp vis-à-vis the SS, and were called to account by the SS in that capacity. Without being appointed by the inmates, their job was to represent the inmates and to implement SS orders directed against the prisoners. Thus, a structural perversion of social representation was concealed behind the facade of self-administration. The prisoner-functionaries were not supposed to act as spokespeople or representatives, but as accomplices of the SS. They had no power of representation up the hierarchy; down the hierarchy, however, they exercised wide-ranging official power. It was not the prisoners who gave them their orders, but the SS.

Direct supervision of the prisoners was in the hands of the superiors in the residential blocks. With the permission of the SS, the senior camp prisoners appointed a block chief in every barracks; he or she was responsible for everything that occurred there. With the approval of the SS block chief and the senior camp prisoner, the block chief appointed room chiefs (*Stubenälteste*) and barrack-room assistants who then helped keep the prisoners under surveillance. The block personnel had a broad array of tasks: distributing linen and daily rations, obtaining basic foods, procuring blankets, dishes, clothing, and shoes, checking on hygiene, assisting sick prisoners. This wide range of activities offered diverse opportunities for granting favors to some prisoners, putting others at a disadvantage, engaging in harassment, and making shady deals. At times, the power of the block chiefs resembled that of military regimental commanders. There were hundreds of prisoners under their surveillance in the mass barracks. In accordance with the principle of dual subordination, they were under the direct command of both the SS block leader and the senior camp prisoner. This not only sparked role conflicts, but also provided the block personnel with a certain degree of independence vis-à-vis their superiors. Even if prisoner self-administration was largely dominated by one category, members of the opposite group could often maintain their position in the block with the backing of the SS. Under a red camp administration, there were green block leaders, and vice versa. It was impossible for the *Lagerälteste* to run the camp as they saw fit.[6] Dual subordination made a chink in the orb of power of prisoner administration. In a serious case, the block leader was able to rely on the *protekcja* of the SS, and could oppose the top echelon of the prisoners. Thus, the rivalry between factions within the prisoner elite was already a built-in feature of the formal structure of self-administration.

The Kommandos were under the command of the Kapos; the Kapos in turn were subordinate to the respective SS Kommando leaders. Larger Kommandos consisting of several hundred prisoners had a head Kapo and several sub-Kapos, as well as a number of supervisors. These supervisors were excused from other work; their only tasks were to divide up the prisoners and to push them to work harder. Specific professional skills did not become important until prisoner labor was brought into the program of systematic economic exploitation. In the stone quarries and the construction or underground Kommandos, their job was limited to control functions and terror. In formal terms, the Kapos were largely independent in the administration of the camp. The Kommandos also provided a field of activity even for those prisoner-functionaries who had been booted out of the main camps and transferred to the satellite camps.

The power of the "guys with the armbands" (*Bindenträger*) was incalcul-ably immense. Unlike the SS, such prisoners were ubiquitous. The influence of the administrative prisoner-functionaries was less clear; they were concen-trated in two prisoner offices—the *Schreibstube* and the labor statistics office (*Arbeitsstatistik*). The entire span of internal administration was the responsi-bility of those working in the orderly room. They registered new arrivals, assigning them to blocks. They planned the allocation of supplies, kept the catalog records, and prepared the daily reports and roll calls. In each block, a *Schreiber* kept an account of the prisoners there and had to report any change to the orderly room. Those working there assembled all information into a report, which the SS then only needed to check at roll call. Although these workers were directly subordinate to the SS rapport leader, the daily round of office work was largely beyond his perusal. The rapport scribes (*Rapport-schreiber*) and their helpers worked in a central zone of uncertainty; they were not exchangeable ad hoc. Office work required organizational talents, preci-sion, a knowledge of foreign languages, and familiarity with filing operations and routines when recording unpredictable events. Because the SS had itself adopted bureaucratic bookkeeping and completeness as a method, it became dependent on a band of auxiliaries who retained an overview of what was happening on the ground in the turbulent environment of the camp.[7] The clas-sic bureaucratic dilemma of delegation and control also applied in the case of the *Schreibstube*. Set up for the purpose of total surveillance of prisoner soci-ety, it gained influence to the extent that it became the only office that was able to guarantee exhaustive and thorough monitoring.

The second office operated by prisoners, the labor statistics office, was in a similar position. Using a card-file catalog with data on prisoners' qualifica-tions, these workers put together the Kommandos, prepared transfers, and de-termined the transport lists for the satellite camps. For the most part, they were given general orders regarding the number of workers required; actual selec-tion, changes in registration, and record keeping were left to those in the office. The labor statistics office was also an important support base for administra-tive power. As in the orderly room, its workers monitored a zone of uncer-tainty. Without the knowledge of the SS, they were able to ship off undesirable prisoners from the camp and send them elsewhere. They could protect com-rades in special danger by removing the prisoners' names from death trans-ports or transferring them to better external subcamps. Because one's Kom-mando assignment often determined whether one lived or died, labor statistics amassed enormous power. A prisoner's name on a Kommando or transport list could mean the difference between survival or certain death. This power grew parallel with the growth and differentiation of the camps. The greater the camp complex, the more external Kommandos there were, and the more diverse the types of labor deployment, the more options were open to the office of labor statistics. With the economic mobilization of prisoner labor toward the end of the war, it developed into a full-fledged office, employing more than fifty workers in each of the larger camps.

The category of prisoner-functionaries also included prisoners working in the various supply and service facilities. Work in the kitchens, laundries, storerooms, and workshops allowed access to vital goods that could then be used to build up a network of *protekcja*. Although these positions were not invested with any immediate disciplinary power or power of decision, they were a source of economic power in the camp "market" and social capital. Monopolies on scarce but essential goods provided prisoner-functionaries with an opportunity to obligate grateful fellow prisoners to provide support and allegiance, and to retain them as dependent clients. Work in the *Revier*, a preferred power base of the political prisoners, had similar advantages. Because every prisoner had to expect that he or she might be injured or fall ill, the attendants and doctors were positioned at a central node where numerous contacts could be made. Medical assistance was limited, but sick fellow prisoners could nonetheless be cared for and protected from harassment and persecution behind the walls of the infirmary. The members of the SS avoided setting foot in the camp hospital because of the danger of epidemics, so in many camps the hospital became an illegal meeting place for the resistance. In addition, the camp leaders depended on the prisoner doctors in order to reduce the numbers of the sick and maintain the workforce. The more important labor deployment became, the greater the opportunities were for the self-organization of medical care, and even for negotiations with the SS. In light of the danger of epidemics and the excessive number of sick prisoners, various hygienic measures were implemented and foreign and Jewish prisoner doctors were allowed to offer medical care.

The SS did not pursue a uniform strategy in recruiting prisoner personnel. For disciplinary posts, it generally gave priority to those prisoners it could exploit as willing tools. Although initially the only prisoners available were political (red triangle) prisoners, the SS was able from 1936 on to fall back on the pool of (green) prisoners in "limited protective custody" (BVs) as well. Though such prisoners were always in the minority (except in Buchenwald), the SS was able to break the dominance of its political opponents with their help. From that point on, the criminal prisoners formed the core of the higher levels of supervisory personnel in Flossenbürg, Mauthausen, Groß-Rosen, Auschwitz, and Majdanek. In Dachau, with one brief interruption, the political prisoners were able to maintain their position. The fiercest struggles between reds and greens raged in Buchenwald and Sachsenhausen. In late 1938 in Buchenwald, a number of criminal prisoner-functionaries who, along with the camp SS, had robbed the new Jewish arrivals of their belongings and failed to send the pilfered valuables to the state authorities, were removed from their posts, sent as Kapos to external Kommandos, or transferred to Flossenbürg.[8] In Sachsenhausen, despite the red-dominated *Schreibstube*, green cliques provided many of the Kapos and block chiefs. A unified self-administration controlled by a firm political hand, such as existed among the red prisoners in Dachau, was no longer possible in Sachsenhausen.

In staffing the administrative posts, the SS had to make certain concessions, take professional skills into consideration, and grant leeway, which the prisoner-functionaries were then also able to exploit to protect fellow prisoners. In most *Schreibstuben*, the red triangle predominated. As a rule, foreigners were given disciplinary power only when there were not enough Germans available. But foreigners were absolutely indispensable in the orderly rooms. The leading German scribes had repeated success in adding foreigners to the staff; they argued that for proper record keeping, assistants were needed who were fluent in all the languages represented in the camp population. Thus, for example, the labor statistics office in Buchenwald in 1944 employed twenty-eight Czechs, twenty-four Germans, seven Russians, seven Poles, three French prisoners, two Austrians, and one prisoner each from Belgium, the Netherlands, and Spain.[9] That same year, the *Schreibstube* of the main camp in Mauthausen had two Germans, two Czechs, one Spaniard, one French prisoner, and one Austrian; the registration Kommando employed an additional fifteen to twenty-one prisoners from a variety of national backgrounds.[10]

SS personnel policy was subject to conflicting tensions generated by organizational growth, personnel shortages, delegation of power, and social control. The expansion of the camp system required increased efforts and expenditures for surveillance and administrative functions. Because the camp SS had been chronically understaffed since the beginning of the war, and there was a constant drain of its personnel to the front, the scope of required surveillance and the need for the delegation of power increased as the numbers of prisoners climbed. This is why the camp leadership delegated more and more tasks regarding the administration and the maintenance of order to the prisoners, withdrawing from the daily operations of the camp.[11] Because there was at the same time a shortage of German prisoners, many foreigners were appointed prisoner-functionaries in the external subcamps. The hierarchy of social categories was thus partially undermined, and the economic mobilization of the camps forced a limited deviation from the ideological model of prisoner classes.

The gradation of power presented the SS with a number of problems. Delegation was intended to close gaps in power and make surveillance complete; at the same time, however, it generated centrifugal tendencies and created areas where latitude was possible. In order to gain cooperation and underpin the system of power by organization, the SS was compelled to grant options for action that could also be used against it. By providing prisoners with power, it breached the boundary line separating the lowest ranks of SS personnel from the prisoner elite. The communists, otherwise persecuted as political archenemies, were moved up in the pecking order, specifically because of their organizational iron discipline. Criminal prisoners were given a higher rating because of their readiness to obey orders, even though that rating was diametrically opposed to their civilian status as social outsiders. Finally, the SS exposed it itself to possible corruption from below. The impenetrable wall between personnel and inmates that characterizes every total institution became porous. Fissures opened; the domain of the camp personnel overlapped with that of the prisoner elite.[12]

There were other risks. When administrative tasks are delegated, a zone of uncertainty often is created that eludes monitoring. The elite prisoners were able to feather their nests without paying the necessary tribute to the central authority. Monopoly control over administrative services could be used for various protective measures. Under cover of self-administration, resistance and sabotage were organized. And the SS itself became more and more dependent, the more indispensable the central administrative tasks became. By contrast, the camp leadership pursued classic strategies of power politics. It partially diminished incalculability by means of standardization. Tasks were set down in fixed form by regulations,[13] and had to be documented in writing. Informers and spies were smuggled into areas of possible activity that eluded surveillance—a second, secret, auxiliary band of traitors to keep tabs on the official band of accessories. When prisoner-functionaries grew too independent, their rivals were built up, and one elite was replaced by another. The struggle between the reds and the greens functioned like the mechanism underlying the guided circulation of elites. The SS kept its body of auxiliaries submissive and obedient by aggravating antagonisms, thus lessening its own dependence. Consequently, the overriding power of personnel remained ultimately unaffected—the power to grant or deny personal protection for survival; the sovereign prerogative to replace order by arbitrary whim, discipline by terror.

Yet the system was not static: power was not distributed irreversibly once the positions had been staffed. The gradation of power was a constant process of displacements, coalitions, and intrigues. Although it was a formal structure, self-administration was also a political process, a figurative movement. Just as the SS attempted to channel the power to delegate, the prisoner elite developed strategies in order to grapple with the structural problems arising from their intermediate position. Nonetheless, this power process encompassing the elite, their clients, and those on the periphery was anything but balanced. Though the relationship was reciprocal and interdependent, as in any social configuration, it was heavily skewed. The gradation of power was marked by a fundamental asymmetry. The SS was dependent on its auxiliaries; these, in turn, were dependent on the *protekcja* of the camp leadership. Yet this changed nothing in respect to the asymmetry and transitivity of the *power to kill*. The SS could cast aside or liquidate its accomplices at will. Open resistance was hopeless. The dictatorship of the center was ultimately based on a general power to kill. By contrast, the power to kill invested in the auxiliary staffers extended only to those prisoners under their direct supervision.

What were the strategies by which the prisoner personnel were able to maintain and defend their position? Like those in any intermediate position in a hierarchy, they could orient themselves up the pyramid toward the camp leadership, or downward toward the stratum of their fellow prisoners. But they could also try to carve out room to maneuver between the fronts in a bid to garner as much independence as possible. One cannot presuppose a natural solidarity between the elites and other prisoners or a general chumminess with the SS. There were quite a few political prisoners who adapted to the SS, and green prisoner-functionaries who hated the SS, though this did not mean they did much to help their fellow prisoners. All three strategies had specific problems. Initially, it was not of decisive importance to what category the actors belonged, and by what convictions they were guided. All prisoner-functionaries, red and green alike, were caught up right from the start in a social structure that decided on life and death.[14]

If the auxiliary band stuck close to the center of power, it was able to exploit the weakest prisoners, thus bettering its own situation. To make themselves the representatives of prisoner society was not only extremely dangerous; it also entailed giving up the advantages accruing from their intermediate position: freedom from physical harassment, powerlessness, hunger, and death. In general, collaboration certainly has its rationale. And none are more conservative in their concern for maintaining their advantages than the accessories of dictatorship. They are the born accomplices, the traitors to their fellow prisoners. The more unassailable, the more impregnable the center of power, the greater their readiness to partake of the privileges of tyranny. Only when the advantage of the center threatens to collapse do they switch their sights and allegiance downward in a bid to ally themselves with those they had terrorized and exploited only a short time before. Once despotism has been overthrown, the bitterest revenge is reserved for its former associates.

In the concentration camps, there were three strategies for adaptation to the center of power: mimetic servility, total obedience, and economic common interest. Mimetic servility was manifest where prisoners sought close contact with the camp SS and adopted its modes of behavior. The spectrum ranged from the imitation of brief gestures to demonstrative subservience to identification with the dreaded authority and duplication of its external appearance. Mimetic servility is a special mode of social exchange. The helper curries the personal favor of powerful individuals, seeking to gain their attention. The prisoner-functionary demonstrated loyalty by treating fellow prisoners as brutally as the SS did, if not at times exceeding their brutality. The Kapos shouted louder than the guards, and were quicker to swing their clubs and strut around like petty potentates, reading on their masters' lips their every wish. At times, a symbiotic relationship developed between masters and servants. The supervisors hardly needed to take action themselves; they were able to leave everything to their servile lackeys. A flick of the finger, and the assistant responded—the elongated arm of the master, or an accomplice ready to perform torture. Often there was no need for a gesture from the master—the servants took the initiative on their own. Submissive accomplices do not merely obey an alien dominant power to which they are subject. *Protekcja* is also involved: they are obedient to an authority that shields them, although at the same time they must fear that superior power. This social relation should not be mistakenly confused with the unconscious identification of the victim with the aggressor.[15] What from the perspective of others often appeared to be an identity between the SS and the prisoner elite was, despite all similarities in behavior, ultimately an antagonistic relation. Nothwithstanding the value the superior may have placed on the submissiveness of the servants, the superior was able to cast aside, degrade, or kill the servants at will. The actions of the accomplices had a meaning totally different from those of the master. The master permitted them to act because the servants enhanced the master's power. But the servants had to fear for their very existence. They mistreated fellow prisoners; they harassed and even killed them in order to prove to the guards how assiduous the servants were, how capable. Their violence confirmed that they were the right people for the job. They imitated the master because the latter would never punish an imitation of what the master did. They acted like their master in order to remain what they were—privileged prisoners. They followed this model in order to survive.

Servility transforms absolute power into authority, dependence into submissiveness. The strategy of total obedience should be distinguished from servility. Servility is an attitude; obedience is a way of acting. Obedience lacks the elements of assimilation and bondage peculiar to the believer in authority who attempts to survive by pandering to power, by courting the favor of superior authority. Those who do everything demanded of them do not need to be convinced that the commands are just and proper. In the camps, total obedience was generally not based on agreement with the camp power; it was founded on self-protection, pure and simple. The prisoners obeyed because disobedience was lethal, not because they condoned the orders of the SS. That is why they did not ask for reasons or worry about consequences. The prisoners obeyed every order because the compulsion to submit seemed overwhelming. And they even did more than their duty. Those who wished to hold onto the privileges they enjoyed had to do more than they were ordered to do. Absolute power issues regulations, but it prefers broad orders that allow subordinates enough latitude to make mistakes, permitting superiors to take action against them at any time. Absolute power delegates arbitrariness in order to preserve its own arbitrary will.[16] It demands more than mere blind obedience. The prisoner-functionaries were always expected to act in the interest of the regime. Because a lack of initiative could immediately be interpreted as insubordination, they had to do more than was explicitly ordered. However, they could not determine whether the extra effort would be recognized. Even obedience was no protection from the uncertainty of terror. The prisoner could carry out orders immediately or even try to surmise the will of the guards—but it was they who retained the absolute power of definition.

Servility and obedience leave absolute power untouched. This situation changes when social exchange is altered into an economic relation. Again and again, cells of corruption containing SS members and prisoner-functionaries formed in the underground of the camps; working together, they would undertake to plunder the blocks of new arrivals or loot the environs of the camp. The spoils were subsequently smuggled into the camp, divided up, or channeled to the black market. SS officers coerced private services from prisoners, granting them limited protection in return. In the canteens and storerooms, food, clothing, and valuables were misappropriated or shunted off elsewhere.[17] Usually the prisoners would assume the more risky role in such activities. They smuggled the forbidden items through the checkpoints; if they were discovered, under no circumstances could they reveal the names of their bosses. If they were caught, they could be punished, but if they betrayed their accomplices, they were killed as accessories who knew too much.[18]

Under normal circumstances, corruption binds accomplices to each other. It is a transaction based on reciprocity, obliging both sides to maintain silence. This symmetry was also annuled in the camp by the regime of power. It is true that inmate and supervisor formed a kind of secret coalition whose machinations were occasionally investigated by external SS commissions. But such checks shed little light on corruption's dark recesses, and thus did not generate any symmetry. The prisoners always remained dependent on the mercy of their accomplices. At times, they were able to play off one SS officer against another, but *protekcja* was not something one could extort. In an emergency, the SS would quickly dispose of its witnesses, transferring them to a death Kommando or liquidating them itself. In its pure, unadulterated form, corruption is a coerced relation among equals, a forbidden exchange of equivalents. In the camp, it was subject right from the start to a dictatorial compulsion that could not be offset.

The prisoner-functionaries had to pay for their support from the SS with extreme dependence. Those who offered services to the SS were completely and utterly at the mercy of its arbitrary will and caprice. For the accomplices, there was no way back into the society of the prisoners. If the accomplices were rejected by the camp leadership, their days were numbered. The antagonism between the personnel and the inmates confronted the prisoner-functionaries with an insoluble dilemma. Those who got involved with the adversary, serving as informers or executioner's assistants, forfeited their lives to their fellow prisoners. The *protekcja* of the SS exposed them to the vengeance of their comrades. The Kapos attempted to make themselves indispensable by exercising the power delegated to them in an excessive manner. They were known and feared everywhere. Yet as soon as the SS removed the truncheons from their hands, their hours were numbered.[19] The threat of being lynched by the prisoners drove the prisoner-functionaries ever deeper into the clutches of the SS. This was one reason for the sheer unboundedness of cruelty and violence. In order to protect their own backs, the prisoner-functionaries had to prove they were faithful minions. In order not to be killed themselves, they had to stay in power at any price and intensify the level of terror meted out to those below. But the more they harassed the prisoners, the greater was the threat of a kangaroo court and summary lynching. Their only option was further to curry favor with the powerful, to demonstrate additional submissiveness and violence.

Solidarity with fellow prisoners was hardly less dangerous. The SS demanded unconditional obedience, mercilessly pursuing a redefinition of the prisoners' role. The camp leadership tolerated prisoners using the power of their positions for their own benefit as long as the tasks of surveillance and administration were fulfilled to its liking. The egoism of the band of auxiliaries easily meshed with the dictatorship. Such selfishness only intensified the degree of dissociation among the prisoners. However, if a prisoner-functionary shifted over to the side of the prisoners, there was a threat that hierarchical delegation could be undermined. A consistent policy in favor of the prisoners would have reversed the polarity of power in self-administration. The prisoner elite would no longer have been the proxy of the SS; it would have been the representative of the camp. Instead of closing the chinks in power, it would have pried them further open. It is not surprising that such a development was snuffed out by the SS at an early stage. To fight for the interests of the camp would have enhanced the status of the prisoner-functionaries among their fellows, but in so doing they would have jeopardized their central source of power: the backing of the camp leadership. Those who tried to protect the lives of others necessarily risked their own.

Moreover, options for solidarity altered with changes in the prisoners' material situation. The worse the living conditions in the camp, the greater was the threat of death should the prisoner-functionaries lose their privileges. Even if they were protected from lynching, prisoner-functionaries who had been removed from power were doomed to misery. The possibility of genuine proxy representation is material as well. As long as prisoner society was comparatively homogeneous and the prisoners lived under relatively equal circumstances, the distance between them and the elite was small. Yet in extreme distress, any and every advantage was crucial for survival; indeed, survival itself became a privilege. Where food rations languished far below the required minimum, prisoners could only survive if they partook of the privileges of power. To risk one's position by leniency or through solidarity was to risk death.

Nonetheless, there were prisoner-functionaries who took up the cause of their fellow prisoners and tried to protect them. Roles in supply or administration opened up various options for direct assistance. Upon admission, newcomers were given vital pointers for survival; the *Schreibstube* transferred prisoners in danger to other blocks; fellow prisoners were freed from the clutches of brutal Kapos by the office of labor statistics. Yet shielding of this kind was extended only to certain individual prisoners, not to all. Practically speaking, representation of the interests of the entire camp was simply out of the question. Instead, the effects of the gradation of power reached into the furthest corners of prisoner society. Just as the band of auxiliaries was dependent on the *protekcja* of the SS, the prisoner-functionaries gave preferential treatment to a select clientele of their own. Criminal prisoner-functionaries kept private lackeys and bodyguards whom they protected and for whom they arranged extra supplies. In return, these servants had to perform all sorts of personal and sexual services.[20] This second stage in the gradation of power was not a formal structure but a system of personal patronage, an instrumental friendship that was extremely risky for the clients. It was based solely on the fortuitous inclinations of the individual prisoner-functionary. Selection of the favorites was an act of individual mercy that could change at any time into repression.[21] This increased the power of the prisoner-functionaries in an unusual manner. The patrons enjoyed personal physical protection from the attacks of rivals, and could thus give free rein to their whims and moods. They would kill one prisoner while generously pardoning another. Absolute power does not simply mean the power to kill another person at any time one desires; it also entails the power to let him live. Acts of mercy are always part of the repertory of freedoms absolute power has at its disposal. The prisoner-functionaries had unrestricted control over such options.

The recruitment of private clients was a preferred practice of the green camp elite and those political prisoners who were not part of the secret resistance effort. Yet the political prisoner personnel also had a band of auxiliaries at its disposal—an organized cadre kept together by personal trust and a shared ideology. The resistance group protected its prisoner-functionaries against encroachment and attacks by other cliques, and profited in turn from their power. Red self-administration consisted not of collaborators but of disguised adversaries. Yet it too was subject to the laws of power gradation, and operated according to the pattern of clientele formation. Preference was generally given to reliable comrades and fellow prisoners who strengthened the ranks of the secret resistance group. The parceling out of *protekcja* aimed above all else at preservation of the group; it determined the selection of the prisoner-functionaries. Only in individual cases did the core of the communist resistance effort co-opt prisoners of another ideological stripe or from a different category. Its ideology guided the dispensing of assistance. The pressure of harassment and repression demanded strict reliability and group loyalty from each and every member of the secret fraternity. To expand secret protection beyond one's own group would have meant placing that group in immediate jeopardy.

The political group reflected the camp; in turn, it was represented by its prisoner-functionaries. According to the law of transitive representation, the political prisoner personnel thus represented the camp society. But it represented the others by controlling them, registering them, and often disciplining them with violence. Isolated assistance was only possible if one became an accessory to the order of terror. To maintain themselves over the longer term, the prisoner-functionaries had to give preferential treatment to the group that supported them, while excluding the others from support. The favoring of a small number of beneficiaries was a prerequisite for the self-preservation of the red camp administration. The dilemma of a consistent resistance strategy lay in representation ultimately having to be restricted to one's own core group. But by acting to assure its own survival, the red camp administration had to become an auxiliary executor of terror.

Successful self-preservation of the prisoner elite demanded independence vis-à-vis those above and those below. This middle strategy required the drawing of a line of separation on all sides; it necessitated an energetic struggle on multiple fronts against the temptations of power, the attacks of rival cliques, and the claims for protection of the subordinate prisoners. Naturally, options for independent action were heavily circumscribed. It was impossible to break the power of the SS. Yet there were certain interstices where latitude existed— legal and illegal techniques of resistance the auxiliaries could use to defend or bolster their position.

The most important precondition for the autonomy of the auxiliary personnel was the prevention of corruption by power in their own ranks. In order for them not to become totally and completely dependent, any incipient similarity to the SS had to be combated. This required constant surveillance of the prisoner-functionaries by the resistance group. Not only did the prisoner elite have to check up on the others; it also had to keep tabs on itself. This self-surveillance was ruthless; it showed no consideration for the individual person.[22] The resistance group disciplined its own members. If possible, decisions were taken collectively, and possible deviants were eliminated at an early stage or transferred elsewhere. The group was assisted in this effort by rigorous organizational discipline and the compulsion for conspiratorial behavior. It kept surveillance on each individual, pursuing every genuine or presumed traitor, rooting out deviation. In this way, it strengthened the authority of the prisoner-functionaries in the camp while diminishing the temptation to make common cause with the SS.

If their own ranks were united, the prisoner-functionaries could then proceed to exploit contradictions and antagonisms within the SS. The SS was anything but uniform and united. Various offices vied for authority. While some officers gave preference to criminal cliques, others lent support to a political self-administration that relieved them of administrative burdens, guaranteeing an orderly daily routine in the camp. Many SS officers were interested in private enrichment and were susceptible to bribery. The structure of command and surveillance was not firmly established and cemented, nor were the aims of the individual cliques consistent. A resolute band of auxiliaries was able to exploit all this for its own purposes. In order to finesse one or another improvement, it could cite the need for organizational effectiveness, the threat of epidemic, or the necessities of labor deployment. Corrupt supervisors could be bribed with valuables; some block leaders were given scarce food items from parcels as a form of hush money. Of course, such activities were only successful as long as group self-monitoring prevented a mutual chumminess from crystallizing. As the SS did from above, the prisoner elite pursued a power strategy of divide and rule from below in order to undermine the structure of power.[23]

In addition, prisoner personnel were threatened by attacks by rivals. The battle for power and privileges was a struggle for life and death. The relationship between reds and greens often assumed the character of mortal enmity. In the scramble for power, everything depended on occupying key positions and blocking every opportunity for the opposite side to gain the upper hand with the help of the SS. This practice was thwarted by intrigues and denunciations, or by eliminating opponents. Political prisoner-functionaries who came under a green regime in a *Strafkompanie* or a Kommando were "done in" there by their antagonists. Criminal prisoner-functionaries who had raged unrestrained in the camp were either ousted from the camp by the red prisoner administration or delivered over to internal mechanisms of prisoner justice.[24] Transfer to another camp had serious consequences. Those who had been expelled formed a new core group in the new camp, and were able, unopposed, to replicate their former regime of terror there. Terror was merely shifted to another site within the concentration camp system. One camp was freed from its scourge, while another felt the storm all the more vehemently.[25]

To defend the pockets of latitude, a minimum amount of compulsion and oppression was unavoidable. In order for the elite to remain what it was, it had to fulfill its tasks and reject the claims to protection by the subordinate prisoners. Lenience would have undermined the discipline on which it based its regime. As long as the camp ran smoothly, the SS had little occasion to intervene. Yet this required strict and drastic measures, and consistent punishment for any infraction. In order to avoid causing a stir, prisoner personnel had to suppress anything that might bring the SS into the arena. In order to protect one's fellow prisoners, there had to be discipline everywhere. Justice meted out on one's own authority lessened the dilemma of the duty to denounce other prisoners. The prisoner-functionaries were required to report irregularities. Yet if they reported offenders, their own lives were often finished. There was the threat of collective punishment, and the prisoner-functionaries discredited themselves as accomplices of the regime. But if they ignored the incident and let offenders get off scot-free, then they encouraged others to do the same. For that reason, the arm of internal justice proceeded rigorously against thefts, laziness, or disobedience. The prisoner-functionaries penalized offenders without issuing formal reports. They took over the role of the SS in order to prevent SS encroachment.

Yet this was only one side of the picture. The prisoner-functionaries also had to demonstrate their indispensability. For that purpose, they repeatedly needed chaotic situations in which they could take demonstrative, resolute action. The deathly quiet of complete discipline would have endangered their privileged position. Complete order would spell ruin for the band of auxiliaries. If order were total, they would be totally superfluous. For that reason, the prisoner-functionaries had to prevent all attempts at self-organization by the prisoners. There had to be a certain amount of disorder during the distribution of meals so that the Kapos could show they were indispensable.[26] Some incident actually had to occur in the blocks so that the block chief could demonstrate his or her function. To that extent, the prisoner elite had a vested interest in limited disorganization. It justified the system of the gradation of power and the necessity for an elite. Disruptions of order were imperative; discipline could never be allowed to become total.

Self-administration provided absolute power with an organizational substructure. The gradation of power raised an elite above the other prisoners. It turned prisoners into accomplices of the guard personnel, and thus into enemies of the other prisoners. It undoubtedly opened up options for a minority of responsible and incorruptible prisoners to organize resistance and save human lives. The moral courage, discipline, and solidarity of these functionaries was of inestimable value. Yet they too were unable to resolve the structural dilemma of the gradated system of power. Assistance for everyone was a sheer impossibility in the concentration camp. Aid always entailed preferential treatment for a select few. Yet in order to help at all and prevent something worse, the prisoner had to become an accomplice. Intrinsic to the functional logic of the system was the link between solidarity and coerced collaboration. One can hardly imagine a greater power than that which transforms victims into accessories to their own execution.

12

The Aristocracy

Our Kapos said: we're all buddies. We're all concentration camp
prisoners, we're all buddies here. The one who kills you is your
buddy. Paul, the senior camp prisoner, had a genuine studio apart-
ment set up for himself in the new barracks, complete with a sofa,
radio, books. He dined sumptuously. He was waited on by a Polish
prisoner. He was very elegant, and often changed clothes. He was
the lord of the brigade. He received the aristocracy in his apart-
ment, especially the French clerk, a criminal. This clerk, who had
plenty to eat, would dash around sometimes in the barracks naked
from the waist up to let others admire his physique, since he was
not emaciated. At the slightest incident, he wanted to start a fight.
By the way, he wasn't the only one who was so obviously proud of
the fact that he still had some flesh on his bones. He regarded that
as a personal success and, with a quite natural impulse, despised
those other mediocrities. Applying SS logic, he thought they were
scum. When he ran around half-naked, he knew he was handsome.[1]

THE ARISTOCRACY had everything the other prisoners lacked: enough to eat,
warm clothing, sturdy shoes. The Prominents had longer hair; the men were
clean-shaven. They did not need to work and had beds for themselves. When
they were sick, they were given preferential treatment at the infirmary. The
brothel was open to them, and when they felt bored, they were entertained by
boxing matches, bands, or drama groups. During the day, they spread terror in
the camp, supported and admired by their servants and lackeys. In the evening,
playing cards, they consumed the day's loot—a bottle of liquor, some cigarettes. In the midst of hunger and misery, the aristocracy lived in its own
special world.

There were numerous categories and classes in the concentration camp,
but only one social estate.[2] Only the Prominents had any chance to live a
decent life. The others had nothing—were nothing. Only the aristocracy was
able to develop some sort of lifestyle, a rudimentary culture of distinction.
By contrast, the miserable prisoners in the mass blocks were locked in a
daily struggle for sheer survival. The social antagonism ran along the dividing
line between life and survival. On the one side, a relatively secure living
standard; on the other, distress and misery. Power and prestige, counterposed

to anxiety and defenseless. Here the prominent individual, there the mass of the nameless. The distance between the normal and privileged prisoner exceeded even the most glaring differences in civil society. It was founded on the difference between status and its lack, a tolerable lifestyle and the struggle for basic survival.

Initially, one's place in the system of classifications and power gradation decided on who belonged to the prisoner aristocracy. The category channeled access to the elite of the prisoner-functionaries, and thus to the world of the aristocracy. But not every prisoner-functionary belonged to this upper crust. The innumerable inspectors for bunks, lice, and scabies, the runners, sweepers, and pot washers were nothing but servants of the masters. Prominence is always a question of social definition. Status must be ascribed by others and confirmed by one's equals. And the prominent person must also ascribe that status to himself or herself, expressing it in personal behavior. Material advantages are a necessary condition for this, though by no means a sufficient one.

The criterion of social definition permits one to demarcate the prisoner aristocracy. Prisoner-functionaries concerned with fostering solidarity enjoyed respect among the inmates, but not with the SS and the dominant elite. From time to time, the SS gave preference to those prisoners who were considered authorities in the camp. Yet assistance for those in misery conflicted with the self-image of a leadership stratum that flaunted its special position. On the other hand, the aristocracy encompassed more than just the "political" prisoner-functionaries who behaved like the green elite that was predominant in many places. It also included those prisoner-functionaries who saw themselves as the avant-garde of the resistance, and carefully differentiated themselves from the ranks below. This group shared the privilege of temporary protection from harassment with the criminal prisoners, as well as a pronounced interest in the institution of the camp and its power relations and intrigues—an orientation that far surpassed the limited horizon of the lower classes. Their motives and interests differed fundamentally from those of the green aristocracy. The self-monitoring of the resistance group prevented any individual demonstration of special status. In the political group, personal modesty and self-discipline were regarded as supreme values. The means of distinction were ideological steadfastness, iron discipline, and moral superiority. Moreover, the necessary conspiratorial approach precluded public self-presentation. The resistance group was an exclusive circle, a secret faction within the aristocracy. For that reason, the lifestyle of the Prominents was shaped primarily by the prisoner-functionaries, generally green, who made a public display of power and possession.

However, under the conditions of absolute power, it is not only those who can demonstrate that they know how to live who achieve prestige. The survivors are also accorded a mark of distinction. In a society where death can overtake anyone, the mere fact of survival is a conspicuous sign. The veteran prisoners with low numbers enjoyed a quite peculiar and special respect among the prisoners.[3] They had surmounted the greatest dangers, they had struggled on, they had seen countless others die. Their most elementary success was that they were *still* alive.[4]

Of course, age in the camp was a relative variable. The greater the pressure for annihilation, the shorter the time needed to turn a prisoner into a veteran concentration camp inmate. Thus, it was not just the German prisoners from the prewar period who belonged to the group of veterans. In the Auschwitz main camp, the survivors of the first Polish transports were also part of the prisoner aristocracy. In the women's camp at Birkenau, along with the German *Asoziale*, for the most part prostitutes, the ranks of the prominent prisoners also included the small number of Jewish women from Slovakia who had been confined there in the spring of 1942 and had survived a series of selections. Most were no older than eighteen or twenty, but they already formed the first generation in the camp.[5] In Monowitz and the attached satellite camps, several hundred Jews from the first transports were part of the aristocracy, along with the German prisoners.[6] In a situation in which a prisoner's life expectancy averaged a few weeks, or several months at the most, anyone who had survived the initial period somehow was already regarded as an experienced inmate, an "old hand."

There was a deep gap between the old prisoners and the newcomers. The small core group of old-timers occupied most of the prisoner-functionary jobs and the easier Kommandos, and blocked entry to newcomers. The new arrivals entered an alien world that had been constructed by the veteran inmates. The veterans had arranged their lives in the camp as well as possible, and had techniques of survival at their disposal of which the new prisoners did not have the faintest conception. The seasoned prisoners had gone through the hell that still awaited the newcomers. They came from a world the veterans had inwardly divorced themselves from long ago. In any case, they constituted an additional burden. The old-timers routinely completed the tasks connected with admission of new prisoners, at best giving them a pointer here or there, or a bit of advice. They drummed the required discipline into the newcomers; they even drove undesirables to their death.[7] A deadly cycle arose: by monopolizing possessions and knowledge, the old-timers secured their special status and diminished the chances for survival of the new prisoners. It was not accidental that seasoned inmates, with their distinctive set of characteristics—an amalgam of intolerance, inner callousness, indifference, vigilance, and taciturnity—were on the other side of the divide when it came to many of the new arrivals. They did not interest the seasoned inmates, who did not wish to be like them. The veteran inmates were prominent because they embodied the camp. And since they had known the camp over a period of months, even years, and had outlived countless comrades, they had the self-assurance of an elite that looked down condescendingly on the newcomers.

In order to reckon themselves among the ranks of the camp aristocracy, veteran prisoners had to go through a process of inner colonization.[8] They turned aside from the world outside the camp, concentrating all their efforts on the here and now of camp life. In no sense was this displacement in thematic relevance a form of identification. It involved sealing off the field of consciousness against all events that could have posed a threat to a laboriously achieved success. In order to remain alive, the prisoners had to live in the camp. But to do that, they had to internalize its laws of survival. This predicament cannot be measured using an external yardstick, the values and morals of civil society. What might appear to the outsider as demoralization was the morality of a serial society, one in which every individual was superfluous. Those who wanted to escape its lethal seriality had to make sure they did not sink into the lower classes. Since they could not allow themselves to become like the majority, they sealed themselves off. The hardening of the veteran prisoners was a method of self-defense, survival, and social distinction.

The prisoner aristocracy was controversial, its prestige often negative. The only prisoner-functionaries who had authority were those who visibly tried to help the prisoners. Most of the Prominents were not friends but opponents, even enemies, of the other prisoners. Although they lived in close proximity, they nonetheless belonged to another world. The aristocracy's ties to the SS, internal coalitions, and power struggles were inscrutable to the prisoners in the block. What those prisoners could see and experience directly was the Prominents' flaunted wealth and unbroken physical strength—the cudgel in the hands of the Prominents. Esteem and respect were not the bases for the attribution of prestige—it was founded on anxiety, powerlessness, and hatred. It is incorrect to assume that recognition is always the result of positive assessment. Just as it is expedient to give recognition to those superior to you, expedience also suggests according the same recognition to those you must fear. Faced with the camp aristocracy, the prisoners experienced just how defenseless and powerless they were. The enemy not only wore the uniform of the SS; it also wore the stripes of prisoner society.

In the camps, prestige was not a function of education and profession, but of possession, power, and violence, the elementary criteria of survival. The first sign of the Prominents was brute violence. It documented the prerogative they enjoyed to beat, torment, and kill. People have generally tried to attribute the excessive violence exerted by the prisoner-functionaries to moral depravity or sadistic brutalization. In individual cases that may have been true. But the violence of the aristocracy had a clear social meaning. It demonstrated the priority of the Prominents over the superfluous. To kill one's fellow is the simplest form of survival.[9] It is an act of triumph. One person's death is another's enhanced self-esteem. To kill is to feel that you still exist, while your fellow does not. The killer experiences an exceptional strength: the power of being someone chosen. All prisoners were subject to the guards' absolute power to kill. But among the prisoners, only the aristocracy had the privilege of carrying and using weapons. By means of brutality, many prisoner-functionaries demonstrated that they were still alive, while so many others were not.

It is no accident that numerous prominent prisoners staged their acts of violence as a spectacle.[10] The milieu of the aristocracy, especially that of the criminal prisoners, was an ambience of violence. They showed the rung they occupied in the pyramid by the number of victims they had chalked up, and the forms their violence took. Prisoners who physically exhausted themselves by clubbing others were below those who did in their victims with a quick flick of the wrist. And those prisoners, in turn, enjoyed less respect than those who assigned accomplices to do their violent dirty work and did not need to lift a finger themselves. Cruelty was a mark of distinction in competition for rank and prestige. The more feared a prisoner-functionary, the higher his or her position in the aristocracy, and the greater his or her standing with the SS. At the same time, violence demonstrated social solidarity. The Prominents confirmed to one another that they belonged together. Violence marked the social boundary line marking the divide between them and prisoner society. Encroachment on others bolstered their feeling of togetherness, sealing off their circle to the outside.

To acquire and maintain prestige, it is not enough to be powerful and wealthy. Power and possessions must also be flaunted. Just as violent acts provide a visible demonstration of power, consumption stages wealth. Just as violence strengthens the consciousness of being someone select, visible consumption is conspicuous: it attests to being free from hunger and misery. Yet in the general distress of the camps, the conspicuous consumption of the camp aristocracy acted as a provocation.[11] The neatly ironed prisoner's uniform, the warm overcoat, the brightly polished boots, the whip, the watch on one's wrist—all this showed the others that they were nothing and the Prominents were everything.[12] The provocative distinction was a double humiliation. The prisoner saw that he or she had nothing, and could do nothing about it. Physical strength and clothing documented prosperity and affluence. It was similar when it came to the semipublic consumption of food items. It is true that Prominents would distribute sausage, coffee, or fruit—the symbols of luxury—to their accessories. But that was generally done in the shadowy recesses of their milieu. Standard rations were distributed in front of everybody, so all could see who was given preferential treatment and who was discriminated against—who got nothing but a thin, watery soup and who was given scraps of turnips scrapped from the coveted bottom of the pot. By contrast, the private packages, with their rare delicacies, holiday roasts, potato pancakes, or alcohol, were consumed discreetly, though not secretly. After all, the others were supposed to take note that the aristocracy knew how to live. But it was a dictate of prudence not to put on a banquet in public. In order to avoid having to chase away the hungry, the privileged preferred to dine among themselves. The set table, that obvious sign of survival, was more than a provocation. It was an affront that engendered envy and hatred.[13]

Now and again, on long summer afternoons, birthdays, and holidays, the cream of the aristocracy put on festivals of generosity.[14] The band played a tune in honor of the patron of the day; the camp aristocracy paid the patron homage with best wishes and gifts. There were large quantities of cigarettes, beer, wine, sliced meats, and cheese. The spectators were entertained by sporting matches, and the patron gave the players a generous reward for their show. The party punctured the dull monotony of everyday camp life and provided the aristocracy with an opportunity to demonstrate its lifestyle to a larger public. The more splendid the celebration, the greater the standing of the patron in the scramble for prestige within the aristocracy. The law of *dépense*,[15] the ostentatious waste of time, energy, and goods, was also valid for the camp's upper crust. Naturally, in this rivalry for prestige, the aristocracy never risked the possible loss of all its goods; it practiced a carefully dispensed generosity in order to bind its minions personally, and to prove that its members were worthy masters.

In many total institutions, there are regularly scheduled presentations in which the actors briefly can suspend their roles as inmates. In the concentration camp, such institutional ceremonies were the privilege of the SS and the prisoner aristocracy.[16] Most prisoners either did not have the strength to visit the presentations or were a priori excluded from them. Just as the SS had its camp bands and was entertained by sporting competitions, the aristocracy cultivated a certain cultural life. In the Auschwitz camp complex, there were a number of orchestras and bands, and musical ensembles even existed in some external subcamps.[17] Initially, there was a gypsy band in Buchenwald; from 1940 on, there was also a brass band, for which special hours for practice were arranged. Sachsenhausen boasted a choir and a string quartet consisting of Czech students, a wind quartet under the supervision of a former musical director of the *Reichswehr* (the German armed forces), and a harmonica group that a barber had started up on his own. Along with concerts for the SS, the prisoners organized unofficial concerts that were tolerated by the camp leadership. Unlike in other organizations, however, these affairs were not regular get-togethers for all prisoners. The barrier between personnel and inmates, aristocracy and camp society, was also maintained on these social occasions. That was even more true when it came to the cabaret or variety programs put on by the political prisoner-functionaries. Although musical presentations did not represent any direct opposition, texts, poetry, recitals, sketches, and dramatic skits were media used to bolster courage. Such shows were usually subject to censorship and demanded skillful encoding of the covert protest between the lines. Thus, numerous cultural presentations took place in a kind of organizational gray area. Unlike the more common practice in total institutions, they did not represent the unity of the institution. They did not cancel out social differences; instead, they underscored the antagonistic values and views that the personnel and the aristocracy had of themselves and others.

Sports events were less controversial and problematical than drama programs and recitals. Soccer and boxing matches were popular both with the SS and the green prisoner aristocracy. In Mauthausen and Gusen, there were national soccer teams of Germans, Spaniards, Yugoslavs, and Poles; in 1943 and 1944, they competed almost every Sunday afternoon. In the main camp at Auschwitz, soccer was already being played as early as the spring of 1941, in Birkenau on a field close to the crematoria.[18] Games were even held in the courtyard of the crematorium—an SS team against members of the Jewish Sonderkommando. Amateur boxers, well-trained prisoners, and even Kapos presented their physical skills and prowess in the boxing ring.[19] They received special rations from their patrons so they could stay fit for upcoming bouts. The spectators consisted of SS personnel and the camp aristocracy. A fight that pitted a Pole or Spaniard against a German in the ring symbolized a kind of proxy revenge for the foreign prisoners. Only in the boxing ring was it possible for a foreigner to knock out a German.

The lifestyle of the aristocracy also included a series of diverse services. The higher their status, the larger the band of servants responsible for the personal welfare of the prominent prisoners. Prisoner-functionaries who thought they "were somebodies" had themselves regularly groomed and massaged. Their clothes were tailor-made, their shoes polished to a gleam every morning. Their meals were served, their rooms cleaned by a servant. They had young boys or prostitutes in the brothel to attend to their sexual needs. For evening entertainment, there were prisoners on tap who could tell stories or jokes,[20] sing songs, or put on acts. The scribes took care of the administrative tasks. A few also kept private nurses whose sole job was to provide medicines for their masters from the *Revier*. Well-known specialists obtained food and valuables on the black market, and the masters had a whole troop of bodyguards at their disposal for their personal protection. This clientele, which the masters bent to their will by the offer of *protekcja*, augmented their standing. The less they had to do themselves, the higher their status. The more lavish their court, the greater their stature in the aristocracy.

This retinue of servants formed a separate stratum of subaltern hangers-on who not only cared for the comfort of their masters, but were also a living demonstration of their prestige. To be able to retain personal lackeys is always a sign of social status. Many of these minions were also relieved of heavy physical labor in the camp, and were given food and other items by their masters. The slaves of the aristocracy thus stood a notch above the ordinary prisoners in the pecking order. They knew their place. In order not be be downgraded in standing, they courted their masters' favor. Their servility was the main source feeding the self-recognition of the aristocracy. The lackeys extended their patrons unrestricted authority, while they in turn satisfied the patrons' need for conspicuous consumption. The possession of servants who hardly had anything to do themselves, who were nothing but "idlers according to plan,"[21] confirmed the masters' unassailable position.[22] In the camp, to serve was still a privilege.

In the universe of the concentration camp, the aristocracy lived in a separate milieu. It was a bizarre world situated between the SS and prisoner society. The camp nobility demonstrated its lifestyle by the basic semiotics of survival: clothing, food, services, and physical strength. The *protekcja* accorded to a personal troop of servants limited the privileges to a circumscribed circle of the chosen few. Physical force defended the privileges against competitors, conspicuous consumption provided prestige and underscored social differences, extortion and violence served to exclude individuals from society. Like any social estate, the prisoner aristocracy secured its advantages by sealing itself off from the outside.[23] In that way, it consolidated and expanded a power advantage that could never be equalized by the prisoners. Only the organized resistance group was capable of mobilizing a counterforce. Yet that power was based on another mode of social closure, the exclusive solidarity of the group. However, that too belonged to the Prominents in the camp. All other prisoners were exposed to material and social conditions that precluded solidarity. Their forms of social interaction were so fleeting, fragile and serial that no counterpower could spring from their matrix.

13

Mass, Exchange, Dissociation

> Basically, most prisoners lived a rather solitary life, or else moved within a small circle. Within his own barracks room, every prisoner who hoped to survive had anywhere from three to five "comrades." These were not real friends; they were companions at work, and more often in misery. But while misery loves company, it does not make for friendship. Genuine attachments cannot grow in a barren field of experience nourished only by emotions of frustration and despair. Other than these comrades, the rest were just acquaintances.[1]

BENEATH THE REGIME of the SS personnel and the aristocracy, the prisoners existed in a tertiary social region, a world of misery and namelessness. The aristocracy and its clientele were only a minuscule upper class. The other prisoners had no access to privileges, no part in power. Although they made up the overwhelming majority, their situation was marked by hunger, powerlessness, and disorientation. The "normal" prisoners were housed in mass blocks, worked under the open sky, were protected by no one, and had little chance for advancement. They were the helpless objects of power. Surrounded everywhere by death, they were incapable of seeing the camp as a whole and gauging the extent of the dying there.[2] Their horizons were limited to the immediate proximate world around them. Tomorrow, the fellow prisoner who had been toiling next to them today might disappear—transferred to another block, the hospital, or another camp, or beaten to death somewhere. The foreigners who understood no German often had no idea where they were and for whom they were working. They learned nothing about the activity of the resistance group and the fierce rivalry between the prisoner-functionaries. The average prisoner eked out a miserable existence, locked in an unfathomable cage of terror.

The camp has been labeled a mass society, not just because of the large number of inmates but also because of the social anonymity and depersonalization that prisoners experienced in its confines.[3] Yet that perspective underestimates the heterogeneity of prisoner society, the antagonisms between national and social categories, the contours of the gradations of power, and the formation of clienteles. The prisoners were anything but equal, and it is hard to imagine greater differences than those that existed between the aristocracy and the pariahs. Nonetheless, the concept of the social mass has a certain justification insofar as it refers to the world of those bereft of power and possessions. The mass is the primary structure of powerlessness, that state of social aggregation which is the ultimate target of absolute power. Yet seriality was not the only social structure. There were camp-specific forms of positive and negative reciprocity, fleeting contacts, illegal barter, and elementary emergency aid. And there were conflicts over space, food, and jobs. In order to construct a proper picture of the social structures of camp society, it is therefore necessary to examine, along with the notion of mass, the other forms of sociation and dissociation.

The social mass is totally in keeping with the interests of absolute power. It lacks the internal links from which counterpower and resistance can sprout. Despite the physical density intrinsic to the mass, its structure is serial.[4] Juxtaposed seriatim, individuals are isolated. Their orientation is not to each other, but past one another; it is tangent. The change in perspectives occurring in any social action is absent here. In the mass, each is for himself or herself. It is a condition of isolation, social atomism, and egoism. The series only attains a unity externally: by the direction in which it is moving, by an event to which all are oriented in parallel, by the compulsion condemning it to passivity. In the mass, every person is exchangeable. The mass grows, but whoever is added is accidental. Equality is negative. The greater the mass, the smaller the space left for the individual. In the coerced mass, each human atom is one too many. One person steals the other's place, the other's air to breathe. Density is transformed into the superfluity of each individual. These laws of seriality correlate directly with the strategies of absolute power. Isolation prevents gatherings that cannot be monitored, external constitution facilitates the steering of movements, density spurs the antagonistic struggle for scarce goods. Superfluity presents the power to kill with a free field for action.

The society of the concentration camp was a mass of a singular kind. It had little in common with the open mass that grows rapidly, discharging its tensions in collective action.[5] Camp power transformed the society of the concentration camp into a closed, coerced mass. This mass grew not externally, but internally. It was unable to extend beyond its set perimeter. Compulsion had immobilized the inner dynamic of social masses. Discharge, outburst, destruction, and exceeding the limits were impossible. Thus, density was intensified in an extreme manner. The movements of the coerced mass were strictly monitored and guided. It did not move on its own; it was moved by others. It did not slacken but was goaded on, stopped, or forced into passivity. At the roll calls, the powerless mass was confronted with itself. With brutal force, the marching columns were compelled to move at double time. In the block, individuals were compressed to the point of motionlessness, of paralysis. Camp power made use of a simple social mechanics to gain control of the inmates.

It concentrated and compacted them, squeezing them together, pushing them to and fro. In this way it suppressed the affect that infused this mass: the fear of danger and violence. Ways of escape were blocked, exits barricaded. None could bolt from the formations of this mass. And panic—that collapse of the mass in the mass—was precluded from the start. Absolute power is so far-reaching that it is able to defuse the explosive power intrinsic to social masses, retaining individuals in a rigid, disciplined series. Power is endangered neither by the density of the mass nor by its growth. The coerced mass is a source not of shared strength but of collective immobility; it is not a process of imitative expansion and unpredictable eruptions, but a crystallized structure.

Mass situations were recreated anew day after day. In general, the mass is an unstable condition between contact and dissociation; it can only be maintained in the longer term by artificial means. Masses dissolve when the occasions that gave rise to them disappear, or split into countless interactions when individuals begin to relate to one another directly. Camp power had to prevent both such events. After the admission ceremony, which made all newcomers externally equal, they spent most of their time in mass situations: at night on their wooden bunks; during the day in marching columns, roll-call formations, and serial work situations. The regime left little time or space for any other forms of sociation. There was a dense throng in the blocks, in the washrooms, at meal distribution. The march and roll-call assembly created a collective mass body; individual labor under conditions where speaking and cooperation were prohibited atomized the Kommando. Though the prisoners were never alone, they were not together with the others. Independent forms of association and community were thus thwarted.

The organized, coerced mass is an extremely pathogenic social relation. It is almost impossible to shift from proximity to distance and vice versa. Although individuals are densely packed, anonymity and social alienation predominate. Anonymity here is less of a torment than is the simultaneity of physical density and social dissociation. The structure of the social world, the strata of the world of work, shared world and distant world,[6] is shattered if other people are immediately on hand yet simultaneously anonymous. They are as near, as intimately present as one's closest partners—and despite this, as alien as any distant contemporaries, an empty type, a nameless schema. It is thus mistaken to term this a forced community. The camp was not a community.[7] The other people were not individuals whose stories you knew. They were not your opposite numbers, but merely the people next to you. Physical proximity was not matched by the presence of an interpersonal "we"; there was no partnership and cooperation hand in hand with the similarity of suffering that all endured. The mass made the other person faceless;[8] it robbed the individual of the possibility to relate to another person, and thus also to himself or herself. In the mass, the significant other, the mirror of the self, is lacking. Violence and deprivation reduced the individual below the animal minimum for existence; the forced condition of the mass destroyed his or her self-relation as a person.

Mass was the dominant structure of powerlessness. This did not completely exclude contact, interaction, or social relations. But reciprocity had to be wrested from seriality, and was generally shot through with negativity, under the pall of envy and distrust, egoism and enmity. Mass is not a neutral state; it tends toward mutual indifference and repulsion. The nameless prisoner was surrounded without surcease by an irritable crowd, constantly scrounging for something to eat. Chronic hunger forced people to steal food and other items from fellow prisoners; it spawned unscrupulousness and betrayal. To posit collective solidarity here is to be blind to the milieu of mutual anxiety, to the hopelessness of a situation that a person could only survive if he or she had no consideration for others in the struggle for self-preservation. That should be borne in mind when examining the social forms that crystallized beyond seriality.

The most fleeting form of social exchange is social contact. Contacts break the mute silence of serial order, while simultaneously maintaining that seriality. Social contacts lack a permanent focus of shared orientation. The social situation remains without a thematic center from which encounters and relations might develop. Contacts are limited to short, ritual statements and physical gestures. There is little mutual accessibility, and the contact is usually over as quickly as it began. Contacts regulate and maintain the structure of seriality. Signals of threat and warning, curses, or abrupt defensive gestures create distance within the mass. Short comments about incidents or third persons produce nothing but a fleeting commonality that immediately dissipates. Contacts fill the interstices in the mass, but without violating its structure. They cement seriality instead of rupturing it. Reciprocity is transitory.

For longer conversations and lasting relations, the prisoners lacked not only the time but a clear code. Once the war began, the concentration camp became a multilingual society. The language of power was German, but only the SS and the small number of German prisoners shared this language. Yet a smattering of some German was crucial for survival; otherwise the prisoner could neither understand orders nor orient himself or herself in the alien camp world. Those who did not understand camp German entered a wasteland of incomprehension.[9] They did not know what the commands meant, and were kicked and beaten as a result. In Mauthausen, for example, the rubber truncheon was nicknamed "the interpreter." There was a babel of national languages among the inmates. Although in the individual camps the language of the largest group of prisoners was predominant,[10] it was at best understood only fragmentarily by the others. The linguistic barriers between the roughly forty different national groups represented in the camps were similar to the barrier separating them from the German center of power. Under these conditions of extreme heterogeneity and constant pressure from commands, all that could arise was a rudimentary colloquial code that allowed for minimal communication, the bare essentials.

The language of the concentration camp was a peculiar mixture of elements from German bureaucratic, barracks, and SS parlance, and from the languages of the largest prisoner groups, especially Polish.[11] It was modified morphologically by the addition of Slavic diminutive forms and plural and gender suffixes, along with multilingual sentences. The prisoners learned many expressions by phonetic imitation, not translation. Language was acquired here according to the pattern of stimulus and response. In addition to the command imperatives and terms for sites and situations in the camp, the lexicon also included numerous words for everyday objects, bodily functions, and typical camp activities, the various groups of prisoners, diseases, and forms of death. Bread was "coke," a foul-smelling cheese was "farmer's foot," fish paste was "cement." Lice were termed "blonds" in camp slang, fleas "brunettes." The row of seats over the block latrine was nicknamed the "chicken roost," the fourth level of the bunks the "mountain nest." The Kommando that returned in the evening to camp, lugging the bodies of dead comrades on its shoulders, was called the "caravan." The isolation block where experiments were performed was christened the "rabbit hutch." Prisoners who hushed up another's death in order to get his or her rations were dubbed "corpse breeders." To survive, they had to do "eye work" or have "eyes in their asses." The expression to refer to prisoners who became conspicuous and were reported was "report and goodbye."

Camp language was direct, terse, and vulgar. There were almost no words to designate feelings, nor were there expressions for statements of satisfaction or retraction. It was a discourse of naming and address, threat and warning, command and demand. Other speech acts—such as descriptions, explanations, the giving of reasons or permission, and promises—were rendered marginal simply as a by-product of prevailing conditions. Camp jargon was a gesticulatory, abbreviated code for fleeting contacts, not for encounters and conversations. Its tone was often as brusque as its expressions were coarse. In the struggle for space and food, one inmate shouted at another, hurling words of rebuke or mockery. A friendly word was a rarity, and for that reason it often received special mention in prisoners' testimony. Conversation generally revolved around food, illness, and items necessary for survival. Situations were standardized, and language was similarly limited. It was an emergency language for an extreme situation. Days were monotonous, and the topics of social intercourse were restricted.

Absolute power forces one to take strategic action. Social relations were also structured by instrumental calculation. Social instrumentality basically means that the other person is treated only as a means to an end. When it appears expedient, one joins forces; where another stands in the way, one fights against him or her. Temporary coalitions or individual initiatives for assistance are quite compatible with such instrumentalism. In numerous total institutions, there are repeated acts of fraternization when inmates suddenly help each other and join together in opposing the system forced on them.[12] But this fraternization is never more than a limited coalition, a spontaneous alliance in the face of external pressure. It has nothing in common with mutual sympathy or the cohesion and and loyalty of social groups. Thus, inmates often gave one another brief helpful pointers, divided and shared their packages, or warned one another regarding the guards. Yet these acts of emergency aid remained limited to an individual situation. These were serial coalitions that came into being solely because of the external antagonism—not because of common ground. The congruence of relevancies was limited to dealing with immediate threats.[13]

Instrumentality also permeated longer-term friendships. The annihilatory pressure transformed the structure of friendship fundamentally. It was not an exclusive dyadic relation based on voluntariness and emotional and personal affection.[14] It is true that at times individual prisoners took considerable personal risks to save a fellow prisoner and extricate him or her from a life-threatening situation. Many newcomers tried hard to stay together with a few inmates from their own transports, be housed in the same block, or be assigned to the same Kommando. And quite a few ran into old friends and acquaintances in the camps from before the time of their incarceration. Yet all such relations were in extreme danger. It was a rare bit of good fortune if your friend did not die, was not sent off elsewhere, did not disappear in the anonymity of the mass. Fluctuation within the camp system destroyed lasting ties. In any case, certain fundamental prerequisites for friendships that developed in the camp were absent: the freedom of choice, the atmosphere of emotional openness, and opportunities for personal self-presentation and mutual confirmation. Misery and despotic power eroded the bases of interpersonal intercourse. It helped for the moment if one was given a friendly word or could give vent to one's sense of despondency. But it was taboo to overburden the others with one's feelings. An inmate had to avoid endangering his or her own protective armor so crucial for survival. One was relieved to see other faces sometimes and not always to have to listen to the same jokes, gripes, curses, or stories. The normal inmate could hardly develop an interest in any topics other than food, harassment, grueling work, and illness. The pressure of everyday routine dried up the reservoir of topics for the development of lasting friendships. Direct material assistance was more important in the camp than symbolic recognition, the exchange of feelings, or mutual confirmation. Fellow prisoners were valued not for themselves but because of their connections and utility. Social bonds were rationalized and made subject to the overriding purpose of immediate self-preservation. Thus, the predominant mass structure not only reduced alliances to fleeting, serial coalitions; it also forced people to forge instrumental friendships and engage in egoistic strategies of reciprocity.

The simplest method of using other people is to enter into an economic exchange relation with them. In social exchange, signs of recognition or rejection are traded; in economic exchange, the trafficking is in goods. There are no obligations here of gratitude or symbolic response. Once the goods have changed hands and the price agreed on is paid, the relation is at an end. But there was one indispensable condition for illegal bartering: a minimum degree of trust.[15] The supervisors had nothing against a trade of bread for soup. These were permitted goods of which any prisoner could dispose. But the majority of items and services that changed hands were forbidden wares. No prisoners were allowed to barter their shirts, because as soon as they were caught without shirts they were beaten for having violated the dress code. To secretly make spoons, pliers, or lighters in the workshops and sell them on the black market was an offense against the rules governing personal belongings laid down by camp power. It was also risky to channel stolen and smuggled goods from the storerooms into the market. Deals with forbidden goods demanded caution and reliability. One had to trust the other person to deliver the promised items, and that the other person would not turn out to be a disguised informer who would rat and tell the SS about the shady transaction.

Although it was officially prohibited, barter was absolutely necessary for the prisoners. No one could survive in the long term living on the sparse alloted rations. Not a single button was allowed to be missing on the zebra-striped uniform. Yet if one accidentally lost a button at work, one had no other option but to replace it on the black market. A prisoner who had lost a cap either had to steal someone else's or pay someone to get him or her a replacement. According to camp regulations, the entire block had to appear every morning in formation with their shoes greased. But boot grease was handed out so rarely that the block chiefs diverted soup rations in order to buy machine oil or grease in the evening for the entire block. The camp code of regulations created a need to obtain certain items that could only be had by illegal trafficking. Hunger's pangs left one no other option but to sell one's last possessions for an additional ration of bread. Prisoners hacked out their gold fillings in order to trade them for three or four rations of bread. Whoever did not want to die or attract attention had to locate a bartering partner or intermediary who was selling a bowl of soup, shirt, or spoon, inevitably at a high price.

The exchange system in the camps was not a closed black market. Trade would have quickly died out without contacts to the surrounding world. Goods came in from various sources. Prisoners who received packages from their families offered for sale or barter what they did not immediately consume. Kommandos that had contacts with civilians smuggled food into the camp, furnishing tools, tobacco, or valuables in exchange. Turnips, potatoes, margarine, and bread found their way onto the black market from the kitchen or potato pantry. From the stockroom and laundry, shirts, caps, shoes, and overcoats came onto the market; from the workshops, paints, handmade cutlery, pliers, and nails. Bands of thieves offered what they had pilfered at job sites or stolen from other prisoners. Medical attendants sold drugs and medicines from the *Revier*, or the belongings of dead patients. Where concentration camps were directly linked with the mass extermination of the Jews, such as in Birkenau, the storerooms were an inexhaustible reservoir. This was used not only by the SS and camp aristocracy but also by the simple prisoners who were working in Kanada. The more items the doomed from the death transports had brought along with them, the better life was in the camp. The mass death of the Jews was one of the most important material foundations for daily survival in the camp.

In the unofficial system of distribution, one's position and market power depended on several factors. There was only a pretense of the abrogation of status hierarchy in exchange dealings when normal prisoners, prisoner-functionaries, and occasionally even SS personnel faced each other as trading partners and accepted cigarettes or tobacco as camp money. It was not uncommon for superiors to renege on their half of the deal and pocket the "money" they had been given without providing anything in return. A prisoner who had just bought a few cigarettes lost them again immediately if threatened with a possible disciplinary report for "inadequate work performance" or a "messy bed," and then blackmailed to hand over the cigarettes. The law of the jungle of the power hierarchy intruded on the market mechanism, abrogating the principle of equal exchange. Moreover, those who had direct access to the sources or outside contacts or were members of a gang that regularly conducted looting raids in the camp enjoyed a definite advantage. By contrast, most new prisoners were at a total disadvantage; they were bewildered, unable to fathom the murky exchange relations and the swirl of constantly changing prices in the market. Tyros were often duped by old-timers and, to the derision of the onlookers, sold their possessions at prices far below their current black-market value. The exchange system was anything but egalitarian. On one side were the professional black marketeers, shrewd organizers, fences, and monopolists; on the other, the countless have-nots who had nothing to offer but an old rag, a piece of cardboard, or half a portion of bread they had stashed away instead of devouring.

The easiest form of barter was the direct exchange of comestibles and services: bread for onions, onions for margarine, margarine for tobacco, tobacco for sewing on a button or fixing a bed according to regulations. Depending on the going rate of exchange, a package of margarine could fetch a robe, a bedsheet, or a sweater. For a large onion, one could get a piece of bacon, and five to eight cigarettes for a plate of thin soup. A plate of dog food was worth three to five times as much as the normal camp food. Prices depended on the prevailing supply situation in the camp. Although the price of soup remained relatively stable, prices for turnips and potatoes were subject to heavy fluctuation because they were connected with the quantity of food diverted from the kitchen. Trade with a general means of exchange was less limited than the traffic in foods. In most camps, bread rations, cigarettes, or tobacco served as camp money. Thus, depending on the market situation, a slice of sausage in Mauthausen cost one to two cigarettes, a belt about three; a dead cat went for twenty cigarettes, a small dog for about thirty.[16] Camp money enhanced the flexibility of exchange processes and even permitted a small amount of profit speculation: with cigarettes in your pocket, you could wait for more-favorable exchange rates. However, in this exchange system, with its limited mobility, it was the intermediaries who reaped special profits. They persuaded newcomers who, either because of the unfavorable location of their jobs or for linguistic reasons, were unable to develop contacts with civilian workers, to sell their packages from home, or to part with their gold dental crowns. They then smuggled these items through the checkpoints and obtained the desired bread or shirt, demanding high premiums for this service because of its inherent risks.

The transactions took place in a precarious field of power. Contacts with civilians were strictly prohibited. Generally, this order could only be circumvented by bribing SS guards. Theft at the work sites of private companies was often pursued by the management, but tolerated, if not furthered, by the SS. Theft of camp property was strictly punished by the SS, but theft from civilians who did not like the SS was regarded as an ordinary procurement measure. Economic exchange was threatened by betrayal and punishment. The social structure of power permeated trading relations as well. Against an alliance consisting of Kapos and black marketeers, the average prisoner was powerless to effect anything.

One way to get around economic exchange was by robbery and theft. Prisoners who had saved some of their food rations had to expect that the bread might be stolen from their bunks during the night. Whatever one did not carry directly on one's person could disappear; it could be filched in a careless moment. Many prisoners found that the shoes they had left at the foot of the bunk beds the night before were gone when they woke up the next morning. At meal distribution, Kapos, block chiefs, and "kitchen cops" regularly pilfered rations in order to rechannel them to the members of their respective cliques. By contrast, stealing food from the average prisoner was severely punished. Theft of bread violated an unwritten law of block comradeship and presented a challenge to the justice meted out by the prisoner-functionaries. Such thieves were beaten by block chiefs and their accomplices, and sometimes even killed. Hunger necessitated the stealing of food from other prisoners, but such thievery was more than mere theft. It was murder, and it was punished by murder. The gangs of thieves who looted storerooms or housing blocks under the cover of the SS or influential Kapos had less to fear.[17] The superiors and their associates protected robbers from the vengeance of the defenseless victims. The ordinary prisoner, who could not count on the support of a few strong comrades, was helplessly exposed not only to violence but also to the looting raids of the prisoner gangs.

There was another danger no less characteristic of the merciless struggle for existence: the ubiquitous presence of informers and spies. An integral component of the system of terror was the development of a network of stoolies. The more crowded the camps, they harder they were to monitor, and the more important the informers became for the SS. They tried to infiltrate the nuclei of political resistance, and also were on the lookout for infractions of camp regulations in the mass blocks and at work sites. The Political Department had its accomplices, and so did the camp leaders and rapport leaders. Many barrack-room assistants were in the service of criminal block chiefs or Kapos, and reported to them which prisoners had come to their attention or had something to conceal. The system of informers served both political and social control. If forbidden contact with a civilian worker, a secret message to the family, or theft from the kitchen became known, the superior could extort the offender and make him or her submit to the superior's demands. This system of spies and informers was just as disastrous for the social relations in the camp as robbery and privation. A prisoner could never be sure whether the inmate next to him or her was a traitor. The informers were rewarded with cigarettes and *protekcja* for their services. However, the others were constantly under the threat of an anonymous danger that contributed directly to the dissociation of prisoner society.

The world of the average prisoner was determined by the compulsions and constraints of individual self-preservation. There were numerous examples of solidarity and support, nourished by political or religious convictions, feelings of national shared bonds, or simple humanity. But the extent of such sentiments of fraternity and comradeship should not be overestimated. This was not a *Leidensgemeinschaft*—there was no community of suffering here.[18] The laws of the jungle prevailed in the daily struggle for survival—a social state of nature in which the person who prevailed was the one who was stronger, more ruthless, and more cunning than his or her fellows. In order not to perish immediately, each had to engage in a grinding struggle against everyone else. The prisoners existed in a zero-sum situation in extremis. Frequently, the only way to survive was at the expense of the others. One prisoner's death was another's bread. In the final phase of the camp system, there were allegedly also some incidents of cannibalism. Where the minimal conditions of survival—food, clothing, and space—were lacking, the only option was pitiless severity toward others, unconditional egoism. Material supplies were insufficient for lasting solidarity. Solidarity is based on the principle of mutual aid and sharing. But where there is nothing to share, except at the cost of common destruction and doom, solidarity lacks a material basis. Hunger, deprivation, and the pressure of annihilation ravaged social relations, inciting individuals, to ruthless self-interest, pitting them one against the other. In the coerced mass, the other person was not indifferent to you—he or she was a potential enemy who cheated you in bartered exchange, betrayed you to superiors, or stole your last crust of bread. Absolute power is based on a cleverly devised system of classification and collaboration, gradation of power, and privilege. This superstructure is raised above the seriality of a mass that permits only fleetingly brief contacts, mutual exploitation, and economic utility. Absolute power thrusts individuals into a condition where what is ultimately decisive is the right of the stronger.

Part IV

WORK

14

Work and Slavery

We work week after week, five to six hundred men, on a piece of land that could be taken care of in four days with two steam plows. That's called "productive labor." We call it "slave labor, sheer drudgery." The foremen think the acidic soil will be OK in maybe another ten or fifteen years. But already by next year, it's supposed to become farmland and be planted. . . . We stand out on the moor for months, often sinking up to our knees in the swamp. Frequently, our spades can't cut through the gigantic roots and tree stumps of the sunken forests in this moor. . . . Often, one of us collapses and is taken to a field hospital by two fellow prisoners and a sentry. And then there's this constant pressure to work, driving us on and on, the humiliating insults, the tormenting feeling you're not human any more. Just some animal. An animal that's herded together in flocks, housed in ten long stables, given a number, hounded and beaten as need requires, exposed to the whims of its drovers.[1]

WORK IS NOT "liberty." The motto above the camp gates ("Arbeit macht frei") was utter mockery. The prisoners received nothing for their labor, neither money nor bread. It was not exploitation; no unequal exchange took place. The prisoners were not made use of—they were hounded, driven until they were drained. All the prisoners received in return was a short postponement, a temporary reprieve until their total depletion. Work was an instrument to shatter them, wear them down, break their power to resist. It was a means not of survival, but of absolute power and terror.

Prisoner labor shares little with customary conceptions of work.[2] Work usually is performed to remove some deficiency or eliminate a situation of scarcity. It serves a purpose beyond itself: the satisfaction of needs held in abeyance until the results have been achieved. At the same time, work is associated with toil and effort, and generally with subordination as well. It is a burden; it weighs down the body, spirit, and soul. It is a repeated activity, not a onetime act. It demands discipline and self-restraint in order for plans to be realized and objective demands to be met. Work is aim-oriented, planned, constant action that befalls human beings as a burden. They bear its weight, voluntarily or under compulsion, in order to eke out an existence, ensure their survival, and create the conditions for a better life.

Absolute power changes this structure of work fundamentally. It breaks free from the rationale of utility, effectiveness, and their associated aims, and subordinates work according to the law of terror. Labor relations are always social relations. They are determined by the relations between human beings. The configuration of power in the camps was not geared to exploitation, but to terror. Work was organized in keeping with this political purpose. Even where prisoners worked on large-scale projects and rapid success was the professed aim, the system of absolute power had not been abrogated in any way. It continued to determine the organization of labor. The social structure of labor was not ruled by ideology or economy; it was shaped by violence, terror, and death.

Power would not be absolute if it had to subjugate itself to the dictates of functionality and productivity. The camp economy was a political economy in a radical sense. Power dominated, determining the core meaning of labor. The camp economy cannot be comprehended using the rationale of cost-effectiveness. There was a boundless squandering of human labor, an extravagant waste in the midst of incalculable misery. The aim of work was not profit, utility, life, but pure loss—the sovereignty that casts off all purposes: death. The regime of terror was less interested in performance and output than in the process of drudgery. In this way, prisoners were faced with a virtually insoluble dilemma. Those who could not work any more were superfluous. They were weeded out and killed. But if you worked, your strength was exhausted in a few weeks if you did not manage to get into a protected Kommando. Work did not secure life; it ravaged it. Only if one withdrew from labor could one preserve the strength that work destroyed and maintain the requisite fitness for work, the stamina that shielded one from death.

Although work determined the day's round, the concentration camp was not a labor camp. A labor camp is set up so that its inmates can fulfill a productive task. They are there to work. In the concentration camp, people worked because they still happened to be alive. The concept of forced labor is also misleading.[3] It is true that the prisoners were forced to work, but labor was principally a means of torture and abuse. Prisoner labor should likewise not be confused with the penal labor in prisons. It was not meant to inculcate new habits that would release the wrongdoers from the bondage of their passions. It was not a punishment designed to expiate for a crime and reform the culprit. As a rule, even penal labor does not serve ends of economic productivity or education; it is aimed at the disciplining of body and spirit.[4] Penal labor is meant to condition prisoners, transforming them into obedient workers who fulfill their set tasks with complete regularity. Nothing like that existed in the camps. No permanent habits were instilled; rather, absolute power processed its victims for death. The time of survival was hardly more than a few months. In the camps, labor was constant, but the intention was to seal off time hermetically, to plug its every pore. No one here was supposed to be improved or rehabilitated. None of the prisoners was supposed to return to life outside.

One counterargument that can be brought against the thesis of the priority of power is that the camps were a modern form of mass slavery.[5] That theory is based essentially on four historical arguments. First of all, the SS leadership embarked on a functional shift in the camps beginning in the winter of 1941–42, involving a limited economic mobilization of labor.[6] The camps were placed under the supervision of the WVHA, and, in the wake of several waves of arrests, hundreds of thousands of laborers were shunted into the expanding concentration camp system. Several commandants were successively replaced and specifically ordered to intensify labor deployment.[7] Camp doctors were urged to lower mass mortality;[8] guards were told to spur inmates on to work without the use of violence.[9] Restrictions on the receipt of packages were eased, and an attempt was made to limit official camp punishments. The number of prisoners deployed in camp operation activities was to be reduced so as to deploy as many as possible in the new external subcamps, whose inmates were loaned out as cheap hired labor to private firms. Second, the beneficiaries of prisoner labor—the SS economic enterprises, the special staffs for arms manufacture, and private industry—had no interest in the wholesale annihilation of human beings; their concern was to accelerate the economic plans for the war and boost productive capacity. Third, the SS itself initiated a vocational skills program and had prisoners trained in the stone quarries as stonemasons and bricklayers.[10] It introduced a system of premiums as an incentive for productivity in a bid to increase motivation by easing the conditions of confinement and providing extra rations. Fourth, it is claimed that the high mortality was not due to the work itself, but to the material deprivation rampant in the camps, the unforeseeable pressure of overcrowding and supply bottlenecks because of the war.[11] There was no reason, it is argued, to posit a praxis of "extermination by work." Mass death was not the purpose of work, but rather an unintended by-product of the disastrous conditions prevailing in the camps.

Yet this theory of the slave camp remains unconvincing, for reasons both systematic and historical. First, it confuses the plans and goals of the organization's top echelon with the concrete reality on the ground. Even if the central office is assumed to have pursued the goal of reducing the pressure of annihilation to a few specific prisoner categories, this does not mean there was a concomitant fundamental change in the *actual* work situations. As in many large hierarchical organizations, the plans and orders coming down from the apex are only one causal factor behind what occurs at lower levels. Social reality can only correspond to the will of the top echelon in totally regulated, rigidly structured organizations. Yet the concentration camp system was marked by a high degree of decentralization and the relative independence of the local camp SS. Where the middle ranks predominate and lower offices have considerable latitude, many central orders suffer seepage on their way down the hierarchy; they are deemed impracticable, altered, or simply ignored. Certainly, internal SS orders, unlike the hyped-up reports of success directed to external offices, were not propaganda. Yet they ran up against the usages and habits of a guard personnel that was accustomed, through years of practice, to perceive the prisoners as worthless "enemies of the people," as human trash, and to mistreat them around the clock. Just as the camp doctors had no influence on food supplies and working conditions, the permanent staff had no interest in any curtailment of its immediate power and right of disposal over prisoners. To replace violence by orders, drudgery by productivity, not only would have contradicted standing practice but would also have entailed a serious loss of power. There was not enough personnel to shift from a praxis of terror to a system of slavery. Other key elements were also lacking: a thorough and fundamental reorganization of competence, an abrogation of terroristic habits, and a radical change in the configuration of power. Consequently, what is decisive is not whether a functional change was propagated, but that the organization of the concentration camp was not restructured in such a way that labor could have changed from a means of power into its purpose and chief end.

There was no corresponding improvement in the material supply situation in conjunction with the orders handed down by the WVHA for increased labor deployment.[12] There was far more interest in keeping the mortality rate constant than in reducing it drastically. There were no concessions when it came to the policy of induced starvation introduced in 1938–39. Rations, clothing, housing, and medical care were not altered in such a way that the capacity for work could have been effectively maintained. At the beginning of 1944, there was another drastic slash in rations. Reductions in the wearing time spent in roll-call formations always meant more hours on the job. Long periods spent going to and from work and shifts of eleven or twelve hours quickly led to total exhaustion. The work destroyed the capacity to work. Actual effective performance lagged far behind planned objectives. Instead of improving living conditions and increasing productivity, the SS pursued a policy of inadequate maintenance and the replacement of prisoners. Because the overwhelming majority of prisoners was always replaceable, expendable, their capacity to work had little value. If the camp population died off, it was replenished by a new batch of workers.[13] The mass dying demanded an ever-new influx in order to offset losses. Even if labor was not defined by the private beneficiaries as a means of annihilation, it was nonetheless a major cause of mass death.[14]

To maintain and boost a laborer's capacity for work contradicted the rationale of security. Hardy, strong prisoners can also engage in resistance, and thus constitute a danger for the camp regime. The "system of piecework and bonuses" introduced in the spring of 1943 brought a certain degree of relief, but only for a small number of privileged, (mainly German) inmates and foreign skilled laborers. They were allowed to wear their hair longer, frequent the camp brothel, and buy tobacco with bonus coupons in the camp canteen.[15] It is absurd to contend this was an effective incentive for performance and an abrogation of terror. The system of rations linked to performance was part of the policy of class differentiation. Moreover, terror organizations always have an interest in locking up as many people as possible in order to maintain a deathly quiet. The larger the number of prisoners, the greater the danger appears to be which the regime must hold in check. The expansion of the concentration camp system in the final years of the war was also justified by reference to the shortage of civilian workers. However, that enlargement was particularly in keeping with the internal dynamic of an organization that wished to extend its sphere of power to economic activities, while at the same time pursuing a policy of promoting its own indispensability. The larger the camps, the greater the power to negotiate vis-à-vis external beneficiaries, and the more indispensable the entire apparatus of security. As contradictory as the measures for expansion of labor deployment may initially seem, there were no real antagonisms among work, annihilation, economy, racist ideology, and terror. The intensification of prisoner labor was solely a change in the specific means of terror. Absolute power is distinguished by its ability freely to determine the value of a human being. It can decide whether it will kill by violence, starvation, or labor. It can determine when to let up briefly on killing, exploit labor power, or be paid in cash by outside beneficiaries. There is a fundamental contradiction between the rationale for this power and the conventional economy of forced and slave labor.[16]

The concentration camp was not a slave factory. Nonetheless, a comparison with the social form of slavery has heuristic value. It helps elucidate the transformation of human labor into *terror labor*. Slavery is always a social relation of domination and production.[17] Slaves are part of the physical property of masters, working for them under coercion, and totally dependent on their personal arbitrary will. In contrast with wage labor, labor power is not a commodity; it is the human being himself or herself. The slave is a human being, but qua slave, he or she is a thing, an object like all other objects at the master's disposal. By social definition, the slave is therefore not a member of human society. Slaveholders have total power to dispose of their property as they wish. That power is unlimited in every respect. Slaves are deprived not only of control over their labor, but also over themselves as people. Their owners can force them to work without a break, beat them, torment them, or hound them to death. Nonetheless, unlike the concentration camp, the world of slavery ultimately is not geared to terror and death, but to exploitation. The slave, especially under the conditions of commercial slavery, has a value and going market price. The master does not acquire slaves in order to kill them, but to put them to work for the master's benefit. Power remains a means of exploitation. Slavery is primarily a system of labor.

The personal dependence typical of slavery was lacking in the concentration camp. The prisoners were also exposed to arbitrary will and whim, yet they were not the personal property of masters but the inmates of an institution.

They belonged to no one. They were controlled by an apparatus that had hunted them down and incarcerated them. It forced them to work, and in the final years of the war also leased their labor out to external beneficiaries. The SS did not operate as a slaveholder in the marketplace. Rather, as a formal agency, it defined the status of the prisoners by decree and violence. For that reason, the prisoners had neither a value nor a price. They were not traded as commodities or sold. What private companies were required to pay for prisoner labor was not a price, but an administrative leasing fee. The prisoners were subjected to a far more radical reification than any victim of slavery ever experienced. In terms of status, a slave is not a person but a thing. Yet as a living creature, the slave is a human being who has a certain property value. By contrast, the prisoner was actually depersonalized by humiliation and misery, stripped of humanity, transformed into an animal-like bundle of reactions, and ultimately killed. As barbaric as the owners often were in dealing with their slaves, the death of a slave was a loss. For power, however, the vegetating and death of the prisoners was a victory.

Slave labor is not ineffective per se. Slavery does not exclude skilled labor or personal trust between the master and servant. In contrast with other forms of involuntary labor, total power of disposal has a clear advantage for the slaveowners: they can deploy the slave in a mobile manner and rid themselves of undesirable laborers. Despite the enormous costs of surveillance, slave labor is by no means limited solely to repetitive manual labor. The more skilled the slaves are, the greater their value, and the greater their chances to be protected and cared for by their masters. To that extent, slavery is in accordance with the economy of value maintenance and enhancement. It was radically different in the concentration camp. In its pure, ideal form, terror labor does not maintain the value of labor capacity, but squanders it. Prisoner labor did not serve the purpose of self-preservation; it accelerated a prisoner's ultimate end. The camp invented numerous senseless tasks that had only one purpose: to drain and emaciate individuals, to grind them down. Absolute power strips labor of its purposive structure, expanding it endlessly. It has no interest in products or results. It is oriented to the process of working itself, to the duration of suffering. It transforms hard effort and strain into a deadly pressure for annihilation. The social relation of power overlays the objective relation of labor, shaping it almost totally. Violence is not a means for labor; labor is a means of violence. The prisoners did not belong to a slave class of outsiders. They were part of the class of the expendable and superfluous, the wretched and lost.

15

The Beneficiaries

Since the arrival of the Kommando, this was the tenth
fuselage assembled in the plant. Of these ten, only
one, the very first, was sent on to Heinkel in Rostock.
It was returned because the thing was faulty. The
other fuselages were first stored in a shed, and later in
the church we'd just cleared out. They would never be
delivered and we knew it. Rostock, where the Heinkel
aircraft plant was located, had been destroyed, and the
necessary materials were not being delivered to the
factory. The only purpose of work was so that the
management and master workmen, almost all of them
Nazis, who had no interest in being sent to the front,
could avoid being drafted.[1]

NUMEROUS organizations profited from the labor of the prisoners. The concentration camp was integrated into a complex field of offices and firms that expanded over the course of the years. Two parallel developments can be discerned in the organizational history of prisoner labor. After the concentration camp system had initially sealed itself off from the outside, it gradually opened up to external beneficiaries—first to the plants locally, then to the economic enterprises of the SS, and finally to the interministerial special staffs and the private arms industry. At the same time, the Economic Administration of the SS expanded its domain until by the spring of 1942, the camps were completely under its administrative wing. These shifts were accompanied by various conflicts. The offices and firms competed for cheap labor. In particular, it was a matter of heated controversy whether labor deployment was compatible with police security, racist mass annihilation, and the interests of organizational power aggrandizement. There were prisoners in profusion. But to use them was only appropriate if they augmented power, strengthening the position of the SS. These processes of opening of the system, competition for power and limited economic mobilization can be examined in detail via a closer look at the specific beneficiaries of prisoner labor.[2]

The first facility that made use of prisoner labor was the camp itself. A concentration camp had to be built up from scratch. If there were no buildings available, barracks had to be erected, paths laid, perimeters secured. Once in operation, it had to be supplied on a regular basis, continually maintained and expanded. A fully developed camp had to guarantee the same functions as any self-sufficient society. Along with kitchens, workshops, and storerooms, there were nurseries, timberyards, stables, administrative offices, hospitals, crematoria. There were also countless tasks associated with clearing, transport, and cleaning. The sole purpose of all these activities was to maintain the camp. By means of their own work, the prisoners constructed and then maintained the institution in which they were caged until their death.

Economic aims did not determine the construction and maintenance of the completed camp. The work was supposed to be exhausting, severe harassment. The personal needs of the prisoners were of no interest to the terror regime. Economic pressure was minimal. Efficiency was not even an important factor in the construction of new camps, the most murderous phase of camp labor. When a barracks was to be finished, whether meals were distributed on time and there were enough places in the bunks—all that was of secondary importance. There were preferential occasions here for mistreatment and excesses. The more some work might prove useful to the prisoners themselves, the less its results mattered.

The inmates themselves benefited least of all from their labor. For the camp masters, on the other hand, it was not only a source of power but of personal wealth. Absolute power of control over prisoners' labor opened wide the door to general enrichment. Right from the start, the personnel had prisoners working to meet their needs. Although scarcity was ubiquitous, the personnel used the workshops in Dachau, which already employed five hundred artisans in 1933, for its own private orders. This was the origin of the system of graft and corruption in which many members of the commandant office staffs were implicated later on. When the Dachau workshops were transferred from the supervision of the central *Inspektion* and placed under Pohl's Administrative Office, that move met with fierce opposition from the clique of commandants. The shift to commercial principles curtailed their private power of control. This line of conflict between the economic administration echelon and the camp SS also resurfaced in differences over the later deployment of prisoners in arms manufacture.

A second group of organizations likewise owed its existence to the labor of the prisoners. Most of the economic enterprises of the SS were linked with the concentration camps right from the start.[3] Prisoner factories were the source of their growth. The enterprises were under Pohl's supervision; in 1940, they were merged into the conglomerate Deutsche Wirtschaftsbetriebe GmbH; in 1942, management was taken over by Section W in the WVHA. The antagonism between security and economy did not just exist between the RSHA and the WVHA, but was also reflected in tensions between Sections W and D within the WVHA. The roots of that antagonism were already present in the path of decision making and the distribution of supervisory authority. The managers of individual plants sent their requests to Office DII; its job was to direct prisoner deployment from a central point. The selection of workers and their guarding was left to the local camp leadership. The Kommandos were under the commandant's office. The authority of plant personnel, generally civilian employees of SS firms, was limited to directives regarding division of labor and skilled supervision.

A constant conflict smoldered between camp leadership and factory management. Naturally, the commandant's office was not particularly interested in losing supervisiory powers over its inmates, while factory managers were more interested in efficiency and effectiveness. Thus, the continuity of production was often disrupted by fluctuations in the workforce.[4] The camp leadership sent experienced prisoners to other camps or retained them for questioning, or removed skilled workers from the plants and deployed them in camp workshops. Weak or unfit prisoners were dismissed from their jobs and had to be sent back to the camps. If an epidemic broke out in camp and a quarantine was imposed, none came to work. The plants were idled, often for weeks or months on end. In the local structure of power, camp management always retained the upper hand. The enterprises were dependent on the office that provided them with prisoners. Replacements were hard to find. For that reason, the camp administrations could largely dispose of their reservoir of prisoners as they saw fit. Those they wished to keep were retained; those they wanted to get rid of were shunted off elsewhere. Orders from the central office did little to change this. In order to combat fluctuation, Pohl appointed the camp commandants as plant managers in April 1942, giving them a financial bonus for combining the two functions. But the effect was precisely the opposite. Although it was dependent professionally on the plant personnel, the sphere of power of the commandant's office now encompassed the factories as well. That office was able to intervene directly in the production process without having to busy itself any further with business matters. Camp power reached into the plants, subjugating them to the tried and tested practices of terror.

Aside from the modest financial incentive, the camp leadership had no direct benefit from the profits of prisoner labor. It had to give everything it took in it from the plants to the Reich treasury, from whose budget the concentration camp system had been financed since 1936. To the end of 1942, the SS enterprises paid .30 RM per day per prisoner; effective January 1, 1943, wages were increased to 1.50 RM for skilled workers, .50 RM for women and unskilled laborers. Beginning on April 1, 1944, wages for skilled workers were boosted to between 4 and 5 RM for skilled workers, and between 3 and 4 RM for unskilled labor. This corresponded to the daily wages that private firms in the defense industries were paying. The substantial profits that accrued due to low wage costs, which was far in excess of the profit margin permitted by war economy regulations, had to be passed on by Section W to the Reich. Along with the protests from private industry about low wages, the reason wages for prisoner labor deployment were increased was probably that excessive reported profits could be reduced in this way, and profits could be retained within the system of camp financing.

The local struggle over authority appears in a new light if one considers the organization of the SS as a whole. Under the primacy of power, the maximization of profits is less pressing than the policy of power aggrandizement. In expanding and centralizing its economic enterprises, the SS pursued the aim of strengthening its financial power and thus extending its political latitude. An organization that was able to equip its armed units itself, implement its settlement plans using its own construction capacity, and supply its personnel by itself was largely independent of outside funding. It could operate as an independent body vis-à-vis the army, the ministries, and private industry. Using prisoner labor, the SS expanded its power zone, gaining additional resources for implementing its political and racist schemes of terror. To a degree, the link between labor and annihilation was inherent in the system.[5] This also becomes evident when the SS enterprises are examined in detail.

The most notorious prisoner factories were the production facilities of the Deutsche Erd- und Steinwerke GmbH (DEST), founded in 1938. In the final years of the war, the company operated fourteen plants: stone quarries and granite works, brick and clinker works—factories that served the camps as mills of mass annihilation. In Flossenbürg, Mauthausen, Groß-Rosen, and Natzweiler, prisoners were employed in stonemason workshops. Using hammers and chisels, stone was worked into square blocks, slabs, stairs or curbstones. Some 20 to 25 percent of the workers were involved in loading and transporting the leftover stone. DEST also operated brick, gravel and building material plants in Sachsenhausen, Berlstedt near Buchenwald, Neuengamme, Auschwitz, Hopehill, Stutthof, and Treblinka. In Treblinka, some four thousand men were deployed in a gravel pit located about two kilometers from the death factory. Plans for large-scale brick factories in Dessau and Linz were not realized. Instead, an experimental facility, a blast furnace slag plant, was put into operation; its basic capital was raised in equal parts by DEST and a subsidiary of the Hermann Göring Works. It was supposed to process the slag from the steel plant in Linz into coarse gravel, sand, and broken stones as bulk for roadbed sub-basing. During the second half of the war, DEST leased its grounds and facilities to the aircraft industry: Messerschmitt in Flossenbürg and Mauthausen, Steyr in Gusen, and Siemens in Sachsenhausen. In Natzweiler, it took on the overhauling of aircraft engines from Junkers. On its own, it reextracted raw materials from captured war equipment in the stone processing plant in Oranienburg. Numbering more than three thousand prisoners, this "Kommando Speer" was the largest single work site of the concentration camp Sachsenhausen. In addition, DEST was busy extracting new building materials from the ruins of German cities. In Essen and Düsseldorf, it operated small plants for reprocessing rubble; Buchenwald supplied prisoners to work in these facilities. Production in the brickworks at Sachsenhausen and Neuengamme was constantly increased due to the steadily rising need for building materials as a consequence of the destruction of urban areas by aerial bombardment. The number of deployed prisoners rose concomitantly.[6] In May 1942, there were 9,421 prisoners deployed in the enterprises of DEST; 3,844 of these were in Mauthausen and Gusen, and 1,700 in Flossenbürg. By September 1944, they numbered more than 23,000.

Work in the stone quarry or brickworks was extremely dangerous, lethal. Physical exhaustion, accidents, and the unlimited excessive power of the supervisors depleted a prisoner's strength in a matter of weeks. The prisoners deployed for such terror labor were primarily those who were subject to special persecution: Jews, "non-Aryan" foreigners, Russians, Poles, and veterans of the Spanish Civil War. Stone quarries were preferred sites for mass annihilation. The death of the prisoner was an inseparable part of the job. Nonetheless, there was no shortage of workers. The dead were exchanged for the living.

The firm Deutsche Ausrüstungswerke (DAW) was set up a year after DEST; it specialized in wood and iron manufacture. Most of the workshops in Dachau were under its control, and additional factories in Sachsenhausen, Buchenwald, and Auschwitz were added in the summer of 1940; in the following years, these were supplemented by plants in Lublin, Lemberg, Stutthof, and Neuengamme. The array of production ranged from beds, wardrobes, and stools to filing cabinets, small wooden houses, rabbit hutches, wood screws, and wrought-iron work. With the shift to war production, stress was placed on the repair of cases for ammunition, shell casings or rifles. The total work force soared from 1,220 prisoners in 1940 to 15,498 in 1943.[7]

Another prisoner-based enterprise was the Gesellschaft für Textil- und Lederverwertung GmbH (Texled) that operated production facilities in Ravensbrück.[8] Its main output was clothing for prisoners and troops,[9] but it also made furs, mats, and bedside rugs. While only 699 women were deployed in these factories in March 1941, their numbers jumped to 5,082 by September 1942, leveling off at between 3,000 and 3,500 from early 1943 on. The textile plants were equipped with machinery and had a relatively high level of rationalization. In the sewing department, where some 600 women worked, thirteen belts were installed, each with twenty-six sewing machines. In the knitwear section, there were automatic ribbers, and the weaving mill set up in 1943 had ninety-six hand-operated and forty-four mechanical looms. Productivity reached a level of 40 percent of normal civilian work performance, an unusually high figure for prisoner labor. However, the mortality rate in Ravensbrück being lower than in other camps cannot simply be attributed to the higher technological level of textile manufacture. Though there was no murderous drudgery as there was in the stone quarries, the day and night shifts were ten to twelve hours each, and the shop floor was under a regime of beating, extreme pressure, harassment, deafening noise, and workload quotas.[10] Operating the machinery called for a certain set of skills, though these could be learned in a short period of time. In the closed factory and workshop halls, it took just a bit longer to reach the point of total exhaustion.

The third beneficiary of prisoner labor was the SS construction administration that had been set up in 1933 on the basis of the Dachau building office. It was reorganized in 1936 and again in 1939, and integrated in 1942 into the WVHA as Section C. It supervised the construction of barracks for the Waffen-SS, along with residential quarters and service and other camp buildings, though this area of activity was cut back during the war. At the end of 1941, eighty-eight hundred prisoners were deployed on the building sites of the SS; in the summer of 1942, mobile construction brigades were formed, generally numbering about a thousand men, whose tasks were to repair bomb damage in the cities, detonate blind shells, and recover bodies from the rubble. In Normandy and on the Channel island of Alderney, thousands of half-starved Poles and Russians were deployed under the surveillance of the Wehrmacht to build fortifications, tunnels, and launching ramps. Other small building projects included the establishment of weapons factories in direct proximity to the concentration camps: Krupp in Auschwitz, Metallwerke in Neuengamme, and Zeppelin near Sachsenhausen.

During the final phase of the war, the gigantic projects of the special staffs in the SS and the Armaments Ministry assumed a far greater importance.[11] Although these immediate emergency measures were classified as top priority, here too, the strategic struggle for power predominated over economic usefulness. Hitler appointed Saur, the service director in the Armaments Ministry, as head of the Fighter Staff (*Jägerstab*), whose task it was to mobilize all reserves for aircraft construction. Göring, who had previously been in charge of aircraft production, attempted to offset his loss of power by forging an alliance with the SS. With Hitler's approval, he appointed the head of Section C of the WVHA, Hans Kammler, as director of special construction projects. Himmler, who sensed an opportunity here to expand his area of power to production as well, proposed to Göring that he could triple the number of prisoners offered.[12] Göring promised him that the SS would soon have its own air squadron. The formal position of the Special Staff Kammler (*Sonderstab Kammler*) in the thicket of diverse authorities and competencies opened up a direct path for the SS to penetrate into the domain of the Armaments Ministry.

Kammler maintained a network, independent of the WVHA, of district special inspectorates and local head staffs for every construction job. He was personally and directly subordinate to Himmler, over the head of Pohl. Neither Pohl nor the members of Section DII, responsible for labor administration in the camps, made decisions on prisoner deployment; that was the prerogative of Kammler as personal Special Deputy of the Reichsführer-SS. Although officially subordinate to the Armaments Ministry, he was also deputized at the same time by Göring, the head of the Aviation Ministry. This intermediate position gave him a great deal of latitude. And the section of the *Sicherheitsdienst* (SD, the security service) under his personal control could be used as an instrument against anyone who stood in his way.

The only possible protection against massive air raids was to relocate production into bombproof underground facilities. As early as 1943, Kammler deployed prisoners in work on the expansion of mines and stone quarries. There were already plants working for the aircraft industry in the granite works of Flossenbürg and Mauthausen, where Messerschmitt had transferred roughly 35 percent of its production after the destruction of the Regensburg facilities. Starting in early 1944, some 11,000 prisoners were deployed in Sankt Georgen near Mauthausen digging shafts and tunnels into the mountainside for a facility to produce the jet fighter Me 262. Further projects in Ebensee and Melk each deployed 7,000 laborers. In Neckarelz, there were 3,000 workers; in Ohrdruf, where an underground Führer Headquarters was to be built, there were more than 10,000 workers on the job.[13] But the largest single bunker complex came into being in the cave network in the Kohnstein Mountain in the southern Harz. Under the code name "Dora," subterranean production halls were built here to manufacture the secret weapons V1 and V2. Dora was initially operated as a satellite of Buchenwald; from August 1944, it became an independent camp complex with thirty-two external subcamps and seven construction brigades, and was the exemplar for the underground relocation of industry. As aerial bombardment continued, more and more firms sought a secure production site, and a fierce struggle erupted over the scarce footage available underground. Three million square meters of subterranean production surface were planned; by January 1945, 425,000 square meters had been made ready, at fifteen underground alternative protected sites.[14]

The Kammler staff could fall back on a source of power no longer available to any other office: the labor of tens of thousands of concentration camp inmates. The reserve army of foreign workers had largely been exhausted, and only the SS was still in a position to deploy prisoner labor on a massive scale and without any consideration for losses. For all practical purposes, it had a monopoly on mobile labor reserves. Consequently, it did not lease out workers to private industry on the construction projects, but kept control in its own hands. It was in the expansive interests of the SS that, after completion of the production halls, Kammler also took over production of the V2, then the deployment of the rockets, the manufacture of all jet planes and, at the last minute, the direction of the entire complex of air defense industries. However, the SS did not reach the zenith of its power until 1945, at a moment when there was no longer any arms production.

The turbulence of the final phase of the war directly affected the prisoner's chances of survival. The time pressure was murderous. The large-scale projects were railroaded through at breakneck tempo. The closer final defeat came, the more quickly the production facilities decisive for "final victory" had to be completed.[15] In Dora, the prisoners were deployed on digging tunnels immediately, even before housing was ready. In Kaufering, which was under supervision of Organisation Todt, some deployees vegetated in holes in the ground. Losses were immense. In Dora-Mittelbau, 2,882 of the 17,000 prisoners deployed there died in the period from October 1943 to March 1944. Down to evacuation, some 60,000 were sent to the facility as forced laborers; only two-thirds of these prisoners survived.[16] New transports were constantly brought in to compensate for losses and attain the targeted labor force. Invalids were shunted back to the main camp, an infirmary or a camp for the dying, and replaced by fresh laborers. The precipitate and brutal deployment of prisoners triggered a deadly cycle: since the Kammler staff did not wish to forgo the planned numbers of those deployed, but was unwilling to feed and maintain them properly, there had to be a constant influx of new prisoners, whose fate was the same as that of their predecessors. Replacement was no problem at the construction sites of the Kammler staff. This was exclusively an operation for unskilled mass labor. For the overwhelming majority, production here did not mean industrial skilled labor, but menial drudgery on the construction site. The value of a human being plummeted to the level of what his or her body was able to deliver for a few short weeks.

Work for the Kammler staff, the SS enterprises, and the camp remained within the sphere of power of the SS. Although the field of power was expanded around the Armaments Ministry and the mixed special commissions, the organizational rules of the concentration camp system were not abrogated in any way. That situation changed only after a fourth group of beneficiaries entered the picture: the private arms manufacturers. These firms were not in the service of SS policies of power and annihilation. They were more concerned about cheap labor than about political expansion. For the camp regime, the opening of the gate to system-external firms was thus rather risky. It endangered the principle of the sealed site, closed to the outside. There was the threat of a loss of political power if such firms could not be attached to the camp territorially and in terms of organization. Although there were close ties between the top echelons, there could only be smooth and successful cooperation if the laws of terror and the demands of production could be reduced to a common denominator.

When the SS began to propagate the idea of direct involvement in arms production in the spring of 1942, initially its own power interests loomed paramount.[17] It invited private companies to set up production facilities in the camp enclosure or in the immediate vicinity. In so doing, its aim was not just to retain the power of disposal over prisoners, but also to take over control of production under its own auspices. However, this ran up against opposition from private firms—and from the Armanents Ministry and the Wehrmacht, which were linked with them. They regarded SS defense industries as a potential unwelcome competitor in their own bailiwick. Though they were interested in cheap prisoner labor, they had no interest in a new rival in the central sector of the National Socialist economy. In addition, there appeared to be no guarantee for economically useful deployment unless the prisoners could be integrated into ongoing production. On September 16, 1942, a temporary compromise was found: Speer agreed the SS could engage in construction in Auschwitz, while the WVHA proposed it would make larger numbers of prisoners available for deployment in arms manufacture. The plan was to staff entire factories using prisoners, or transform them immediately into concentration camp plants. After a renewed attempt by Himmler to get approval for an SS-controlled sphere of production, Speer was able to obtain a key decision from Hitler on September 20 and 22, 1942: prisoners were only to be deployed directly in private firms. This institutionalized the principle of leasing out forced labor. As compensation, the SS was promised war matériel for equipping its divisions. Nonetheless, it did not entirely abandon its program of expansion. Again and again, experienced workers who had learned the ropes were removed from a given plant and transferred for deployment in SS enterprises.

Down to the summer of 1944, the following decision procedure was in force: private companies, on their own initiative, reported their needs to Office DII of the WVHA. If prisoners were available, the SS checked the housing facilities and whether the plant was secure from escape, and then issued the permit. Company representatives could choose workers themselves in the respective assigned camps, and these were immediately transferred to a satellite camp near the work site. The rate for hiring on such laborers was six RM per day for skilled workers, four RM for unskilled workers. The Armaments Ministry was initially not involved in the decision process. But that changed in June 1944 when Speer's ministry took over the application procedure, instructing the WVHA by courier after a positive decision had been reached. It thus wedged itself as an intermediary between the SS and private industry. Now there was no longer to be any direct contact between private firms and the SS during the process of application.

For a long time, reservations on the part of the SS vis-à-vis system-external organizations acted to limit prisoner labor deployment in private industry. In the summer of 1943, 160,000 prisoners were registered. Twenty-two percent of these were reported as unfit for labor, 15 percent were involved in repair work on the camps, and the remaining 63 percent, some 100,000, were distributed among the construction projects of the SS, its economic enterprises, and various private companies.[18] As late as the spring of 1944, the Armaments Ministry listed only 32,000 prisoners directly deployed in industrial production.[19] At that same time, the Oranienburg *Inspektion* recorded a total of 20 main camps and 165 external subcamps.[20] The system of hiring out prisoners did not experience a dramatic expansion until the second half of 1944. Most of the external Kommandos came into being then, after the reservoir of POWs and civilian forced laborers had finally been depleted. Only the SS was in a position, such as after the occupation of Hungary, to conscript a veritable army of prisoners. At the end of 1944, the entire number of concentration camp inmates was some 600,000. Of these, 480,000 were fit for deployment: 140,000 were with the Kammler staff, 130,000 deployed under Organisation Todt, and 230,000 were in private industry.[21] The number of satellite camps also soared. At the end of 1942, as far as can be ascertained, there were 82 external camps and satellites; in December 1943, there were 18 main camps and 186 subcamps; by June 1944, that number had surged to 341. In January 1945, the concentration camp system encompassed 13 main camps and at least 662 external subcamps.[22]

The list of the beneficiaries reads like a guide to German industry.[23] To name but a few: Siemens leased some 7,400 concentration camp prisoners for its plants in Bobrek near Auschwitz, Ravensbrück, Nuremberg, Berlin, Neustadt, Ebensee, and Jungbuch. AEG-Telefunken employed 1,500 Jews in Riga-Kaiserwald, 650 in Freiburg in Lower Silesia, and 850 in its rolling mills and cable plant in Berlin. The firm Braunkohle-Benzin AG (BRABAG), whose synthetic fuel was supposed to reduce dependence on foreign oil, deployed up to 8,000 prisoners in four plants; in Zeitz alone, 5,000 Jewish prisoners were deployed. From 1941 to 1944, some 35,000 prisoners were deployed in the Buna plant of I. G. Farben in Auschwitz-Monowitz. They were selected from the extermination transports and exploited as laborers; invalids were sent back to Birkenau to be gassed. The life expectancy of a Jewish prisoner at Buna was three to four months, and just one month in the nearby coal mines. Of the 35,000 deployed at Buna, at least 25,000 perished.

Krupp leased 520 Hungarian Jewish women to charge the steel-tempering furnaces and carry out welding operations, among other tasks, in its Rolling Mill II in Essen. In the Neukölln section of Berlin, 500 Jewish women from the Lodz ghetto who had been confined in Sachsenhausen were working at the subsidiary Krupp-Registrierkassen GmbH (Krupp Cash Registers, Ltd.). Their job, part of the galvanization process, was to submerge hot iron parts barehanded in cold water. In October 1943, Krupp brought in 1,500 Jews from Auschwitz for the construction of the Bertha Works in Markstädt near Breslau, a production plant for light field howitzers; they were incarcerated in a new external subcamp of Groß-Rosen. A few months later, there were 4,000 prisoners confined in this concentration camp Fünfteichen. The company Rheinmetall-Borsig deployed 900 Jewish women in Unterlüß, sixty kilometers north of Hannover; their job was to dig trenches, build roads and bunkers, and work at the conveyor belt filling cartridges and grenades with corrosive explosives. In Hundsfeld, near Breslau, some 1,000 Jewish women were busy producing condensors, electric instruments, and small parts for V2 rockets. The firm deployed about 5,000 prisoners.

Some 1,300 prisoners from Buchenwald were hired out to the Bayerische-Motoren-Werke (BMW) for its plants in Eisenach and Abteroda. Roughly 1,500 inmates were leased from Natzweiler to their plant in Neunkirchen, and about 3,500 initially were sent from Dachau to Allach (a section of Munich). They were used there for bunker construction and the production of cylinder heads. Toward the end of the war, Allach became a transit station on evacuation marches. The camp, built to accommodate 4,000 prisoners, was at times packed to overflowing, housing 17,000 to 20,000 men and women. At the VW plant in Fallersleben, 1,800 prisoners were deployed in munitions production; at Conti-Gummi in the Stöcken section of Hannover, some 1,000 Jews were reportedly working in tire production before they were handed over to the Kammler staff and set to work building subterranean factory tunnels for Conti in Ahlem.

The aircraft industry was a special focus for deployment. The aviation firm Junkers leased concentration camp prisoners, mainly from Buchenwald. According to camp statistics for March 25, 1945, Junkers leased 5,084 prisoners for eight plants.[24] Heinkel Works used prisoners from the camps Kraków-Plaszow, Sachsenhausen, Ravensbrück, and Mauthausen. In Oranienburg, some 6,000 laborers produced cockpits for the He 177, among other tasks. In Barth, 1,721 women were deployed in the manufacture of aerial torpedoes; in Schwechat, 2,065 Mauthausen prisoners put in a total of 468,206 hours in January 1944 in production of the fighter He 219. When the factory halls were destroyed by Allied bombs, production was relocated into the cellars of the breweries; in the grotto at Hinterbrühl, a production surface of 12,000 square meters was completed in two tunnels. Heinkel had a maximum of 2,737 prisoners available for construction measures and production of the *Volksjäger* fighter He 162.[25] Messerschmitt deployed laborers in its plants in the stone quarries of Flossenbürg and Gusen, as well as in Augsburg, Dachau, Kottern, and Gablingen; these workers totaled more than 3,500 in February 1944. Steyr-Daimler-Puch AG, a firm that produced rifles and machine guns as well as airplane engines, cabins, and frames, was among the best customers of the Mauthausen camp. More than 14,000 prisoners worked for the company at various locations, including subterranean construction projects in Melk, Ebensee, and Gusen.[26]

Work in the weapons industry cannot be equated with civilian skilled labor. A job with a private company was not some sort of protected niche in the system of absolute power. Not all prisoners in the external camps had roofs over their heads. Although there were, as in the main camps, preferentially treated internal Kommandos for the self-maintenance of the camp, units that employed 5 to 10 percent of the total subcamp population, the depleting tasks of construction, transport, and cleanup also had to be taken care of in private companies, just as in the projects run by Organisation Todt and the Kammler staff. At Buna in Auschwitz, labor in the initial years did not involve the chemical industry; it was concentrated on construction. Prisoners hauled sacks of cement, laid railroad track, or pulled heavy freight wagons. A number of the dead were tossed into the ditches dug for cable lines and covered over with concrete.

Even employment in industrial production was no guarantee of survival. As a rule, prisoners worked under wretched conditions. Many jobs involved extremely heavy physical labor with a high risk of accident. Shifts were generally ten to twelve hours, and little time was left for sleep and recreation. Pressured work, mistreatment, and harsh penalties, especially for foreign and Jewish prisoners, were the order of the day. Some civilian supervisors were almost as sedulous as the SS in this regard. The prisoners suffered from hunger and were housed in cramped and filthy blocks that were seldom heated in winter. Medical care was minimal; there was no clothing to protect the prisoners against the damp and the cold. There was the same structure of power and organization in the leased-out subcamps as in the main camps. The advantageous jobs were generally taken by the few German inmates. The material and social situation of the others showed little improvement. External subcamps were nothing but concentration camps on a smaller scale. However, the dying were generally not put to death directly in the camps. Prisoners whose labor power could not be further used were sent back to the main camp, to Auschwitz or, in the final months of the war, to Bergen-Belsen. Work in arms production did not offer a way to survive. Prisoners were worked to death in private companies as well. Private industry was not interested in the life of those deployed. Although it was more concerned about cheap workers than terror, it accepted mass death as unavoidable—part of the bargain if it served to boost production. Thus, the external subcamps were for many only a brief reprieve, a death sentence temporarily postponed.

16

Work Situations

The transport Kommando pushes the wagons loaded down with salt
to the shaft, and brings back the empty cars, or bags of cement,
gravel, or stones. A simple and stupid job, but without any break.
Frenchmen, Greeks, and Russians are all put to work at it, no preference given. You walk all day long, bent over behind the wagon:
one man for an empty wagon, three if it's loaded with stone or salt,
four for concrete. The stooped backs and extended buttocks are
perfect targets for the blows of the civilian master workmen . . . and
the jabs of the sentries with their rifle butts. The strong prisoners
form into a group quickly. The *Muselmänner* always find they have
the same wagons they can barely get rolling. With one initial
glance, the shrewd prisoners can spot the wagons that roll well,
because many of the cars are rusty. . . . We know that they can wear
two men out even when they're empty. The track runs for many
kilometers, and at some points it's too wide, that can always end
up in a catastrophe, especially at the switches. The transport Kommando lives in constant fear of a derailment.[1]

NOT ONLY DOES absolute power permeate social relations; it also saturates the
objective relation to work. It shapes the content and course of activities. Terror
is not a marginal condition of the work situation, but constitutes its very core.
A sociological pathology of prisoner labor must proceed from this fact: in the
concentration camp, work too was terror. Terror determined the structure of
work, transforming it into a lethal situation. Consequently, one of the greatest
privileges was to be freed from work. Prisoners who had recognized the true
meaning of work tried their best to slow the murderous tempo and conserve
their strength. Since labor itself threatened life, it was crucial to save one's
energies. Resistance did not begin with organized sabotage, the production of
defective waste pieces, or the destruction of tools and machines. Even the
slightest attempt to work as little as possible, to husband one's strength, was
an act of refusal and opposition. Prisoner work was a constant labor struggle,
a struggle against the destructive force of work.

Prisoners were deployed at various tasks.[2] They had to level the ground, lay
terraces and streets, build barracks, and haul railway track. Artisans were deployed in the workshops; outside the camp, they drained moors, plowed fields,

dug canals, quarried stone, and excavated tunnels. In the workshops, they mounted parts of airplanes, repaired engines, and filled grenades with powder. Prisoners built factories and ferreted for unexploded bombs in the rubble of houses. An exhaustive descriptive account of all work situations is not adequate to reveal just how human labor was mutated into terror labor. The approach adopted here uses the perspective of work analysis:[3] workload, the structure of tasks, time and objectives, cooperation and monitoring. The intention is to delineate how terror transforms the social structure and task structure of labor into a situation of life and death.

The first feature of much prisoner labor was the systematic overburdening of the worker. Without any chance to regenerate their strength, workers were exposed to a ruinous regimen of physical exploitation that quickly exhausted all energy reserves. Even the strongest among them were reduced after a few short weeks to physical wrecks as a result of the depleting drudgery. The brutal excessive physical demands forced the laborers into a constant and hopeless struggle against themselves, one that completely destroyed the somatic self-relation.[4] When labor can only be performed if coupled with constant torment, the body collapses. It is no longer a tool for action. One's intentional relation toward the world contracts; attentiveness to the needs and dangers of the situation atrophies, and is replaced by the passive condition of suffering. Continued physical harassment annuls the constitutive relation of human self-distance, subjugating a person to the dominance of his body. The consequence is defenseless, emaciated human beings, who drag their bodies wearily through space, as if in slow motion. They can move their limbs, but only with great pain, helpless in their exposure to that one final act of violence that will end it all.

Typical of this form of labor were activities in stone quarries and tunnel construction, in the underground and transport Kommandos. In the stone quarries,[5] prisoners had to smash rocks and boulders with picks, then lug the stone blocks on their shoulders or on wooden frames, moving at double time. They had to shove freight wagons uphill and push wheelbarrows over difficult terrain, spurred on by blows and lashes from the Kapos, most of whom were from the green elite. There were frequent accidents, caused in many instances by the supervisors themselves. Safety precautions were nonexistent. Technical equipment in stone quarrying was minimal. Only gradually were conveyor belts installed, and cranes and power shovels made available. Prisoners on the verge of total exhaustion were usually given especially dangerous work. For example, they had to load heavy slabs of stone on their shoulders, transporting them around until they were finally pressed down and crushed under the enormous weight.

Canal construction and brickworks had the same function elsewhere as the stone quarries in Flossenbürg, Groß-Rosen, Natzweiler, and Gusen. Beginning in 1938, between 1,500 and 2,000 prisoners were deployed in the "brick-works Kommando" in Sachsenhausen. There was only primitive equipment on hand for clearing the land and expanding the harbor facilities: saws, shovels, wheelbarrows. Sacks of cement, bricks and machines always had to be hauled at double time. Work on the brickworks was halted after it was discovered that the planned technique of dry pressing could not be used because the available raw material was unsuitable. The meter-thick concrete foundations were demolished using hammers and chisels; pipelines were torn up and the plant was built anew. The brickworks in Sachsenhausen turned out to be a gigantic blunder, a crackpot venture that cost hundreds of lives.[6] Some 1,200 prisoners were deployed in construction of the brick factory in Neuengamme in 1941. After the extremely modern facility was put into operation, only 170 semiskilled laborers were deployed in brick production; another 250 were in the pits to dig clay and move and unload freight wagons. The most difficult Kommando, at times numbering more than 1,000, was charged with the task of controlling the Dove Elbe River and constructing a branch canal up to the brickworks. Slopes had to be smoothed out, mud shoveled onto carts. If a cart veered off the catwalk, prisoners were beaten mercilessly. There were many cases where exhausted prisoners were simply tossed into the water and drowned.[7]

While the amount of annihilatory labor in stone quarries and brickworks declined during the course of the war, the construction of underground tunnels became more and more important. In Ebensee, prisoners had to excavate tunnels as high as a two-story house into the side of the mountain, and then lay down track and cover the tunnel walls with concrete. In Melk, with prisoners working in three shifts, six tunnels measuring several hundred meters in length were dug out. Except for a few hundred skilled workers who were deployed making ball bearings, most worked as stonecutters, in rubble removal, laying cable, and manufacturing support beams. In Neckarelz,[8] prisoners were deployed as unskilled laborers on the expansion of a plaster pit. Because there were no safety precautions, there was constant danger from falling stones and the inrush of water or mud. Prisoners were never employed as skilled mechanics in aircraft construction, installing airplane engines or single parts for planes. In Porta-Barkhausen,[9] prisoners working on twelve-hour shifts had to expand a multilevel tunnel system for an underground refinery for lubricating oil, a ball-bearing plant, and a factory in which radio tubes were made. Here too, the more-demanding jobs in mining and other areas were handled by civilian skilled workers; prisoners were mainly given the menial jobs of excavating and laying concrete. As a result of excessive physical strain and accidents caused by landslides, the mortality rate soared. Of the fourteen hundred prisoners deployed there in the autumn of 1944, some five hundred to six hundred died.

There were several causes for physical exhaustion: the catastrophically in-adequate rations, long, grueling marches to and from the work site, extended working shifts of ten to twelve hours a day, and the constant, brutal pressure from the supervisors. Above all, however, these tasks were seriously under-mechanized. Prisoner labor has always been work without mechanical equip-ment, primitive manual labor. What it took hundreds to achieve with their bare hands, picks, shovels, or hammers could have been done far more rapidly using compressed air drills, excavators, cranes, winches, conveyor belts, and tractor-trucks. This systematic undermechanization was not due to the irregu-larity of work tasks or variation in the materials—it was rooted in the principle of terror labor itself. Nonskilled menial labor guarantees despotic supervision. The supervisors did not require any specialized knowledge; their arbitrary will was not limited by the specific time frames generated by some technology or device. Their power of surveillance was unrestricted. They were able to beat prisoners, working them like slaves, as whim and wish dictated. Under-mechanization secures the power of disposal over the work process, and is thus in complete accord with the needs of absolute power.

Yet even tasks at a higher level of organization and mechanization did not protect workers from being exploited and depleted. Even in industrial produc-tion, the law of terror labor remained in force. This can be illustrated by two examples. In Salzgitter-Drütte, prisoners were deployed in a mill to manufac-ture shells.[10] A Kommando of 150 men, working in alternating shifts, was given the task of hauling steel blocks to the presses, tooling the machines and then extracting the broken pieces, each about fifty centimeters long, and stack-ing them in equal piles. The Forge Kommando heated the steel blocks, took them from the furnaces to the presses, and then transported the still-glowing blanks to a further site. Work at the furnaces and presses was exceptionally heavy and dangerous menial labor, performed under extreme time pressure. Transport of the material and charging of the furnaces was done manually, without protective clothing. The Kapos passed on the orders from the supervi-sors, peppering their instructions with a hail of blows. The civilian manager also took part in beating the deployees. Despite this, the performance levels reportedly reached 95 percent of the targeted goal. Yet each day had its human toll: the prisoners would have to haul several fellow workers who had died of exhaustion back to the camp.

The level of standardization was higher where material transport was mech-anized and prisoners carried out repetitive component tasks at conveyor belts. This was the case, for example, in the serial installation of cylinder heads in the BMW plant in Allach,[11] the production of machine guns in the Steyr plant in Gusen,[12] in the sewing factory in Ravensbrück or in gas-mask production at the Conti plant in Hannover-Limmer. Some 250 women were deployed there, installing about twelve thousand masks per shift on a piecework basis; they had been provided initial training lasting six weeks.

The conveyor belt moves at a certain speed, which they set in accordance with our dexterity. We respond to every attempt to crank up the tempo by deliberate clumsiness. Which leads to more violence from the "pigs." The upshot's always somewhere in between. Over the nine months, no one was able to bring us up to the targeted tempo. We wanted to impede production. But more than anything else, we wanted to protect our health, since the gas masks were only of minor strategic importance. The women sit all around the conveyor belt. When it's your turn, you lift the iron head, hang it on a hook, perform the required precise hand movement, and then place the mask back on the belt. The next head is already waiting for you. You can't waste any movement, otherwise the head will slip on past before you can get to it. At the end of the conveyor belt, the "pig" is watching. If a head's sent back, that means you're going to be punished. Especially later on toward morning, when your weary arms can hardly lift the iron heads and your open eyes have an empty stare, the masks become greedy gods: they demand human sacrifice. The conveyor belt is insatiable; it constantly feeds us new heads. No sooner is one finished than the next one is there. There are ten, twenty, thirty on the belt, and they move on ahead, slowly, regularly, rigidly. And we have to serve them. For weeks on end, our sleep is haunted by this image.[13]

This job situation shows all the features of repetitive partial tasks. To that extent, it is the precise opposite of unregulated and unmechanized terror labor. Task structure is fragmented; action is reduced to a few quick movements of the hand and body that have to be repeated schematically at the same tempo. Simultaneously, the field of consciousness is restricted to a single theme, blinkered, without any internal or external horizon. The situation contracts to a single theme-horizon; it is monothematic. The tempo of bodily movement is determined by the speed of the belt, but the rapid and even repetition produces a duration in which the individual acts of the worker flow undisturbed, one into the next. Time-consciousness loses its contours and dissolves. Work acts degenerate to permanent activities, to an incessant busyness. However, the objective theme and the temporal monotony are overlaid and molded by social terror.[14] The labor entails a high stress level because of possible punishment, and thus demands supreme concentration. Despite the even and steady repetition, a worker's movements must be constantly observed and self-regulated. A mistake invariably means a beating. It is not the difficulty of the tasks that forces a belt worker to concentrate, but the persistent threat of violence. Thus, the situation is not just monotonous, as is any repetitive partial task—it is a situation of total dominance as well.[15] The danger of terror constricts the field of consciousness to a single thematic core: precise movement in order to avoid violent punishment. Although the work becomes a habit, the situation calls for extreme vigilance. The women had apparently succeeded in preventing any speedup in the tempo of work—most came from the French Resistance and formed a homogeneous resistance group—the mechanized work was subjugated to the regime of brute force. Arbitrary will vitiates the advantages of mechanization. The atomized structure of tasks breaks up action into tiny chunks, but the ever-present terror punctures habitualization incessantly, forcing constant caution and concentration.

Along with physical overexertion and undermechanization, the third feature of terror labor is its pointlessness and endlessness. Even if the factory managements were pursuing economic aims, this does not mean that the individual work situations and partial tasks had any purpose that guided action on the job. To haul the same metal parts or sacks day after day, to dig tunnels one meter after the next into rock, to lay concrete over kilometers of roads or lay railroad track, to dig ditches until one collapses or drag heavy carts—there is simply no end to such activities; they go on interminably. Just as repetitive partial tasks expand the time of action into a monotonous stretch, these task forms destroy the temporal and goal-oriented structure of human labor. This applied in particular to the category of "gigantic tasks":[16] work loomed like a mountain, its end in some distant future. Many of the tasks in construction and cleanup on the grounds of the bombed-out armaments factories, which have been improperly classified as work in "industrial production," were precisely of this type.

But there were gigantic, labor-intensive tasks in the camps from the beginning. They conformed perfectly with the temporal law of the camp system: the principle of the eternal present. In the camps of the Emsland, enormous stretches of moorland were placed under cultivation. Drainage ditches were dug out with blunt spades, and the slabs of turf were then stacked up in long walls. The steam plows that had been available to criminal prisoners before 1933 had been sold off by the SS. Hundreds of concentration camp inmates now took their place; day after day, they marched with shovels and picks into the moor to work on the bog.[17] Work on the large farms likewise had little in common with civilian agricultural and horticultural labor. No matter what the weather, the prisoners had to haul stones, fill in ponds in the swampy land, lay ditches and put down humus—constantly driven on by their brutal supervisors, with no prospects on the horizon for an end to their plight.[18]

Although gigantic tasks can be conceived as having some rationale, however meager, that is quite impossible in the case of the toil of Sisyphus. Such work is interminable. The end of one sequence is always the beginning of new drudgery. Sisyphean tasks are terror labor in pure and unadulterated form, without any productive secondary purpose. Their sole aim was to harass and deplete the prisoners. For the supervisors, it was a welcome occasion for violence; for the victims, an endless torment, a vivid demonstration that all their efforts were totally worthless, devoid of meaning. There were hardly any limits to inventiveness here.[19] In Dachau, prisoners were forced to push a cart with rubber wheels, the notorious "Moor Express," loaded with heavy stones, back and forth through the deep morass. In other camps, prisoners had to construct stone walls, layer by layer, pull them down the next day, and then rebuild them the following day. Prisoners were forced to haul heavy railway tracks back and

forth at double time, dig trenches and then fill them in again, or shovel mountains of sand from one spot to another. Sisyphean tasks destroy the purposeful
structure of human labor. The effort had no meaning outside itself. Basically,
it made no difference whatsoever whether the prisoners worked, or were assigned to stand rigidly for hours in a *Stehkommando*.[20]

Absolute power tries its utmost to prevent the formation of ties that elude
control, and to retain human beings within the straitjacket of a serially structured mass order. This technique of power also impacted on the cooperative
structure of numerous work situations. Cooperation itself is a force of production. By orienting their activities to shared goals and pooling abilities and
skills, workers conserve time and energy and enhance the effect of their labor.
Yet the camp regime had little interest in that. Not only did it waste the labor
power of the individual, it also squandered the potential of collective cooperation. In many Kommandos, there was a strict prohibition on talking. Most
unskilled tasks had a low degree of functional differentiation or objective need
for coordination. Stable work roles with interdependent links were the exception. Work was generally organized along the lines of serial individual labor,
at best coupled with cooperation on a set task as a labor brigade (*Kolonne*).
This segmentary division of labor proved extremely disadvantageous for the
prisoners in tunnel, moor, or construction Kommandos. Workers who swung
their shovels a bit more slowly than their peers immediately attracted the attention of the supervisors, and were beaten mercilessly. Prisoners who were faster
than the others wielding their spades animated the supervisors to put more
pressure on everyone else. For that reason, the members of a brigade had to
find an even tempo that all could maintain, even the weakest among them. Of
course, this tacit understanding was only possible if the group preserved a high
level of solidarity. Yet even when this secret cooperation proved successful,
the sentries repeatedly intervened, using violence to disrupt the work cycle.[21]
Absolute power does not create cooperation, it destroys it.

Where transport tasks could only be handled by a combined effort of the
brawn and muscle of many, the prisoners were forcibly gathered together and
pressed into mechanical collective bodies. Tree trunks, wood planks, and iron
girders could be transported only in *Kolonnen*. It was absolutely crucial here
that no one stumbled or collapsed under the burden. Because of the danger of
accident and injury, everyone depended on the worker by his or her side:
weakness or faltering could spell a possible mishap.[22] Laborers were also used
as beasts of burden—human draft animals. In Dachau, prisoners on the road-
construction gang were forced to pull a steamroller. In Sachsenburg, and then
in Buchenwald, Sachsenhausen, and Auschwitz as well, fifteen to twenty men,
generally Jews, were hitched to a heavily laden wagon, ordered to sing, and
then driven by whiplash at a gallop. The SS coined the expression "singing
horses" for this spectacle.[23] Even cooperation was transformed into a means of
harassment and humiliation. Carters and slaveholders are also accustomed to

beating their draft animals. But only the accessories of the camp regime came up with the idea of sitting majestically in a wagon, pulled by coerced coolies to the crack of a whip through the camp streets.

While they were working, the prisoners were under multiple supervision. The SS sentries secured the camp enclosure, escorted the marching work brigades, and surrounded the work sites to prevent escape. These surveillance duties did exclude the possibility of driving the prisoners ever harder, or using excessive violence. Officially, however, their job was restricted to guard duty, waiting hour after hour for some incident to occur.[24] Only the SS Kommando leaders could intervene in the work process. They had nearly unlimited power over their Kommando, but in the case of larger groups of prisoners, were not always able to be present. Frequently they could do little more than conduct spot checks. In order to close this chink in their power, they reacted by using terror to teach the prisoners a lesson. The brutality of many Kommando leaders was the result of a basic law of random checks: if permanent surveillance is impossible, reckless violence, applied randomly, creates a climate of constant intimidation.

But the true lords and masters of the Kommandos were the Kapos. They were always on hand. The organization of work in the concentration camp would have been inconceivable without the Kapos. They kept the work sites under surveillance, distributed work tasks, and were responsible for their groups being complete. Although dependent on the favor of the SS, they enjoyed considerable latitude. They were authorized to report prisoner infractions and "saboteurs," and could use gratuitous, arbitrary violence. They were to blame for a great deal of excessive drudgery and a great many of the killings. Unlike the SS sentries, the Kapos had a definite interest in output. If their Kommandos showed no visible results, they were threatened with the possibility of replacement, and later with the vengeance of their fellow prisoners. Where there was a piecework or bonus system,[25] they received special premiums if their Kommandos fulfilled the required quota. This heightened the annihilatory pressure on the weak and ill. For a bonus of four to six RM, more-productive workers were able to purchase various goods in the canteens, and thus better maintain their labor power. The weaker inmates, unable to keep up with the pace, received no bonus, declining all the more rapidly as a result—a vicious circle. The Kapos were interested in high-output workers, and thus pushed the others out of their Kommandos.

Many Kapos used violence to secure their primary source of power based on functional indispensability. Although they were interested in order and performance, their discipline always had to have gaps; it could never be total. In order for inspectors to be considered indispensable, there had to be repeated infractions and deviations that they must penalize. The Kapos justified their own role by forcing prisoners to perform at high levels, demonstrating at the same time that such levels of performance would never have been achieved without them. It was disorder, not order, that legitimated the Kapos. Consequently, their violence always had a double function: it drove prisoners to work harder, while at the same time generating the requisite amount of disorder needed to justify renewed force. By destroying labor, terror itself created the occasions for further terror.

The fourth category of surveillance personnel was made up of the civilian workers and supervisors from the private firms. Their behavior toward the prisoners varied, depending on their political convictions and possible national or racist prejudices. The spectrum ranged from immediate human sympathy to indifference and hostile reserve, informing on and denouncing prisoners, and even active violence. German supervisors, master workers, pit bosses, or managers who were favorably disposed toward the Nazi regime often treated foreign and Jewish prisoners with the same contempt and brutality as did the SS.[26] Conscripted civilian workers who were opposed to the regime sometimes forged contacts with German political prisoners. Polish and Russian foreign workers were closer to the prisoners, especially their fellow Poles and Russians, than to the German civilian laborers. However, direct contacts demanded great caution and secrecy. In many private companies as well, there was a strict ban on talking. Like the prisoners, civilians had to fear possible punishment if they were caught passing food secretly to a prisoner, smuggling out letters and news, or even just stashing cigarette butts in a secret cache. Prisoners could expect flogging; civilians had to face penalties for "aiding and abetting prisoners." For that reason, the orders of civilian superiors generally were passed down indirectly via the Kapos. Formal charges and denunciations were channeled through the Kapos to the SS. Although communication would have improved the cooperation and effectiveness of labor, the system of power was bent on preventing social mingling and endeavored to keep prisoners separate on the job.

When work is tantamount to a life-and-death struggle, resistance surfaces early on, at the point where tasks are distributed. Prisoners wanted to land jobs where they had a roof over their heads and a stove in the corner, where they could get hold of extra food or other items for exchange, and could elude the ever-present panopticon of surveillance. The so-called inside Kommandos were among the most choice, sought-after places to work: the kitchen, storerooms, offices, and workshops. However, these jobs were generally occupied by prisoners who had good connections with the *Schreibstube* and could prove they had (or could feign) special skills. On an external Kommando, out in the open, there were few chances to avoid physical depletion, aside from the post as Kapo. Nonetheless, a fair number of inmates succeeded in presenting themselves as indispensable, though without having to work very much.[27] In any case, the conventional wisdom for all types of labor was: do not work with your hands, work with your eyes. Surveillance was mutual. Just as the supervisors monitored the prisoners, the prisoners kept an eagle eye on the supervisors. As soon as they were busy somewhere else, the inmates cut their movements down to a bare minimum. If you were being observed from a safe distance, you simulated being eager and busy; you shoveled with gusto, but filled the shovel only one-fourth full. For the great majority of prisoners who had no chance of being shifted to an inside Kommando, deliberately "putting on the brakes," going slowly, and interrupting work were the only options for conserving their energies.

Spontaneous and organized forms of disguised labor struggle must be distinguished from such individual acts of resistance. They required maximum cover, absolute reliability, technical ingenuity, and an orientation beyond the immediate situation. Sabotage was aimed not at husbanding physical energies but at harming the adversary, whether for reasons of personal revenge or for military or political motives. Consequently, it was largely limited to the core groups of the political and national resistance.[28] Along with the communist opposition, many Russian, French, and Polish prisoners played a prominent role. Organized and spontaneous sabotage frequently meshed. The direct destruction of machines or the turning out of defective, unusable pieces were possible only at considerable risk. Sabotage demanded subtle methods in order to disguise the origin of the fault. In the camp, the first point for sabotage was where materials were distributed and data processed. In Dachau, the card catalog of prisoners' qualifications was manipulated by the labor-statistics office so that skilled specialists were not transferred to armaments plants—instead, the companies were given workers they first had to train. On the other hand, politically reliable skilled laborers were channeled into key positions in order to organize sabotage directly on the spot. At the Gustloff factory in Buchenwald, prisoners succeeded in systematically reducing the production of carbine barrels over a period of months, while at the same time wearing out enormous numbers of special tools. In Natzweiler, during the disassembly of damaged airplane engines, prisoners also damaged the parts that were still intact. At the Heinkel Works, young Russian prisoners from Sachsenhausen regularly removed valves that were extremely difficult to replace. In rocket assembly at Dora-Mittelbau,[29] prisoners diverted materials being transported, disposed of small parts on the sly, rendered tools unusable, and welded seams in violation of all technical specifications. The success of such acts of sabotage rose in direct proportion to the extent the SS itself was involved in monitoring production. It had too few officers to pinpoint the causes for the fault. On the other hand, turning out defective pieces demanded a high level of technical knowledge on the part of the prisoners, lest these faults be discovered during production or final monitoring, and the workplace responsible be identified.

In a system of terror labor, the effects of sabotage are mixed. Sabotage could do little to counter the depletion of physical strength and violence, or squandering of human labor and the resources of cooperation. It exploited isolated chinks in the system of power, though it was unable seriously to endanger that system. The courage and ingenuity it required were considerable. The saboteurs were always risking a possible death sentence if caught. Yet sabotage did not lessen terror. On the contrary: it intensified terror by providing it with new opportunities. It is true that successful acts of sabotage gave prisoners a feeling they could still act, still do something against the dominant power. Yet its concrete damaging effect was less important than its symbolic meaning. Sabotage served as a shield against demoralization, providing tiny, often hidden victories over powerlessness. But it was unable to rupture the iron law of terror labor—the inversion of production into destruction. Labor in the concentration camp was lethal, a means of annihilation.

Part V

VIOLENCE AND DEATH

17

The *Muselmann*

Their life is short, but their number is endless; they,
the *Muselmänner*, the drowned, form the backbone of
the camp, an anonymous mass, continually renewed
and always identical, of non-men who march and
labor in silence, the divine spark dead within them,
already too empty to really suffer. One hesitates to
call them living: one hesitates to call their death
death, in the face of which they have no fear, as
they are too tired to understand.[1]

THE *Muselmänner* are persons destroyed, devastated, shattered wrecks strung between life and death. They are the victims of a stepwise annihilation of human beings. Before absolute power kills using immediate physical violence, it pursues a policy of deliberate misery, the transmogrification of the *conditio humana*. The mere external appearance of the *Muselmänner* bespoke profound dehumanization. In a final stage of emaciation, their skeletons were enveloped by flaccid, parchmentlike sheaths of skin, edema had formed on their feet and thighs, their posterior muscles had collapsed. Their skulls seemed elongated; their noses dripped constantly, mucus running down their chins. Their eyeballs had sunk deep into their sockets; their gaze was glazed. Their limbs moved slowly, hesitantly, almost mechanically. They exuded a penetrating, acrid odor; sweat, urine, liquid feces trickled down their legs. The rags that covered their freezing frames were full of lice; their skin was covered with scabies. Most suffered from diarrhea. They ate anything they could lay their hands on—moldy bread, cheese wriggling with worms, raw bits of turnip, garbage fished from the bins.

Their increasing emaciation eradicated the dividing line between life and death. It was no accident that the *Muselmänner* were reminiscent of the "living dead."[2] They were only shadows of their former selves. Their actions had sunk below the animal minimum for survival. They hardly heard or saw anything, and reacted only when shouted at or prodded. When action is extinguished, life implodes, contracting to mere existence. In action, people mark a beginning to some sequence, show who they are, express themselves, communicate to and with others.[3] Action is the medium of identity and sociality. A person robbed of action is a nonentity, a no one. The *Muselmann* embodies the anthropological meaning of absolute power in an especially radical form. Power abrogates itself in the act of killing. The death of the other puts an end to the social relationship. But by starving the other, it gains time. It erects a third realm, a limbo between life and death. Like the pile of corpses, the *Muselmänner* document the total triumph of power over the human being. Although still nominally alive, they are nameless hulks. In the configuration of their infirmity, as in organized mass murder, the regime realizes its quintessential self. The *Muselmann* is the central figure in the tableau of mass dying—a death by hunger, murder of the soul, abandonment; dead while still living.[4]

We cannot know what really took place in the consciousness of the *Muselmänner*. The reports of prisoner doctors describe their physical decline and changes in behavior. Their psychological and mental condition has been interpreted as a loss of the will to live, an enigmatic apathy and surrender to fate.[5] Psychopathology talks about "affective anesthesia," an "annihilation," a radical destruction of the meaning of life.[6] In terms of clinical diagnostics, the *Muselmann* syndrome should not be confused with symptoms of radical starvation or with the trancelike state of shock often encountered in the wake of natural disasters.[7] To compare their condition to some mode of resignation akin to that which can seize the dying after one last final rebellion is totally mistaken, and downplays its severity. In fact, the fate of the *Muselmann* bears nothing in common with what is commonly termed "dying." The *Muselmann* perished in misery because he or she could not go on any more.

It is debatable whether the *Muselmann* can be properly grasped using established nosological categories. Although hunger is the basis for numerous diseases, misery is not an illness. Nor is the extinction of the field of consciousness, nor social isolation, nor persecution. These facts characterize a material and social situation of absolute helplessness lying beyond what can be labeled "absolute deprivation" or "loss of milieu."[8] It is an object not for psychology, but rather for a social anthropology of misery. The mental and psychological changes to which the *Muselmann* was subject were closely linked with physical emaciation and the destruction of social relations. Immiseration implies a simultaneous destruction of the social sphere, the *vita activa* and *vita mentalis*.

Every prisoner encountered hunger almost immediately, in the first few days after admission to the camp. Those who regularly received packages or got into a Kommando where there was an opportunity to lay their hands on extra clothing or food had a chance of escaping the fate of the *Muselmann*. But without "organizing" supplementary supplies, the situation was hopeless. Official camp rations were pegged at a level so low that death by starvation had to occur sooner or later; it was preprogrammed. In the beginning, prisoners were still actively engaged in a search for food and involved in black-market transactions. If a prisoner had nothing more, he or she looked around at the work site for something edible: roots, grass, acorns, scraps of garbage. In the evening, small groups would linger near the camp kitchen; they invented a variety of tricks to get themselves a second portion. Some robbed their fellow prisoners in the barracks, and were robbed in turn. The loot was stashed in a bag somewhere, hidden under a straw mattress, or gulped down immediately if there was no safe hiding place.

A prisoner who had nothing but the camp rations deteriorated drastically after only a few weeks. Chronic hunger led to a general physical debility.[9] The body accommodated to the environment by consuming itself. Muscles atrophied; vital functions sank to a minimum. The pulse slowed; blood pressure and temperature dropped; the body shuddered with cold, even under several blankets or next to the stove, the favorite spot of the *Muselmänner*. Breathing slowed; the voice grew weak; every movement took enormous effort. If a person was afflicted by the ravages of diarrhea due to starvation, deterioration was accelerated. Wherever they could, the *Muselmänner* retired to the latrine, dragging themselves constantly back and forth between the infirmary and the barracks toilets. Many remained lying in their own excrement in the bunk, or slouched feebly in some corner, waiting. Action lost its somatic prerequisites: physical strength and bodily mobility. Gestures became nervous and uncoordinated. When they sat, their torsos rocked back and forth. Although their skin no longer could feel, the *Muselmänner* scratched under their shoulders involuntarily, performing mechanical movements without purpose. They could no longer lift their legs to walk, and slowly shoved their feet forward. In the end, they had to use their hands to place one foot in front of the next, manually. They were no longer the masters of their own bodies. The soma collapsed into its component parts. The unity of bodily existence was dissolved.

Hand in hand with somatic disintegration, there was a radical decline in mental activities and affect. The *Muselmänner* withdrew increasingly from the world. They lost their memory and the ability to concentrate. Memories faded and disappeared: many no longer even knew their own names. Expectations about the future flickered and dimmed; the temporal horizon of the field of consciousness narrowed to a monothematic fixed point: food, nourishment. In the beginning, the *Muselmänner* still combed the surroundings for something edible. Hunger-spawned fantasies and visions of sumptuous feasts drowned out the gnawing pain of starvation. But then the horizon of perception also contracted and was sealed off; attentiveness numbed; the senses were blunted. They no longer felt the hot sun beating down on their heads, and were blind to the dangers lurking ahead. They only could see what was held up directly in front of them; they only could hear when shouted at. They reacted without resistance to blows and lashes, as though these were not meant for them. Stimulus defense and mechanisms to ward off anxiety led ultimately to total numbness and indifference toward the world and themselves. They lived neither in the society of the others, nor with and by themselves. They were abandoned by their fellows, and abandoned by themselves. Eccentric positionality—that self-distance from which a person can observe himself or herself at a remove—had been deleted. They now lost the present, as they had lost the past and future. Feelings froze and stultified. Their spirits and minds emptied, sclerosed to a inward wasteland. Just as gestures and actions forfeited their intentional goal-directedness, intentionality of consciousness withered. Mental agony reached staggering proportions. The intellect dimmed, and along with the disappearance of intentional acts, the content of consciousness vanished. Conciousness was no longer awareness of something, point-focused. The prisoners were powerless to act, to think, to feel. In order to salvage the hulk of the body, the psyche self-destructed. In the final stage of decline, the prisoners no longer felt hunger, no longer perceived pain. They refused to eat and were unable to speak. Anxiety and excitation reached a final state of crystallization beyond tension; all defense mechanisms had collapsed, and the prisoners were in a condition of total apathy and subjugation.

Veteran prisoners could tell after a few days whether new arrivals had a chance for survival. Death appeared like a stigma inscribed on their bodies. They became negligent about cleanliness, went to sleep in their clothes despite the prohibition, relieved themselves where they stood. They avoided any exertion, dragged themselves to and fro, and came repeatedly to the attention of the others. Fellow prisoners had to haul them to the roll calls and prop them up against the barracks wall. Occasionally, the pointed admonition of an attentive fellow prisoner was enough to encourage them to greater physical self-discipline. Although there was little soap and washing facilities were limited, the effort to maintain cleanliness was not just a dictate of hygiene. It was a precept of self-respect. Erect posture, an upright gait, clothing worn in accordance with the camp code—these were not only concessions to the required discipline; they were also measures against external and inward dereliction. These were necessary last residues of civilization needed for sheer survival.

The *Muselmänner* repeatedly violated this self-discipline. They stood in the way everywhere; because they were weakened, they were unable to work as well as the others, and the Kapos punished them brutally for this. They developed edema and boils; they were filthy, stinking, oblivious of what was happening to and with them. They were totally superfluous for the camp's everyday routine. They were shoved aside, shouted at, beaten, flogged, derided, and mocked. They called forth feelings of disgust and self-defense; they provoked irritation and anger. At first, they were shooed away like unwanted stray dogs; later, they were no longer noticed. Thus, they sank to the lowest rung of the social hierarchy. They vegetated at the periphery of camp society, isolated by their torpor and the indifference of the others. They gave up on themselves, and the others gave up on them too. The indifference of the others was in keeping with the apathy of the *Muselmänner*. Their bodies expired, their spirits perished, and simultaneously they died a death that was social.[10]

The fate of the *Muselmänner* was a social concern. They were subject to a process of dissociation in which their fellow prisoners also played a part. As they increasingly withdrew from the world, the others turned away from them, withdrew their interest in them, persecuted and isolated them. There were occasions when a few *Muselmänner* would congregate, rubbing their backs and shoulders one against the other in order to snatch a bit of warmth. The only topic they shared was their hunger: the number of pieces of potato in the soup, the hope for second helpings, the daydream of the grand feast. If a favorable opportunity arose and they still had a sliver of strength left, a number of them might pounce on someone carrying a pot of food. But most of the time, they squatted side by side in silence, seeking a physical nearness that supplanted language, a mute animal togetherness. Those who could still work were gathered into special Kommandos. After the morning roll call, the block leaders and Kapos rounded up everyone they had picked up by chance out on the camp grounds. The *Muselmänner* marched out as the last Kommando, holding hands, in rows of five. At the timberyard in Auschwitz, one of the most notorious Kommando assignments for *Muselmänner*, they had to unload wagons and haul boards. In Neuengamme, they were forced to crawl on the ground and pull out tufts of grass with their bare hands. In other camps, they worked in stone quarries or subterranean shafts; they dragged dump cars and shouldered heavy loads until they collapsed under the strain. Although physically at the point of exhaustion, they were deployed on the heaviest types of work. In the evening, their Kommando was the last to return to camp, usually with dozens of dead in tow.

Most *Muselmänner* came from the underclasses of the outlawed and superfluous who were locked out of the camp distribution system. The majority were Jews, Russians, and Poles—the camp pariahs. As a result of their physical decline, they sank even below the lowest rung of the system of social classes. The *Muselmänner* became the butt of crude jokes, humiliation and cruelty. Their lethargy was frequently mistaken for laziness, or a form of passive resistance against the orders of the supervisors and prisoner functionaries. Since they repeatedly violated the rules of order and cleanliness, they were singled out as scapegoats. If one had holed up in some corner of the barracks, the others had to stand and wait at the roll-call assembly until the *Muselmann* was found. In the barracks, they dirtied the halls, bunks, and blankets. At meal distribution, they tried to push their way to the front, were shoved aside, and had to look on as the others ate. They relieved themselves in soup bowls; they begged and stole. They did not care about punishments. Thus, many prisoner-functionaries declared war on them. They chased the *Muselmänner* into the latrine or washroom and made them sleep there. *Muselmänner* were a nuisance, superfluous; their movements were grotesque in their mechanical helplessness. If they were shouted at, they were momentarily startled, and did nothing. Punched in the face, they did not react. They were kicked but they felt no pain. They were whipped and beaten, yet in vain. Their apathy was provocative; it stirred the rage of their tormentors. The excess of violence was vented specifically against the *Muselmänner*. Orders accomplished nothing. Even violence fell flat; it was ineffective. The passivity of the *Muselmann* was an insult to power.[11]

In the end, contempt changed to indifference. Those who no longer can respect themselves forfeit the attention of others. And those who spark no interest in others soon lose interest in themselves. The *Muselmänner* were left to their own devices. Abandoned, they wandered aimlessly about the camp, finally slipping into a daze in some corner. As action was extinguished, social action also withered, and with it their orientation to the norms of camp society or toward other individuals. The indifference was mututal. The *Muselmänner* were surrounded by a wall of social isolation. What were the reasons for this defensive indifference and heartless lack of interest? It was more than just disgust for these filthy persons, or anger over their disorderly ways, rage toward those who had abandoned any semblance of self-assertion. Indifference makes one deaf to one's own anxiety. It forms a thick armor against the perception of one's own powerlessness. The *Muselmänner* embodied an irretrievable hopelessness that affected one and all. They were mirrors of the misery in which others had to recognize their own reflected image. One's own death was constantly present in cameo form in the *Muselmänner*. What befell the *Muselmann* could happen to each and every prisoner. They anticipated the future of the others. Because they were prisoners themselves, the prisoners avoided them; because they were too close to the prisoners, the prisoners banished them from their sight. Because they demonstrated to the prisoners their helplessness, the prisoners failed to assist them. The prisoners wrote them off—in order not to have to write themselves off. To watch the *Muselmann* die was to preview one's own dying, a dying that was more frightening than death.

The *Muselmänner* confuted the collective conceptions of death in civil society. They died anonymous, nameless deaths. Their fate was a mass fate. But where death occurs en masse, the end of a single individual is not noticed. Death is no longer the *principium individuationis*, the final criterion of individuality.[12] Death was not an exceptional event in the camp—one for which camp society required rituals of transition and replacement in order to cope. The death of an individual did not jolt the structure of the group; it did not threaten any social unit. Because the society of the camp was serial, individual death made no hole; it left no gap. In the series, every person is one too many. His or her place is taken immediately by someone else. On the other hand, mass death threatens society as a whole. Individual death leaves the existence of the collective unaffected. By contrast, dying in massive numbers involves a fundamental disorientation. The death of an individual can be understood; if need be its causes can be accepted. But mass death shatters the concept of the peaceful continued existence of society, the idealization of an immortal society. If any person can be struck down, survival becomes provisional. Camp society existed only on call, until further notice. As a result of mass death, camp society was divided into a dyad, a double mass:[13] on one side, the burgeoning mass of the dead; on the other, the mass of those still alive, from whose midst sprouted the mountain of the dead. It was not just that the regime prohibited all customary rituals of mourning, making them a punishable offense. Mass death could not have been comprehended or coped with by such practices in any case. A society threatened by annihilation was no longer able to cut loose from the dead. All it could do was to try to ignore the dying and erect a wall of social indifference.

The difference between the living and the dead was negligible. Where the demarcation line between life and death has been eradicated, death is no longer an event, a negation of life, a cleft between two states. The expressions "the living dead" and "the tottering corpses" should be taken literally. They designate a specific modality of time. The *Muselmänner* embodied a creeping death, a sequence and transition, not a point in time. Although still among the living, they were already dead. Although they were corpses, they still moved. No taboo could liberate society from the ambivalence of this threshold state. Instead, it resorted to the mechanisms of social death: reduction in social class, persecution, ignoring. It tried to draw a new line of separation. By treating the semidead as irksome individuals, banning them from social intercourse, it anticipated their final end. In this way, the physical death of the *Muselmann* was hardly noticed. A large number met their death on the march or at work, under the truncheon of a Kapo, from the blow from an SS rifle butt, or simply from total, lethal exhaustion. Many who still showed signs of life were locked up by the SS in segregated blocks for the infirm, and then murdered by injection, cold showers, or gas. Others died suddenly, while still chewing a hunk of bread. They dropped dead everywhere: at roll call, in the latrine, in some corner, at night on their pallets, without their bunkmates even noticing. In the morning, the others climbed indifferently over the pile of bodies that the hut assistants had dragged out in front of the barracks for removal.

18

Epidemics

Lice were everywhere, even on the crust of bread we
ate. Our gray horse blankets were totally infested. If
you looked closely, you could see that the blankets
were absolutely crawling with them. Whoever felt
very cold didn't care much about the lice. Whoever
was freezing because he was dead was abandoned by
the lice. The krauts hated epidemics. They set up a
quarantine barracks and never showed their face
there. Jewish doctors and their assistants took care of
the patients. I succeeded for a time in keeping away
from the barracks. It had become the vestibule to the
mass grave beyond the hill above the camp, the daily
destination of the corpse-bearers.[1]

MANY OF THE overcrowded concentration camps were ravaged by epidemics
during the war. Camp society was a society of the sick. Along with edemas
from hunger and pneumonia, there were epidemics of scabies and deadly infectious diseases.[2] In the winter of 1941–42 in Dachau, some 250 prisoners
suffering from scabies were isolated in a quarantine block; their rations were
reduced and they were left standing naked in front of the showers. Many contracted pneumonia and died. At the end of 1942, an epidemic of typhus and
typhoid fever broke out. The camp doctor placed the camp under quarantine
for two months; of 1,400 who came down with the disease, 526 died. At the
end of November 1944, when Dachau was already serving as a reception camp
for evacuation transports, another typhus epidemic erupted; it took thousands
of lives over the following months. The first dysentery epidemic in Flossenbürg, shortly after Christmas 1939, caught the camp leadership by surprise,
totally unprepared. Since the camp was still in the stage of construction, there
were no barracks for the sick and no medical care. Work in the stone quarry
was suspended for a month, the whole camp was closed and sealed off, and the
prisoners were left to fend for themselves. In the winter 1941–42, 208 Soviet
POWs died of typhus in a special camp. When an epidemic also broke out in
the main camp in the autumn of 1944, two quarantine blocks were fenced in by
barbed wire. During the winter, as many as 50 prisoners a day died in these
blocks, nicknamed "Chinatown" in camp jargon.

Soviet POWs were also incarcerated in a separate camp in Neuengamme in October 1941, where 477 died of typhus. When the epidemic spread to the main camp, all external work operations were suspended and the camp was declared a "no-go" area. The SS no longer entered the camp. Mortality rates rose rapidly. In February 1942, the Hamburg health authorities placed the SS residential area under quarantine as well, because an SS guard had also come down with the disease. This led to an improvement in the supply of medicines, and the ban on entering the camp was lifted. More than 1,000 people died from the epidemic there. Because of a dysentery epidemic, a special sick bay was set up in Mauthausen in September 1939; during the two following years, prisoners sick with dysentery were gathered together in a room of Block 20. The only beds were for personnel. Some of the sick lay on the barracks floor; initially, it was covered with a thin layer of straw, and later with paper sacks filled with straw and smeared with pus, blood, and excrement. From July to September 1941, during a typhus quarantine in Groß-Rosen and Auschwitz, the sick were regularly killed by injection directly into the heart.

In Majdanek, a typhoid fever epidemic raged almost constantly for the entire duration of the camp's existence. At the end of November 1941, half of the 1,500 Soviet prisoners of war there were ill or convalescent. Whoever was suspected of having typhus was hanged or shot. In June 1942, the SS selected two hundred of the sick from a transport of Czech Jews and shot them in a nearby wooded area. At the beginning of 1943, the epidemic spread to the entire camp. The SS set up a quarantine barracks in every section, letting the sick die there. Only after forty SS personnel had also come down with the disease did they ask the WVHA for disinfection and washing facilities for the sick-bay buildings. At the end of October 1943, the epidemic reached its culmination in section 3, where Jews from Warsaw and Bialystok were housed, along with sick prisoners transferred from Buchenwald, Dachau, and Sachsenhausen. Three infirmary barracks were built, the section was declared a "no-go" area and closed for a month, and the barracks were disinfected after hundreds had died. In addition, tuberculosis was widespread. It probably claimed a similar number of victims, especially from the end of 1943 on, after many prisoners sick with tuberculosis were transferred to Majdanek to die there.

In Auschwitz, paratyphoid fever, malaria, and diphtheria appeared in waves; dysentery and tuberculosis were chronic. Typhus was brought in with prisoners from the Lublin jail in April 1941, and could not be checked until the end of 1943 after disinfection tanks had been set up in all the camps. Over the years, more than 10,000 prisoners probably contracted typhus in the main camps. The epidemic in Birkenau in 1942 took a dramatic course. The first cases were reported in March; by July, the epidemic had spread to the entire camp. Hundreds a day were dying during the summer months, and in the infirmary, SS doctors regularly carried out selections of dozens of sick prisoners, sending them to the gas chamber. On August 29, 1942, more than 700 sick prisoners were selected in the isolation blocks—not just acute cases, but also patients who were recovering from the disease. From August to October, work in the Buna plant in Monowitz had to be interrupted. The camp leadership finally took belated countermeasures after construction work had been delayed and numerous SS personnel had also come down with the disease. In the Gypsy camp, the first cases of typhus were discovered in May 1943. On May 25, 1,033 prisoners either sick or suspected of being infected were taken from the camp and gassed. A delousing was then carried out. By autumn, the epidemic had subsided, since almost all the inmates had in the meantime contracted the disease. At the same time, it reached a climax in the women's camp. Despite disinfection measures, it was impossible to limit the spread of lice. As elsewhere, special death blocks were also set up in Auschwitz: Block 20 in the main camp, Block 25 in the women's camp, and Block 7 in the men's camp in Birkenau. Those sick with typhus were concentrated here, and selections were carried out regularly. These blocks were nothing but "waiting rooms for the gas chamber."

This brief overview indicates that the development of epidemics cannot adequately be explained by deterioration in general conditions as a result of the war. The epidemics had their own time and context. Their course depended on the pressure of annihilation to which specific groups were subjected, the policy of labor deployment, and measures taken (and not taken) by camp management. After the catastrophic period in 1941–42, the situation improved until early 1944. When the concentration camp system started to disband, typhoid fever and typhus raged once again in the overcrowded camps during the final phase of the war. In general, an infectious disease can only develop into an epidemic under specific material and social conditions: there must be a large number of persons who can be infected, and an ecological soil for causative agents and carriers. The danger of epidemics always mounts with increasing density and mobility of population. The more crowded the camps became because of mass transports, the greater was the density of contact, and the worse the concomitant hygienic conditions. The mobility in the concentration camp system, the constant admissions and transfers, transported not only people from camp to camp but their diseases as well. They injected the causative bacilli into the system, linking the individual camps into a chain of infection. The prisoners were susceptible in any case. Chronic malnutrition and a lack of vitamins had reduced their resistance to infection, and physical strains and extreme psychological stress had radically heightened their disposition to illness.

Material conditions also provided fertile soil for epidemics: inadequate water supply, a lack of latrines and sewerage, drinking water contaminated by sewage. Contaminated wells and food, dirty and overcrowded mass housing facilities—all these promoted infection by dysentery and typhoid fever bacilli. In the densely packed conglomerations of people, infection by airborne tubercle bacilli was virtually unavoidable. The filthy underclothing, rags, and blankets that were changed or washed very infrequently formed an ideal breeding ground for the clothing louse, the transmitter of typhus. The condition of the infirmary and the quarantine barracks was such that it precluded effective therapy of any kind. The infection barracks were nothing but centers for the spread of an epidemic.

What occurs in a society when an epidemic breaks out? A cursory look at the historical record indicates just how closely the sociology of epidemics is bound up with the sociology of power.[3] History knows two typical strategies in social hygiene to combat epidemics: exclusion of the infected from society, and inclusion of society in a closed space. After having been reported to the authorities, the lepers of the Middle Ages in Europe were ostracized from the community by a religious or secular court, and banned to institutions located beyond the walls of the city. In the leprosariums, they then eked out a life of deprivation until their deaths. Sometimes lepers were permitted to stay at home; some founded a villagelike community in the countryside and engaged there in agriculture. In periods of collective mass hysteria, they were persecuted as scapegoats. Their houses were stormed; the sick were massacred. However, leprosy never reached the epidemic proportions of the plague, smallpox, or cholera. Its incubation period is more than two years. Leprosy is an epidemic that affects the individual, not the masses. Explosive epidemics took a quite different social course. They often started as a rumor, and the authorities concealed the danger in order to avoid a panic. The wealthy fled from town early on. If the pestilence took on alarming and uncertain proportions, rigorous measures were instituted. The city gates were sealed, residential quarters were divided into sections, and the residents, whether sick or healthy, were confined to their houses. Soldiers patrolled the streets, and officials kept a daily record of who was still alive. Social monitoring was total. Any absence from one's assigned place was punished severely. After one week, work commenced on purging the neighborhoods, house by house, street by street. Contaminated objects were burned; rooms were sprayed with aromatic substances. Total surveillance was the prerequisite for total disinfection.

Elements of both power strategies can be found in the concentration camp. This does not mean that historical models were simply repeated. The camp regime was interested less in stemming epidemics than in the destruction of the inmates. So long as prisoners were not needed as laborers, their deaths meant nothing, and were even desirable. They were considered to be the "dregs of humanity," "bearers of racially alien blood," "sick with hereditary diseases," "persons alien to the folk community," "pests" from whom the "healthy folk body" supposedly had to be protected.[4] The ideological model of the politically and racially pure community itself used categories of "health" and social "contamination" borrowed from medical metaphor. To that extent, the institution of the concentration camp resembles a social leprosarium, exaggerated to a murderous level, where all who had been excluded from the *Volksgemeinschaft* were isolated and then murdered. The fact that persons perished from disease was nothing but "natural selection" in the eyes of the SS, "political hygiene."[5]

Moreover, epidemics confirm absolute power in a quite unusual manner. Before its eyes, it transforms the infected into a dead mass. As long as its associates are not infected, absolute power is a witness to the grand spectacle of dying. It looks idly on and triumphs over death. Death cannot affect it. Power participates in the triumph of those still living over the dead. Epidemic's aim is death. It relieves power of the dirty work, while providing it with the satisfaction of a task accomplished. The epidemic is a natural ally of absolute power.

It is only the other side of the coin that the battle against epidemics was always a power struggle waged against the mortal enemy. Measures to fight epidemics had to be wrested from the reluctant SS; medical care was largely in the hands of the medical attendants and prisoner doctors. Medicines had to be organized by bribery, or smuggled into the camp. In the housing blocks, the prisoners tried to control the diseases using the most meager, makeshift methods.[6] To fight diarrhea, they ate charcoal made from burned bread crusts or pieces of wood. To quench the bleeding, they inserted suppositories made of paper or linen into the anus. They rubbed the main areas infected by scabies with urine, or a salve made of slaked lime and lubricating oil. Scarce bread was bartered for soap or clean underwear, and underpants were cleansed with a warm infusion made from herbs. People went without sleep in order to remove the lice manually at night. Against typhus, the only effective remedy was to apply cold compresses—or to hide the sick. Medical self-help was also a method of social self-defense. These practices were passed on from one prisoner to the next; they were elements of a collective knowledge that aided in resistance. As hopeless and ineffective as the measures often were, their aim was to retain the prisoners for as long as possible within the regular round of camp life and prevent their being sent to the *Revier*.[7] Sickness meant immediate mortal danger. Selections and killing of the sick were the order of the day. Consequently, keeping infections a secret was a limited lifesaving act. Attendants and prisoner doctors sent unsuspecting sick prisoners who were supposed to be admitted to the infirmary back to the blocks—in order to save them from the clutches of the executioners. They concealed the diagnoses and falsified the lists of patients to prevent a selection from taking place. Covering up the epidemic was a form of resistance against the system of absolute power.

On the other hand, it was quite in keeping with the mentality of the camp leaders that they initially took no steps whatsoever to combat the epidemic. Their first reaction was to ignore or hush up its presence.[8] Diarrhea, tuberculosis, and scabies were accepted as permanent fixtures, part of normal, everyday camp life. Only after their own people had been infected did they take steps against typhoid fever and typhus. They were cautious when it came to official measures. To report an epidemic to the central *Inspektion* or the local civil administration was to show conditions in the camp in a bad light. Moreover, a camp quarantine usually also meant a freeze on leave for the SS. An amalgam of organizational sloppiness, indifference, ignoring of the facts, and terror allowed the epidemic to take its own course. In any case, nothing was done to change the conditions underlying the epidemic, such as catastrophic overcrowding and the lack of proper hygienic and sanitary facilities. Measures, if they were taken at all, were half-hearted, ineffective, harassing, or lethal.

The surest prophylactic against typhus was mass delousing: the disinfection of the persons, their clothes, and their accommodations. The procedure was time-consuming, and it interrupted the normal camp routine. For it to be effective, thousands of people had to be kept under constant monitoring. It demanded the surveillance of each individual prisoner, a precondition that was a sheer impossibility in the mass society of the camp. In many camps, the disinfection of new arrivals was an obligatory stage in the admission procedure. In addition, there were lice-control checks—sporadically, weekly, or even every evening after the final roll call. These were measures of a rigorous permanent regimen of discipline that would have been impossible to implement without the assistance of the prisoner-functionaries. Although such checks were in the obvious interest of the prisoners, their reaction to these measures was often frightened and defensive. Disinfection was an integral component of the dictatorial camp code, and was accompanied by harassment, excess, and humiliation. Inmates were forced to wait naked in the cold for hours for clean wash from the laundry. As in the induction ceremony, their hair was shaved and their private parts were wiped with dirty rags or sprayed with disinfectants. A number of prisoners were submerged and drowned in the vats containing the viscous liquid. If a louse was found on a prisoner, he or she was beaten or killed by the SS, the medical attendants, or the block leaders. The procedure was anything but efficient. Generally, cleaning was only superficial. Many blocks were reoccupied too quickly, and clothing was often given a quick, superficial wash. Whole colonies of nits remained in the seams, producing new lice within a matter of hours. Delousing, far from being an effective medical measure, was also a situation of terror.

If the epidemic appeared to be serious, the SS set up special infirmaries or infection blocks. This procedure fell back on the model of spatial separation. The epidemic was combated by isolating the sick prisoners in a closed area. The intention of such exclusion from camp society was to reduce the danger of infection and concentrate the center of the epidemic in one place. The infection block was an asylum inside the camp, an area surrounded by barbed wire and under strict quarantine. It was immaterial whether the prisoners went on living or died in its confines. The sole purpose of the block was to isolate the sick, not to cure them. Occasionally, there was the semblance of clinical organization.

Patients with tuberculosis were in a separate facility, those with typhoid fever were segregated from inmates suffering from malaria or diarrhea. But this medical classification dissolved as the barracks became more crowded. The infection block turned into a death ward where all those were shunted who were considered incurable, and thus superfluous. It was a jail for the sick, one whose inmates had been written off.[9] Rations were cut. The prisoner doctors and *Revier* Kapos had hardly any means at their disposal for effective care. When people were not dying fast enough, the SS carried out selections in order to make room.

Like other invalids, those ill with infectious diseases were a preferred target for deliberate liquidation actions. For the SS, killing was the simplest means to combat an epidemic. In this way, it saved on food, space, and medical and other care, and rid itself of the burden of time-consuming permanent supervision. Killing did not upset the camp routine; it served to slash the numbers of the sick. This approach was not merely in harmony with the barbarous rationale of the camp regime. Epidemic and power stand in a distinctive relation to each other. On the one hand, the victims of an epidemic are completely superfluous to power. Faced with someone sick, power is at a loss: it cannot truly demonstrate its hegemony. The patient is only a helpless victim of epidemic infection. The only true trophy of power is persons who have been killed. They fill power with a special self-confirming strength.[10] On the other hand, power fears it may itself fall prey to infection. Although they are power's natural ally, epidemics are difficult to predict. They can also strike the mighty. In the infection block, the epidemic was only localized—taken, so to speak, into custody. But killing was a final vanquishing of the epidemic. Thus, the camp regime was not satisfied with mere passive observation of the mass dying. It took the initiative. How can power better prove itself than by victory over that anonymous elusive enemy, the adversary who can strike down one and all: friend and foe alike, young and old, weak and strong? Here is the defeat of an enemy that makes no social distinctions, and knows nothing but the mass of the dying and the dead.

If the epidemic could no longer be contained, there was one last-ditch resort. The SS sealed off the entire camp and fled from the infected area. At the most, it dared to enter the prisoner camp only for roll call. Work was halted; the Kommandos no longer marched off to their sites. The quarantine transformed the entire concentration camp into a camp of the sick. In such cases, the camp leadership did nothing to combat the epidemic. There was a total lack of everything. Barracks were not disinfected. The prisoners had almost no water to wash, and no laundered clothing. The tyrannical regime of order and cleanliness was abruptly abrogated. The camp deteriorated into a cesspool. The way now stood clear for the epidemic to rage unchecked.

The quarantine led to internal disorganization.[11] The withdrawal of the SS left a vacuum of social power. Unlike the historical instance of the city plagued by pestilence, the regime chose to forgo total surveillance, their micropolitical control over a closed internal space. It cleared out, vacating the field, abandoning it to the unbridled struggle for survival, the struggle of all against all. The sick inundated the infirmaries. The hungry, ill, and dying lay packed together in the bursting blocks. Separation and isolation were virtually impossible. One barracks after another was contaminated by infection. Piles of corpses amassed in the camp streets and along the paths, since the body carriers and the crematorium could not keep up with the headlong pace of dying. Medical attendants abandoned their posts, withdrawing for safety to the last uncontaminated barracks. Veteran prisoners and Prominents barricaded themselves in their blocks. Only where self-administration was underpinned by a stable group structure and a broad consensus was it possible partially to close the power gap. But the epidemic also thinned the ranks of prisoner personnel. Now, the only way to establish a modicum of makeshift order was via the solidarity and self-organization of the prisoners. Because there was no arrangement to conscript prisoners for work in the infirmary blocks, they had to rely on volunteers. Courage and pity, a sense of responsibility and readiness to sacrifice, the mustering of the last ounce of physical energy and willpower—these were the final resources available in the battle against the epidemic. Some who had survived typhoid fever and recuperated made themselves useful as attendants. Because of the lack of medical supplies, doctors who were found in the newly arriving prisoner transports were able only to institute administrative measures. They classified the sick, attempting to divide them into separate groups. Dysentery patients were placed near the latrines; special blocks were reserved for those sick with typhus and typhoid fever. Purification squads were organized, and, in a risky move, brushes and brooms were gathered to clean the blocks. Matches and lighters were taken from the storeroom to set fire to the contaminated sacks of straw. By burning down the legs broken off from wooden chairs, charcoal was prepared as a treatment for diarrhea. Sick patients were given a "diet soup" made of water mixed with a bit of flour or groats. The tiny groups of survivors trying to assist were unable to change much. There was a fundamental lack of supplies necessary to stem the epidemic. Moreover, no central point coordinated the various ad hoc assistance efforts. The internal dissolution of the closed society behind the barbed wire accelerated the spread of the epidemic. Social power had retreated, surrendering the stage to another all-powerful enemy.

19

Terror Punishment

I witnessed a situation where some prisoners who had tried to escape were brought back to the camp. We stood in ranks, arranged by blocks, out on roll-call square. There was a company of armed SS militiamen in formation in front of the execution site. Four prisoners who had attempted to flee from the construction Kommando were taken to the gallows that stood on the *Appellplatz*. The band, headed by Magnus, the camp senior prisoner, went on ahead of them, marching along. A hanging was organized like this: the second prisoner sentenced to be executed hung the first, the third hung the second, the fourth man hung the third prisoner. The fourth prisoner was then strung up by Magnus. The third man brought for execution was one of the Kapos in the construction Kommando, a green prisoner, a German guy . . . he had close connections with the construction office. He was handsome, blond, tall and slim, about twenty-four or twenty-five years old. The man stood beneath the gallows, smiled at the assembled prisoners and said quite audibly: "OK, you guys, so long!" The camp commandant shouted at him angrily: "Shut your trap or. . . ." The commandant was from Bavaria and liked to use the word "or." The prisoner asked the camp commandant: "What did you say, sir? Or . . .? Or what?" The commandant replied: "Shut your trap or I'll shoot you down like a mad dog!" The prisoner continued to smile, tore open his shirt and said: "Well, that'd be a lot better for me, camp commandant, sir!" So then they strung him up.[1]

THE CAMP DESTROYED human beings by humiliation and psychological murder, by dissociation and repression, by labor, starvation, and epidemic. But power also took direct action in countless incidents of excessive violence, massacre, and industrialized mass murder. Yet before it shed all restraining fetters, power resorted to the social mechanism of sanction. It made threats, imposed sentences, and carried out punishments. Nonetheless, in the great majority of cases, it was not what could be called a rule-bound, orderly procedure. Despite the existence of a formal disciplinary code, the transition from a penalty according to the rules to *Terrorstrafe* (terror punishment) was fluid. Absolute power jettisons regulations and restructures punishment, paving the way for excessive brutality and cruelty. The present chapter focuses on the procedures and situations in which penalty sanctions were transformed into *Terrorstrafe*.[2]

Penalties generally are a response to a deviation from norms, regularities, or social expectations. The offender is made to suffer a disadvantage designed to demonstrate that deviant behavior is unacceptable.[3] Punishment is the final link in a chain of situations strung together via the social mechanism of sanction. This chain begins with a threat that forces the actors to decide among alternative paths for action:[4] if they do what is demanded they incur no penalty; if they violate the required norm, they trigger a sanction in response. This is followed by the situation in which the actors decide in favor of conformity or deviation. Subsequently, their deeds are judged and the degree of deviation established, generally with recourse to a normative schema that assigns an appropriate sentence for the transgression. Finally, the threat is realized; the sanction is implemented. This general model provides an analytical frame within which to trace the process whereby sanctions are transformed into terror punishment.

Genuine sanctions always count on human beings to act. The threat defines punishable offenses that the threatened individual can elude by conforming and obeying. To that extent, punishment can always be avoided, no matter how great the cost. Threats leave a way out, an exit via obedience and subservience. They keep alternatives open. Customary threatening power channels action but does not destroy it. Its target is obeisance, not absolute impotence. Its instrument is deterrence, not unending terror.

Absolute power operates in a quite different manner. It creates a "jungle of punishable offenses,"[5] a condition of constant punishability, in which even obedience is no guarantee for avoiding sanctions, and power can intervene at will. In the camps, this "punitive jungle" had a distinctive configuration: first of all, alongside the official prohibitions, there were a large number of informal regulations; not even the veteran old-timers could know all of them. In any case, new arrivals were not *informed* about the rules; they were beaten into them.[6] Consequently, the prisoner had only a vague, imprecise idea of what was subject to penalty, and what punishment could be expected for a given violation. To compound matters, many prohibitions had been kept nebulous so that the supervisors could arbitrarily define what was an infraction. This absolute power to define the situation used another method: it made demands that could not possibly be met, extending the perimeters of threat to the point that behavior in accordance with the prescribed norms was a sheer impossibility. For example, in making one's bed, it was not humanly possible to smooth down the cover of the straw sack to make it appear as if it had been freshly ironed. If prisoners were not harassed for this at morning block inspection, that was more likely because of the chance leniency of the supervisor than because of the painstaking precision with which they made their beds. The third technique of absolute definition employed a special ruse. Linking two contradictory rules, it constructed a trap so that no matter what the victims did, it could be interpreted to their disadvantage. Thus, there was a penalty for dirty shoes, because this violated the code concerning cleanliness. On the other hand, clean shoes were a sign that a person had avoided working, and thus had violated the general obligation to work. If the prisoners followed one rule, they automatically broke the second: damned if you do, and damned if you don't. A fourth technique was that terror constantly created its own punishable offenses. It maneuvered people into situations in which they had to violate some regulation or other. For example, at "morning sports," prisoners were forced to crawl through the mud; afterward, they were beaten for having dirty trousers. Or they were sent to deliver some message during work, and were subsequently reported to the camp head office for "unauthorized absence from the job." Absolute power is not curtailed in any way by a formal set of norms. Rather, it uses that code as a tool of terror, a means to exercise arbitrary power. Organized terror erects a rigidly regulated disciplinary order that generates intentional disorder, opening up an array of possibilities for manipulating punishable offenses. Camp power was less interested in preventing infractions than in being able to take action itself whenever it wished. It transformed calculable, concrete threats into incalculable, anonymous danger.

Because anything could be defined as a punishable offense, the prisoners were left with only one way out. There was only one path of action that could take you through the thick jungle, though it was far from safe. Its precepts: exercise extreme vigilance, never become conspicuous, make yourself invisible.[7] The overriding rule of thumb for personal survival was to avoid any contact with the camp personnel. The prisoners set up a collective warning system,[8] a red alert that signaled the imminent approach of an SS man or a Kapo. At roll call, one had to disappear somewhere in the middle rows, and suppress any urge to cough or sneeze. In the marching column, one needed to get oneself a position roughly in the middle. The maxim was: avoid the exposed outer edges. In the barracks, a berth on the top bunk was an advantage; at work, one had to arrange a location behind a shed with a friend stationed as guard out front. If one crossed the field of vision of the supervisors, one had to move at a normal speed if possible—not too fast, not too slow. It was always dangerous to loiter inactive at the corner of a barracks without any obvious task, or to wander aimlessly across the roll-call yard. By keeping one's own activities secret—indeed, by keeping one's own existence out of sight—one was able to avoid the second situation of the mechanism of sanction. Unnoticed, one was in no danger of being selected as a victim of some punitive operation.

In terroristic penal praxis, judgment and punishment often coincide. Many perpetrators did not wait for a proper penalty to be decided on; they took action immediately. The punishment procedure was radically abbreviated and punishment was carried out directly on the spot of the "infraction," based on the total power the superior enjoyed. For many perpetrators, an official report was only tedious paperwork that transferred the power of judgment to superior authorities, thus restricting the personal power they enjoyed. The price for the camp command of delegating terror to subordinates was reduced control over staff. But this approach relieved the administration of having to deal with "trifles," and consolidated the fundamental law of social terror: the suddenness and indeterminacy of a possible attack. Any central bureaucratic guidance of punishments would have undermined the effectiveness of terror. By transferring the power to punish right down the pyramid to subordinate functionaries, the individual supervisors had discretion to decide whether they wished to initiate a formal procedure or exercise their power immediately. Internal lists of offenses and official disciplinary codes played an important role in this process.[9] They defined a large number of punishable offenses and provided the supervisors with various pretexts for wholesale flogging. Social rules have constitutive as well as regulative functions. The disciplinary rules generated the matrix for arbitrary punitive action, the countless situations providing an occasion for veritable orgies of beating. They constituted a gray zone of unofficial and spontaneous punitive measures—without direct hierarchical monitoring or any regulation of the degree of punishment, yet always under the shield of official rules and regulations. The transition from punishment to arbitrary excess was fostered, not blocked, by the bureaucratic superstructure.

The functional logic of terror punishment was not contradicted if superior authorities repeatedly attempted to bring criminal proceedings into their bailiwick. Terror was accompanied by disputes over punitive authority. Although the most minor supervisor, the lowliest Kapo, beat prisoners on a daily basis and often murdered them, the central *Inspektion* insisted again and again, though in vain, on maintaining its monopoly over authorization for corporal punishment. This fight was a bureaucratic sham, and it demonstrates that the *Inspektion* central directorate had lost effective control. Officially, the camp commandants were not allowed to impose corporal punishment themselves. In the case of male prisoners, the decision was the prerogative of the *Inspektion*; for female inmates, Himmler himself had to decide. However, for the most part, actual authority lay with the subordinate offices. The guidelines requiring the exercise of restraint in punishment in order to maintain a prisoner's labor capacity, and the obligation to file for permission for corporal punishment from the *Inspektion*,[10] contrasted with a long-standing local practice that could hardly be checked by means of a central order.[11] De facto, the power of judgment regarding official penalties lay with the local commandant's office or the camp leader. They determined what cases, if any, would be reported to Oranienburg. In many instances, the punishment was carried out first; a go-ahead confirmation was obtained after the fact, and this was used as a pretext for a second punishment. Thus, prisoners were frequently flogged twice for the very same "offense." The formal procedure served as a device permitting the camp SS to double the penalty.

The implementation of terror punishment was barbaric in both means and scope. In numerous cases, it was tantamount to a covert death penalty. Many official punishments linked the bureaucratic procedure with excesses and torture. Whoever was placed in the *Strafkompanie* or sent to an isolation cell in the prison bunker fell into the clutches of torturers who had a completely free hand. Arrest often meant torture and death. The *Strafkompanie* involved total isolation inside the camp and hard labor at double time, even after regular work hours and on Sunday afternoons. It also meant cancellation of meals, constant mistreatment by the Kapos and the SS, and the danger of being "shot while attempting to escape." In dealing with the prisoners of the punishment company, no holds were barred. Although the upper limit for penalties was six weeks, the punishment company ravaged even the strongest, quickly reducing them to the point of collapse. Those who survived and were released were often so badly injured that they did not live much longer after the nightmare.[12]

Even the punishment of standing at the camp gate or out on the *Appellplatz* was linked with SS harassment. Depending on the transgression, the prisoner was compelled to stand without moving for hours or days, no matter what the weather, without food or protection from the blows of block leaders who chanced by. The prisoners who managed to survive the ordeal depended on the support of their blocks. In Dachau, a relief service was organized in the early period. Bread was put aside and saved for prisoners whose rations had been cancelled, and other prisoners helped out by cleaning the punished prisoners' lockers so that they were able to be in bed by lights out. Because they were forced to stand out at the gate until the final whistle, they had no time left to fulfill their customary duties as prisoners. Only the assistance of their fellow prisoners in the block spared them further offenses and penalties.

Collective punishments had a special social impact. In such cases, prisoners were penalized for things they did not even do. As a punishment for some minor irregularity, all the prisoners from a barracks were compelled to run across the roll-call yard weighed down with various "enclosures"—until they dropped from exhaustion. If one inmate was missing at barracks roll call, all the others were forced to wait until that inmate was found. The collective had to bear the punishment by proxy for the individual—a method that necessarily triggered the mechanism of the scapegoat. In addition to the sanctions meted out by the SS, the offenders had to fear those of their fellow prisoners as well. Rage over the injustices suffered was transferred from supervisors to the culprits, the prisoners responsible for bringing the entire group into that situation. Collective punishment shifted terror into the internal sphere of the group, thus exacerbating the pressure on every single individual. Terror reached deep into prisoner society. It had to make sure that each prisoner watched the next. In order to avoid intervention by the SS, infringements of discipline were reported to prisoner-functionaries, who then called the culprits to account in the name of the collective. The system of internal justice meted out by the prisoners protected the collective from penalties and relieved the SS. It was the executor of terror in the prisoners' own ranks.

The demonstrative punishments carried out at the end of the evening roll call had another meaning.[13] They were a public staging of terror that transformed it into a ritual drama. Official corporal punishment was carried out in the following manner.[14] After a verdict handed down by the camp leadership and medical attestation by camp doctor, two prisoners carried the whipping block, a wooden frame with a troughlike plate made of wooden strips, out to the roll-call square. The culprits were called forward; the camp leader read the verdict. The camp doctor was standing there as well, to give the impression that what was about to happen was under medical supervision. The prisoners were then tied to the block, face down, buttocks up. The torturers yanked up the inmates' shirts and jackets, and pulled down their underpants or the linen trousers of their overalls, so that the blows would strike exposed skin. In the early years, not only were all prisoners summoned to take part in this ceremony as spectators, but a platoon of SS guards with steel helmets and rifles was also present. That was meant to provide the spectacle of corporal punishment with a ritual frame and harden the young SS recruits.[15] Later, after corporal punishment had become a customary part of camp routine, the SS dispensed with such formalities. The site for the punishment was often shifted to a bathroom or the detention-block yard, where prisoners were then flogged brutally, one after the other, without any spectators.

Public corporal punishment was a stage presentation of absolute power. Thousands were compelled to watch as their fellow prisoners, initially reduced to total defenselessness, were then forced to lie in a humiliating position and flogged. The helplessness of the victims symbolized the powerlessness of the entire prisoner society. The shameful ordeal was aimed against not only the delinquent prisoners, but the onlooking public as well. It was meant to deter, intimidate, humiliate, and degrade. One should not underestimate the suggestive power of the ritual, its raw brute force and cruelty. It attested to an unassailable power that smothered the first signs of any protest. The spectators were condemned to follow the staging of the punishment as it unfolded motionlessly, with no show of emotion. Although they were in the overwhelming majority, they could do nothing. To that extent, the configuration of camp punishment differs from the historical festivals of public torture. On such occasions, spectators would gather in throngs, eager not to miss the spectacle. They demanded the head of the culprit, and only reluctantly passed on the job of joint killing to the executioner. By contrast, the prisoners in the camp were *forced* to watch as one of their number was brutally beaten. Camp power transformed the historical audience into a rigid, motionless mass. Anger, rage, and hatred were repressed. At its finish, the spectacle left its audience with nothing but the apathy of their absolute powerlessness.

The effect of the blows was devastating. The assistants pounded the prisoners with clubs, sticks, or bullwhips, which they had dipped beforehand in water to make them more supple. If torturers did not demonstrate enough gusto and élan, they were replaced. Prisoners who were forced to carry out the punishment and attempted to spare their fellow prisoners were threatened with the same corporal ordeal as a penalty. The first few blows lacerated the skin, and each new blow or lash struck deep into the bleeding wounds, widening them further. Experienced torturers directed some lashes in between at the prisoners' backs, severing the kidneys with a few well-placed blows. Some inmates succeeded in suppressing their cries of agony and, as the procedure demanded, counting the blows out loud as they landed. Whoever suffered a nervous collapse or lost consciousness was rudely awakened with a pail of cold water, and the torture commenced again from the beginning. To aggravate the punishment, double blows were administered, with two SS men striking the prisoners simultaneously, though only one blow was counted. Or the pace of flogging was slowed down in order to make the victims feel each individual pang of pain. Those who had survived the torture were forced to do deep knee bends in order, as flogging discourse put it, to "strengthen the muscles." Then the victims were carried to the *Revier*, where the camp doctor painted their lacerated flesh with stinging iodine; or they were tossed in detention cells, where they soon perished from the complications of internal injuries and festering, untreated wounds.

Public execution, even more than corporal punishment, demonstrates the supreme perfection of absolute power. The death penalty eliminates the victim immediately. The camp masters certainly did not need to prove that they could kill at will. They murdered tens of thousands lined up in front of the backstop at the rifle ranges, in shooting alleys, against the death walls next to the detention blocks, in gravel pits or installations for execution by *Genickschuß*. However, these massacres usually took place without witnesses, outside the normal camp routine. They were not punishments but collective excesses, carried out at concealed execution sites—*Sonderaktionen* ("Special actions"—a euphemism for liquidation operations) designed to wipe out large numbers.

Public execution had another meaning. It was a punishment for real or presumed acts or resistance, mutiny, sabotage, or attempted escape. It did not elude the public eye; on the contrary, all were made its witnesses. The event was meant to be imprinted indelibly in memory, extinguishing any thought of insubordination. Its primary purpose was not deterrence but exemplary retribution. Prisoners were all too familiar with the risks of disobedience. In administering the death penalty, camp power avenged itself for an act of conscious revolt, an insult to itself. Using a single case, power demonstrated that it knew no lenience if someone dared to leave its sphere of power or throw down the gauntlet, challenging its dominance. Absolute power tolerates only objects bereft of will. Whoever refuses to obey, confronting it with courage and daring, has declared war against its reign. Power cannot countenance that audacity. It might provide a dangerous example for others. The brutality of the punishment and the mocking of the victims restored power's sway. The execution was far more than a mere proof of power. It was an act of vengeance, of collective degradation and dishonoring.

The course of the execution confirms this interpretation. As a rule, prisoners were executed by the rope. If there was no gallows out on the *Appellplatz* as a symbol of camp power, workers hauled in a portable frame and set it up at the edge of the grounds. Once roll call had been completed and the SS officers were gathered, the condemned prisoner was led from the prison to the execution site. Occasionally, prisoners who had escaped and been recaptured had to wear a sign proclaiming: "Hurray, I'm back again!"; "Happy to be back again!"; "Was a bird came a-wingin' . . .!"[16] The band played an appropriate accompaniment. The commandant or camp leader gave a speech, replete with threats to the inmates and scornful remarks about the condemned prisoner. Afterward the commandant gave the executioner, selected from the ranks of the prisoners, exact instructions. The victims had to stand on boxes, the executioner tied the nooses around their necks, the cover of the box was opened by a lever, and the men plunged abruptly, falling a few centimeters. The painful death was drawn out, often lasting several excruciating minutes. In most cases, death did not occur from a broken neck, since the rope and distance of the fall were too short; the inmates died from suffocation or the cutting off of circulation to the brain. Death on the gallows was death by strangulation.

As a rule, the SS delegated the job of executioner to the prisoners. In some camps, the prison Kapo assumed the role. The position is worth a closer look. The executioners were themselves under the threat of death. To resist the order to carry out the execution was virtually impossible. They freed themselves from this predicament by becoming killers. The obedient executioners had nothing to fear. They even received a small reward. Thus, they killed in order not to be killed themselves. The order to kill doubled the effect of the death penalty. The executioners passed on to others what was a mortal threat to themselves. Above them was a power to which they were totally subordinate, and which they recognized for that reason. But because they carried out immediately what they were required to do, no residue of the act committed under orders remained within to torment their consciences—no feeling of guilt, no thorn that pricked them into rage. The order to kill cut straight through the executioners like a bullet, a clean exit. They simply did their job. This is the reason underlying the curious composure, the equanimity with which many performed the dirty work of executioner.[17]

Death by hanging has always ranked among the most shameful forms of the death penalty.[18] The culprits are degraded—they are not worthy of weapons. They are subjected to a spectacle of dishonoring, a degradation aimed not only at the condemned, but also at the spectators from whose circle they come. The victims in the camp were forced to carry mocking signs; the proclamation of the verdict derided one and all. The victims had no right either to a blindfold or to a final statement. For the SS, it was an outrageous provocation if the condemned prisoners, at the last second, shouted final battle cries of reassurance to their fellow prisoners, or tried to beat the executioner to the punch.[19] Execution in the camp shared little with the traditional ceremonies of public execution. Though it also restored a previous state of power, there was no pomp and circumstance. Even the most severe demonstrative penalty, a public killing, was a means for the SS to debase the prisoners. By stripping the execution of the ritual elements of civilian or military tradition, the SS demonstrated its contempt. Power found its final satisfaction not in killing, but in the public humiliation of all the others; it was a ritual of shaming, an enactment of impotence. At the end of the performance, it sometimes ordered the blocks to march by the gallows in formation—to show respect not to their dead comrade but to the gallows, the emblem of absolute power.

The executions and *Terrorstrafen* in the concentration camp were a pale reflection of those historical festivals of public torture that preceded the modern disciplinary institutions.[20] Nonetheless, they did absorb certain elements of their historical predecessors and models: collective deterrence and retaliation, the manifestation of power, the extolling of sovereignty. Although the degree of penalty was fixed in the written camp disciplinary codes, terror punishment shattered the regulated mechanism of social sanction. Even the ancient, premodern forms of punishment had their terrorizing effects. They too spread fear and anxiety. But they were tied to rules; despite their immoderacy, they were integrated into a legal procedure before a court, and a ritual of execution. There was no dimension of absolute arbitrariness. In the camp, terror punishment broke free, step by step, from the framework of sanction, paving the way for the excesses and massacres whose cruelty was far more inventive than that of the old forms of torture. It was brutality unbridled.

20

Violent Excesses

Nothing would be more mistaken than to assume the
SS was a horde of sadists who tormented and mistreated thousands on their own initiative, out of passion, goaded by an itch to satisfy their desires. Those
few who did act in this way were in the small minority. But their image is more clearly etched upon the
mind, because it has a sharper profile than that of the
more colorless ruffian, the brute who took care of his
daily workload of brutalities according to regulation—bureaucratically, so to speak—without ever
having to miss his lunch break.[1]

HUMAN BESTIALITY is inventive. It appeared in countless variants in the
camps. There was spontaneous killing, routine flogging, tormenting of prisoners out of a sense of tedium, and collective massacre during searches. Nonetheless, murders for reasons of passion were relatively rare. Many acts of brutality took place without aggression, rage, or feelings of revenge. For that
reason, they cannot be likened to the mad frenzy of those who run amok or the
bloody deeds of soldiers who overcome their battlefield anxieties by cutting
down anything that moves. Ecstasy and panic were alien to the excesses in the
camp. Few perpetrators lost their senses or self-control. Some simply terminated a torture or cut it short, to be continued later. Camp excesses bear the
greatest similarity to a form of military barracks harassment raised to a barbaric level, a brute and vicious hazing come unhinged. It was no accident that
acts of violence in the early camps, which were the training grounds where
many perpetrators learned their craft, bore a striking resemblance to traditional
military practices. They began with punitive pack drills, endurance runs,
forced crawls, or knee bends. If one's energies were exhausted and the orders
barked from a distance had no effect, there was a hail of whiplashes and blows
from clubs and bamboo sticks. Those who tried to crawl away were kicked in
the head and belly until they could no longer move.

If the lust for blood and murder had been the driving force behind barbarity,
cruelty would never have been so inventive as it actually was. Perpetrators
driven by nothing but blind hatred, instinctual destructiveness, or the pure
pleasure in tormenting others lose control over the situation—and over them-

selves. They would hardly have been capable of carrying out the atrocities that were committed on the side—in passing, so to speak. Lust for blood desires the sight of blood; the lust to kill only wishes to increase the number of its victims. These forms of lust lack the creativity of excess, the cold-blooded cruelty of seizing a victim, trying out a new method, experimenting. Excess bursts the framework of regulated violence. It is not a punishment, a torture, or an execution. Punishment follows an infraction; its severity depends on the crime. Torture is an operation of calculation and comparison; it seeks to extort a statement from its victim. Execution is a public ritual of deadly power. Excess has nothing in common with these. At best, it takes punishment and torture as a welcome occasion for its own devices. Yet it usually comes to pass without any motivating occasion, without any command or purpose. In excess, power runs riot, letting off steam through the outlet of the defenseless. It is rooted in a situation of omnipotence. In excess, the perpetrators demonstrate their triumph over the other. They show just how free they are. Excess is violent force for its own sake: terror per se.[2] It has no goal; it is not a means to an end. Cruelty wills nothing but itself, the absolute freedom of arbitrary action, which it realizes by countless new ideas and variations.

In the camps, excessive violence was an everyday phenomenon. The prohibition on killing operative in civil society had been abrogated. Even before the machinery of annihilation was set up in the death factories, there was a broad range of routine cruelty. This should not be overlooked when attempting to assess the camps. The perpetrators behind their desks and many junior-level, whip-wielding associates were neither perverse nor sadistic—they were frighteningly normal. Their cruelty was a part of the regular routine of camp operations. Where terror has been let off its leash and its accessories need fear no punishment, an essential barrier is removed. Violence, always an option in human action,[3] has a free hand, its way now clear. The perpetrators never were obliged to torment and murder, but they always could if they so desired—as individuals or in a group, in any and all situations, in passing or on an impulse, with or without rage, with or without desire, with a purpose or without.

What social facts furthered this unhinging of brutality? What structure marked the situations of violence? In what sequence did they unfold? In order to work out a sociological causal explanation for excessive violence, to focus solely on the specific motivation driving the perpetrators is of limited utility. Although the associates had all the power they needed to express their motives in action, such a perspective sheds little light on violence that was largely useless, without motive, or on the social dynamics of cruelty and brutality. The psychological approach shifts the problem of excess from the social situation to the psychological plane. By contrast, a sociological analysis must proceed from the assumption that cruelty has a social meaning, that it occurs in a social context. In the camps, it was based on the collective readiness of the personnel to engage in violence toward helpless inmates. The manner and course of violence depended not only on the internal structures of the group of perpetrators, but also on their relation to the victims and the methods of violence employed. Cruelty was more a methodical mode of behavior with a complex configuration of power than an eruption of uninhibited physical urges on the part of an individual. Consequently, the analysis here will explore both the suprasituational factors responsible for the unleashing of violence and, based on selected cases, the situational dynamics of excessive actions.[4]

The first precondition for the unbridling of brutality was the institutionalization of terror. From the beginning, violence was regarded in the camps as a means of repression and discipline. Readiness to use violence was an objective in the training of personnel, and an essential feature of the collective *habitus*. This laid down criteria in terms of which all the SS officers had to orient their actions. But more than that, it reproduced a behavioral pattern of arbitrary force that dominated virtually all social situations in the camp, taking on lasting validity. Other forms of social exchange were increasingly excluded. Yet when violence becomes a routine and is exercised routinely, situational power in action is transformed into "objective" absolute power. The camp was violence, and violence was the camp. Once solidified as an institution, habitual violence had a recoil effect on the perpetrators. It consolidated their *habitus* and that *habitus* continued on with the habit of violence, unquestioned and unquestioning. The perpetrators carried out what was only a general pattern of behavior. This relieved them of the need to furnish motives anew in every situation. They whipped and clubbed as the others did, as they themselves had always done. It was routine behavior. If a prisoner stumbled across their path, they struck immediately, without pause for thought or decision. The automatism of the habit saved them from having to make time-consuming decisions, shifting the trigger mechanism for the action to the object.[5] Anything conspicuous set the habitual pattern into operation, provoking immediate violence. The institutionalization of terror made violence a law of action that was executed with routine. Consequently, the perpetrators were largely able to avoid being implicated in the deeds qua persons: they could keep them*selves* out of it, as it were.[6] The frictionless operation of the terroristic function supplanted the intentions and decisions of the individual.

Institutionalized terror produces habitual perpetrators who do without reasons for their actions. The actions in Sachsenhausen are characteristic of this form of violence, and resemble occurrences in other camps as well.[7] The perpetrators seized their victims at roll calls, on joint sweeps, or in chance encounters. Generally these victims were from four categories: Jews, the weak and frail, university graduates, and new arrivals. They were brutally beaten, kicked to death, or killed by blows from shovels, clubs, or water cans. They set the beard of a seventy-three-year-old Jewish man ablaze and then beat him to death. Another Jew was drowned in the muck of the latrine. To the roaring laughter of the onlookers, two other Jews were seized and a water hose placed in their mouths; the faucet was then turned on full blast, until their internal organs burst from the pressure. In February 1942, sixty to seventy Jewish prisoners were forced several times to exit from their barracks. At the door, each man who passed by was hit on the head with a club. Afterward, the men had to lie down in a row on their stomachs in the snow, and two SS men ran back and forth over their backs for ten minutes. The infirmary was "cleansed" by a removal operation: prisoners suffering from diarrhea were lifted up from their bunks by shovel handles, dropped to the floor, and then trampled to death. For the habitual perpetrators, the prisoner was nothing but "fair game"—helpless prey that they could humiliate, torture, or kill at will, indiscriminately. But they were quite discriminating in their means. Excess arose on the foundation of habitual violence; it intensified that violence in order to alter the habit.

After institutionalization, violence can be organized in terms of a division of labor. As in the death factories, cruelty in the concentration camps developed a certain level of specialization. Beating and kicking were engaged in by many supervisors. In addition, however, there were special sites for excess. Specialists in cruelty plied their trade there, concentrating on tormenting the prisoners in any and all imaginable ways. Habitualization to violence gradually extinguished inhibitions among most SS men and Kapos, blunting their sensitivity to the suffering of their victims. Yet their main task initially was discipline and repression. A different situation prevailed in the central killing sites in the camp: the *Strafkompanie*, prison bunker, and interrogation cells of the Gestapo. There, torture, torment, and murder were a trade, a handicraft.

The excesses perpetrated in the bunkers and *Strafkompanien* exceeded even the brutality of the habitual deeds.[8] Any prisoners sent to the camp jail were generally written off by their fellow prisoners. In the bunker, they passed into the clutches of torturers who could do as they wished. Frequently, it was an unspoken instruction or common practice that those detained should not be allowed to return to the camp. Every prisoner confined here was deprived of meals and subjected to orgies of flogging and clubbing and a host of humiliations. In the "dog cells" in Dachau, the prisoners had only enough room to lie if they cowered on the floor. Before they were brought something to eat, they were forced to beg, barking like dogs. In the *Stehzellen* (standing cells) in Sachsenhausen, prisoners had just enough space to stand erect. In Natzweiler, inmates were locked up in small recesses 131 centimeters high and 30 centimeters across, so that they could not lie, sit, or stand.

The forms of torture were frequently an extension of torture practices used in interrogation. However, the transition from torture intended to extract a confession to pure, purposeless torment was fluid. In torture, if a prisoner dies it is a mistake, a miscalculation. Excess emancipates itself totally from such considerations. Whether a prisoner confessed was secondary. The main point was the process of torment. Prisoners in Buchenwald were handcuffed to the heating pipes before interrogation, and then beaten with rubber truncheons or lashed with bullwhips. Those who fainted were brought back to consciousness again and again by being doused with cold water. In this way, some died even before being questioned. During interrogation, prisoners were strung up on a grate door, their arms tied behind their backs, their feet dangling several centimeters above the floor. Others were hung upside down by their feet; their legs were then torn asunder by the repeated opening and slamming of the door. A special form of torture was to tie a rope to a male prisoner's genitals and then swing him back and forth as he hung on the door. Another technique was to dip the genitals alternately in cold and boiling hot water and, once the skin was lacerated, to douse it with iodine. One variation on the Buchenwald method of stringing up the prisoner was the "swing" in the Political Department in Auschwitz. The victims were forced to sit down with their knees pulled closely together on the floor, and then clasp their bound hands up over their knees. A rod was inserted below the hollows of the knees and above the lower arms. These were then lifted and attached to a wooden frame. The prisoners hung with their heads down, and were "swung" back and forth. During each swing, they received a blow to the taut buttocks or directly to the genitals.

Smashing fingers with blows from a hammer, crushing the skull with iron clamp screws, suspending prisoners and then manhandling their genitals—such forms of human bestiality suggest the presence of a sexually pathological personality on the part of the perpetrator. In individual cases, that cannot be ruled out. However, it should not be forgotten that such practices derive from the traditional expertise of seasoned torturers.[9] The bunker in the camp was a world of its own. The specific, cold objectivity of the ordeal of torture engaged in here differed from the numb and deadened cruelty of the habitual perpetrator. Here the predominant aspect was one of active experimentation. The bunker was the laboratory of calculated excess, a camouflaged site of professional torture. Habitual perpetrators were routine accomplices; torturers, by contrast, were artisans of cruelty. For them, the victim was nothing more than a physical body, a piece of quivering flesh they subjected to manipulations. Their success was evidenced not by a confession, but by the pitch of the screams of the victim. The transition from torture to pure torment did not lie in the method employed. What in torture is solely a means to an end becomes an end in itself in torment. Perpetrators tried out how much victims could stand; they experimented to see what could be done with and to the prisoners. Sometimes the torturers interrupted the procedure in order to smoke cigarettes in the room next door, or have a bit of breakfast. And if the victims unexpectedly survived the ordeal, they were summarily disposed of: shot, beaten to death, poisoned. Or—and this also occurred on rare occasions—released and given a gift of tobacco.

The agony of the victims is beyond description, unspeakable. At best, we can attempt to determine the anthropological meaning of torment. "A person

... under torture, overwhelmed by pain, experiences his body as never before. In self-negation, his flesh realizes itself totally. . . . Only in torture is human corporeality total: screaming with pain, in the clutches of violence, bereft of any hope for help, incapable of self-defense, the tortured victim is nothing but a body."[10] Torment renders individuals absolutely helpless. All they can do is scream; they can no longer even whine for mercy, or try to avoid the blows. Their bodies are bound tightly. Torment is carried out on objects that have been fastened down and immobilized. The ability to speak has been obliterated by the pain. For that reason alone, the demand of the tormenters for the victims to confess is nothing but pure mockery. Torture only wishes to prolong the agony, expand it, reducing the victims to quivering bundles of flesh. It is thus the most radical negation of sociation. Excess manipulates the living body as though it were a lifeless thing. The perpetrators are more than lords over life and death. Their sovereignty intensifies absolute power: sovereignty over death and the manner of dying is greater than mere killing. It turns a person into a gutted wreck, still breathing. The butchery mutates human beings, reducing them to the creaturely minimum.

A third complex of causes behind the unbridling of violent force lay in the group structure of camp personnel. If violence is considered normal in a social collective, it gradually becomes a binding norm. The collective *habitus* is more than a mere disposition to act in a customary way. At the same time, it is a normative demand addressed to the members of the organization. It calls for conformity with the values and habitual practices of the group. The more isolated a group is from the surrounding social environment, the more unquestioned is the validity of its internal norms and ideals. The members of the camp SS were, for the most part, removed from the world of their former civilian social roles and relations. They had been transplanted into a milieu that was beyond external control, an ambience in which an independent world of norms could develop. Obedience, loyalty, comradeship, and "steeled severity" determined the guiding image of the SS. Personal commitment was demanded of both SS members and prisoner-functionaries. Individuals demonstrated commitment by acting, on their own initiative, with greater brutality than their orders called for. Thus, excess did not spring from mechanical obedience.[11] On the contrary; its matrix was a group structure where it was expected that members exceed the limits of normal violence. They were expected to make actual use of the license given them. Brutality was considered an accomplishment, a mark of distinction. Thus, an atmosphere of mutual stimulation to engage in ever more extreme cruelty prevailed within the ranks of the personnel; it was a competition in barbarity.

The demonstrative form of excess was in keeping with this state of affairs. Torture took place in the concealed area of the bunker or the crematorium. Here the perpetrators were alone with their victims. By contrast, demonstrative excess was a performance, a spectacle directed to an audience. It was a staging meant to spread fear and earn respect. The more feared the Kapos, the greater was their prestige in the prisoner aristocracy. The more brutal the SS officers, the higher their standing among their superiors and accomplices. The guard who had repeatedly foiled "attempted escapes" at the camp perimeter was officially praised and rewarded. The block leaders who killed "superfluous" prisoners on their own initiative were regarded as zealous vassals. To be able to choke a person with one hand, or kill with a single sharp blow of the hand, was a mark of special strength. Perpetrators also gained prestige demonstrating their sharpshooting or skills at stone throwing. Thus, for example, on May 1, 1943, in the Buchenwald stone quarry, SS officers dreamed up a special contest, wagering for six cigarettes or two glasses of beer. The aim was to kill a prisoner by throwing a single stone. If they missed, they lost their patience and simply shot the prisoner. The result of this exercise in group dexterity was seventeen dead and wounded prisoners. That same day, another incident occurred in the nursery: a Pole was ordered to carry away a large stone. It was impossible even to lift the massive block. An SS sentry then threw a brick at the Polish prisoner, striking him; he collapsed, covered with blood. Several guards doused him with a pail of cold water, bringing him back to consciousness. They then set the prisoner up against a tree, using him as a live target for rifle practice.[12] In Auschwitz, the head of the large crematoria used to place four persons in a row, one behind another, at the edge of a burning pit, and then shoot all four with a single bullet.[13] Whoever tried to duck down was thrown alive into the fire. This man also hung a prisoner by his arms and then fired repeatedly at the man's arms until they ripped apart. After that, he repeated the same procedure, hanging the man by his legs.

In a subculture of violence, demonstrative deeds of excess earn the actor respect and standing. In this atmosphere, the atrocities involved are not even directed primarily against the victims. For the perpetrators, the victims are nothing more than stage props in the performance, trophies for their self-aggrandizement. The more dead bodies subculture members could chalk up, the greater was their fame; the more adroit and imaginative their brutality, the higher their rankings in the in-group pecking order. Special recognition was given to those who could simultaneously entertain the onlookers. Brutality in the camp not only served as a stage for self-presentation; it also relieved boredom and satisfied the public's hunger for stimulation, its need for diversion and entertainment.[14] During the endless watch on guard duty, to chase prisoners loaded with heavy stone slabs up and down an incline until they collapsed was a welcome break in the tedium, and it was relished with laughter by the other supervisors. Both for perpetrators and for spectators, the humiliation, harassment, and killing of victims provided a distraction and source of amusement. This had nothing to do with anger, hatred, or rage. The identity of the victim was totally immaterial. In demonstrative excess, the direction of signification of the brutality committed shifts from the victim to the onlooking public. Torment is directed totally against the tormented victim. Its meaning lies in the destruction of human existence. But performance is aimed at the audience. Its significance derives from the personal distinction of the perpetrator. Its function is the distribution of prestige, the confirmation of the collective *habitus*.

Group pressure, however, was not a compulsion that left no alternatives. No prisoner-functionaries were compelled to distinguish themselves by special brutality; no SS officers were constrained to exploit their total license. Implicit in absolute power is the liberty to refrain from atrocities at will. No one had to fear official punishment as a consequence. In addition to the habitual perpetrators and torturers, the camps also contained supervisors who took part only with reluctance, who attempted to keep out of such acts, or who even aided individual prisoners. On the other hand, however, loyalty demanded a certain conformity with the usages and rules of the group. Whoever wanted to belong had to join in, beating, shooting, and laughing along with the others. Deviations did not incur penalties, but they did have repercussions that resembled sanctions.[15] Those who chose openly to be different, not to go along with the others, risked their base of personal support in the community. Violence was considered proof of group membership and solidarity. New recruits repeatedly had to confirm this in initiation tests, as they did later on. Under such scrutiny, it was specifically the anxious and inhibited who felt constrained not to make a worse showing than the others, and thus distinguished themselves by their brutality. In this configuration, inner conflicts and guilt feelings arose not as a result of killing, but because of infractions that violated in-group expectations—that is, the failure to kill. By performing demonstrative deeds of excess, the perpetrators proved they were like the others, and showed that they belonged.

The fourth precondition for cruelty was the diffusion of responsibility.[16] Integrated in an organization, the actors could see their violent deeds as the fulfillment of anonymous duties as members. The responsibility of individuals fused with the orders and fate of the organization. They did not view themselves but rather the camp and its routine, as the originators of their own use of violent force. The perpetrators were able to see themselves totally as performers of a role—as participants *in*, not originators *of*, action. Even arbitrary excess was only considered the execution of an order from others, a group assignment. For that reason, insofar as the question ever arose in their minds, they ascribed responsibility not to themselves but to the organization. The individual deed took on the character of an act of participation, even when it was committed based on one's own decision. The self-image of the individual was directly linked with the identity of the group. Responsibility was depersonalized and assigned to the organization.

Various categories can be distinguished in relation to the degree of actual participation. First, there were actions taken on one's own initiative that were covered by the camp leadership or at least silently condoned, although they contradicted the rules governing the correct and proper treatment of prisoners. Thus, there was no regulation specifically ordering personnel to kill prisoners or harass them to death; de facto, however, this option was open to each and every subordinate prisoner-functionary, and covered by the informal norms of terror. Taking counteraction here would not only have meant disrupting a common practice, but undermining the tried and tested foundations of terror.

Deeds of excess could also take place as a result of an excessive alacrity to comply, based on an anticipation of the actual or presumed expectations of one's superiors. One of the established methods of calculated terror is, instead of issuing direct orders, to merely hint and allude or indicate aims that the subordinate must register mentally—or even just "feel" or intuit. The superiors were able to claim that they had given no specific instructions, and the subordinates were able to persuade themselves that all they had done was to carry out someone else's decision. Thus, no formal order had been given, which had advantages for both sides. It let both commanding superiors and lower-level executors off the hook. From September 1941 to January 1942, an undetermined number of prisoners—estimated at three thousand—were "bathed" to death in the showers.[17] The prisoners, most of whom were sick or invalid, including a large number of "red Spaniards," were brought to the open shower building and forced to stand for up to half an hour under ice-cold showers running at high pressure. No one was allowed to leave. The debilitated prisoners either died immediately of hypothermia or lost consciousness because of an acute circulatory collapse, dropped to the floor, and were held by SS officers under water until they drowned. Any survivors died soon thereafter from pneumonia. If the number of victims was insufficient for a collective *Badeaktion* (bathing operation), the SS camp leader had smaller numbers of prisoners drowned by the senior camp prisoner in buckets filled with water. When the *Lagerälteste* complained that he was becoming notorious in the camp as a mass murderer, the SS camp leader ordered all block chiefs and block scribes to drown at least one prisoner of their own choosing. This, in part, was then carried out. Significantly, there was no concrete order of killing for the overall operation. There had only been subtle hints as to the "wishes" of the superior officer in the regular consultations with the camp leader. Yet based on previous experience, he knew what he had to do to please his superiors.

There was another factor operative in the case of "frame orders." Here, an entire group of victims was delivered over to excess. The order to "remove" all prisoners unfit to work from a barracks, or all Jews from a Kommando, was a kind of carte blanche, opening wide the door to unbridled barbarity. The official frame order set out the result to be achieved, not the procedure to be used in getting there. It stated *what* should happen, not *how*. The perpetrators were allowed considerable leeway. To make use of that leeway was not only permitted but required. Initiative and arbitrariness were delegated down the command chain. As a flexible instrument of terror, the frame order was especially effective. It instructed its recipients to exercise arbitrary will, demanding independent action and active involvement.

Collective acts involved the least degree of individual participation. The perpetrator here was solely one accomplice among many, acting like the others. The situation had no individual actors—only a group of perpetrators, and a multitude of victims. The massacre is a collective form of atrocity that can proceed according to plan or unregulated, with or without orders. Massacres differ in terms of their degree of organization. They can take place with a strict division of labor and cooperation, or without any leadership and joint action. The less organized a massacre, the greater its excess. The more it resembles an orderly military operation, the fewer the individual atrocities perpetrated.

Mass shooting by firing squad reflected the greatest degree of organization in the camp system. There was no individual perpetrator, no executioner or torturer. Each member of the firing squad took part in the killing. No one could avoid participation, because the firing squad is a military formation trained to fire on command as a single body. On command, the fusillade is fired that cuts down the victims. Joint fire is coordinated to the fraction of a second. The firing squad operates like a precision killing machine, its members integrated cogs. While the weapon is lowered and reloaded, assistants are already busy pushing up the next group to the wall or the edge of the pit. The sequence was interrupted only for a superior to check the accuracy of the shots and finish off victims still alive with a bullet to the base of the skull. The procedure was both effective and integrative. The perpetrators acted as a cooperating military unit. Action was replicative: each did the same as the one next to him. All could rest assured that the others were doing exactly what they themselves did. In a firing squad, even the smallest gestural deviation is noticeable. The group kills "with a common hand." Its unity is realized in the moment of killing. It is the killing itself that creates and confirms the common bond between the actors; the deed constructs the unit.

In a number of mass shootings, there were certain evident deviations from the organizational principle of death by firing squad.[18] In Majdanek on "bloody Wednesday," November 3, 1943, when some eighteen thousand Jews were shot within the space of a few hours, the victims were driven on foot to the mass graves. They were ordered to climb down in rows of ten into the graves, and to lie flat. They were then fired on from machine guns mounted at the edge of the pit. The next group was ordered into the pit, forced to lie down on the dead who had just been killed, their heads on the feet of the bodies beneath them. In this manner, the grave was filled up layer after layer, and finally was covered over with earth. In Auschwitz in July 1941, some three hundred Soviet POWs were murdered in the gravel pit next to the camp kitchen over the course of several days. The SS officers took up positions at the edge of the pit and fired at will down at the prisoners working below. Any prisoner who was not killed by bullets was beaten to death with clubs and picks by the Kapos. The mass executions at the "death wall" in the main camp were generally achieved by bullets to the nape of the neck. Thousands of men, women, and children were shot at this site. In Dachau as well, mass executions were carried out in the yard of the bunker or the garden of the crematorium, generally by bullets to the nape of the neck. Groups of fifteen to thirty prisoners were forced first to disrobe completely and then to kneel down in a row. The associates went from person to person, pressing a pistol to the base of each skull and pulling the trigger. This procedure had no military tradition behind it: killing by *Genickschuß* was a method first used by the secret police. Although the act of killing here was done by an individual, the sequence of slaughter was just as anonymous as in the case of a firing squad. The perpetrator saw the victim only from behind. Direct eye contact was precluded. Soldiers condemned to death stand erect and await a hail of bullets to their faces. Honor demands that they stand directly facing the enemy. By contrast, the concentration camp inmates were forced to kneel down, bending their necks forward, and were then liquidated in rows, one after the other.

The dynamics of a slaughter during a hunt differed substantially from that of an organized massacre. The firing squad operates according to the principle of automatic obedience; the sharpshooters fire indiscriminately, but together. In a hunt, the victims are chased by a pack, ferreted out, and slaughtered on the spot.[19] It offers a framework in which individuals can stand out. Those who grab their prey most quickly have the right to strike first and kill it. For that reason, more and more join in the action. The collective excesses of a human pack draw many into its vortex, even those who initially were uninvolved. All are oriented totally to one aim: to kill their prey. Participation is without any danger whatsoever. Lynch justice abrogates all rules, and the victims are totally defenseless. But the longer the hunt lasts, the more greedy the pack becomes, and the more bestial the atrocity once the pack seizes its hounded prey.

Hunts took place after attempted escapes and during the death marches that marked the final stage of the concentration camp system. One of the best-known massacres entered the chronicle of Mauthausen under the SS name of the "Mühlviertel rabbit hunt."[20] On the night of February 2, 1945, some 500 Soviet POWs, many of them officers, broke out of the camp. To escape, they threw wet blankets and pieces of clothing over the electrified barbed wire fencing, thus shorting out its circuitry. Using fire extinguishers, they managed to capture a guard tower, and were able to put a second out of commission by machine-gun fire. A total of 419 prisoners escaped from the camp area. But many only got a few meters from the camp. They left a trail in the snow and were soon captured and beaten to death or shot. The SS then ordered a large-scale hunt with instructions "not to bring back prisoners captured to the camp alive." Along with the camp SS, units of the Wehrmacht, the SA, and the Nazi party, groups of Hitler Youth, the *Volkssturm*, local fire departments, and many civilians from the surrounding area took part in the search. A kind of mass hysteria spread through the population because the escapees had been labeled "dangerous criminals." So a general hunt was declared: one and all could join in to track down the Russians. A report prepared by the gendarmerie in Schwertberg a few weeks later gives a graphic account of events:

> The slush in the street turned red from the blood of the men who had been shot. Everywhere people encountered them—in homes, car sheds, stables, up in the loft, down in the cellar—if they weren't dragged out and killed at the next house corner, they were shot right on the spot, no matter who happened to be present. . . . A few had their heads split open with an axe. . . . The bodies remained lying where they fell. . . . Intestines and genitals were exposed to open view. The next morning, the murdering continued. Again, blood was shed, atrocities were committed that one could never have expected the Mühlviertel population capable of. . . . At the Lem villa, there was a certain Mr.———. . . . During the evening, his wife had heard some suspicious sounds in the barn while feeding the goats. She went and got her husband, who dragged an escaped prisoner from his hiding place. . . . The farmer then stabbed the poor man in the neck with his pocket knife, and blood began to gush out. His wife joined in, punching the dying man in the face.[21]

Of the five hundred who originally escaped, only seventeen survived the Mühlviertel massacre.

Along with the institutionalization and specialization of terror, group conformity, and diffusion of responsibility, there was a fifth causal complex of special importance for the unleashing of violent force: the extreme distance between victimizer and victim. Despite the direct physical effects, numerous excess situations were characterized by a microsocial distance that reduced immediate aggression. In contrast with most acts of murder in civilian society, excess in the concentration camp was marked not by social proximity but by distance. It is true that aggression might be intensified if the victim whined in agony, begging for mercy. Moaning and pleading sometimes triggered an outbreak of rage on the part of the perpetrator, who then stopped at nothing.[22] However, indifference is more powerful than hatred, anger, or rage as a driving force of the absolute power to kill.[23] Indifference toward the suffering of the victims forms a defensive armor against everything the perpetrators do. It renders them seemingly blind and deaf, liberating them in the process from any inhibitions of pity or guilt. Indifference generates distance. And the greater the distance, the greater the indifference. In the end, the victim is no longer perceived as a feeling, thinking, or acting person. For the perpetrators, the victim is not a human being, part of the same species to which they belong, but a subcreature. The mechanism of distancing releases cruelty from its restraints.

If one traces the stages in such distancing, the first is the familiar design of the image of the enemy. However, its significance should not be overestimated. Images of the enemy construct the adversary as malicious, dangerous, and inferior. Counterposed to that negativity, one's own group is seen as the embodiment of higher values, specially chosen, exceptional. Such stereotypes are transmitted by indoctrination and propaganda. They unite the group against a supposedly menacing external world, justify force, and generate shared feelings of hatred. They enhance self-esteem and channel internal conflicts toward outside scapegoats. There is no doubt that among the camp personnel, political and racial stereotypes, especially of the Slavic and Jewish *Untermenschen*, were common and widespread. But this was not the usual type of xenophobic imagery. Absolute power has no enemies that could endanger it. The SS camp leadership may have occasionally feared the possibility of collective escapes. But no SS officer ever encountered a form of resistance in the camps that enjoyed any prospect of success. Images of the enemy posit adversaries who are dangerous and devious, yet equals nonetheless. They construct a relation of struggle for life or death. Yet it is difficult to believe that the starved and ailing prisoners were actually perceived by their supervisors as enemies. Day after day, the violence the supervisors exercised proved just the opposite. No excess, no massacre had anything in common with a struggle waged with an adversary. To attempt to derive the brutality of the associates of the SS from the images of the enemy propagated by regime propaganda would be naive: it would mean being taken in by the ideology of the system. And to regard the prisoners as the scapegoats of the personnel would entail a serious error: that of mistaking a system of absolute power for ordinary tyranny. The camp was not a battlefield but a slaughterhouse. Death was not a victory over dangerous enemies, but a slaughter of powerless victims. The prisoners ranked far below the enemy in status.

A far more important factor than images of the enemy was the anonymity of the victims. The victim was only one among countless many, a nameless multitude. Violence was not directed against an individual, but against some prisoner or other who differed from his or her fellows by some minor conspicuous feature: he happened to wear glasses, or she had inadvertently stuck her hands in her pockets while crossing the camp's main street. In a direct person-to-person relation, the most brutal supervisors or Kapos might be quite open and personable; they could even be helpful. However, they were not hampered by any personal relations vis-à-vis the nameless. If the victims are all the same, it does not matter who is affected or what happens to them. Anonymity is the foundation stone of indifference. The anonymous other is nothing but an empty type. Anonymity is a question less of the quantitative number involved than of the degree of typification. Even before the expansion of the camp into a mass society, this practical design paved the way for cruelty and atrocities. On one side, the victimizers; on the other, the nameless, faceless inmates, whom they confronted with consistent violence.

In keeping with this anonymity, there was a practical deindividuation of the person. The prisoners were not only defined as *Untermenschen*, they were actually transformed into subhumans.[24] Excess was often preceded by systematic degradation and misery. At the point when deadly violence finally struck them down, many had been harrowed, reduced to mere ravaged husks of their former selves, emaciated figures of total misery, lice-infested, filthy, wrapped in rags. The camp had already degraded them to the vegetative minimum of existence, so that excess only completed the physical destruction of creatures already drained. The prisoners had already been robbed of their human attributes; they had been alienated to the level of animals. Thus, the perpetrators did not need to deny the personhood of their victims. At best the *Muselmann* evoked nothing but feelings of repugnance or defensive aversion. For that reason, there was no longer any need to tear down an essential barrier to the use of violence. Killing simply completed the process of destruction.

As a rule, deindividuation only lasted a few weeks. But excess was able to compress this process into a few hours. The following incident was reported to have occurred in the transition camp Neue-Bremm in Saarbrücken:

> One morning they brought in a German Jew. First they beat him brutally with a rubber truncheon; then the panther [deputy of the camp commandant] shoved him into the water pool. After this spectacle in the swimming pool, he was pulled out of the water, beaten once again, and then placed in the disinfection block. Yes, the disinfection block. He left the block in a very sorry state, naturally covered all over with burns. But only in order for the entire sequence to be repeated once again, without a break, down to the middle of the afternoon. The poor Jew could no longer stand, he was burned all over his body. The man drowned after he had been tossed once more into the pool. The rods lying near the pool provided a bit of help in drowning him, though it wasn't necessary to do much more. He now was just a poor wretched figure—trying desperately, as they beat him, to keep his head above the water. In the span of five hours, this man, who had a rather robust constitution, had been reduced to a wreck and hounded to his death.[25]

In this instance, the public ordeal was gradated in temporal stages; violence was staggered. Force was intensified, interrupted, then applied once again. The torturers allowed it to take effect, repeated the violence, and combined it with another method. The torment was drawn out in order to prolong the pain. Excess transforms killing into a process. Nothing would have been simpler than to shoot the victims immediately. But they were made a show of, as if part of a performance: publicly mutilated, burned, drowned. Excess experiments with time and varies the tempo of cruelty, the pacing of atrocity. It tests just how long is needed to destroy a strong and robust human being.

Distance was not only a precondition of cruelty; it was also created by the methods excess employed. The violence of absolute power is a mute physical act that annuls social interaction and response. The victim had no chance for self-defense. There was no struggle. Many excesses employed procedures that sundered the social bond between victim and perpetrator. Some victimizers delegated the cruelty to accessories, or simply harnessed the laws of nature. In order to clarify this mechanism of the deed at a distance, it is necessary to examine certain individual practices of violence in detail.

Some excesses were carried out without any bloodshed whatsoever. The perpetrators hardly touched their victims, but rather let the force of nature, earth, water, or gravity do the deadly job. They avoided direct influence, and their hands remained clean and free of blood. Although the victims died a miserable death, nothing stained the perpetrators' pride. The oldest method of banishing individuals from the circle of society is to bury them alive. In the *Strafkompanie* in Sachsenhausen,[26] the broom cupboard next to the washroom served this purpose. It was a tiny room, one square meter in area, with no windows, almost airtight. The leader of the punishment company would arrange to have up to eight prisoners squeezed into this tiny space—the "little corner," as it was known in prisoners' jargon. The victims clutched at each other, climbing one over the other until the door was closed. The keyhole was stuffed with paper. The knot of human flesh became so tightly entangled that those who suffocated could not drop to the floor. The method was considered so effective that it was adopted by other SS men for the *Stehkommandos* with dozens of prisoners. The procedure required no further action on their part. Once the door was sealed, the perpetrators could attend to other tasks. No reactions were audible or observable; no shouts, no resistance, no blood. Just as in the gas chambers of the death factories later on, death occurred behind a locked door, invisible.

The deadly power of water is no less brutal. In many camps, it was common to force the prisoners to shower in ice-cold or hot water and then to let them stand naked for hours waiting for their clothes. Rain and snow in the camp were potentially lethal. In winter, prisoners were doused with water until they had frozen into solid blocks of ice. Sometimes their corpses had to be hacked out with picks from the frozen ground. In the washrooms, victims were not simply drowned; another method was to direct streams of cold water against their hearts or carotid arteries until death occurred. To the amusement of the spectators, they forced the shrieking victims to jump back and forth. The deed resembled a game with a defenseless cornered animal: letting loose for a short while, then grabbing it again—a shift between power and violence until the victim finally collapsed.

The excesses that resorted to natural gravity took a similar course. In the stone quarries, many prisoners were crushed under arbitrarily engineered rockfalls. In Flossenbürg, members of the punishment company were compelled to load heavy stones on their backs at the foot of the slag heap and run around with them in the morass until they finally collapsed. There was also the "moor hole," a swamp one hundred meters long and forty meters wide in a small hollow; at its deepest point, a grown man could stand with his head barely protruding above the surface. Granite blocks were loaded on the backs of prisoners, and they were then forced to run at double time down the slope. Those who collapsed under the heavy load while still on dry ground were beaten and forced to rush further down into the moor hole. They were supposed to "rest" down there for a while, with the stone slabs supported on their shoulders. If they still had some strength, they survived; if they were too weak, the stones pressed them down into the swampy morass.[27] In Natzweiler,[28] individual prisoners were pushed down the steep side of the stone quarry, a drop of fifteen to twenty meters. The supervisor waited above for the prisoners, who laboriously hauled their wheelbarrows back up the slope. Once they were in reach of the supervisor, they were shoved down the slope again; the full barrows were turned over and also sent tumbling down the incline. The stones and wheelbarrow pushed the victims further and further down the side of the quarry. At the bottom was the boundary of the line of sentries. If the prisoners reached that point, they were shot by a guard on duty, alerted to the "prisoner trying to escape" by shouts from above. Caught between the supervisor on top and the sentry guard ready to fire, the victims attempted in vain to make their way up the incline—a hopeless game of abuse. The SS used a different method in connection with mechanized stone quarrying. Shortly before an explosive charge was laid, prisoners were lined up in rows of five in close proximity to the rock face. While the SS officers, Kapos, and supervisors ran to safety, the victims were not allowed to move. They were unable to protect themselves from the hail of broken rock scattered by the explosion. Thus, there were injured prisoners after every detonation, and sometimes dead ones as well. A massacre was carried out here without any direct intervention whatsoever. It had the external appearance of an accident at work. The perpetrators crouched in the protective bunker and left things to chance. Afterward, they checked to see how many had been injured and killed this time around.

The converse of the stoning process was the arranged fall. In June 1941, 348 Dutch Jews arrived in Mauthausen. Three weeks later, not a single one of them was still alive. Most had fallen victim to a method of killing that was considered a Mauthausen specialty: "parachute jumping."[29] In the stone quarry called Wiener Graben, boards were placed on the prisoners' shoulders and loaded down with extremely heavy stones. Then the prisoners were forced to ascend the "death stairway," a series of 186 stairs fashioned of irregular rocks at the edge of the abyss. After a few steps, the stones fell off the boards, crushing the feet of those climbing up beneath them. Many lost their balance on the rock stairs, plunging down the rock face after being giving a helping shove by a supervisor. Others committed suicide by hurling themselves to their deaths, or were pulled down by their fellow prisoners. In these excesses managed from a distance, the perpetrators needed to do little or nothing. They could calmly watch what was happening. Their triumph was less the act of killing itself than the mortal agony that gripped the victims. The victims toiled to the point of exhaustion; the perpetrators waited. The victims ran for their lives, collapsed, dragged themselves to their feet again, and fell once more. The executioners observed the event, laughing. The end was preprogrammed and unavoidable. All tribulation and torment were ultimately in vain. But the perpetrators acted as though their victims still had a chance. They let the victims wriggle and run—and were always there, watching and waiting. The mortal agony gave them a kick; it was a source of amusement. And the less they had to do themselves, the greater was the triumph of power. Prisoners were harassed to death, without the perpetrators having to expend much physical effort—just a voice, a shout, a command barked from a distance. The word was lethal. Thus, many deeds of excess were carried out less *on* orders than *through* orders.

A complicated variant of such deeds has been documented for a shaft Kommando in Buchenwald.[30] The construction supervisor ordered two Jews whose strength appeared to be waning to lie down in a pit. He then commanded a Pole to fill it in and to bury the two men alive. When the Polish prisoner refused, the supervisor beat him with a shovel handle, ordering him to lie down next to the two Jews in the pit. The two Jews were then commanded to cover the disobedient Pole with earth. When all that could be seen was the Pole's head, the supervisor halted the operation and had the man dug out. The Jews had to lie down once more in the pit, and the Pole was told once again to cover them. This time he obeyed. In the meanwhile, the other prisoners continued with their work—in order to play it safe and not call any attention to themselves. When the pit was filled in, the supervisor, laughing, stamped the ground solid. Five minutes later, he called over two prisoners to dig the Jews out again. One was already dead; the other still showed weak signs of life. Both were transported to the crematorium.

The perpetrator picked up the shovel here, but only to use it for beating. The task of burying was given to an accomplice chosen on the spur of the moment. When this man refused, he reversed roles. He forced the victims to do the dirty work of the associates, and threw the executioner into the pit in order to incite him against his victims: what they do to you, you should do to them. The mechanism of revenge worked. The other prisoners, who were following the scene out of the corners of their eyes, continued to work in mortal fear. The perpetrator behaved like a laughing third party, inciting his victims against one another. In the moment of triumph, after his accomplice had obeyed and filled the pit, he stomped the ground solid himself. Shoveling is slave labor; by contrast, giving orders and killing are the privileges of the master. Excess helped him to a threefold victory. He broke the resistance of the accomplice, liquidated two exhausted workers, and demonstrated to the others what could happen at any time. The shift in orders back and forth entangled the victims in a deadly game, presenting the perpetrator as the mighty master who did not even need to dirty his hands. To finish the job, he stomped around on top of the fresh grave with his boots.

In excesses and massacres, absolute power was transformed into absolute power in action. Cruelty exceeded all boundaries and inhibitions. The grotesque physiogonomy of this power was varied: atrocities performed out of habit or conformity, the torments of the torturers, the demonstrative performances, massacres, and hunts; finally, the deeds done at a distance, achieved by using natural forces, accomplices, or mere verbal commands. Far from being a consequence of authoritarianism or a sadistic disposition, cruelty arose from a constellation of total power. Inhumanity is always a human possibility. For it to erupt, all that is required is absolute license over the other. Conventional terror still expects adversaries it must defeat. By contrast, excess manipulates bodies. Whether as public spectacle or disguised torture, excess is not intended as a means to spread fear or suppress resistance. Death is not even its primary aim. What it desires is to prolong pain, suffering, dying—to stretch them out. Excess transforms killing into a process. It takes all the time it needs. Like the pile of corpses, it shows how absolute liberty is transformed into absolute abuse.

21

Selection

An SS officer stands in front of us, *Obersturmführer*.
He's addressed that way by a sentry. Probably a
doctor. Without a white coat. Without a stethoscope.
In a green uniform. With a death's head. We step
forward one by one. His voice is calm. Almost too
calm. Asks about age, occupation, general health.
Asks to see hands. I hear a few answers. Metal-
worker—to the left. Administrator—to the right.
Doctor—to the left. Worker—to the left. Storeroom
clerk for Bata—to the right. . . . Cabinetmaker—to
the left. Then it's my father's turn. Unskilled laborer.
He goes the way of the administrator and the storeroom clerk. He's fifty-five. That could be the reason.
It's my turn. Twenty-three years old, healthy, road-
construction worker. Callused hands. How wonderful
the calluses are. To the left.[1]

THE SCENE AT THE ramp in Auschwitz is familiar: the first station in industrialized genocide. However, selection did not take place only in the forced ghet-
toes and when transports arrived at the extermination centers. It was a more
common procedure: a general organizational schema by which "superfluous"
human beings were sorted out from workers and then liquidated. Selection also
took place within the concentration camps, in the overcrowded infirmaries,
and in the external subcamps. Its scope was broad: for that reason, in any
attempt to grasp the magnitude, process, and function of the selections, the
focus should encompass the entire concentration camp system. The nature of
this unparalleled situation of absolute power varied according to the context
in which it was embedded.

After an agreement had been reached between Himmler and Philip Bouhler,
chief of the Führer Chancellery and head of Euthanasia Program T4, efforts
were begun in the spring of 1941 to sort out undesirable and frail prisoners in
the camps and to transfer them to euthanasia installations to be gassed.[2] The
operation was handled administratively through the *Inspektion* in Oranienburg
under the code name *Sonderbehandlung* (special treatment) 14f13, and the T4
program supplied the personnel. Commissions of doctors traveled from camp

to camp, conducting the selections. In its initial stage, the operation was targeted principally at the category of "asocial" prisoners, who were now redefined in the discourse of racial euthanasia as *lebensunwertes Leben*—life not entitled to live, human trash. However, when the program of institutional euthanasia faced a halt in the autumn of 1941 and T4 personnel were threatened with possible unemployment, the SS expanded the selection criteria to include prisoners who were unfit for labor or racially or politically "undesirable." In order to ensure the continued existence of the T4 organization, the number of victims in the camps was multiplied. Not until the camps were shifted to the supervision of the WVHA in March 1942 and the SS began to implement the labor-deployment program did the Oranienburg *Inspektion* take steps to restrict the program of extermination.[3] In the meantime, however, the practice of selections had been taken over by camp personnel, eliminating the need for the presence of representatives from external offices.

Selection by the doctors' commissions had nothing in common with a professional medical activity. The procedure was bureaucratic. In order to accelerate the process, the questionnaire section of the registration forms previously used in the mental asylums for euthanasia candidates was substantially reduced; forms were now filled out in advance by the commandant's office. Frequently, no medical data whatsoever were recorded—just "previous convictions," political attitudes, or simply a person's "racial affiliation."[4] Under the guise of medical diagnosis, the SS carried out racial and social selection, a "mustering out" of undesirables. Requests by the camp SS were regularly and routinely fulfilled. Cooperation with the T4 medical staff went smoothly and efficiently. Reasons to justify a decision could always be found, since the lines separating illness and social deviance and racial stigma were inherently fuzzy and ideologically imprecise. The examination was generally carried out pro forma, initially just visually, based on appearance, and then by a quick glance at the files. In the case of Jews, a summary collective diagnosis was sufficient. In this way, even healthy workers, not just prisoners no longer fit for work, were placed on the death lists. For the camp SS, the operation was a welcome opportunity to "cleanse" their local bailiwick, with official authorization from above.

The prisoners were deliberately deceived regarding the purpose of the procedure. Before the arrival of the medical commissions, volunteers were requested to report to the *Revier* if they wished to be transferred to what was called a "rest camp." The unsuspecting *Schreibstuben* were even asked to put together lists of workers who were chronically ill or war-disabled; hundreds of prisoners reported to the block chiefs to have their names included.[5] Thus, the apparatus of prisoner self-administration was harnessed as part of preselection processing. If the "examination" was conducted in a room of the infirmary, the prisoners were hurried through at a brisk pace: a brusque once-over by the doctor, a confirmation stamp, a death sentence. In Dachau, all camp inmates were marched in goose step past doctors at roll call. They decided on the spot whether a prisoner should step out to the left or right. Distrustful prisoners thought the doctors in their white coats were disguised Gestapo agents. Trusting souls cherished hopes that the promised "transfer" to a "rest camp" was not a ruse, and adhered to the prohibition on talking. It did not become clear what was actually happening to these "transports of invalids," as they were known in camp parlance, until the personal belongings of the deportees were unloaded from the returning freight cars and taken to the camp storeroom.

The prisoners were not murdered directly in the camp; killing was carried out at a euthanasia installation. Transports from Dachau, Flossenbürg, and Mauthausen went to Hartheim Castle near Linz in the state of Upper Austria; those from Sachsenhausen, Buchenwald, and Auschwitz were sent to Sonnenstein in Saxony. Victims from Groß-Rosen, Ravensbrück, and Buchenwald were sent to the Bernburg facility on the Saale River. After Sonnenstein and Bernburg were shut down in 1943, the only facility that remained in operation was Hartheim. Officially, however, the victims were listed as having died in the camps. A natural cause of death was recorded on the death certificate, and dates of death were spread over a number of weeks in order to avoid awakening any suspicions among the relatives of the deceased.[6] Despite its limited scope, *Aktion* 14f13 was of central importance for the history of selections. The euthanasia program was the direct precursor of the death factories— ideologically, organizationally, and in terms of personnel. The extermination operation known as 14f13 transferred the practices of the euthanasia program to the concentration camps. The camps were linked with external liquidation centers, thus taking on a double function as labor and extermination camps. Cooperation with T4 established the principle of selection in the camps. To a certain extent, 14f13 furnished the welcome model, willingly taken over by the camp system. After external offices had provided the impetus, the camp personnel continued the practice on their own. At the same time, the procedure used in the mental asylums was generalized and extended to new categories of victims: first the "mentally ill" and handicapped, then those unfit to work and political and racial persecutees. Selection cast off its pseudo-medical legitimational anchorings and was accommodated to the pragmatic needs of the camp operation.

Camp selections marked the entire history of the concentration camp system throughout the war. They were the instrument for creating a balance between labor and death, productivity and annihilation. Prisoners who appeared weak or who were regarded as superfluous were regularly weeded out and killed. The camps functioned as a kind of revolving turntable of death. To make room for new arrivals, the SS liquidated exhausted inmates, exchanging them for fresh prisoners. And in order to close the gaps created by the pressure to annihilate, new groups were incarcerated, and then they too were replaced. In the bureaucratic logic of the system, the selections were a murderous means for system maintenance and guided organizational growth.[7]

Selections took place at roll call or during work, in the barracks and in jail, and, most often, in the infirmaries. The victims were either shot immediately in the camp, "bathed to death," gassed, or poisoned by an injection into the heart. They were locked up in special blocks to starve to death, or put on a transport headed for Auschwitz, Majdanek, or a *Sterbelager* to be liquidated there. Depending on the situation, the local SS went about its task using improvisation and original initiative. Four examples of camp selection will now be examined in detail: selection at roll call, in the barracks, in the sick bay, and in the external subcamp.

Selection at roll call linked two procedures: daily inventory and weeding out. The SS sometimes summarily ordered all prisoners belonging to a specific category or from a given barracks to step out and undergo a selection. Or it suddenly scheduled a special roll call whose sole purpose was to muster out the unwanted. Because of the security risks involved, mass selections carried out among tens of thousands of prisoners were rare. The SS preferred the semiofficial situation of a partial roll call. Only when it felt totally secure did it use the mass roll calls as well. In Majdanek, the SS appeared almost every week on the individual sectional fields of the camp grid, gradually combing the entire camp. In the women's section, it was mainly Jewish women who were sorted out from the rest. In the men's sections, invalids of all categories were weeded out; they were then placed in the "donkey blocks" until there was room in the gas chamber.[8] In the women's camp in Birkenau, selections were scheduled after the Kommandos had returned, or at special roll calls. Wearing their heavy wooden clogs, women were required to march several meters in goose step formation. Whoever limped or was too slow was fished out from the ranks with hooked poles and placed to one side.

Selection at roll call proceeded according to one of two basic social patterns: either as a parade review of the victims, or as a pacing down the ranks of the assembled formations. In the first pattern, prisoners marched past the SS tribunal; in the second instance, an SS officer accompanied by others walked through the ranks. The first method was the series in movement, the second the series in stasis. Both situations, however, had a social structure typical of all modes of selection: the contrast between serial mass and individual perfection of power. The verdict was always handed down by a single individual. It is true that the "judges" had their auxiliaries—other SS officers, block chiefs, or Kapos—who used violence to help things along. And they had an audience that watched the proceedings attentively. But despite all its businesslike trappings, selection had a cleverly devised dramaturgical meaning. It staged the absolute power of the individual over the mass. The judges were the unchallenged centerpoints of the situation, the powerless mass the mirror of their might. They triumphed over the mass by transmuting it momentarily into a row of visible individuals. With curt gestures, a flick of the finger or a pointer, a slight turn of the head, the judge realized the social law of seriality: fortuity and superfluity. The arbitrary will of the absolute master determined who was one too many. Even if the total number of victims to be chosen had been agreed upon beforehand, the appraiser had a free hand during the actual procedure. The judge selected one inmate because he wore eyeglasses, another because she looked dirty, a third because he was a Jew. None could run from roll call. It could strike anyone. Yet one person's death was another's life. Selection atomized the serial order. Each hoped that he or she would not be chosen, that it would strike the next person.

The parade was a ritual of review and humiliation. The individual prisoners stepped forward and were appraised. This was a macabre march of emaciated husks, trying in vain to move nimbly, and appear sprightly. Sometimes they were ordered on the spot to run or do a few knee bends; generally, however, a short glance at the prisoner's physical condition sufficed for a death sentence. Inmates with varicose veins or edemas on their legs, those covered with festering boils, those with a disfiguring scar or scabies were all sorted out. Frequently the victims, particularly the women, had to parade naked. Defenseless, they were at the mercy of the evaluating glances and the mocking laughter of the onlooking Kapos and SS officers, who laughed at the grotesque attempts by the terrified marchers to cover their nakedness with clumsy gestures of shame.[9] The review parade certainly had a sadistic aspect. The victimizers' power found its satisfaction in the anxiety and degradation of the victims. The more visible their anxiety, the more perfect the victimizers' power. Selection was more than a mustering out of the unfit. It was a staging of absolute power that assayed its victims individually and then passed sentence.

The parade set the series in motion; pacing down the assembled ranks forced the series to freeze, motionless. Calm and composed, the judges paced up and down the rows, stopping here and there, suddenly changing direction. They could always return. They alone moved freely; the victims stood at attention as if fixed to the spot, straining to stand as erect as they could. Passing by, the judges scrutinized each individual, handing down a final judgment in a fraction of a second: "Raus!" The helpers grabbed the victims by the arms, yanked them from the row, and wrote down their numbers. The others waited in tormenting uncertainty until it was their turn. The closer the judges came, the greater the danger. Legs threatened to buckle, hands trembled, pressing themselves tighter and tighter against the upper thigh.

When the selecting officer came toward us, none of us knew what to do and how to behave. Should you boldly return his murderous glance, which normally meant that you could say goodbye to life? Or should you lower your eyes and avoid his? Should you even plead for pity, beg with your eyes for mercy, implore him for the gift of one's life? Because sometimes it was the right decision if you stared insolently right at them, straight into their criminal face. And other times, it was the wrong thing to do. But who could look into their minds? It was an internal mental measuring of strength. . . . I was completely conscious. It was clear to me that my fate hung in the balance, was being decided that very second. Suddenly everything around me started to whirl. I glanced briefly into his eyes, then to the ground, looked once again at the SS men who were facing me. I felt their glance boring into my depths. My thoughts congealed, seemed as though paralyzed. For a moment, I didn't know what was happening around me, whether their eyes were still upon me, if they were even still standing there, right in front of me. I can't say what went on inside my brain. But then, not sure when, the world had me back again.[10]

It is as though the entire situation were concentrated, reduced to its quintessence in this imperceptible micro–power struggle of glances. The glance of the inspecting officers was a lethal force. To look boldly or proudly into their eyes spelled certain death. Their defeat would have been transformed immediately into rage. But to beseech them would have stirred their pity, most certainly provoking a sentence of revenge. Although a supplication for mercy appeals to the sovereignty of the superior, it also touches an inviolable zone: the pitiless indifference of power, its ruthless disinterest and aloofness, a power that demonstrates its perfection by proving that it does not let itself be shaken or swayed by anything or anyone. Yet in the moment of deadly confrontation, all reflection failed; one's thoughts gave way. The glance of the powerful master overwhelmed the paralyzed victim, turning him or her into a squirming bundle of anxiety.

Roll-call selections were usually sudden and unexpected. There was more warning time with barracks selections. They were often preceded by rumors. Whoever had heard something from prisoner-functionaries about what was up kept the information secret—in order to switch on the sly at the right moment over to the *Revier* or to a barracks that the commission had already seen and left. If the rumors multiplied, the prisoners tried to instill courage in each other. They displayed their chests, legs, and buttocks to one another for mutual reassurance. Some arranged for a quick last-minute shave at an exorbitant price; others stuffed rags under their clothing to appear heavier, or rubbed their cheeks briskly in order not to look pale. If there was a ban on leaving the barracks, then it was too late. The block personnel bolted the door; the SS stormed in and herded up all inmates in a single smaller room. The inspector then positioned himself at the outside door and had each prisoner run through the dayroom. A look at the prisoner's front, a look at the back; the slips with the prisoners' numbers placed on one side or the other. The victim hardly had a chance to see on which pile his or her slip had landed. In a few minutes, a block with two hundred or three hundred prisoners had been sorted out, the selection completed.

Selections in the barracks and at roll call were handled by the camp leadership, while the procedure in the infirmaries was under the authority of the SS doctors, the medics, and even the *Revier* Kapos. The medical trappings were pure sham. The outpatient room functioned simultaneously as a site for selection, the hospital as a waiting room for death. Selection had nothing in common with triage on the battlefield. Triage is an extreme emergency situation within the sphere of medical competence, the sorting of the wounded according to a system of priorities geared to maximizing the number of survivors. By contrast, selection in the *Revier* followed the same rationale as at roll call: prisoners were only permitted to live if they worked; if they did not, they had to die. Selection at sick bay was not limited to weeding out the "incurably ill." It also removed patients whose treatment had just a few more weeks to go. And if the SS could not round up enough sick patients to meet its target, it simply included the convalescent as well.

At times, selection in the infirmaries became a part of normal camp routine.[11] In Dachau from 1942 on, any prisoner who had been in the *Revier* longer than three months was regularly registered and then killed by injection or sent to the gas chamber. In the autumn of 1944, faced with an especially large number of sick patients, the head SS doctor in Flossenbürg carried out selections at his own discretion, killing the patients with phenol. The number of victims is estimated to have been between seventy and three hundred. Beginning in November 1944 in the "small camp" in Buchenwald, a "depot camp" for newly arrived transports, several thousand prisoners were sorted out several times a week by the block chiefs of the makeshift barracks. They were then taken to Infirmary Block 61, where they were either admitted for treatment or immediately "given the needle." At the Mauthausen main camp, between 1939 and March 1945, up to twenty weakened prisoners were weeded out in regular selections once or twice a month and then killed by an injection into the heart. In nearby Gusen, this was done almost on a daily basis. The largest *Revier* selections were carried out in Auschwitz. All Jews, as well as other sick prisoners whose treatment had lasted more than four weeks, were murdered "discreetly" using phenol, hexobarbitone, or prussic acid, or were taken to the gas chamber after a large-scale selection. From September 1941 to April 1943, over a period of twenty months, SS doctors and their auxiliaries, including prisoner paramedics, murdered dozens of patients daily by poisonous injection. From August to December 1942 alone, 2,467 victims were liquidated in this way.

Selection in the hospital followed the model of doctors' rounds on the wards. In more-extensive selections, all the sick were dragged outside where they were sorted out. "Normal" selection took place during the daily rounds of the SS doctors. In the outpatient room of Block 28 in the Auschwitz main camp, the procedure was as follows: every morning, the prisoner doctors introduced each new "admission," summarizing the patient's record. The SS doctors scrutinized the patient briefly from a distance of three meters and decided on the basis of the papers at hand whether the sick prisoner should be taken into the infirmary for treatment or sent on for *Sonderbehandlung*. Patients' records for Jews and *Muselmänner* were placed on one pile, and all the others on a second pile. At noon, in a room of the ward for infectious diseases, the unsuspecting victims were then given poisonous injections, one after another. A procedure that had the outward appearance of an examination for hospital admission was nothing more than pretense, a medically disguised selection.

The doctors' rounds through the wards were sometimes staged as a patients' parade. The camp doctors ordered the living skeletons to march for a few meters, naked, in Prussian step, and then pronounced the verdict. Or the doctors passed silently between the beds: tossing back the blanket here or there, they glanced at the patients' records and had some patients chased from their bunks by an auxiliary. The names of those selected were noted down, and they were picked up a few hours later. It was a well-kept secret in many camps that they were being killed by poison. Hundreds of victims were killed before the truth came to light. The facade of the *Revier*, the medical personnel, the administrative documentation—all this was deceptive. It did not initially give the impression that there could be a scheme of systematic murder underway. That illusion was maintained down to the last moment: the injection of the lethal liquid. Before the method was adopted of giving the patient a forced injection directly into the heart, everything looked like a normal clinical procedure. There was cotton on the table, a container with alcohol, a rubber tube to wrap around the patient's arm. The murderer, sometimes a doctor but more commonly an SS medic or a prisoner attendant, administered the shot intravenously, following standard injection procedures.

Only a small number of prisoner attendants knew what was actually happening.[12] They alone had the chance to save some patients from certain death.[13] At admission to the *Revier*, they sent sick patients who were sure candidates for selection back to the camp. Patients whose length of treatment had exceeded the prescribed limit were released back into the camp at the proper time, and were then readmitted a few days later as "new admissions." The registration numbers of selected patients were exchanged for the numbers of those who were critically ill, or even already dead; some slips for patients who had been selected were simply laid aside. If attendants had managed to get advance knowledge of the date for a selection, patients were hidden, or at least advised to look as sprightly as possible at the parade.[14] The constraint of triage was not a factor for the SS. However, prisoner doctors and attendants in active opposition had to carry out a priority-based preselection, placing the critically ill on the lethal list in order to save others. This dilemma was deliberately created by the SS. If the prescribed number was not reached in preselection, the SS ordered it to be reached by taking barracks assistants and medical attendants.

Under the threat of death, it forced *Revier* personnel to put the full number of sick on the trucks. Attendants could only save their own lives by allowing the deaths of the patients.

Selection procedures incorporated familiar patterns of modern discipline: the doctor's round, the review parade, the pacing off of the rows, the examination of the bodies.[15] But it was a hasty, often completely summary procedure, sharing little or nothing with a genuine medical examination. It was not a question of gathering knowledge or statistical data about a patient. That numerous selections were carried out by doctors was more often the result of the need to construct a false front than of their medical expertise. At most, it was bound up with their professional *habitus*, their experience in assaying the human body, their familiarity with death. In truth, selection was nothing but a series of death sentences. The inspecting physician was an executioner; the examinees were candidates for death. Selection knew no measure or limit, no gradations. There was only a single disjunction: to the right or to the left, yes or no, life or death. It realized the sovereignty of the individual over the mass, doing so in the process of a judgment, the handing down of a final sentence.[16]

To arrive at their verdict, the judges required neither reflection nor time. They did not let themselves be swayed by anything. Judgments were handed down with an uncanny composure, a sense of certainty that was virtually routine. This swiftness was itself a sign of absolute power. Unhesitating indifference toward the suffering of the victims was the prerequisite for the quickness of the instantaneous decision. The passing of the sentence was a kind of sorting process, a classifying of bodies and objects. Nonetheless, the selectors had a strong sense of inner satisfaction. Selection provided the perpetrators with a strange gratification. They were absolute masters over life and death. They alone had the power to categorize the victims filing past, to regroup and juxtapose them. Selection atomized the rows, and the verdict divided the series into two mutually exclusive classes, the living and those doomed to death. No one was allowed to cross the dividing line. The triumph of total power was mirrored in the mortal agony of the victims. The greater the powerlessness, the greater the judges' gratification. The smoother the selection, the greater their satisfaction; the swifter the sentencing, the greater their passion.

The SS carried out selections in the satellite camps as well. The practice of mustering out the unwanted extended to the periphery of the camp system. The subcamps of Auschwitz were directly connected with the mass annihilation in the main camp. The infirmaries there were too small to take in all the sick. And the private beneficiary firms were always interested in maintaining the percentage of fit prisoners, and holding down the numbers of the sick.[17] The regulation in Monowitz was that there could never be more than 5 percent of the total prisoner population in the *Revier* at any one time. During 1942 and 1943, regular selections took place every other week. The number of victims in these operations is estimated to have been in the neighborhood of 8,000. Bedridden prisoners who needed more than two weeks to recuperate were sent to Birkenau to be gassed. From November 1943 to January 1945, between 1,300 and 1,600 were selected from the nearby camps of Janinagrube, Eintrachthütte, Jawischowitz, and Neu-Dachs. On January 18, 1944, 254 were weeded out in Neu-Dachs, and 247 of these were then gassed in Birkenau. Even prisoners who had been transferred from Auschwitz into the Reich had not escaped the gas chambers of Birkenau. Thus, on September 18, 1944, some 1,000 Hungarian Jewish women were transported by freight car to Hessisch-Lichtenau, a satellite of Buchenwald southeast of Kassel. After a selection there, 206 women were returned to Auschwitz on October 26. All were sent to the gas chambers immediately after their arrival.[18]

Selections also preceded the transports on which the sick or superfluous were sent back from external subcamps to the main camps or directly to a *Sterbelager*. Undesirable prisoners were generally not murdered directly on the spot, but were starved to death and liquidated in "rest camps." The SS set up special barracks in the main camps or established special death camps, where conditions were nothing short of catastrophic: minimal sanitary facilities and medical care, jam-packed housing blocks; there was no water, food rations had been slashed to the point of starvation, epidemics raged. Thus, the camp at Vaihingen an der Enz northwest of Stuttgart served from November 1944 on as the central death camp for the subsidiary camps of Natzweiler in Baden and Württemberg. Prisoners mustered out in Dautmergen, Leonberg, Echterdingen, or Mannheim-Sandhofen went to Vaihingen to die. A total of 2,442 victims was registered.[19] From the end of March 1944, Bergen-Belsen had the same function. This camp was not only the destination of many evacuation marches, but also operated as a reception camp for sick prisoners from other concentration camps. The first transport arrived at the end of March: a thousand prisoners from Dora, most suffering from tuberculosis; only fifty-seven of these survived to the end of the war. In the following months, the men's camp in Bergen-Belsen developed into the largest *Sterbelager*, absorbing transports of sick prisoners from the entire concentration camp system. Thousands were freighted there, from Sachsenhausen, Neuengamme, Friedrichshafen, Magdeburg (Brabag), Ohrdruf, Flossenbürg, Leitmeritz, and Leonberg.[20] The *Sterbelager* had the function of relieving the subcamps by absorbing sick prisoners and lowering the mortality there. The death blocks and *Sterbelager* had the same function for the camps inside the Reich as the Birkenau gas chambers had for the subcamps of Auschwitz.

In the concentration camps, it was the "superfluous" who were selected. The situation was just the opposite in the extermination centers of Operation Reinhard.[21] In Belzec, Sobibór, and Treblinka, the SS only selected as many from the arriving death trains as it required for the smooth running of the program of mass extermination; all the rest were liquidated immediately. Infants, the sick, and the aged were shot at the edge of ditches, where they were buried; the healthy were sent on through the various stations of the death factory and gassed. In the beginning, several strong men were chosen from each transport to carry the frail to the pits, sort the clothing of the dead, and search the bodies for gold and other valuables. Afterward, they too were shot and thrown into mass graves. Only after the camp leadership recognized the value of an experienced team of so-called "Jews for work" (*Arbeitsjuden*), who could relieve the guards and improve the continuity of the extermination work, were permanent Kommandos set up. In Sobibór, the number of these *Arbeitsjuden* fluctuated between three hundred and six hundred; in Treblinka, it ranged between five hundred and one thousand. They were housed in a separate section of the camp, and assigned to fixed Kommandos.

These working prisoners also became victims of selection. Whoever came to the attention of the supervisors, looked weak or sick, or had injuries as a result of being beaten during the day, was placed in the *Lazarett*, a disguised area with a wooden shack and a pit for the dead. The shack had a bench inside. Outside was a Red Cross, the Jewish prisoner-functionaries sported Red Cross armbands, the Kapo wore a white gown—all a deceptive sham, disguising an execution site. Extensive selections in their ranks depended on seasonal fluctuations in the business of killing. If there were no transports, a certain number of the *Arbeitsjuden* became superfluous and were eliminated. Part of the logic of extermination operations was that the survival of the workers was directly linked to the magnitude of the work of annihilation. The more people there were to be gassed, the longer was the respite of survival granted to the Sonderkommandos. The fewer there were to kill, the greater the danger of a camp selection. Of course, the opposite also held true: the greater the interest of camp leadership in a seasoned team of working prisoners, the less likely the prospect that new candidates would be chosen from the arriving transports.

Another law was operative on the selection ramp at Auschwitz. Auschwitz was not only the largest extermination camp but the largest concentration camp as well. As in the death camps, selection at the ramp was a selection of new arrivals; the SS left only as many alive as the camp could absorb or as were needed as workers in the concentration camp system. Unlike the death factories, Jewish prisoners here were deployed at all kinds of jobs. At times prisoners were also selected as a stock in reserve, a kind of labor pool, even though no jobs were yet available. This did not mean that all those fit to work were granted a respite, a period of survival. The personnel had total power to define categories. The practice of classifying prisoners depended on several organizational and situational factors. Ramp selection was a procedure for recruiting workers. At the same time, it was a focus of bureaucratic rivalries and a power situation of a special kind.

The practice of selection among new arrivals was initiated on July 4, 1942; previously, the SS had sent arriving transports as a group to the gas chambers.

To date, it has been impossible to determine exactly how many trains of the RSHA arrived in Auschwitz, how many selections took place in the period until the beginning of November 1944, and how many were gassed immediately. The files of the Political Department with reports on the selection figures were removed by the SS. Nonetheless, there are individual figures that provide some notion of the actual selection quota. Of 69,025 Jews deported from France, 27,200 (39.4 percent) were given prisoner numbers, while 41,805 were murdered immediately in the gas chambers. Of 24,906 Belgian Jews, 8,435 (33.8 percent) were registered and admitted to the camp; of the 56,545 Dutch Jews, 18,270 (32.3 percent) were registered; of 53,789 Greek Jews, 12,757 (23.7 percent) were processed into the camp.[22] Of the 458,000 Hungarian Jews brought in the early summer of 1944 to Auschwitz, 350,000 were gassed and 108,000 (23.6 percent) sent for labor deployment, including many younger women, since the Hungarian army had already inducted many young men into their work battalions earlier.[23] On the basis of 329 transports whose numbers can be reconstructed,[24] one can calculate an average admission rate of 25.9 percent, although, because of the lack of reliable individual figures, the data do not include the massive 1944 deportations from Hungary. Of the 417,727 victims here, 108,244 were processed and registered on the camp rolls in the period in question, while 309,483 were killed immediately. Only in 43 of these selections were more than half of the new arrivals admitted to the camp.

It is difficult to believe that 70 to 80 percent of the persons arriving were actually unfit for work, too old, or too young—even if one takes into consideration the transport time (often several days) spent without adequate food and water and the miserable physical condition of those sent from the ghettos or work camps. Even after the introduction of selections at the ramp, the SS still sent a number of entire transports straight to the gas chamber. The selection quota fluctuated from month to month, day to day, even hour to hour. An example from the final two weeks of August 1943, when the large crematoria were already in operation, is presented in table 3.[25]

How can one account for the unusually high rate of admission during this particular period? Data on the organizational context of selection is provided by other events in this same time span: on August 18, 1943, 532 prisoners were transferred from Auschwitz to Sachsenhausen; on August 19, 1,094 were sent to Buchenwald. On August 25 and 27, 1,000 were transferred to Neuengamme, and 500 were sent to the concentration camp in Warsaw.[26] After a selection conducted in the women's camp on August 21, 1943, 498 women were sent to the gas chambers. In a mass selection in the men's camps in Birkenau on August 29, 4,462 men were chosen for liquidation. The prisoner population was reduced in Auschwitz and subsidiary camps by 8,086 inmates. Consequently, the absorption capacity of the camp had risen, so it was possible at the

TABLE 3

Transports and Selected Admissions to Auschwitz, August 18–31, 1943

Date	Size of Transport	No. admitted		Origin
Aug. 18	1,800	271	(15%)	Saloniki
Aug. 21	500	66	(13%)	Pomerania autobahn camp
Aug. 23	2,000	1,032	(52%)	Kolo labor camp
Aug. 24	100	0	(0%)	Markstädt labor camp
Aug. 25	50	27	(54%)	Berlin
Aug. 26	1,001	236	(24%)	Westerbork (Holland)
	1,500	938	(63%)	Zawierc ghetto
Aug. 27	1,500	805	(54%)	Zawierc ghetto
	205	0	(0%)	Eberswald labor camp
	1,026	1,016	(99%)	Wolsztyn labor camp
Aug. 28	800	667	(83%)	Küstrin labor camp
Aug. 29	2,000	1,392	(70%)	Rawicz labor camp
	1,600	227	(14%)	Koluszki ghetto
Aug. 31	3,000	1,075	(36%)	Bochnia ghetto
Total	17,082	7,752	(45%)	

ramp to categorize an above-average number of prisoners as fit for work, and thus for camp admission. Fitness for work was therefore not a fixed attribute: it was a label changed pragmatically by the SS and adapted to the given situation. It had less to do with actual vocational abilities, age, and physical strength than with the organizational context of selection, and the absolute power of category definition enjoyed by the personnel.

The practice of selection was tied to the concrete need for labor and the absorptive capacity of the camp. If a new external subcamp was about to be set up, the prisoner population was to be expanded, or a large-scale transfer was being prepared, the number of those selected for admission rose for a brief time. Extensive selections inside the camp made room for new prisoners and increased the admissions rate at the ramp. The more who died in the camp, the greater the chances for a new arrival temporarily to escape the gas chamber. Death in the camp reduced death at the ramp. However, it was also true that the better living conditions were in the camp and the fewer the number of camp selections, the less the absorptive capacity—and the more who were killed immediately upon arrival.[27] Similarly, the more concentrated the arrival of transport trains and the greater the number of inmates recently admitted, the smaller the chances for survival at the ramp. In the deadly logic of the system, organizational chance decided on the fitness of arrivals for work. If they arrived at a time when a particularly large number had died in the camp and only

relatively few new prisoners had been admitted, their chances to be catego-
rized "fit for work" increased. If the camp was already filled beyond capacity
because a large number had been registered a few days earlier, their situation
was virtually hopeless.

Selection at the ramp was the linchpin between the social system of the
concentration camp and the process of genocide. Like any organizational
management team, the camp leadership was also interested in managing events
so that the existence of the system was not endangered and the administration did not collapse. When the transports increased and, in a certain sense,
the external pressure of the environment rose, the leadership employed a
familiar method of organizational management: it created buffers and "cleared
present capacities"—that is, it killed thousands in order to make room. In
May 1944, when trains were pouring in from Hungary and, at the same time,
demand was rising for more forced laborers for deployment in the war economy, the SS set up a "transit camp" for "depot prisoners," who were not given
registration numbers and not tattooed. Tens of thousands of younger Jewish
women were crowded together without water, clothing, or underwear in
Section BIII ("Mexico") and the barracks of BIIc, which had been used previously as storehouses. Camp BIIb, which in May had still housed eleven
thousand prisoners from Theresienstadt, was cleared on July 12, 1944, by a
mass selection that claimed more than four thousand victims. Subsequently,
the empty barracks served as reception camps. Jewish deportees from Hungary
and the Lodz ghetto, earmarked for shipment to the Reich, were placed in
Section BIIe, the "Gypsy camp," which had been liquidated on August 2,
1944.[28] The admissions quota did not depend unidirectionally on the mortality
rate in the camp. Mass admissions increased the pressure for annihilation
inside the camp. The more people were admitted to the camp, the more extensive were the camp selections. However, it was by no means the case that
all "depot prisoners" were transferred for labor deployment. Only if a concrete need for workers was made known were they shipped off to the Reich,
or recorded in the official camp register. Mortality in these sections of the
camp was extremely high, and the hygienic conditions were far below the
level of the other camps in Auschwitz. The SS regularly conducted selections
here. At the beginning of October 1944, "Mexico" and BIIc were liquidated.
At least fifteen thousand Jewish women were murdered in the gas chamber
within a few days.[29]

At the ramp in Auschwitz, the antagonistic interests and rationales of the
SS offices collided head-on. For reasons of police security and their overall
political mission, the RSHA, under whose aegis the deportations were carried
out, and its local branch, the Political Department, were interested in killing
as many as possible. The WVHA, whose task was to provide workers for
construction and armaments projects, aimed at retaining the maximum number
possible as laborers, even if they should later die as a result of the nightmare

conditions on the job. The commandant's office pursued the policy of selecting only healthy and strong Jews.[30] Finally, the SS doctors, who conducted
most of the selections or at least were in charge as supervisors, thought in
terms of a "hygienic camp ecology."[31] They agreed with the commandant's
office on the restrictiveness of criteria, though from a medical point of view.
Their rationale was that older prisoners and those who were only condition-
ally fit would soon become unfit for work in any case, further worsening the
already disastrous health situation in the camp. They would aggravate the
danger of epidemics and crowd the already overburdened infirmaries, which
would then require additional personnel. Yet that surplus personnel was not
available.[32] So in the eyes of the SS doctors, it appeared expedient to dispose
of any persons who did not have some chance for survival, sending them to
the gas chambers immediately. The selection of new arrivals was a focus of
bureaucratic conflict, and consequently also a bone of contention between
various factions. This dispute was ultimately decided in favor of the doctors,
though not until the spring of 1943. Until that time, and contrary to the regulations and instructions from Berlin, the camp head office had directed selection; it had sent persons even still fit for work to be gassed, in order to avoid
overburdening the camp administration. At the initiative of the camp medical officers, the doctors now gained supervisory authority.[33] Selection became
a pseudomedical task, a procedure of "medicalized killing."[34] The doctors
took control of selection and, together with other SS leaders, coordinated the
rate of admission. By acquiring official authority over the fate of the transports, the doctors expanded their power sphere in the ramified bureaucracy of
mass annihilation.

The selection process was carried out in accordance with a tried and tested
pattern, and with an organized routine. First, the commandant's office was
informed of the imminent arrival of a transport. It immediately dispatched the
waiting guards and the prisoner Kommandos assigned to ramp duty, and informed the medical department. In turn, that department sent word to the doctor on duty and the motor pool. The trucks drove up to the loading site,[35] and
the guards took up their positions. Supervisors divided the prisoners into
groups: one for opening the boxcars, a second for unloading them, a third to
move the transportable wooden stairway. Noncommissioned SS officers arrived on motorcycles; officials of the camp Gestapo stood by with their brief-
cases; other SS personnel waited, thin riding crops in their hands. If the train
was delayed, those waiting paused for refreshment: a glass of mineral water in
the wooden shed. In the winter, the waiting party kept warm with a glass of
glühwein. Before work began, the ramp was a meeting place to exchange the
latest gossip, a social site for camaraderie.

The freight train backed up to the platform. If the people inside the sealed
cars started banging against the walls, a sentry fired a warning shot on command. Then all was quiet. There was a final warning to the prisoners not to

steal any valuables, and the operation began in earnest. The boxcars were opened; a surge of fresh air rushed in over the exhausted and thirsty human freight in the stifling semidarkness inside. They pushed over the lying bodies toward the open door, loaded down with their suitcases, packages, and bundles. "Everybody out! On the double, get it moving! Take everything, okay, all your stuff on the pile! Form up in rows of five!" Out on the ramp, the dense throng was thickening. People searched for their baggage, children cried out for their parents, translators gave orders, questions were asked of the prisoners. People tried to stay together. The baggage had been unloaded. The prisoners grabbed the belongings from the hands of the new arrivals; they tore their overcoats off their backs. In all the swirl and commotion, the new arrivals had to assemble into formation so that they could be counted.

Based on everything we know, the arrivals on the ramp were torn between emotions: fear, despair, and a glimmer of hope. Dogs barked threateningly on all sides; on all sides sentries were posted, armed with machine guns or fixed bayonets. At night, blinding searchlights bathed the scene in an eerie glow. Few could suspect what all this meant. The prisoners, who began immediately to clear the boxcars and pile up the baggage, were hardly responsive; now and then they offered a soothing word. A few meters away, an SS officer was beating someone to the ground. There was not enough time to gather one's thoughts, to think clearly. The first selection: as the men were separated from the women, there was a renewed flurry of agitation. Mothers did not want to part from their children; many men tried in vain to keep their families together. The two formations, in rows of five, now stood only a few meters apart, side by side. Whoever crossed the line from one side to the other was brutally shoved back. In a few minutes, the arrivals had been separated from everything that had constituted their former lives: first the loss of personal possessions, then their closest family.

After the mass of new arrivals had been arranged in columns, the second selection commenced at the end of the ramp. The first batch was herded over the wooden stairs onto the backs of the waiting trucks. In his notebook, an SS officer marked down one line for every full vehicle. The waiting row moved up quickly. Perhaps a prisoner who chanced by asked "What's your age?" Response: "Fifty." "No, forty, you're forty, got it?" Up front, two groups were forming, one near the trucks, the more robust off to the other side. The officer—in an immaculate uniform, with the composed, confident attitude of someone who does his duty daily, his right elbow resting on his left hand—asked "Occupation?" "Age?" "Are you ill?" His questions had a matter-of-fact tone; they were not unfriendly. An appraising look, a flick of the finger or his crop, and the next person moved up. After a few minutes, the parade had passed. The truck drove off to the crematorium, the selected column marched into the camp. The prisoners loaded the baggage, filled their pockets with bits of food lying about, and dragged the dead from the boxcars onto a pile. SS officers went along the ramp once more, and the Red Cross ambulance pulled away.

The situation at the ramp was a mass state. A transport often included more than one thousand people, sometimes two thousand, faced by only a handful of SS. Nonetheless, firearms were almost never resorted to. Resistance was virtually impossible—and not because once the SS reserves had arrived, everyone would have been mowed down anyhow. No: the situation itself did not permit any form of resistance. The SS was organized as an experienced military force, well trained and ready. The officers knew exactly what they had to do. By contrast, the victims arrived either alone or with their families, crowded together in a dense mass in the cattle cars, drained by the long journey, full of fear and uncertainty. While they were still trying to keep their belongings together in the hubbub, or searching for their families in the throng on the ramp, the SS was already carrying out the first selection. It created order by dividing the crowd up, forcing it into serial columns. Though the victims were hardly able to see beyond the immediate area, the SS had a commanding overview of the entire situation. There was a practical reason why it delegated the task of unloading the freight cars to the prisoner workers, and stayed to one side; they did so in order to be able to take action if the need arose. The new arrivals lacked the coordinating bond indispensable for resistance. They faced the organized unit as an atomized crowd or a serial column. Already in this confrontation of social forms, the contours of power were clear, its distribution unmistakable.

This power was buttressed by the tactical combination of reassurance and violence, intimidation and pacification. Although regulations prescribed "correct" treatment for new arrivals in order to avoid panic and maintain the deception, the SS did not forgo violence when it was deemed necessary. In meeting transports from ghettos or nearby camps (where rumors about Auschwitz were rampant), they proceeded with extreme brutality, herding the crowd, unselected, straight to the gas chambers. In the case of other transports, they made do with threats and forceful intervention, like a police unit charged with the task of maintaining order in a crowd.[36] Instead of shouting and beating, they adopted a cordial tone; the SS officers provided information; they promised food and work. Only when there was unrest did they resort to violence. Selection made use of a tactical division of labor in exerting power. Some subordinate squad leaders behaved with brutality. The sentries stood menacingly in the background, while the doctors, with the ranks of officers, simulated friendliness and cordiality. In contrast with the uniformed thugs, they had a pacifying effect. They inspired confidence. Not that this was enough to allay all fears or dispel mistrust. The weapons of the guards were in evidence—ubiquitous. But anxiety was mingled with hope, uncertainty laced with a sliver of expectation that people could cling to. It was precisely the systematically created ambivalence of the situation that generated confusion and inhibited decisive action.

The people were overwhelmed instantaneously by the force of events. There was extreme time pressure. The SS was intent on completing the operation quickly, so that no one had time to come to their senses and reflect, or gain some distance from what was taking place. The headlong pace hurled the victims into the situation. What was relevant contracted to one's most immediate world: baggage, breathing space in the crowd, family. Caution and circumspection were impossible. The precipitate speed of events generated shocklike ruptures. Phases of waiting or thinking were radically suppressed. From the start, victims had no chance to work out even the rudiments of a plan for action. The plan worked like a preprogrammed machine. Before one could turn around, it was all over.

The great majority of the victims were unable to understand what was happening, let alone to react by fleeing or trying to resist. The few who suspected or even knew something were in no position to seek a way out. There was no exit. Recognition of the imminent end culminates more often in resignation and apathy than in resistance. However, most were successfully deceived. Selection on the ramp was a cleverly constructed situation of "as-if," a lethal manipulation, a massive hoax. Perception was deluded. People failed to see that under the guise of a medical diagnosis, summary death sentences were being handed down seriatim, in a split second. It was beyond the powers of the imagination to comprehend that absolute power, here, on the ramp, was busy realizing the fundamental social law of the series, the superfluity of one and all. The perpetrators performed their duty—composed, routinely, without any special thoroughness. Their concern was in making sure that everything was over and done with quickly. The victims were helpless, in the grip of a situation whose meaning they were unable to grasp.

22

The Death Factory

The long hall, its surface perhaps 160 square meters, was filled with acrid dense smoke. In the middle stood two large, rectangular oven complexes, each equipped with four chambers. Generators had been installed between the ovens to ignite the fire and keep it burning. The ovens were coke-fired, the fuel was hauled over in wheelbarrows. The mass of flames leaped down, passing through two underground flue channels that connected the ovens with towering chimneys, and out, upward into the air. The force of the flames and the heat were so strong that everything trembled from the roar. Several soot-blackened, sweat-covered prisoners were busy scraping a white glowing substance from one of the ovens. It had accumulated in grooves cut in the concrete base under the oven grill. As soon as this mass had cooled off a bit, it turned white-gray. It was the ashes of a person who had been alive just a few hours before, and had departed the world after an agonizing ordeal, without anyone taking any notice. While the ashes were being scraped from one of the oven complexes, the ventilation was turned on in the complex next to it, and all steps were taken to prepare for a new charge. A large number of bodies lay in wait on the damp concrete floor.[1]

A DEATH FACTORY is a work organization whose purpose is the annihilation of large numbers of human beings, without a trace. On a twenty-four-hour basis, victims were murdered, their corpses disposed of. Kommandos of prisoners collected the belongings of the dead and brought them to the sorting sites. The bodies were checked for gold teeth and thrown into mass graves or pits or burned in cremation ovens. Mass annihilation was organized on the basis of a division of labor. The process was integrated into a kind of assembly line, its stations coordinated in temporal sequence. Killing was mechanized by the installation of stationary gas chambers, into which hundreds of persons were lured and then poisoned by carbon monoxide or hydrocyanic acid fumes. The death factory was an apparatus that functioned smoothly, virtually trouble-free, working at a high capacity and speed. A death train arrived at the ramp in the morning; by the afternoon, the bodies had been burned, and the clothing brought to the storerooms.

Death factories were the main installations for the annihilation of the Jews and the Roma and Sinti (Gypsies). The SS set up such death centers in the camps of Operation Reinhard—Belzec, Sobibór, and Treblinka—as well as on the grounds of the two concentration camps at Auschwitz and Majdanek.[2] Prisoners from the camps here were also killed in the gas chambers. The first extermination site, Chelmno, established in December 1941 in the woods forty miles northwest of Lodz, was not a camp but a site equipped with mobile vans, using engine exhaust fumes for extermination.[3] Belzec, Sobibór, and Treblinka were pure death factories, with no organizational link to the concentration camp system. According to previous calculations and estimates,[4] some 225,000 Jews were murdered in Chelmno, 250,000 in Sobibór, 600,000 in Belzec, and an estimated 974,000 in Treblinka. In Majdanek, about 200,000 perished; roughly one fourth of these were murdered in the gas chambers. The number of Jewish victims there is estimated at between 50,000 and 60,000. In Auschwitz, more than 1,000,000 died in the death factories.

Belzec, Sobibór, and Treblinka were set up based on a primitive pattern, and were marked initially by a high degree of improvisation.[5] On several hectares of land, an area was set off for the barracks of the guard personnel and the camp administration. Nearby was the "reception area": a railway ramp, disrobing barracks, and storeroom sheds for clothing and valuables. There was a narrow passageway, dubbed the "tube" (der Schlauch)—and nicknamed the "way to heaven" (der Himmelsweg) by the SS—leading from the reception area to the annihilation sector. This path was bordered on both sides by barbed-wire fencing; the wire had been covered with brushwood to block visibility. At the beginning of the path or about midway down it, there was a hairdressing barracks where prisoners shaved off the women's hair. The annihilation area was secured by fences six feet high. The gas chambers were disguised as showers, and were packed full for a gassing. At the start, no camp had more than three chambers. After the construction of large buildings in the summer of 1942, Sobibór and Belzec boasted six gas chambers each; Treblinka reportedly had ten large chambers. In Treblinka, at the entrance of the building, a dark ceremonial curtain from a synagogue had been hung, bearing the Hebrew inscription: "This is the gate through which the righteous enter" (Psalms 118:20). Beneath the gable, a Star of David had been mounted; there were flowerpots on the stairway leading up to the entrance. Each factory was equipped with diesel motors whose exhaust fumes were pumped into the gas chambers. The dead were loaded on rail wagons that were pulled by Jewish Kommandos to the mass graves. There were no crematoria. In the autumn of 1942, however, efforts were begun to dig up the corpses and burn them on massive grills made of railroad tracks. The piles of ashes and remains of bones were then dumped back in the empty graves, some ten meters deep, and covered over with a thick layer of sand and refuse.

The personnel of these killing centers was not recruited from the ranks of the concentration camp administration; it came from the euthanasia installations.[6] A core group of some one hundred workers was seconded by the Führer Chancellery, to which Organisation T4 was subordinate, to the SS and police leader of Lublin District, Odilo Globocnik. Globocnik was in charge of Operation Reinhard. These office heads, registration officials, and medical attendants already had experience with the gassing of human beings through their involvement in the euthanasia program and Operation 14f13. A number of them had been recalled from the eastern front after temporary deployment there in order, based on their practical experience, to direct the construction and operation of the three death factories of the Reinhard program.[7] The top leadership echelon in each camp consisted of no more than between twenty and forty German SS officers and noncoms. The guard personnel was staffed by units of Ukrainians and ethnic Germans who had been given previous training in the Trawniki camp. In Treblinka, the guard staff ranged between 90 and 120; in Sobibór, it numbered about 90. These guards carried out patrols, observed from the watchtowers, kept guard over the Jewish Kommandos, and took up positions as sentries at the ramp and along the path of annihilation when trains arrived. Each platoon of Ukrainians was under an SS supervisor. These auxiliary forces were equipped with black uniforms, carbines, and leather whips. The German personnel that handled administration and supervisory tasks had only pistols and whips. There were several machine guns and hand grenades kept in readiness for a possible emergency. Thus, each death factory was operated by a total force that numbered not more than 120 to 150, outfitted with minimal infantry gear. Counterposed to them on a daily basis were hundreds of prisoner workers and thousands of deportees. It was not military superiority that secured the functioning of the machinery of mass annihilation, but rather a cleverly devised system of organization, deception, intimidation, and violence.

Majdanek and Auschwitz were under the central concentration camp administration. Consequently, it was not necessary to look for personnel and bring them in from outside; they were already available in the camps. A large proportion of the Majdanek personnel had come in from Buchenwald to help construct the camp. Because there was a constant lack of materials and the Reichsbahn (German railways) refused to provide the transport capacity requested, Majdanek never was able to move beyond a situation of permanent improvisation.[8] For a long time, the mass killing of Soviet POWs and Jewish and non-Jewish Poles was carried out by shooting the victims. In July 1942, the camp was finally provided with a small crematorium. In September 1942, a gassing facility was completed. Initially, it consisted of two chambers in a wooden barracks. Later, three chambers, with a total capacity for gassing up to six hundred persons at one time, were set up in a concrete structure. During gassing operations until September 1943, the mass executions by shooting were halted. Unlike in Operation Reinhard, the new arrivals were generally not herded immediately to the gas chambers. Because the capacity of the extermination facilities was insufficient, the Jews were temporarily confined in Section 2, where they had to wait several days outside for selection. On November 3, 1943, when the gas chambers were no longer in operation, all Jews still alive in the Majdanek camp complex were murdered in a major massacre, code-named "Harvest Festival" by the SS. Construction of a larger crematorium was not completed until this time. In Majdanek, many of the dead were burned on enormous pyres before the crematorium was finished. The remaining bone was ground in a mill to a fine pulp; ash and bone meal were used as fertilizer for the SS vegetable gardens.

The largest death factories were built in Auschwitz. This was not done as part of a long-term plan, but rather under the pressure of the ongoing program for mass murder. The increase in the number of death transports and extreme overcrowding in the camp made it imperative to boost killing capacity. The first gassings were carried out by the SS in September 1941 in the basement of Block 11 in the main camp. Then the morgue near the crematorium was put to use as a gas chamber. Because of the lack of secrecy and limited effectiveness of the crematorium, operations were shifted in 1942 to Birkenau; two farmhouses in a wooded area were converted, one at at time, into gas chambers. The corpses were transported by narrow-gauge railway to the pits located several hundred meters away, where they were initially buried. In the autumn of 1942, however, they were exhumed again and the remains burned. Since these provisional installations likewise proved insufficient, construction was started in July 1942 on the four large death factories, which were put into operation between March and June 1943. These factories centralized and mechanized all stages of the extermination process. Each unit had disrobing rooms, gas chambers, and retort furnaces for reducing the bodies to ashes. In crematoria 2 and 3, the gas chambers were located underground. The corpses were transported by an electric freight elevator up to the area for burning. Table 4 provides information about the death factories in Auschwitz and their respective periods of operation.[9]

According to design, the crematoria were constructed to handle a maximum of 4,756 bodies a day. However, this was solely a technical value that included time for servicing the units and removal of cinder from the ovens. Actually, up to 5,000 bodies a day were cremated in crematoria 2 and 3, and up to 3,000 a day in crematoria 4 and 5. The capacity of the pyres near the bunkers was unlimited. In the summer of 1944, during the deportation of the Hungarian Jews, bunker 2 was put into operation once again. During this peak period, some 24,000 persons a day were killed and burned.

How was it possible to murder some three million persons in these death factories over a period of about three years? My concern here is not the social

TABLE 4

Death Factories in Auschwitz and the Immediate Vicinity:
Capacity and Period of Operation

Main Camp, Auschwitz

Crematorium I	Gas chamber, three ovens for 340 bodies; early 1942 to the spring of 1943

Birkenau

Bunker I	Two gas chambers for 800 persons, disrobing rooms, mass graves; 1942
Bunker II	Four gas chambers for 1,200 persons, disrobing rooms, burning pits; 1942, remodeled in the spring of 1944, and used during the day as a reserve
Crematorium II	Subterranean installation with five ovens, daily capacity of 1,440 bodies, gas chamber for up to 3,000 persons; March 1943 to November 1944
Crematorium III	Subterranean installation with five ovens, daily capacity of 1,440 bodies, gas chamber for up to 3,000 persons; June 1943 to November 1944
Crematorium IV	Aboveground installation with two ovens, daily capacity of 768 bodies, four gas chambers for approximately 3,000 persons; March 1943 to October 7, 1944 (destroyed by prisoners)
Crematorium V	Aboveground installation with two ovens, daily capacity of 768 bodies, four gas chambers for approximately 3,000 persons; April 1943 to November 1944

prehistory of the persecution and deportation of the Jewish population of Europe, the ideological and practical radicalization of the program of annihilation, or the complex bureaucratic field of the offices involved. Rather, the key question is: how did the the death factories themselves function? The analytical focus is thus not on the causal factors behind the genocide, but the preconditions for what took place within the perimeter of the death camps and concentration camps after the arrival of the transport trains.[10]

The first prerequisite for smooth operations was the organization of the killing and the disposal of its traces. Organization involves a coordination of schedule and concrete tasks. Task areas are defined and roles are allocated in such a way that an interdependent network of procedures is created. Sequences are frequently standardized and made permanent. A hierarchical ordering of responsibility for decision making is constructed and centralized in a small number of offices. Organization saves time and labor and implements routines, thus enhancing performance and augmenting power. Individual activities are combined and bundled into collective action. It was less the mechanization of violence, as is sometimes maintained, than the high degree of organization of the process of killing that made the death factories into such an unprecedented and unparalleled machinery for extermination.

Organization integrates work processes and sequences. After selection, the victims were brought to the disrobing rooms. Simultaneously, the ovens were fired up in the crematoria, and wood was piled in readiness next to the burning pits. The victims were told that after showering, they would be given back their clothing, or they were promised warm soup. In the death camps, they had to hand over their valuables at a special window. Then they were hurried on in groups, separated by sex, through the "tube." The women were told to be quick—otherwise the shower water would start getting cold. While the first groups were jammed into the gas chambers, prisoner Kommandos were already at work bringing their clothing to the sorting site and packing it there properly for shipment. On command, a Ukrainian assistant turned on the motor. If it did not start right away, the victims sometimes stood for half an hour, crowded together until they died. In Auschwitz, the victims noticed quickly that the shower heads were a sham. Lights were turned out, and the executioner, who had driven up in a Red Cross ambulance and wore a gas mask equipped with a special filter, shook the Zyklon B crystals into the shafts. After fifteen minutes at the most, all were dead. The giant fans were turned on to clear the chamber, the door was unbolted, and the members of the Sonderkommando, wearing rubber boots and gas masks, hosed down the corpses with water and dragged them out. The members of the transport Kommando hauled them to the freight elevator or to the morgue. Dentists pulled the gold teeth and fillings from the jaws of the dead, barbers cut off their hair, the stokers filled the ovens. After a short while, the dead had been reduced to ashes. The disrobing room and gas chamber were cleaned and readied for the next transport.

The meshing of the functions into a virtually trouble-free assembly line accelerated the process of liquidation and ensured simultaneous activity at several sites. While the last batch of the dead was burning down to ashes in the ovens or on the pyres, the next batch was already being slaughtered. Such organizational integration transformed the annihilation of human beings into a continuous process. One function was linked to the next. The killing itself was now only a single stage in a series—not an individual act of violence, but a single step in a planned sequence of operations. It is inaccurate to speak of the executioner's act in this context. Turning on the motor or throwing Zyklon B into the shafts resembled the activating of a device: a cool, objective operation. Killing was mechanically mediated; it was a deed performed at a distance, one whose effects the perpetrator did not see. The "disinfector," as the executioner was euphemistically dubbed, got into his vehicle and drove off. He had nothing further to do with the "utilization" (*Auswertung*) and disposal of the bodies. Killing was solely a function within the regulated division of labor, a repetitive activity. The death factory rationalized killing, transforming it into labor that required no internal involvement—not even cold-bloodedness. All it asked was for one to be matter-of-fact, efficient, and exacting.

A further condition for the smooth functioning of the death factory was the systematic deception of the victims. For a trouble-free operation, it was necessary that no one become suspicious or panicky or put up resistance. The SS was dependent on the victims' cooperation: they had to disrobe willingly, put their belongings in order, and then enter the gas chambers without any hesitation. To send thousands to their death simultaneously was not an operation that could be carried out using violence alone. Brutality costs time and delays smooth operations. So the victims were lured into the deadly trap. Trees were planted around the crematoria, or victims were brought to a pastoral site: a farmhouse in the midst of a thriving birch woodland. Innocuous signs were put up so that the final stop looked like a train station. In Sobibór, a special barracks was erected before the arrival of the transports from the Netherlands, where the new arrivals were told to deposit their baggage for "safekeeping." There was a wooden booth in Treblinka, the *kleine Kassa* (small cashier's office), where prisoners left all their documents, watches, and jewelry. In the disrobing rooms, clothes hooks and numbers were put up; signs on the walls in several languages instructed the victims to hang their clothes, along with their shoes, laced together, on the hooks. They were told to make careful note of the number in order to be able to find it more easily after showering. Signs pointed the way to the gas chambers; the rooms were sometimes tiled and equipped with dummy showerheads. In order to buttress the ruse, the SS gave little speeches. In Sobibór, an SS squad leader donned a white doctor's coat and lied to the victims: prior to labor deployment, he said, several hygienic measures had to be taken. For that reason, they would initially have to shower. He embellished his talk with a few remarks about a Jewish state that was to be set up in the Ukraine, earning applause and cheers from his audience for this promise. In Treblinka, the sick and frail were promised medical treatment in the sick bay. Then they were brought to the edge of the burning pits and shot in the nape of the neck, falling headfirst onto the blazing pyres. In Auschwitz, the SS leaders sometimes mounted the podium together, giving their talks in the yard of the crematorium. One delivered the salutations, a second the instructions, a third chimed in if the noise began to get out of hand.[11] In the beginning in Auschwitz, filled with a sense of unchallenged superiority, the SS gave speeches that were nothing but diatribes. But later it changed its tactics to gentle declarations and empty promises in order to lull the victims into a feeling of security and dispel their distrust.

Despite the camouflage, the extermination sequence did not always go off as smoothly as planned. The situation in the yard of the crematorium or the disrobing rooms was just as precarious for the SS as that on the ramp. The victims of the camp selections who were loaded onto trucks generally knew that they were heading for certain death. However, the *Muselmänner* were usually already so weak that they were unable to put up any resistance. During the initial phase at Treblinka, the new arrivals could see mountains of decomposing bodies, since the process of extermination was still totally disorganized. New transports came in before the last batches of corpses could be disposed of. Many reacted to the shock by suffering a nervous collapse, and were driven on through the "tube" by the lash. In Auschwitz,[12] Jews from the Sosnowitz ghetto put up passive resistance at one point, but it was crushed by extreme brutality. In the mass panic, people finally tore the clothes from their bodies to avoid the blows of the SS for undressing "too slowly." After the arrival of a transport from Bialystok, a woman who had been informed about what was happening by an acquaintance in a Sonderkommando ran screaming hysterically from group to group. At first, no one paid her any notice, but then mistrust and fear began to spread, and the crowd pushed menacingly toward the exit where three SS officers were standing. The throng was finally pacified by a combination of whistles, polite reassuring words, and the appearance of heavily armed SS sentries and a snarling pack of SS dogs. The most dramatic incident on record occurred with a transport from Bergen-Belsen. A Jewish woman killed an SS man in the disrobing room, his comrades fled from the room, and it was bolted shut immediately. In the darkness, a panic broke out. After the arrival of the commandant, all those still inside the room were mowed down by machine-gun fire. Those who had fled in the dark into the gas chamber were poisoned there by the insertion of Zyklon B.

If deception failed, the SS resorted to direct violence; violence was a constant presence in any case. The people were forced to rush, first by orders, then by blows. The sick were dragged from the freight cars and thrown with the dead onto the dump cars. Occasionally there were deeds of excess on the ramp: bloodhounds were let loose,[13] or hesitant victims were yanked from the crowd and dragged away. In Sobibór, some supervisors distinguished themselves by seizing small children they found left behind in the boxcars by their tiny legs and smashing their skulls against the walls of the cars.[14] In the reception of arriving transports from Hungary in Auschwitz, the SS dispensed with long-winded speeches and deceptive formalities, herding the victims immediately and violently into the waiting gas chambers. During executions at the edge of the burning pits, all inhibitions were cast aside. Whoever resisted, begged for mercy, or pleaded was thrown alive into the flames. In the eyes of the SS killers, these persons were already dead anyhow; their fates were sealed. Deception was only one element in the staging. As in the selections, victims here were misled, simultaneously intimidated and pacified, shocked and reassured. It was precisely this amalgam of anxiety and expectation, suspicion and trust, despair and hope, reassurance and mad rush that shattered the victims' orientation and paralyzed them, entangling them in a situation from which there was no exit. It is quite mistaken to allege there was some sort of "submissive willingness" to die. These persons were lured into a deadly trap, one whose camouflage was often incomplete, but ambivalent enough to smother any stirring of resistance. Manipulation worked.

The final condition for the effectiveness of the death factories was the forced labor of the Jewish Sonderkommandos. The SS deliberately had Jews burn Jews, as though it wished to prove that the members of the subrace accepted any degradation and even killed one another: as though it wished to shift the burden of guilt onto the victims themselves. The sorters, barbers, corpse carriers, stokers, and gravediggers were the personnel who performed the grisly manual labor of the death factories. The fate of the Sonderkommandos is among the most appalling chapters in the history of the concentration and death camps. These prisoners were left alive for a time in order to dispose of their relatives, neighbors, and fellow Jews. Their behavior cannot be judged by the conventional moral conceptions of civil society. The institution of the Sonderkommando shows to what point human beings can be brought by permanent threat of death. Just as the death factory was kept operating by the constant labor of the Sonderkommandos, their temporary survival depended on the continued operation of the death factories. Each new death transport prolonged the lives of those whose job it was to burn the bodies of the dead.

Prisoner workers in the death camps were chosen during selection on the ramp. The SS wisely assumed that recruitment would be easier if it selected the candidates from the frightened and disoriented new arrivals, shattered by the ordeal of the transport, drained of any power to resist. Only after interest shifted to the building up of a stable organization did the SS set up permanent Kommandos and assign the work to specialists. In Sobibór,[15] the new arrivals were received by a *Bahnhofskommando* (station Kommando) dressed in caps and uniforms; another group took the possessions of the victims to the sorting site, where a third group sorted and packed the items according to regulations. Jewish shoemakers had to make shoes and boots for the German personnel. There was a laundry, kitchen, and workshops to supply the camp with goods and services. In Treblinka, a Kommando of so-called *Goldjuden* was formed, made up of goldsmiths, jewelers, and bank clerks. Twice a day, carrying small cases, they went to the warehouses and collected the valuables. In the *große Kassa* (main cashier's office), a small barracks next to the commandant's office, they sorted the rings, jewels, banknotes, and gold teeth brought in after gassing. The corpse workers in the extermination areas, each Sonderkommando numbering about 150, were housed in segregated barracks and, under threat of death, were not allowed to establish contact with the other prisoners. Their job was to empty the gas chambers, examine the orifices of the dead bodies for possible valuables, extract gold teeth from the victims' jaws, and then stack the dead in the pits. The *Waldkommando* (forest Kommando) had the task of chopping down wood in the nearby forests and hauling it to camp for use in the burning of corpses.

With the establishment of the Sonderkommandos, internal subcamps were set up alongside the death factories; their rules resembled those of the concentration camps. The Kommandos were subordinated to Jewish Kapos, who had unlimited power to mete out punishment. The day was punctured by the customary roll calls. Material facilities and medical care were minimal. Toward the end, the prisoners in Treblinka were even given numbers. The SS had the prisoner-staffed workshops produce items for their own needs. It maintained an orchestra and put on boxing matches. Nonetheless, these death camps cannot be equated with concentration camps. The number of worker prisoners was never more than a few hundred, a thousand at the most. The fate of the inmates was sealed from the start. As accomplices, they were "living on borrowed time." Although the skilled workers in whom the SS had a personal interest were treated somewhat better by comparison, the corpse-processing Kommandos were under a barbaric and brutal regime. Whoever appeared to be working too slowly was beaten to death or shot. Replacements could be found every day from the transports. If "seasonal work" slackened because there were no transports for a time and the death factory stood idle, the SS immediately depleted the Kommando ranks and murdered the superfluous prisoners. These camps can be compared only with the Sonderkommando units in Auschwitz. They too had only one function: to keep the death factories operating.

In Auschwitz,[16] the first Sonderkommando, consisting of some eighty prisoners, was assigned the task of burying the victims gassed in bunkers 1 and 2. It was liquidated in August 1942. The second Sonderkommando, made up of from 150 to 300 prisoners, had the job of exhuming the corpses buried until November 1942—about 107,000—and burning their remains. On December 3, 1942, the gravediggers were gassed in the crematorium of the main camp. Both Kommandos were considered provisional from the start. The SS recruited workers in the men's camp and isolated them in bunker 11. Later on, young men were taken directly from the ramp without being processed for admission to the camp. From mid-1944 on, the Sonderkommando was housed in attic of the crematorium building. In their "leisure time," some played soccer down in the yard, even competing against a team of the SS. The Kommando reached its peak strength of about 1,000 men during the death transports from Hungary, when the dead were burned in two shifts, day and night. It consisted of 450 Hungarian, 200 Polish, and 180 Greek Jews, and was commanded by 19 Russian POWs, 5 Poles, and a German Kapo. After that peak period, part of the Kommando was liquidated. On August 30, 1944, 874 prisoners were deployed in the four Birkenau crematoria. Unlike in the death camps, the Sonderkommando in Auschwitz did not need to sort the belongings of the dead. Additional workers, including many women, were deployed for that task in the section known as Kanada; these workers had nothing to do with the Sonderkommando.

The Sonderkommando had to perform gruesome death work. Data from three work situations can serve to illustrate their duties: the clearing of the gas chambers, the servicing of the ovens, and activities performed at the skull-examination site of the pyres. After the door to the gas chamber was unbolted, the "hauling Kommando" sprung into operation.

> The corpses are not lying scattered around the room, but are piled high one on top of the next. That's easy to explain: the Zyklon B tossed in from outside develops its deadly fumes first near the ground, spreading gradually to the higher levels of air. So the poor victims trample over one another, one person climbs over the next. The higher they are, the longer it takes for the gas to reach them. . . . I can see infants, children and the aged at the bottom, the stronger men are lying above them. There they lie, their limbs intertwined, their bodies lacerated from scratches, bleeding from the nose and mouth. Their heads are bloated and blue, disfigured beyond recognition. Nonetheless, the men of the Sonderkommando often spot their relatives among the bodies.[17]

Whoever was still alive directly next to the door was shot by the SS. The haulers surrounded the pile of corpses and hosed them down. Then they pulled apart the entangled bodies, tied leather straps around the fists of the dead, clenched in death's agony, and pulled the bodies through the hall into the morgue or onto the freight elevator. After a signal from a bell, the elevator, with a capacity of about twenty bodies, was sent up. There the doors opened automatically, and the second carrier Kommando dragged the corpses across the concrete floor to the "utilization station." There the toothpullers opened the mouths of the dead with crowbars, removed any gold teeth, and placed them in a solution of hydrochloric acid to remove any flesh and bone clinging to the teeth. The body carriers required five to six hours to remove three thousand bodies from the gas chambers of a crematorium. After this, the rooms were cleaned. The stokers charged the ovens by placing three bodies on a litter, and then shoved this on runners into the chamber. When extracting the litter, the bodies were held with a pitchfork so that they stayed inside. After the chamber door was cranked down, cremation began. In order to save fuel and make sure the mass burned evenly, a commission of SS officers and civilian technicians devised a new procedure in the autumn of 1943: "express work."[18] The dead were sorted into four piles according to physical constitution, and a suitable combination of physiques was placed on the litter so that when they had caught fire, the bodies would continue burning without having to add extra coke: two well-nourished men plus an emaciated woman, or two *Muselmänner* and a strong, muscular man. Nonetheless, the oven capacity proved insufficient. The chambers had to be left to cool, the chimney ducts had to be cleaned, internal surfaces had to be repaired. For that reason, the normal load was constantly exceeded, and more than three bodies were burned at the same time. Only when there were official inspection visits did the SS Kommando leader make sure the prisoners were working according to the regulations.

As in the death camps, the dead were also burned on gigantic pyres in Auschwitz in the summer of 1944. Behind bunker 2, prisoners working in alternate shifts had to dig deep ditches. A Kommando of twenty-five men piled the corpses in three layers on a large iron grating. Fifteen stokers laid sawed-up beams, wood shavings, and pieces of wood into the pits, ignited them with torches and rags drenched in oil, and then tended to the fire. They constantly jabbed with long iron pokers between the charred smoldering carcasses, and poured oil, methanol, or boiling human fat that had accumulated in the receptacles at the two ends of the pit into the flames. It took about five to six hours to turn the twelve hundred corpses in a pit into ashes. Then water was directed from all sides onto the ashes and remains of bones. As soon as the surface had cooled somewhat, wooden floorboards covered with black metal plate were tossed into the pits. The thirty-five men of the *Aschenkommando* now climbed down into the pit and shoveled out the glowing-hot ashes. The only flimsy protection the men had against the danger of being burned or blinded was flat caps and protective goggles. The remains were transported in wheelbarrows at double time to the ash-deposit site. The charred limbs and torsos were removed with special forks there, and burned a second time in a smaller pit. The remaining ash was pounded to a pulverized mass on a rectangular concrete surface.

> You could have thought you were on some large-scale construction site where the foundation for a large building had just been completed. There were numerous metal sieves with coarse, medium and finer mesh standing here and there on the concrete floor. Behind these were many many piles of finely pulverized, whitish-gray ash. . . . A large group of prisoners was out on the concrete surface, busy eradicating the final traces of the mass murders that had been carried out in the gas chambers. They were almost all Jews from Greece. Some of them were engaged in pulverizing the ashes, working with massive iron pounders at a steady rhythm. During this dogged, monotonous work, they sang . . . a melancholy song, over and over again, carefree, with sonorous, expressive voices. It seemed as if they were trying to keep the beat with their iron pounders in time with the melody. Others worked untiringly, shoveling the ashes up against a metal sieve. What did not pass through the mesh was crushed again and again—until the ashes were pulverized so fine that even sieves with the finest mesh were no longer an impediment.[19]

The agonies suffered by members of the Sonderkommandos defy description. Attempts at interpretation must necessarily remain superficial. Nonetheless, some comments on this most extreme form of forced collaboration are in order. These individuals worked in a situation of the constant threat of death and paralyzing violence. The SS let them live in order to work. Whoever refused was put to death. On July 21, 1944, when four hundred Jews from Corfu who had spent three weeks in the quarantine camp refused any involvement with the Sonderkommando, they were gassed.[20] Whoever wished to live another hour had to work. The only way out was suicide—martyrdom. It is known that some did commit suicide while being admitted to the Sonderkommando or immediately thereafter. In addition, there was no certainty whatsoever about how long a respite one might have. No one could predict when the SS would liquidate the Sonderkommando. Yet one often clings to the slimmest of hopes so long as the end is not imminent, even if virtually all facts speak against it. The sheer will to survive triggers rigorous defense mechanisms that brush aside even the greatest dangers. The death of the other person is not your own. Even in a situation of certain death, people frequently do not react with rebellion, but with apathy. One becomes indifferent to the environment; behavior turns mechanical. The protective armor of apathy permits habits to form, and these habits bolster indifference toward one's own actions; they blunt perceptions and the sense of morality.[21] Alcohol was also a factor. This was compounded by a radical foreshortening of the temporal horizon that warded off the fear of death. Now what loomed all-important was the next hour or day—the immediate presence of survival. To achieve that, everything was permissible. If the SS gave the order, members of the Sonderkommando beat the victims who were too slow in disrobing. In executions, they dragged the victims to the edge of the pit and held their heads, so that all the executioner had to do was to pull the trigger. Although it was officially forbidden, the SS allowed the Sonderkommandos to enrich themselves by taking food, shoes, or valuables from the possessions of the gassed. In the block of the Sonderkommando in the men's camp in Birkenau, there was a brisk trade on the bartering market.[22] How long the Sonderkommandos would continue to survive depended on the death transports, as did their "standard of living."[23] They took from the piles of belongings what those who had been gassed had left behind. As a result, the Sonderkommando members were both envied and despised by the other prisoners. The personnel of the death factory lived off the factory's operation and "output."

Revolts in the death factories could be launched only by the Jewish Sonderkommandos. They were the only ones in a position to plan and prepare an uprising. They were familiar with the spatial and military situation, and had the time to procure weapons, form fighting groups, and set up secret information channels. Organized labor in the death factory was the prerequisite for organized resistance. The uprising in Treblinka was prepared over a long period of time.[24] When, in the spring of 1943, the prisoners learned of the ghetto uprising in Warsaw and the number of death trains declined, it became clear that the SS would soon liquidate the Sonderkommando. Attempts were made to purchase weapons from Ukrainian guards, a second key was clandestinely prepared for the SS weapons storeroom, and small conspiratorial groups were set up in individual camp sections. These activities were constantly threatened by informers and demanded top secrecy. The plan envisioned disposing of the main thugs, disarming the sentries, cutting telephone lines, and destroying the facilities of the death factory. Then the penal camp located two kilometers away was to be liberated, and a partisan group would be set up together with Poles in the nearby woods. On August 2, 1943, after the leadership had postponed the date several times, the revolt finally erupted. Everything went off according to plan, until the prisoners, in the early afternoon, accidentally caught sight of an informer speaking with an SS officer, and had to fear possible betrayal. Events then unfolded precipitately. Although not all of the weapons had been distributed, shooting broke out between the prisoners and the Ukrainians in the watchtowers. The barracks started burning, the gasoline tank exploded, and prisoners stormed the perimeter fences. However, they were not successful in cutting the telephone lines, and the gas chambers remained standing. The SS raised the alarm and sent for reinforcements, pursuing on horses and in trucks those attempting to flee. During the raid, many escapees were robbed by anti-Semitic Poles and handed over to the SS. The number who succeeded in breaking out is estimated at some 200; 150 are believed to have reached the wooded area several kilometers away. It is unlikely that more than fifty or sixty of these escaped prisoners survived to see the end of the war.

The revolt in Sobibór came about in a similar situation of utter hopelessness.[25] Several attempted escapes and plans for an uprising had proved abortive. The kitchen staff was supposed to mix poison with the food for the SS. In another plan, a tunnel was to be dug passing under the boundary fortifications; in still another scheme, barracks were to be set ablaze, and in the ensuing commotion, prisoners would attempt to escape. At the end of May 1943, the last workers were brought from Belzec to Sobibór and shot. The female sorters discovered notes in their clothing on which the victims had written where they came from. The fate awaiting the Sonderkommando in Sobibór was now clear to them. A small group attempted to forge ties with Ukrainian guards whose aversion to the SS was apparent. But those guards escaped alone to join the partisans. The SS response was to bolster perimeter fortifications by preparing a supplementary mine field. Time pressure increased, and an SS supervisor who was in sympathy with the prisoners passed on the information that Sobibór was coming to an end. On September 23, 1943, a group of Russian Jews who had served as officers in the Red Army were admitted to the camp. They took over the military preparation of the uprising. A second tunnel collapsed after a sudden rainstorm. Now the only remaining option was direct confrontation. On the evening of October 9 or 10, the SS permitted the prisoners to conduct prayers for Yom Kippur in one of the barracks. This provided the staff with the pretext for informing the others about the plan. While the women prayed loudly, orders were distributed in one corner of the barracks. The artisans were to lure individual SS officers into the workshops and kill them; another group was supposed to break into the weapons depot; the task of the women and girls was to steal weapons from the SS residence barracks. On October 14, 1943, the day had finally arrived. In the late morning and early afternoon, eleven SS officers were killed and their weapons distributed. However, an SS officer unexpectedly drove a truck into the camp to unload it and became suspicious, and the entire disguised operation was uncovered. After a premature whistle signal, a disorganized crowd of prisoners who were not initiated into the plan gathered and then stormed the weapons depot, where they were met by machine-gun fire. Sentries began firing from the watchtowers. In the general mayhem, the prisoners rushed to the gates and fences. Some three hundred escaped from various sections of the camp; however, none succeeded in fleeing from the extermination section. Many were blown to bits in the minefields, yet they blazed a path for others to follow. During the subsequent pursuit by the police and the Wehrmacht, airplanes were reportedly also used to hunt down the escapees. In the following days, some one hundred escaped prisoners were captured and executed along with those who had remained in the camp.

Because of the sheer size of the camp area, a mass breakout in Auschwitz was an even more hopeless venture than one in the death camps. It was inconceivable that a large number of weapons could be procured from SS depots, and it was just as unlikely that foreign guards could successfully be bribed. The rebels were facing a force of 2,000 SS men, not 150. The SS was omnipresent on the grounds of the crematoria where the Sonderkommando had been locked in. To complicate matters, the Sonderkommandos enjoyed numerous material privileges in comparison with the other prisoners, and the SS kept them submissive by providing these favors. In an uprising, the Sonderkommando had something to lose. However, this situation changed in the summer of 1944 when the death transports from Hungary began to taper off and the SS carried out a first selection among the roughly one thousand prisoner workers. As in the death camps, the rebellion broke out in Auschwitz when the situation appeared hopeless and there was no alternative.[26] Conformity and obedience had become just as senseless as fatalism and indifference. The Sonderkommando had already planned an organized breakout for mid-June 1944. Tasks had been assigned, the prisoners were ready for a fight, the date had been fixed—but at the last minute, the resistance group in the camp called off the revolt. The Sonderkommando had connections with the underground in the camp, and had obtained from them a small amount of explosives that the women had smuggled out of a munitions factory. Nonetheless, there was a fundamental clash of interests between the Jewish death workers and the non-Jewish resistance group. Although the latter hoped for liberation by the approaching Red Army and did not want to expose the camp to German mass reprisals, the Jews saw no further chances for survival in continuing to hold still and bide their time. The difference in the pressure of annihilation between the camp and the death factory split the resistance.

On the afternoon of October 7, a part of the Sonderkommando risked going it alone in a final act of desperation. They were armed with stones, three hand grenades, hand-made explosives, and a few flat-nosed pliers to cut through the barbed wire. Several days before, the SS had taken two hundred men from the Sonderkommando under the pretext that they were to be transferred to the Gleiwitz labor camp, and had secretly gassed them in the disinfection barracks of the main camp. Contrary to usual practice, the SS burned the bodies itself at night in the crematorium. The next morning, however, the stokers, poking in the remains, were able to identify their dead comrades. On the morning of October 7, the Sonderkommando received news from the underground that the camp leadership was planning a total liquidation. At noon, the SS scheduled a further selection. Several nights earlier, the Kapos, after heated discussions with the resistance group, had put together a list of three hundred names. When the SS called out the names at the morning roll call, some whose names were on the list had gone into hiding. SS men went to search crematorium 4, and were met by a sudden hail of stones. Shooting broke out, and crematorium 4 went up in flames. When the prisoners in crematorium 2 saw the blaze, they thought the moment had arrived for the general uprising in the camp. They overpowered the German chief Kapo and threw him, along with an SS officer, into the burning oven. Then they tore down the fences and fled. Prisoners in crematoria 3 and 5 did not join in—either because they were not informed, or because the SS had quickly managed to bring the situation there under control. In the camp as well, the hoped-for mass breakout did not materialize, even though the rebellious prisoners had torn down the fence surrounding the women's camp. The camp siren sounded the alarm immediately. Within a few short minutes, mobile SS units had surrounded the wooded area near crematorium 4 and shot the prisoners. In nearby Rajsko, escaped prisoners barricaded themselves in a barn. The SS set fire to the barn and slaughtered the escapees inside. Before the breakout, the strength of the Sonderkommando had been 663; two days later, it numbered 212. None of the rebels escaped. But three SS officers were dead, and twelve had been wounded. Crematorium 4 had been blown up and was unusable.

> Their fate was sealed right from the start. Despite that, this revolt by the Sonderkommando became a symbol. At the site where millions of innocent victims had been murdered, the first SS murderers were killed, felled by the avenging hands of prisoners. And it was Jews who did this. This uprising demonstrated to the non-Jewish comrades-in-fate in Auschwitz what Jews were capable of.[27]

The death factories were based on the principle of extermination without a trace. Nothing was to be left behind to point to genocide. After killing operations were halted in Belzec, the camp was dismantled and the area was planted over in pine trees. After the war, it was discovered that the grounds of the former camp had been dug up. The local population had rummaged there, searching for valuables, and had uncovered the remains of charred human bones and decaying bits of flesh. After the uprising, Treblinka was not rebuilt. Deportees from a few more smaller transports were put to death in the undamaged gas chambers there. Finally, the remaining buildings were torn down, and the area was levelled and planted in lupines. Housed in a newly constructed farm, a Ukrainian caretaker was assigned to watch the grounds. The SS blew up the last crematorium in Auschwitz a few hours before liberation. Right to the end, bodies had been burned there. In the six storerooms still standing, the liberators found 348,820 men's suits, 836,255 women's dresses and coats, 5,525 pairs of women's shoes, 13,964 rugs, and mountains of children's clothing, spectacles, shaving brushes, and dentures. The rooms of the tannery contained seven tons of human hair.[28]

Epilogue

THE CONCENTRATION CAMP is part of the history of modern society. The destructive power of modern technology was tested on the battlefields of mass war, with the slaughterhouses of the concentration camps serving as a proving ground for the destructive power of modern organization. The modern era liberated humanity from incomprehensible forces, yet at the same time immensely increased the power of human beings to kill. Measured against this hypertrophy, earlier forms of power seem fragmentary, irrational, crude in their means, and limited in scope. Born on the threshold of the twentieth century, organized terror reached its most extreme form in the German camps. In anthropological significance, the concentration camp is as important as modern warfare. Using the technology of advanced weaponry, humankind can extinguish itself in a single blow. Using the organization of terror, it can methodically destroy all of humanity.

Contrary to all experience, many people today tend to view the twentieth century as the quintessence of civilized progress. It would seem that the culture of rationality has finally overcome earlier phases of despotism and barbarity. Although cracks have appeared in this ideology, the self-image of the present is still marked by a widespread belief in moral development and trust in the power of reason, peace, and democracy. Perhaps this is one reason why the obverse of modernity, the mammoth burgeoning of repression and force, is so laden with taboos. One can sometimes hear commentators aver that despite all their horrendousness, the crimes of the National Socialists were only part of a historical episode, a kind of cancerous growth on the body of a society that was historically belated in its development. This perspective contends that their deeds sprang from the residue of a dull and obtuse irrationalism, and from specifically German traditions of authority and authoritarian obedience. Dachau and Mauthausen signify a singular "relapse into barbarity," a recidivism that otherwise could not have come to pass.

Such explanations offer a certain consolation. They protect us from the realization that something similar could happen again. They shield us from the disconcerting thought that civilization is only a thin varnish, that organized terror might derive from tendencies intrinsic to the structure of modern society. The nightmare of a "house of servitude" has not come true. It was surpassed many times over by reality. To speak of a "relapse into barbarity" downplays the gravity of the facts and disregards its social prerequisites. Like the war of annihilation, the order of terror and the extermination of entire population groups in special camps and killing sites—set up specifically for that end—do not stand in some no-man's-land beyond the frame of modern civilization. Certainly, Auschwitz could only have come to pass in the special circumstances of German social history. Viewed historically, the creation of camps, torture chambers, and execution sites always takes place in concrete contexts. Yet not everything in the system of the German concentration camps was unique. The camp system evinced features that also appear elsewhere. The German executioners and their accomplices were not unusual individuals. The overwhelming majority of perpetrators were so ordinary and average that, if they were not specifically called to account, they were later accepted without difficulty by civil society. They were reintegrated; they led normal lives beside their neighbors, without calling any further notice to themselves. For their part, the victims only became so for one reason: because they were made into victims, labeled outsiders, enemies, superfluous human beings, that so they could be persecuted, tormented, and killed. And many practices of camp power are reminiscent of other well-established practices in modern society, procedures long since tried and tested.

Along with the state monopoly on violence, rational bureaucracy, and organized work, modernity has also given rise to sites of discipline, surveillance, and conditioning. Modernity has confined human beings for life and trained them to be obedient, docile subjects. The manufacturing plant, industrial factory, and administrative office are the centers of bookkeeping and bureaucratic filing, economic exploitation and political rule. However, the military barracks, prison, penal colony, hospital, workhouse, and insane asylum—these total institutions are the laboratories of power. Here, far from the scrutiny of public surveillance, a special agenda is pursued: the transformation of human beings by other human beings. This is where those strategies of power arose that the regime of the concentration camp appropriated with such ease: collective isolation, zoning, the dividing up and stringing together of serial spaces, the distribution of docile bodies and the shaping of their movements, the gapless ordering of time, total visibility and the documentation of deviations, the classification of human beings and the tableau of categories, the hierarchy of positions, roll call and marching columns, the doctors' rounds, the review parade, the firing squad, the inspection of those still useful and usable. Without this regime of disciplinary power, the concentration camp is inconceivable. It provides terror with a stable platform, an arsenal of simple, universally applicable procedures, capable of being activated at any time, not tied to any special purposes. The prison is meant to rehabilitate criminals, the military to train and drill obedient soldiers, the hospital to heal the sick, the workhouse to produce useful laborers, the insane asylum to banish insanity from society. But in the concentration camp, no one was supposed to be healed, educated, or trained to obedience. Absolute power makes use of the technology of the disciplines, liberates them from their aims, and transforms them into instruments of terror. Its systematic nature is based on this transfer of the disciplines of control, on the coerced unification of action, its *Gleichschaltung*; on minute, total surveillance and control. It is founded on the internment of the excluded, the progressive registration, isolation, and negation of deviations, the program of the planned and structured mutation of the human being.

The SS personnel drew its structures from other traditions: from state bureaucracy, the secret police, and paramilitary fighting bands. Camp leadership used the achievements of formal organization: the division of tasks and offices, rigid command structures and orderly service schedules, bureaucratic record keeping and statistics, hierarchy and delegation of authority. Formalism made sure terror would operate independent of human character defects. Terror generally has no problem in finding suitable accomplices. The more formal the organization and the more uniform its sequences, the smaller the problem of recruitment. Modern terror has no need of big criminals. For its purposes, the small-time tormenter suffices: the conscientious bookkeeper, the mediocre official, the zealous doctor, the young, slightly anxious female factory worker. In order to spread fear and terror, all the personnel had to do was to apply the rules that had been set down. This orderly foundation of camp routine provided the soil conducive to the development of those behavioral patterns that spring from the tradition of quasi-military movements: esprit de corps, camaraderie, personal allegiance, the mentality of the emergency situation, corruption, and the lust for the kill. Linked with formalism, a structure of terror arose. The camp SS was not an anonymous bureaucracy, not a centralized apparatus; it was a decentralized unit with a high degree of delegation, flexibility, local freedom to decide, and spontaneous improvisation. The effectiveness and intensity of terror were, in significant measure, rooted in the temptations of absolute freedom, the excessive power to kill enjoyed by the accomplice. Although the personnel belonged to a total institution with all its associated oppressions, the camp provided the staff with a free field for untrammeled action. The executors of the monopoly on violence were able to shed all external and internal constraints of civilization with impunity. The perpetrators were not subjects or underlings. They did more than they were required to. They did what they were permitted to—and they were permitted to do everything. Sovereignty was transferred down to the lowest man in the ranks.

Given the effective power of modern organizations, the problem of curbing power shifts from the usurpers to their assistants, their accessories. Without the active complicity of tens of thousands, the collaboration and community of interests with the beneficiaries, the camp system would not have been able to exist for very long. It owed its effectiveness to the free despotism in the middle and lower echelons. To attribute responsibility and blame solely to the National Socialist leadership, or even to its charismatic leading figure, may help preserve one's worldview, but it overlooks the dimension of collective crime that is salient here. Without the supervisors, sentries, and administrative officials, the accomplices and accessories from the ranks of the inmates, camp terror would have been impossible. The face of modern systemic terror is not stamped by the all-powerful and inviolable master, but by the unbridled actions of the sedulous servants of power. It is an inconspicuous face, quite mean and shabby, without the grimace of wild frenzy, the ecstasies of brutality, the passions of sovereignty. The triumphs of camp power were in a category apart, different from the glory of despotic, omnipotent force. The dramaturgy of the roll call, the daily degradations, the demonstrative excess, the public execution of terror penalties, the speed of death sentences handed down row by row, the pyre—these had nothing of the gory glory of fame, the magnificent victory of grandiose majesty. The triumph relished by the auxiliary was the laughter of the accomplices, the mortal anguish of the victims, the bottom line on the balance sheet of death.

Nonetheless, although many structures of the camp picked up on historical models, the caesura in the history of power is unmistakable. The universe of the concentration camp is unprecedented in its torture and destruction. Not even the theological image of the horrors of hell can render this reality comprehensible. Over the centuries, religious fantasy has conjured up a world of the dead full of the most horrible torments. Yet this realm of eternal damnation lay beyond human competence. It was a moral prison instituted by the gods, meant to punish the worst crimes and mortal sins, a site of agonizing retribution in accordance with absolute justice. The camp, by contrast, was located in the midst of the social world. No prisoner was punished because of guilt. The victims were cast into an intermediate stage of induced infirmity, and then prepared like biological specimens—turned into living skeletons. What hell performs on the dead, the camp perpetrated on the living. There were no demonic monsters at work here, just simple supervisors and torturers. For that reason, the metaphor of hell is misplaced; it is misleading in the attempt to arrive at an appropriate notion of the radical transformation of power.

Absolute power transforms deterrence into terror, terror into horror. It shapes space, time, work, and society into instrumentalities of itself, plunging its victims into the abyss of helpless anxiety. The destructive power of terror extends into the furthest corners of sociality, the deep structures of human subjectivity. It destroys not just by violence, but by starvation and misery, humiliation and murder of the soul. It is sheer destruction, pure and unadulterated. The innovations of absolute power cannot be grasped in terms of the familiar patterns of purposeful action. In the strict sense, absolute power has no economic or ideological purpose, no productive function. This power does not generate forces and fabricate social energies. It does not create normality or normative order. It is its own meaning. It gratifies itself by prolonging torment, expanding endlessly, intensifying and accelerating its own grip and reach. Once set in motion, it rolls over all opposition. Terror concludes every struggle. It gets the job done. The reciprocity characteristic of all social power is shattered. The powerless attempts at defense, emergency assistance, disguised associations, sabotage—all these must inevitably founder on the superior might of the system.

The strength of absolute power is manifested in the transformation and destruction of the human condition. Terror ravages the universal structures within which human beings move: their relations to the world, to others, and to themselves. Terror strips work of its objectivity and utility by transforming it into terror work. Power does not subjugate people by the material constraints of the task, the grinding regularity of hours, the obligation to achieve results. Terror separates labor from all production value and any moral rules. It intensifies compulsion and exploitation to the pitch of destruction; it transposes production into ravagement. The teleology of human labor is extinguished. The productive meaning of work, the self-preservation of the species, is transformed into its opposite. Nowhere is human labor so directly linked with death as in the concentration camp. Here work does not secure life, it devastates it. This political economy of waste cannot be comprehended by following the principles of calculation and value enhancement. Absolute power overcomes the laws of production. It increases not wealth, but misery.

The deformations of sociality it engenders are no less radical. Absolute power sorts human beings in accordance with its own criteria, erecting a society in the image of its class model. It forces collaboration, compelling its opponents to act as accessories. Absolute power is far more than the possession of a single group. It distributes itself over the social field, permeating and dominating the relations between the inmates. The power of the personnel consolidates itself, becoming the power of the camp, an institutional world of surveillance, anxiety, and brutality, whose laws are constantly reproduced and carried out by the perpetrators. Terror penetrates into virtually all niches, overlaying barter and cooperation on the job, protection, and interpersonality. The elite of the prisoners becomes entangled in the insoluble dilemma of complicity. Brutality and violence are unavoidable means of self-preservation for the accessories. Society is permeated by the informers and accomplices of terror; the victims are driven to a life-and-death struggle for space, shoes, and bread. Although a good many examples of elementary solidarity have come to light, the extent of social indifference, mutual repulsion, and animosity in the camps was staggering. The dissociative strength of camp power shatters the basic rules of social intercourse, fundamental trust in the continued existence of the social world, the prospect for assistance, the certainties of social action, the continuity of time. It culminates in the concentrated coerced mass, the collective massed bodies of the barracks, the marching columns, the roll calls. The camp hurls human beings back into a primal state of nature: the struggle of all against all. The basic tendency of social seriality—fortuity and superfluity—is intensified, climaxing in its deadly terminus. The concentration camp is the modern facility for isolating and destroying the "dispensable." The superfluous are searched out everywhere, seized, confined behind barbed wire, starved, murdered.

The destruction of sociality entails the negation of the human relation to the self. In the concentration camp, the social process of individuation is reversed. The admission ritual robs the person of his or her biographical identity. The regime of violence and misery obliterates individual space, ravages the sense of time, and casts the human being into a permanent condition of dying. Organized terror reduces social life, the foundation of any human selfhood, below the animal minimum. It does not suffice with obedience and subjugation, but strikes people in their entirety, their social, mental, and physical existences. It seizes hold of bodies—not to turn gesture and movement into a blind automatism, but gradually to extinguish all manifestations of life. Absolute power sunders the physical unity of the person, devastates spirit and soul, destroys the ability to act, drains all vitality. Prior to industrialized mass murder, it carries out a transmutation of human nature. The transformation of human beings into matériel and the fabrication of the *Muselmänner*, the waking dead, are its greatest triumphs. In sharp contrast with all earlier forms of power, absolute terror creates nothing. Its work is totally negative, a project of obliteration without a trace. It realizes its freedom in the complete and total annihilation of the human being.

Abbreviations Used in Notes and Bibliography ____

AH	*Auschwitz Hefte*
BA	Bundesarchiv
BGBl	*Bundesgesetzblatt*
DH	*Dachauer Hefte*
HvA	*Hefte von Auschwitz*
IfZ	Institut für Zeitgeschichte, Munich
IMT	International Military Tribunal, Nuremberg
KZfSS	*Kölner Zeitschrift für Soziologie und Sozialpsychologie*
Nbg. Dok.	Nürnberger Dokument
VfZ	*Vierteljahrshefte für Zeitgeschichte*

Notes

1. Entry

1. On the first days and weeks in Dachau, see Richardi, 36ff.; Kimmel, 353ff.; Bastian.

2. Grünwiedl, 3.

3. Higgins, "33,000 Dachau Captives Freed by 7th Army," *New York Herald Tribune*, May 1, 1945; also quoted in Weiß, 26–27. See also Distel.

4. See Bettelheim 1979, 92ff.

5. On the limits of empathy in the face of mass murder, see Claussen, 11, 152, 166.

6. One should not think here only of the bureaucratic murderers sitting at their desks. Everyday routine in the camps was ultimately determined by those average, ordinary perpetrators who, having fulfilled their personal quota of cruelty for the day, depending on mood and caprice, returned to their rooms after work and prayed, or went out on the town to have a good time in some pub or restaurant. See also Arendt 1989, 133–34.

7. See Jäger 1982, 382.

8. Quoted in Bettelheim 1979, 96–97.

9. On the "historians' debate," see, among others, the volume *Historikerstreit*; Meier 1987; Wehler; Jäger 1989, 40–60; and the chapters by Friedländer, Diner, and Mommsen in Diner 1987. In large measure, the systematic parallax distorting this debate is due to a fundamental category mistake. The problem of causation was constantly compounded (and thus confused) with the totally separate question of responsibility for one's actions.

10. Cf. Grosser, 45–46.

11. In critiquing this comparison, Wehler (130ff., 167ff.) has argued that it tends to suppress the differing levels of development and civilization of the "referent societies." But one can certainly doubt whether there can be any historical progress whatsoever when it comes to mores and civilized behavior. How can anyone assert that the historical basis of Soviet culture is less valuable than that, say, of Germany? As if Bach and Goethe embodied the proper cultural level, but Tolstoy and Mussorgsky did not. Moreover, there is no reason why the comparison has to be on the macrosociological level. Comparisons of organizational structures and forms of mass extermination are no less legitimate and revealing. A comparative study of the camp system is ventured by Kaminski. On the comparative analysis of ethnocide, see also Chalk and Jonassohn; Fein; Harff and Gurr; Jahn.

12. See Jäger 1989, 43.

13. There are obvious parallels between Soviet and German concentration camps with respect to the structure of organization, the behavior of the guards, and the systematic annihilation of prisoners by working them to death. Vorkuta and Kolyma far surpassed the camp complexes of Buchenwald, Mauthausen, and Dora-Mittelbau in terms of the length of time the camps were in existence and the number of their victims. In evaluating the Soviet crimes, one should not be taken in by the propaganda of the regime and its weighted discourse: for example, the "expulsion of the Kulaks," "class

struggle," or "forced collectivization." Contrary to what is widely believed, Soviet terror also made use of ethnic and "social-biological" criteria. Mass murder as the result of a deliberately engineered famine in the Ukraine fulfills the criterion of genocide. That mass murder claimed the lives of at least seven million persons in the period from 1930 through 1933, among them three million children. On this, see Conquest 1978, 1988; Grosser, 88ff.; Solzhenitsyn; Rummel.

14. Schwarz (221–22) arrives at the following figures: 399 forced ghettos in Poland, 16 in Lithuania, 3 in Latvia, and 60 in Transnistria (the region between the Dniester and Bug Rivers, to which many Romanian Jews were relocated); 941 "forced-labor camps" for Jews, 230 "special camps" for Hungarian Jews in the Czechoslovak-Hungarian border area of Austria, 78 police detention camps, 106 "labor-education camps," 40 penal camps in the Emsland—and, in Hesse alone, 532 camps for foreign forced laborers. The total number of penal camps and camps for forced laborers is not known, nor can we determine the exact number of camps for infants and small children in Germany, where the children of female conscripted foreign workers were "collected" and subsequently murdered. Schwarz arrives at a total of 10,006 Nazi camps, including concentration and death camps. Regarding camp categories, see also Weinmann (140ff.), based on data from the Red Cross.

15. No adequate sociology of Nazi society will in the future be able to ignore this gigantic system of camps for the "superfluous," social outsiders and slave laborers.

16. The mass murder of the Jews is relevant to a sociological study of power structure and social form in the concentration camp only to the extent that the two crimes were institutionally linked. Consequently, the present study will not address the persecution and deportation of the Jews, the forced ghettos, or the mass extermination at the hands of the *Einsatzgruppen* ("special action" mobile killing units) of the SS. Nor will it focus on the extermination camps except in the concluding chapters (21 and 22), which attempt to examine in detail the way in which the selection process and the death factories functioned.

17. Academic sociology in Germany has seldom addressed the topic, leaving it to contemporary history, psychiatry, the justice system—and the former prisoners. It remains unclear whether that is because of some self-imposed pledge of silence or because of a certain thoughtlessness and a self-defensive posture in keeping with the tenor of the times. Fascism theory, with its decidedly economic tilt, which became an academic vogue starting in the late 1960s, has never dealt seriously with the concentration camps. Among the few studies on which a sociology of the concentration camp can build are: Adler 1960a and 1964; Kogon; Bettelheim 1960; Goffman 1961; Goldstein, Lukoff, and Strauss; Pingel; Kaminski; Wormser-Migot. A first attempt to unravel the internal world of the camps with the aid of a sociological theory of norms can be found in Pohlmann (370–403) and in Kirstein's case study on the Natzweiler camp.

18. On the concept of social organization, see Sofsky and Paris. If one proceeds on the basis of this view of organization, a major objection to the older theory of total systems, as succinctly formulated by Friedländer, no longer applies: "The totalitarian system of domination is a means of annihilation, but is not the explanation (26)." Friedländer views organization solely as an instrument of terror, not as a field of power with its own intrinsic dynamic. Moreover, a strategy of explanation focused primarily on the intentions, plans, and decisions of individual persons or offices remains, in the strict sense, presociological. It fails to capture the figurative mesh of

relations within which decisions crystallize. Above all else, however, intentionalism lacks any conception of an internal dynamic process that itself creates the motives that propel it forward.

19. See Geertz, 10ff.

20. See Pingel, 17ff.; Langbein 1980b, 62ff. On the biographical meaning of various types of eyewitness texts, see also Pollak.

21. Levi 1989, 17.

2. Absolute Power

1. For an earlier version of the following ideas, see Sofsky 1990.

2. See Weber, 544–45.

3. See Paris and Sofsky.

4. See Foucault.

5. The concept of absolute power suggested here proceeds from an intuition similar to that underlying Hannah Arendt's (1986) classic theory of total domination, although Arendt focuses more on the totalitarian state as a whole than on the concentration camp. Arendt was not in a position to work out a detailed analysis of power in everyday camp life because she did not have the categories of the analysis of social forms at her disposal, and also lacked important empirical data not yet known at the time. Thus, Arendt underestimates the importance of work and completely overestimates the salience of an ideological "suprasense" for reality in the camp. However, in a research proposal in 1950 (Arendt 1989, 7–30), she had already radically emphasized that "totalitarian terror" cannot be understood using the customary concepts of the theory of political domination.

6. Nor does National Socialist ideology become more plausible if one views the SS formations as an "objectification" of ideology: "The ideological fictions determined the organization in its entirety, thus making it possible for persons who as individuals were in no way convinced 'believers' to act as members of the organization in accordance with the most insane manifestations of these ideological fictions. The organization was the supreme ideologue, not its individual human part" (Pohlmann, 345). This argument is not persuasive either in theoretical or in empirical terms. It is not apparent how a social formation can function as the incorporation of an ideology if the majority of its actors have not themselves incorporated this ideology as the central guiding motivation for their behavior. From everything we know about the mentality of the SS, especially the Death's Head units, the orientations underlying their actions were far more banal. The organizational reality had less to do with the proclaimed ideals of a "blood elite" than with personal *protekcja* (special privileges and connections), interpersonal rivalry, group conformity, camaraderie, and customary practices—that is, social structures. Only if one is taken in by the controlling perspective of the organization's top echelon can one confuse ideological propaganda with the actual *habitus* (attitudinal disposition) of the members. See also chap. 9.

7. On the antinomy of complete power, see Popitz 1986, 83ff.

8. Probably the best known case of the assassination of a guard occurred on October 23, 1943, in Birkenau: a Polish Jewish woman, rumored to be a dancer, succeeded in grabbing a pistol from SS *Rapportführer* Schillinger, who was on duty in the undressing room, and then shot and killed him. This episode became legendary in the camp. Col-

lective revolts were staged by Russian POWs in Mauthausen and by the Jewish Sonder-kommandos in Treblinka, Sobibór, and Birkenau. However, these were not assassi-nations of camp personnel; they were desperate attempts to break out, the last resort of human beings who found themselves in the jaws of an absolutely hopeless situation. See chap. 22. On Schillinger, see Borowski, 211ff. and Kielar, 249ff.

9. See Améry 1977, 67.

10. See Popitz 1986, 71–72.

11. See Goffman 1961, 188ff.

12. Bettelheim (1979) has made this unmistakably clear: "Any discussion of survi-vorship is dangerously misleading if it gives the impression that the main question is what the prisoner can do, for this is insignificant compared to the need to defeat politi-cally or militarily those who maintain the camps—something that the prisoners, of course, cannot do" (288).

13. Adorno 1955, 326.

14. Canetti, 277–78.

15. Löwenthal pointed this out as early as the spring of 1945 (19–20.). See likewise Bettelheim 1960.

3. On the History of the Concentration Camps

1. See Broszat, 13–37; Pingel, 23–35; Worsmer-Migot, 63–138; Tuchel, 35–158.

2. Before the establishment of Dachau, the camp known as Heuberg in Swabia was set up as a central camp for the state of Württemberg (see Schätzle, 15ff.; Lechner, 61–62.). In Saxony, sections of the prisons in Dresden and Zwickau, the workhouse at Coldlitz, and the camps known as Hohenstein and Sachsenburg were run as state con-centration camps. On the Hamburg detention facilities Fuhlsbüttel and Wittmoor, see Timpke; Klawe. On additional early concentration camps, see Stokes; Wollenberg; Finckh; Lechner; Haardt; Vogt. Schwarz (139ff.) mentions a total of fifty-nine concen-tration camps in the early phase.

3. Regarding the early history of the Emsland camps, see Kosthorst and Walter, 29ff.; Suhr, 27ff.

4. For more detail, see Tuchel, 205–96.

5. See Broszat, 64–65; Aronson, 111–12; Höhne, 188ff. On the basis of documenta-tion, Tuchel (212ff.) has raised fundamental doubts about the thesis, frequently encoun-tered in the secondary literature, regarding the rivalry between the Gestapo and the KZ-Inspektion. However, one cannot conclude from their evident external cooperation that there was completely harmonious internal cooperation. In the sociology of organi-zations, it is well known that struggles over secret plots and intrigues rarely become a matter of formal record. Moreover, Tuchel does not give adequate attention to the local tensions in the camp administrations or the lines of conflict that later emerged between the RSHA and the central Inspektion, incorporated in 1942 into the WVHA.

6. For more detail, see chap. 9.

7. See Broszat, 46–55; Pingel, 35–42; Richardi, 119–54.

8. On the following, see Broszat, 66ff., 76ff.; Pingel, 70ff.; Schwarz, 26ff.; Tuchel, 312ff.

9. However, these were not the first Jewish prisoners. As early as 1933, the SS had placed all Jews in Dachau, who made up roughly 10 percent of the camp population, in

a separate *Strafkompanie*. Although initially taken into custody and interned primarily because they were active on the political left—not because they were Jews—these individuals were a preferred target for harassment and mistreatment from the beginning. It was only after the November 1938 pogrom that Jews were also confined as prisoners in other camps. Right from the start, they were at the bottom of the heap, the lowest in the prisoner pecking order.

10. See Wormser-Migot, 203ff. *Nacht-und-Nebel* operations occurred "under cover of the night."

11. See Billig, 72; Pohl to Himmler, September 30, 1943, Nbg. Dok. PS-1469.

12. See Kogon, 173; Carlebach et al., 1984, 172ff.; Komitee der antifaschistischen Widerstandskämpfer der DDR, 143ff.; Hrdlicka, 46; Pingel, 81, 181ff., 259, 301; Marsalek 1980, 119ff., 131ff., 155ff.; Kimmel, 385; KZ-Museum Dachau, 204; Billig, 75. As a rule, these figures represent the deaths officially registered in the camps. They do not contain the Soviet POWs who were executed, or the victims who died on the death transports or death marches in the war's final phase. On the numbers of dead more generally, see n. 37 below.

13. See Stuldreher, 152ff.

14. Pingel, 125–26.

15. Ibid., 199ff.; Streit, 44ff., 83ff.

16. Pohl to Himmler, April 30, 1942, Nbg. Dok. R-129.

17. Report on Strength, Burger (Head, Office DIV) to Loerner (Head, Office B), August 15, 1944, Nbg. Dok. NO-1990.

18. "Aufstellung über die Zahl der Wachmannschaften und Häftlinge in den Konzentrationslagern, Januar 1945" (List of the Number of Guards and Prisoners in the Concentration Camps, January 1945), BA Koblenz NS 3/439.

19. Memo from Thierack on discussion with Himmler, September 18, 1942, Nbg. Dok. PS-654; Herbert 1985, 244ff.

20. See Broszat, 126; Marsalek 1980, 124.

21. See Pingel, 129; Herbert 1987, 226ff.; Herbert 1985, 154ff.; Herbert 1990, 143ff.; Kaienburg, 302ff.

22. Hilberg 1982, 631.

23. Herbert 1987, 231–32.; Herbert 1990, 172ff.

24. Schwarz 1990, 103ff.; Hilberg 1982, 156ff.

25. See Streim; Schwarz, 169–70, 186ff., 196ff.; on the forced ghettos in the Soviet Union, see also Hilberg 1982, 243ff.

26. See Georg, 25ff., 38ff.

27. For more detail, see chap. 9.

28. See Höß, 136.

29. See chap. 15.

30. These figures are based on calculations using the most complete list of camps compiled to date; see Schwarz.

31. See chaps. 14 and 16.

32. See Marszalek, 243–44.

33. Gilbert, 214ff.

34. See Marsalek 1980, 329ff.

35. Anyone trying to calculate the number of admissions must grapple with the problem of discontinuous accounting: in various camps, registration numbering for

dead, released, and transferred prisoners was not continuous, but was repeatedly begun anew. On this, see Billig, 81; Marsalek 1980, 140.

36. On the statistical manipulation of figures for the dead by the SS offices, see Kárný 1987, 140ff. On methodological problems in connection with the statistical recording of deaths, see Pingel, 16; Billig, 68ff.; Kogon, 175ff.

37. On Dachau, see KZ-Museum Dachau, 204–5; the figures here are the number of admissions and deaths ascertained and documented by the Red Cross. They do not contain persons admitted to camps during the war for the purpose of execution, the 800 Soviet POWs executed in Dachau on the basis of the Commissar Order (*Kommissarbefehl*) (Kimmel, 405), or the victims who perished on the death marches in the late winter and early spring of 1945. Billig (82, 98–99) arrives at a figure of 78,000. This estimate is more than double that of the Red Cross, and is probably too high, even if one takes the high rate of mortality in the camp complex known as Kaufering into consideration. On Buchenwald, see Internationales Buchenwald-Komitee, 83–84. The figure here includes the 8,500 Soviet POWs executed there. Kogon (173) arrives at a total of 33,462 deaths on the basis of the records of the prisoner hospital, but that number does not include those who died on the death marches or death transports. He puts the total number of dead for Buchenwald at some 55,000. On Mauthausen, see Marsalek 1980, 141, 155–58. On Neuengamme, see Bauche et al., 162. On Flossenbürg, see Siegert, 490–91. This figure also includes the approximately 800 Soviet POWs executed there as well as the approximately 6,900 who died on the evacuation marches; it does not contain the roughly 2,000 persons admitted in 1944–45 to be executed who were never registered. On Groß-Rosen, see Konieczny, 20, 24. On Auschwitz, see Piper, 94ff. These figures refer only to those persons who were registered in the camp, and do not include the victims from ramp selection or those who perished during evacuation transports. On Majdanek, see Marszalek, 77, 133; Scheffler, 148. On Dora-Mittelbau, see Bornemann and Broszat, 197–98; Pachaly and Pelny, 105ff. This figure contains the 12,813 deaths listed in the card file of the hospital section, as well as the victims who perished on the death marches and those dead who were not even recorded in the admission report lists. On Bergen-Belsen, see Fassina, 38; Kolb 1985, 40. On the concentration camp system, see Billig, 96ff. In Billig's estimate, the dead in the concentration camps (not including the extermination camps) for the period from 1933 to the end of 1944 amounted to some 800,000. During the first several months of 1945, the period of the death marches, some 300,000 more perished. Kogon (177) places total admissions at 1,540,350, and the number of victims at 1,180,650. To date, the Red Cross has been able to document the names of some 450,000 dead. On the extermination camps, see Benz 1991 (17) and Golczewski (464ff., 495). Piper estimates the total number of victims in the entire Auschwitz camp complex to have been at least 1,100,000, including some one million Jews. This total figure comprises both those victims who were murdered in the gas chambers directly after arrival at the ramp and thus not registered (about 900,000) and the victims from the concentration camp already referred to above. It is important to bear in mind that the figures for victims in the concentration and extermination camps should not be confused with the total number of victims who perished in the Nazi genocide of the Jews. Jews were not only murdered inside the camp system; they were also killed by the mobile death squads of the SS *Einsatzgruppen* and in the forced ghettos, which were not part of the concentration camp complex.

4. Zones and Camp Plans

1. Herzberg quoted in Kolb 1985, 77.

2. On the general sociology of space, see Simmel, 460–526; Halbwachs, 127–63; Konau; Goffman 1971, 109–40; Giddens, 110–61. On space for movement, a summary presentation can be found in Kruse and Graumann; paradigmatic for the spatial analysis of total organizations are Goffman 1961, 227ff., and Foucault, 181ff.

3. See Arndt, 93–101; Krause-Vilmar; Vogt; Lechner; Pingel, 32ff., 236–37; Richardi; Schätzle.

4. The following description is based on camp plans and sketches as well as several descriptions. See *Auschwitz*, 15–39; Czech 1989, 24ff.; Marszalek, 10ff., 29ff.; Komitee der antifaschistischen Widerstandskämpfer der DDR, 19–24; Naujoks, 11, 98–99.; Schnabel 1966, 34–39; Kogon, 74ff.; Zörner et al., 21ff.; Bauche et al., 125ff.

5. See Foucault, 221–22.

6. Where the topography did not offer a level surface, terraces were laid. In Flossen-bürg, the narrow valley bottom was big enough only for the *Appellplatz*, the kitchen, and a few barracks. For the construction of additional blocks, the prisoners had to dig several terraces into the mountain slope; as a result, the water supply to the upper levels of the camp often failed. The Natzweiler camp was built on terraces dug into the northern slope of an eight-hundred-meter-high peak in the Vosges Mountains. There was no central roll-call square. When mustered for roll call, the prisoners had to form up on the terraces in front of their blocks and look upward to the highest platform on the mountainside, where the *Rapportführer* stood next to the gallows. Three steps led from one level to the next; a steep road ran around the camp down to the lowest terrace, where the bunker and crematorium were located.

7. Descriptions of the social geography of the camps are rare in the prisoner literature. They presuppose that the prisoners had the necessary overall view, with corresponding descriptive categories at their disposal, and did not regard privileges as natural and self-evident. One exception is the description by Michelet (112ff.) of Dachau:

> To both sides of the central avenue, behind a row of fraternal poplar trees, rose the green-colored blocks, externally just as uniform as they were different inside. To the right, "Freedom Street"; down it five, then seven, and finally nine *Revier* barracks. . . . After these barracks, the quarantine and transit blocks formed the end of "Freedom Street." They were usually packed to overflowing with a teeming underworld of gangsters. No sooner had the first frost come, and these persons contracted in the internal courtyards into a kind of human ball, a miserably congealed swarm of creatures that crowded together so as to better conserve its bit of animal warmth. . . . After these housing blocks came the filthy parts of the town on the right, the bidonvilles, the slums; on the left were Auteuil or Passy, the fashionable sections. The first blocks of this residential quarter, which bore the numbers 2, 4, and 6, were reserved for the camp nobility and upper classes, Kapos, foremen, prominent Germans of the various aristocracies. . . . A bit further down were the quarters of the middle classes. Poles, Czechs, and Slovenians had moved into identical rooms there around 1943, and French and Belgians followed toward the end of the winter. Behind block 28 was the yeast of the proletariat, namely the Italians, and then came the Hungarians, behind block 28; the last was reserved for the Polish priests, number 30. During the course of the final months, it was transformed into a branch of the *Revier*. To put it more exactly, the morgue for the aged and the ill.

8. These included, for example, the "small camp" and the tent camp in Buchenwald (see Kogon, 210ff.), the special camp for Soviet POWs (*Russenlager*) in Flossenbürg (see Siegert 1979, 466ff.), and the tent camp and sick bay in Mauthausen (see Marsalek 1980, 72ff.).

5. Boundary and Gate

1. Améry 1977, 41.

2. See Richardi, 61ff., 271ff.

3. Höß (120ff.) reports on the unsuccessful experiments to replace guards with trained dogs. Mines likewise did not guarantee that the camp could be totally sealed off, because the prisoners might be able get hold of the sketches showing where they had been planted. "Against human intelligence, one cannot employ either mechanical devices or animals. Even the electrically charged barrier, doubly secured, can be surmounted with a bit of thought and cold-blooded calculation, and with the simplest aids in dry weather. They've done it a number of times" (Höß, 123).

4. See Richardi, 123–24, as well as the "Disciplinary and Penal Code for the Prisoner Camp" ("Disziplinar- und Strafordnung für das Gefangenenlager"), October 1, 1933, Nbg. Dok. PS-778.

5. In Mauthausen, for example, undesirable prisoners—especially Jews, Czechs, Russians, and so-called "preventive detainees" (*SVs*)—were regularly shot dead at the boundary, and then recorded under the heading "death from nonnatural cause" due to "attempted escape" or "suicide." For 1941, 465 such deaths were recorded; 703 deaths in 1942 were registered as "shot while attempting to escape." See Marsalek 1980, 217ff.

6. See Richardi, 146–47; Kogon, 81.

7. Bettelheim 1960, 150–51.

8. See Langbein 1980b, 272ff.; Marsalek 1980, 247ff.; Berben, 165; *Auschwitz*, 164–65.

9. See Arendt 1986, 434–35.

10. See Marsalek 1980, 55ff.; Kogon, 142–50.

11. The sole technical means of surmounting the barrier on information in the camp was the radio. In a few camps, a courageous radio expert succeeded in building a receiver and concealing it in a secret spot. Individual prisoners who worked in the offices, the SS section, or the military garage were able to listen to foreign stations clandestinely, or after bribing a guard (see Langbein 1980b, 256ff.). From the start, however, the dissemination of news, especially on the military situation, was subject to the constraint that the strictest secrecy had to be maintained. Informers lurked everywhere. The threat of the death penalty hung over clandestine listeners if they were discovered during a search. Generally, only the political resistance group was fully initiated and informed about the news; the others got nothing but unconfirmed rumors. The boundary thus divided the camp into those in the know and those who were excluded.

12. For an exemplary view from this perspective, see Wiechert, 73ff., 124; Sachsenhausen Komitee West-Berlin et al., 33–34, 148ff.; Kogon, 97; Marsalek 1980, 49; Rabitsch, 52; Richardi, 143–44.

6. The Block

1. Levi 1993, 58–59.

2. This point was also made by the prisoners themselves—for example, Kupfer-Koberwitz, who was transferred from Dachau to Neuengamme:

> How different everything was here from Dachau. The whole block was a single room. Or, to put it more accurately, a single, barnlike hall. . . . There was no shiny floor, smooth as glass, no lockers; no beautiful windows, no tables with surfaces that had a yellowish gleam; no big tiled stove in the center, no brightly painted walls. Everything was made of wooden boards—the walls, the floor, everything. There was not a bed or cabinet anywhere. On the floor were sacks of straw, one next to the other, arranged in long rows. Between these rows, boards had been laid, the height of the straw sacks; these formed a passageway. . . . There were two of these narrow pathways running the entire length of the barracks. Three tiny iron stoves constituted the only furniture. Maybe they might have been able to heat a small room—but not a barracks of this size. (264)

3. See Fröbe et al., 156ff.; Wysocki 1986, 50–51; Vorländer et al., 134–35; Antelme, 46–47; Kielar, 369ff.; Busch, 6.

4. See Bornemann and Broszat, 166ff.; Pachaly and Pelny, 68ff.

5. On details of housing in the base camps, see *Auschwitz*, 70–76; Marszalek, 97–101; Zörner et al., 54–59; Marsalek 1980, 75–78; Komitee der antifaschistischen Widerstandskämpfer der DDR, 32–35; Naujoks, 98ff.; Kaienburg, 63ff.

6. The barracks blocks that were shown to visitors to the camp were also among the preferred categories of quarters. In Mauthausen, for example, the only block that visitors were taken to see was barracks 2, which housed prisoner-functionaries; flowers were placed on the tables to welcome the guests (see Marsalek 1980, 240). In Ravensbrück, the model block number 3 of the Jehovah's Witnesses was the one showcased when guests arrived; group discipline there guaranteed absolute order. A memorable description is given by Buber-Neumann (200–201), who was *Blockälteste*:

> One barracks locker looked like the next: hanging on every locker door, the dusting cloth folded in the form of a man's necktie; aluminum bowls, cups, and plates, polished to a gleam; in every locker, carefully folded, six sanitary napkins and a belt with the prisoner's number sewn on. Combs were washed daily, and every dark spot was carefully scraped off the shoebrush handles using a piece of broken glass. You weren't supposed to leave any fingerprints on the locker door. The stools stood in a neat line, scrubbed shiny white. Every Jehovah's Witness who had shoes on knew and obeyed the prohibition on touching the legs of the stool with her feet—in order to prevent there being any spots from shoe polish. . . . But the real high point was the dormitories, each with 140 beds. Sacks of straw as flat and taut as boards, blankets folded fastidiously according to the square pattern on the cover—the squares on the cover were counted to make sure they all had the exact same breadth. One pillow after the next, like sharp-edged wooden boxes.

7. Naujoks (188–89) tells about the risky rejection of this spatial privilege. The SS camp commandant had ordered him, as *Lagerältester* (senior camp prisoner), to set up a room for himself in the bathhouse. Naujoks said no, arguing that such a privilege would undermine his standing among his fellow prisoners and act to exclude him from

prisoner society, so that he would no longer be able effectively to perform his job as senior camp prisoner.

8. See Kruse 1980, 147.

9. A dramatic description was given from Natzweiler:

> The block chief had set aside a corner for himself. He received his assistants there, his friends and buddies, often gluttonous young Poles (a few young Dutchmen were also invited to get "buddy-buddy" with him; as far as I know, they never took him up on the offer). In the evening, after food had been distributed, these corners resembled miniature brothels. There was whispering, unnatural high-pitched squeals, singing, billing, and cooing. Sometimes the lightbulbs were tinted pink. There were pictures on the walls, tablecloths on the tables, and always some cans around, jars of marmalade and dishes with "leftovers," soup, oatmeal. You could also find a few portions of bread. At times, the aroma of baking and roasting would reach our nostrils. These were snake pits. (Quoted in Bakels, 201)

10. Virtually every prisoner report from the prewar period contains a description of this form of harassment. See, for example, Langhoff, 140; Bettelheim 1960, 213ff.; Richardi, 73–74; Kogon, 99–100; Naujoks, 76–77. However, the worsening material situation in the overcrowded mass-housing blocks during the war stripped the practice of *Bettenbau* of its basis. Frequently, it was then the job of the block chief's assistants to straighten the straw sacks into some semblance of order after the prisoners had filed out for morning roll call. And because there was no longer any checkered bed linen, the supervisors could not count the squares. Yet see Levi 1989, 116ff.

11. On the distinction between "density" and "crowding," see Stokols; Kruse 1975.

12. As Bakels reported:

> The fact that you were not alone when you went to the toilet was an agonizing experience. If there was some kind of toilet, a lavatory (*Abort*), then it was a common john for all. Outside working hours, it was always occupied by four, eight, or ten men, their pants down, often two to a bowl. . . . But sometimes there wasn't even any lavatory, just a trench with a horizontal board at the edge and—what a luxury—a little awning up above. An open-air fanfare would resound, performed by an ensemble of ten, fifteen, twenty men, squatting one next to the other, like swallows perched on a telephone line. And fistfights might break out too, in the slimy excrement in front of the beam. Someone would come running over, stumbling as he arrived, hands grasping his behind, and try to push his way onto the board, because the guy couldn't wait any longer, was about to explode. Here our degradation knew no bounds. (213–14)

As in other total institutions, only during working hours did the latrines occasionally become an "oasis of peace" (Levi 1993, 68), a space to which prisoners could retire in order to have a smoke or exchange bits of news (see Antelme, 93–94, 141–42). By contrast, in the crowded block, there was virtually no available space, either for the person or for his or her belongings. The only possessions that were certain were what you wore on your back; a cache under your pallet was constantly threatened by thieves.

13. Goffman 1974b, 56ff.

14. Ibid., 51ff.; Hall; Löffler and Sofsky, 415ff.

15. "You always had to try to get yourself a bunk up above; it was warmest there at night, and the others who had to go to the toilet wouldn't climb over their bunk and step on the face of the guy sleeping underneath. Another reason was that then you wouldn't be bothered either by those who just answered nature's call right where they were"

(Bakels, 332). On the other hand, prisoners who had bunks high up were unable to go down to the toilet without disturbing the others and thus incurring their wrath.

16. Along with the latrine, the areas where the dead were kept became the sole places of refuge in the camp:

> I often went over to the morgue to shoot the breeze, have a chat. . . . Down in the cellar was a coke stove. We fried potato pancakes on the stove. We used to sit on the "coffins" around the small glowing stove, the pancakes sizzling. Their pleasant aroma would tempt your nose, and killed the atrocious stench of the chlorine with which the dead bodies stacked there had been doused. We were so familiar with the corpses that they didn't faze us at all. I often played the harmonica, and Ali would sing. There was a nice atmosphere, like at a scout campfire. . . . Everyone avoided the cellar. That was our place exclusively. Nothing threatened us down there. That's where we felt the freest. (Kielar, 54–55)

Similarly, see Frankl, 87ff.

7. Camp Time

1. Frankl, 115–16.
2. See Durkheim, 12ff.; Halbwachs, 78ff.; Elias 1984, xxx–xxxi; on theories of social time, see also Bergmann; Schmied.
3. On the parameters of schedules, see Zerubavel, 88–89.
4. Foucault, 192ff.
5. On the concept of "time tracks" and deviations through "sidetracking," see Lyman and Scott, 191ff., 211–12.
6. On the concept of "deceptive time" and the "erratic time" of uncertainty, see Gurvitch, 31–32.
7. Foucault, 203ff.
8. See *Auschwitz*, 83ff.; Bakels, 267ff.; Bauche et al., 131ff.; Kogon, 101ff.; Marsalek 1980, 51ff., 91–92; Marszalek, 95ff.; Naujoks, 69; Fröbe et al., 230ff.
9. One particular form of harassment was to order a half hour of "early sports" before the usual time for getting up, and to force the prisoners to do gymnastics in a "maniacal tempo" (Kogon, 101), so that they were completely exhausted by the time the day began. Certain Kommandos, such as kitchen personnel and those on cleaning duty for the SS buildings, had to start work earlier, before the others. The kitchen had to have breakfast ready when reveille sounded and the camp was awakened.
10. Antelme evens draws a metaphorical parallel to theophany:

> In Buchenwald, it was necessary to wait for hours during inspection. Thousands were standing there. Then a cry was heard: "He's coming! He's coming!" He was still a long way off. Now you had to be nothing, especially nothing more than the waiting thousands. "He's coming!" He hasn't arrived yet, but he disperses the air, makes it thinner, pulls it in from a distance. Nothing but thousands. There's nothing here, no one. Only the squares of the massed thousands. He's here. No one's seen him yet. Now he makes his appearance. Alone. An insignificant face, an insignificant person. But an SS man, *the* SS man. Your eyes see the face of a person, nondescript, anyone. He is the man. The god with the royal visage. He strides by, inspecting the thousands. And then he's gone. Emptiness. He's no longer around. Once again, the world fills with people. (30)

11. Not by accident, the camp street in Buchenwald down which the prisoners were marched from the gatehouse to the construction sites and the factory halls of the Gustloff Works was known as "Carachoweg" in camp slang. [*Caracho* is twentieth-century soldiers' jargon, dating from World War I, signifying "in a rush," "on the double," great haste and "hustle."—Trans.]

12. There was no need for beating; it was superfluous when exhausted prisoners were simply left lying in the mud of the camp streets. As P. Lewinska commented regarding the street in Birkenau:

> You fall down, you die. . . . As soon as the SS men (who had good senses of humor) saw someone reeling, or having trouble pulling his feet from the clay mud of the paths, they immediately kicked him. The blow would send him sinking into this black, sticky molasses. It's impossible to get up again on your own. And no one will be able to help you. That's why every day, when our work details marched off to work, several of the weakest would remain lying there in the mud, sometimes dozens of us. . . . You can't lean on anything. You don't know where, there's no time, you can't clean yourself or wash. All you can do is lie in the camp street, stuck in the mud, until a special detail collects those who've fallen down, heaving them onto a pile of corpses, even though they're still alive. (Quoted in Pozner, 66–67)

13. The distance from the base camp at Sachsenhausen to the construction site of the clinker brickworks was about two kilometers; from Auschwitz to the Buna plant in Dvory, it was roughly seven kilometers. In the beginning, the Kommandos had to walk that stretch each and every day; later on, they were brought by train, until a separate camp was finally set up in Monowitz. Towards the end of the war, the external satellite camps not directly on the grounds of a plant were often many kilometers away, and this road had to be traveled on foot. To mention just two examples: the distance from the camp known as Hannover-Mühlenberg to the plant gate of Hanomag was approximately three kilometers (cf. Fröbe et al., 466). The Jewish women in Hessisch-Lichtenau (east of Kassel) were marched every day right through the town and then loaded onto a "special train" with three freight cars; from the last stop at Fürstenhagen, they still had to walk uphill about one kilometer to reach the explosives factory of Dynamit Nobel AG. If no train happened to be available, the whole trip on foot was five kilometers. Thus the women would spend some three hours of their work time every day just traveling to and from their jobs (see Vaupel, 52ff.).

14. References to the importance of shoes for survival can be found in many prisoners' reports. The SS laid out a seven-hundred-meter-long "shoe-testing track" around the roll-call square in Sachsenhausen. It had various surfaces. Every day, a *Strafkommando*, the men loaded down with bags of sand, would be forced to fast-march for thirty to forty kilometers over this track, ostensibly in order to test out various types of soles for boots. The real purpose was probably to break in hard leather boots for the SS. See Naujoks, 209; Kielar, 367.

15. In an order to camp commandants dated Novevember 22, 1943 (Nbg. Dok. NO-1290), Pohl stipulated an eleven-hour working day for the winter months as well. However, the order could only be implemented in factories with closed rooms. At work sites in the open air, work was halted at dusk because of the increased danger of escape.

16. For a detailed discussion, see chap. 16.

17. See Bettelheim 1960, 140–41. Antelme provides a description of this internal temporal order, which, however, also had objective points of orientation to latch onto in factory time:

> By 9:00 A.M., three hours have already passed in the factory, half the time 'til noon; at noon, half the day's gone. In the afternoon, the hours become more delicious; they are literally devoured. Four o'clock: two more hours. Back at nine in the morning it was another world. How could you be here at 9:00 A.M., with ten more hours in the factory still to go? How was it really possible for each hour to pass by? Initially, there was that first hour, from six to seven. You had to accept the day, penetrate it. And it was calming somehow that you'd succeeded in pushing into it. The next hour is very long; you still can't appraise what lies behind you, can't gauge it, it's not enough. . . . You could also imagine that the work you're doing is so alien that you spend the livelong day just calculating the quarter hours that have slipped by, and those still to come. You spend your time counting time. . . . But when you look down at your work-piece, time passes by. When you get some blows to the head, time passes by. When you go to the latrine, time passes by. When you take a careful look at the face that you hate, time passes by. (100)

18. On the category of "occasional time," see Rammstedt, 49–50.

19. In the winter, the prisoners propped up the frozen dead bodies inside the block formation.

> In the middle of the square, supported by invisible hands, stood the dead; they were holding out very bravely. They always became stiff pretty fast in the icy cold of the Ettersberg. . . . The SS men would count them, and the number gained—preferably checked twice rather than just once—was then used to determine food rations for the following day. The comrades put together a stock of food from the bread of the dead, their margarine rations, their soup; that was used to help the weakest among the prisoners, and the sick. In this way, the bodies of the comrades who had died during the day performed . . . a proud service for the living out on the *Appellplatz*. They helped vanquish death, which lay in wait for all those still alive, at least temporarily. (Semprun 1981, 214–15).

20. Kogon (104–5.) reports from Buchenwald about two roll calls of this type. On December 14, 1938, during the first phase of overcrowding in the wake of the November anti-Jewish pogroms, the prisoners had to stand outside for nineteen hours in temperatures of negative fifteen degrees Celsius. By the following noon, more than seventy persons had died. Bettelheim (1960, 136ff.) mentions a similar roll call. He notes a process of "depersonalization," one in which the individual is totally absorbed in the mass and loses the fear of death as soon as the collective mood swings to euphoria: "They did not care whether the guards shot them. They were indifferent to acts of torture. The guard no longer held authority, the spell of fear and death was broken. When this stage was reached, a quasi-orgiastic happiness spread among the prisoners. By forming a mass, they had defeated the Gestapo's effort to break them" (137). It is difficult to decide whether this elation was actually due to their having formed a mass, or whether it was a product of increasing apathy. Naujoks (176ff.) describes another murderous, annihilatory roll call from Sachsenhausen, where on January 18, 1940, Höß kept all prisoners of the *Stehkommandos* out on the roll-call square the entire day in temperatures of negative 26 degrees Celsius. The result: "That same day, 78 died; the

night of January 19, another 67 died. Many had fallen fatally ill, and lived only for a few days or weeks. Mortality figures soared from 266 in December 1939 to 702 in January 1940; in February, 488 prisoners died. Many who survived this ordeal had permanent damage from frostbite for the rest of their lives."

21. Thus, for example, Levi (1993):

> We have bored our way through all the minutes of the day, this very day which seemed invincible and eternal this morning; now it lies dead and is immediately forgotten; already it is no longer a day, it has left no trace in anybody's memory. We know that tomorrow will be like today: perhaps it will rain a little more or a little less, or perhaps instead of digging soil we will go and unload bricks at the Carbide factory. Or the war might even finish tomorrow, or we might all be killed or transferred to another camp. . . . But who can seriously think about tomorrow? (133)

8. Prisoner's Time

1. Zywulska, 180–81.

2. A description of the admission ceremony is contained in virtually every prisoner report. Although the ceremony is interpreted in the light of later camp experiences, the reports clearly reflect that the entrance ritual was a profoundly decisive point for the newcomers. See *Auschwitz*, 55ff.; Bakels, 190–91; Carls, 70; Kielar, 16ff.; Kirstein, 80ff.; Kogon, 95ff.; Levi 1989, 39ff.; Levi 1993, 22ff.; Michelet, 62–63; Pozner, 30ff.; Vermehren, 77ff.; Wiechert, 71ff.

3. See Goffman 1961, 14ff.; on degradation ceremonies, see also Garfinkel.

4. See Gennep, 21; Turner, 101ff.

5. Flagellation, like the shaving of the head, is a common practice in many rites of purification, separation, and transformation; cf. Gennep, 85, 167ff.

6. Améry 1977, 55ff.

7. Only in Auschwitz was tattooing of the prisoner number a standard practice, beginning in the autumn of 1941. The procedure was introduced when difficulties arose in identifying the dead bodies. Initially a metal stamp with movable numbers was used; it was pressed against the prisoner's chest. Later the number was tattooed with separate needles on the prisoner's lower left arm.

8. The quarantine camp in Birkenau had a special organizational position. This area was an intermediate stage between the ramp and the concentration camp. During the regular selections there, prisoners were chosen and sent to the gas chambers from among those who had escaped selection on the ramp yet had not been accepted by the SS into the camp as workers. See the "Chronik des Quarantänelagers" by the prisoner doctor O. Wolken in Adler, Langbein, and Lingens-Reiner (111–22).

9. This constitutes an essential difference between concentration camps and other total institutions, where individuals passed through latent "careers" until they became inmates. When one's life was at stake right from the start, one who did not start behaving as an inmate immediately had no chance for survival. Making use of the conventional, three-phase scheme of adaptation, Bettelheim (1960) and Cohen analyze the psychological defense strategies of the prisoners. This may be justified to a certain extent for the camps of the prewar period; however, its validity for the wartime camps is doubtful. Thus, on the basis of his experiences in Monowitz, Frankl distinguishes

between only two phases: the initial shock of entrance and camp life. A developmental model specifically underestimates the element of shock bound up with the camp experience, and the necessity to react to the constant threat of death without any time to learn the ropes of camp existence.

10. The documentary sources contain such a speech by a camp leader from Auschwitz in the early period (Paczula, quoted in Adler, Langbein, and Lingens-Reiner):

> Okay, you guys are in the German concentration camp now. You came in through the main gate. It's got an inscription overhead: "Work liberates." There's only one way outta here: through the chimney of the crematorium. Far as we're concerned, you're not human beings, you're just a pile of shit. We're gonna beat you bloody. You'll have a chance to see for yourselves real quick. For enemies of the Third Reich like you, we Germans aren't gonna have any leniency, we won't show a bit of pity. It's gonna be a genuine pleasure to chase all of you through the grill of the crematorium ovens. Forget your wives, your children and families. You're gonna die in here just like dogs. (14)

11. See Frankl, 114–15.

12. See the collection of prisoner reports in Ryn and Klodzinski 1987b.

13. See Goffman 1974a, 21ff.

14. "Physical condition alone, the psychological power of resistance, personal cunning, and knowledge of foreign languages—none of these was any guarantee for survival; it could not be. Many died in the camps although they had all these qualities and really wanted to survive. What was needed in addition was the proverbial modicum of luck; perhaps that was what decided whether one survived in a specific situation. All the ideological preparation, psychological power to resist, physical fitness, cunning, and so forth were useless if that little bit of luck was missing" (Mylyk, quoted in Jagoda, Klodzinski, and Maslowski, 1987a, 45). "You escaped death just like you pull a lucky number in a lottery. It may well be that there was also a kind of regularity in these unpredictable events; sometimes I thought I'd figured out the law behind it. But in many cases, my actions led to precisely the opposite consequences from those I'd intended; and still, they saved my life" (P. Lewinska-Tepicht, quoted in ibid., 46).

15. See Cicourel, 52ff.; Sofsky 1983, 33ff., 55ff.

16. On the anthropology of human self-relations, see Löffler and Sofsky, 504ff.

17. See Bettelheim 1960, 153ff.

18. "Prisoner society was so permeated by the atmosphere of murder and death that after two or three months in the camp, a prisoner had become fully acclimated to it, and was always ready for death. This atmosphere also found expression in the prisoners' colloquial lingo. Quite calmly and cooly, they'd say things like 'They've come and got him,' 'He was rolled flat,' 'He was finished off,' 'He got the needle,' 'He went up the chimney, 'Our old buddy Heavenly Kommando is already waitin' for you'" (J. Stawarz, quoted in Ryn and Klodzinski, 1987b, 288). "In the course of time, I started getting used to death. Death under the conditions of the camp became something ordinary and everyday, and if it didn't involve someone I was close to, it didn't make much of an impression. Maybe this reaction was something like an instinctive defense mechanism in order to prevent psychological breakdown" (A. Fros, quoted in ibid., 296). See also Rovan, 149.

19. "Particularly during this most difficult phase of camp life, my principle was to survive the day that had begun. Not to think about what would be tomorrow, in a week,

a month, a year. To accept each day as a gift of God" (J. Marszalek, quoted in Ryn and Klodzinksi, 1987b, 307).

20. Bettelheim 1960, 129ff.

21. Ibid., 200ff.; Ryn and Klodzinksi, 1987b, 307.

22. See Pingel, 171ff.; Jagoda, Klodzinski, and Maslowski, 1987a, 24ff.

23. Conversely, the problem of theodicy—the incompatibility of divine providence with the imperfection and baseness of the world—was revealed in no form more jarring and extreme than that of the concentration camp. The camp itself was the hardest test imaginable for the conception that there is a God. Religious belief not only strengthened the common will to survive; it was itself seriously threatened by events in the camps. See, for example, Bakels, 220ff.

24. Améry (1977), in characterizing the devout, believing prisoner, noted: "At one and the same time, he is further from and closer to reality than an individual without faith. Further from reality, since in his basic stance of finalism, he ignores the given content of reality, fixing his eyes on a nearby or distant future. Yet closer to reality, because precisely for this reason, he does not allow himself to be overpowered by the circumstances surrounding him, and is thus able, for his part, to have a powerful impact on them" (36)

9. The SS Personnel

1. Höß, 57–58.

2. See chaps. 11, 12.

3. See chaps. 10, 13.

4. See Kosthorst and Walter, 39ff.; Suhr, 34ff.; Tuchel, 189.

5. On the organizational history of the Death's Head units, see Broszat, 55–66; Buchheim 1967b, 160–82; Kárný 1986; Segev; Sydnor, 3–36; Tuchel; Wegner, 100ff., 122–23.

6. *Statistisches Jahrbuch der Schutzstaffel der NSDAP* 1937, 51.

7. Ibid., 52; *Statistisches Jahrbuch der Schutzstaffel der NSDAP* 1938, 80.

8. See Buchheim 1967b, 168ff.; Wegner, 114ff.

9. Decree of Hitler, August 17, 1938, BA Koblenz, NS 19/1652.

10. See *Statistisches Jahrbuch der Schutzstaffel der NSDAP* 1938, 78–79.

11. Stein, 30.

12. Sydnor, 37ff.

13. *Statistisches Jahrbuch der Schutzstaffel der NSDAP* 1937, 51.

14. Ibid.

15. See Sydnor, 324ff.; Kárný 1986, 247–48, 258ff.

16. See the affidavit of Harbaum, March 19, 1946, Nbg. Dok. D-750.

17. See Boberach; Himmler to Berger and Pohl, May 11, 1944; Pohl to Himmler, June 5, 1944, BA Koblenz, NS 19/1922.

18. To mention several examples: on April 28, 1945, in the Mauthausen camp complex, there were 5,516 members of the Waffen-SS, the air force, and the fire-prevention police, as well as 240 marines (Marsalek 1980, 197). In Hannover-Stöcken, the camp guard was manned by 15 marines together with the SS; in Misburg, the camp and work site were guarded by a force of between 50 and 80 reserve riflemen along with several dozen SS men. The 500 prisoners in Mühlenberg were guarded by 11 SS men and 40

marines (see Fröbe et al., 73, 177, 459). In the Hessental camp, guarding and adminis-tration were handled by 70 men from the air force, plus just 5 seasoned SS men; in Hailfingen, 60 to 70 older air force men made up the guard unit; in Vaihingen, there were some 20 SS men and about 60 soldiers from the army and air force (Vorländer et al., 84–85, 157–58, 186ff.). Where the SS did not have enough of its own men—which was always the case in the countless external subcamps—it followed a policy of mixed personnel. A few SS men with experience in concentration camp service were put in charge of the soldiers or police in order to make sure the proper spirit of service was maintained in the guard unit.

19. For figures on the number of guard units and prisoners in the concentration camps, see BA Koblenz, NS 3/439.

20. This estimate is based on several documented statistics: thus, in April 1945, the commandant staff in Dachau consisted of 245 persons. The strength of guard units was 3,855 (see Kárný 1986, 260). In December 1943 in Auschwitz, there were reportedly some 3,000 guards, 300 on the staff, and 200 working in administration (affidavit of Höß, March 20, 1946, Nbg. Dok. D-749b). In Mauthausen in February 1940, the num-ber of SS men was set down as follows: 190 leaders, subordinate leaders, and enlisted men on the commandant's staff and in the administration, and 1,060 men as guards in Gusen and Mauthausen (Marsalek 1980, 196).

21. The responsibility of the guard units should not be underestimated. They were indispensable to the existence of the camp. The sentries had to guard the work sites, where a policy of "extermination by work" was being pursued, and they were responsi-ble for the massacres on the death marches. In addition, the guard companies consti-tuted a reserve pool of men for the commandant's staff. Many block leaders came from their ranks. See the affidavit of Pauly, March 15, 1946, Nbg. Dok. D-747; the affidavit of Totzauer, March 15, 1946, Nbg. Dok. D-748.

22. See Popitz 1968, 33ff.

23. See Buchheim 1967a, 258.

24. For example, Eicke's order sheet 3, April 1, 1937 (IfZ, Ma 293), states program-matically:

> The foundation of our internal cohesion is the bond of comradeship that must necessarily arise among National Socialists on the basis of our worldview. ... The absolute and overriding obedience that must be demanded of every SS member, whether a commander or a man from the ranks, gives no person any justification for arrogance or the acquisition of special privilege. The highest-ranking commander is just good enough to sit down at the same table with the youngest SS militiaman in the hostel club or barrack room.

25. See Sydnor, 29. Eicke was an exemplary embodiment of the Janus-faced visage of personal authority: at one and the same time, the protective patron and a punitive power to be feared. His nickname, "Papa Eicke," popular among the camp SS, empha-sizes that for many younger, unmarried SS men, he was apparently a kind of father figure. In a letter to Himmler dated August 10, 1936 (BA Koblenz NS 19/1925), in which Eicke voiced his objections to placing the Death's Head units under the authority of the SS regional sectors, he boasted about this principle of leadership: "Very soon now, the dull and spiritless machine of discipline will replace the uniform corps spirit that I have so carefully nurtured. If, back in their rooms, my men refer to me as father, this is a wonderful expression for denoting a community of close fellowship of the kind

that only a superior who always remains in contact with his men can ever encounter—a superior of whom the men are convinced that he not only commands them, but cares for their needs." See also Dicks, 55, 259; Segev, 119ff.

26. Eicke, order sheet 3, April 1, 1937 (IfZ, Ma 293):

> Repeatedly, it is possible to note that when orders are given, they are not immediately obeyed, and are, to some extent, subjected to comment. Of course, it's only natural that there be complaint about some orders. This is not resented, as long as the gripe is expressed with the proper curse. However, the order must be immediately carried out obediently. Whether an order is useful and proper or, as some say, "military," cannot be checked and determined by subordinates. . . . Here too, let me stress that whoever does not obey gladly and willingly is not a true SS man. He is a man of calculation [*Zweck-Mann*], and there can be no greater pleasure for any of us but to be rid of him.

27. Eicke, order sheet 6, July 6, 1937 (IfZ, Ma 293): "The SS commander is only tolerated and a decent fellow if he remains concerned about the well-being of his men on a daily basis. The good commander is also the good spirit of his unit. . . . Commanders and subordinate commanders must therefore be on their guard to make sure that they retain the trust and affection of their men. The task of education is always paramount."

28. On the connections among order, obedience, and excessive violence, see chap. 20.

29. Cf. an undated document from the files of the central *Inspektion*, "Purpose and Structure of the Concentration Camps" ("Der Zweck und die Gliederung der Konzentrationslager"). It was written after the camps had been placed under the jurisdiction of the WVHA (i.e., after March 1942), and contains a detailed organizational plan with descriptions of individual posts (BA NS 3/391).

30. Langbein 1980a, 372, 434–35; Kogon, 83–84.

31. For more detail, see Mitscherlich and Mielke; Lifton.

32. See chap. 21.

33. Wegner, 135ff.; Eicke, order sheet 4, May 4, 1937, order sheet 6, July 6, 1937 (IfZ, Ma 293); Segev, 128ff.

34. Arndt, 104; Müller-Münch, 74ff.

35. Buchheim 1967a, 269–70.

36. That the SS did not correspond to its own elite image should not mislead us into thinking that the SS was basically nothing but a collection of individuals who were socially déclassé, failures, and "all sorts of mentally less gifted persons" (Kogon, 365ff.). Consider recruitment patterns during the war: this theory of marginality cannot plausibly be applied to the guard units. But it is also inaccurate when it comes to the core group of permanent SS personnel, as Heydenburg has demonstrated. Even if we still have no fully reliable mass data on social origins, it can be assumed that most of those on the commandant's staffs came from the lower middle class, from families of artisans and civil servants. They had completed elementary school or even tenth grade and, interrupted by periods of unemployment, had worked as artisans or clerks before they joined the concentration camp service. This also holds true for many camp commandants; on average, however, they were somewhat older (see Segev). Many of them came from the Freikorps and the Wehrmacht; half of them aspired to a career in the military. Of forty-four commandants, three had completed the thirteenth grade and had high school diplomas qualifying them for university study. What brought these individ-

uals to concentration camp service might be professional opportunism, a personal or family crisis, or sometimes just a biographical accident. One cannot discern any connection between the mentality of social outsiders and a disposition toward terroristic behavior. In any case, social origin is of little value in trying to ascertain the underlying causes of barbaric violence. To derive a readiness to torment and kill from a person's social position would support the untenable thesis of social determinism. Lack of social privilege does not predispose people to violence; wealth and education do not protect a person from brutalization. The decisive factors should be sought in the organizational field of the camp, in its group structures, and in the everyday camp routines. Absolute power not only turns the innocent into powerless victims; it also opens the way for quite mediocre, ordinary people to become victimizers.

37. See Wegner, 164ff.; Segev, 47ff.

38. Buchheim 1967a, 231–32.; Segev (95ff.) and Kirstein (54–55) tend to overestimate the significance of ideological indoctrination.

39. See Eicke, order sheet 5, June 4, 1937 (IfZ, Ma 293).

40. See Eicke, order sheet 3, April 1, 1937 (IfZ, Ma 293).

41. See "Dienstvorschriften für die Begleitpersonen und die Gefangenenbewachung" (Service Regulations for Escort Personnel and Guarding of Prisoners), October 1, 1933, Nbg. Dok. PS-778; "Auszug aus der Dienstvorschrift für den Wach- und Sicherheitsdienst der K. L. Bewachung im Konzentrationslager Dachau" (Extract from the Standing Orders for Sentry and Security Service of the C. C. Guard in Dachau Concentration Camp), February 4, 1942 (BA Koblenz NS 4/Da/9) and the eighteen-page "Entwurf einer vorläufigen Wachschrift für das Konzentrationslager Lublin" (Draft of a Preliminary Set of Standing Orders for Guards at the Lublin Concentration Camp), August 15, 1943 (BA Koblenz NS 4/Lu/1). See also the analogous instructions for female guards in Ravensbrück, Commandant Order 3, July 24, 1942 (BA Koblenz NS 4/Ra/1), and a seven-page information pamphlet for weekly instruction, "Aufgaben und Pflichten der Wachposten" (Sentry Tasks and Duties), sent by the Oranienburg *Inspektion* to all commandants on July 27, 1943 (BA Koblenz, NS 3/426, 115ff.).

42. "If the prisoners are to respect the SS guards, then the SS man must be a shining example for the prisoners. While the prisoner performs hard physical labor, it is forbidden for SS members to stand around in a lethargic posture, to lean up against something for support, sling their weapons on their backs, grasp the stocks of their rifles from behind, or place their hands over their muzzles. It is also forbidden to seek cover under trees or wall ledges during rain" ("Entwurf einer vorläufigen Wachschrift für das Konzentrationslager Lublin").

43. This was quite familiar to the camp leadership. Höß describes various types of guards—the rough and malicious and the good-natured and indifferent guard:

> The second category—in the overwhelming majority—are the indifferent men who just doggedly fulfill their duties, their service, insofar as this is absolutely essential, and do this either well or carelessly. To them, the prisoners are objects they have to supervise, things they have to guard. They hardly think at all about the prisoners and their lives. They stick to the given regulations out of convenience, adhering to their dead letter. To act in accordance with the purpose and spirit of the regulation is too much effort for them. . . . But by their indifference, idle convenience, and limited intelligence, they cause much damage; they torment a good many

prisoners, injuring them physically and mentally, albeit unintentionally. Yet they are mainly the ones who make it possible for some prisoners to dominate their fellow inmates in a way that is often disastrous. (60)

44. See Giddens, 73.

45. On the transformation of penalties into terror punishment, see chap. 19.

46. Commandant decree, Dachau, "Disziplinar- und Strafordnung für das Gefangenenlager" (Disciplinary and Penal Code for the Prisoner Camp), October 1, 1933, Nbg. Dok. PS-778; Commandant decree, Esterwegen, "Besondere Lagerordnung für das Gefangenen-Barackenlager" (Special Code of Camp Regulations for the Prisoner Barracks Camp) and "Disziplinar- und Strafordnung für das Gefangenenlager," August 1, 1934 (IfZ, Fa 253) as well as the undated "Blockeinteilung und Lagerordnung im K. L. Natzweiler" (Block Assignment and Camp Code of Regulations in C. C. Natzweiler), BA Koblenz NS 4/Na/8. On the way in which this overregulation operates, see also Kirstein, 85ff.; Pohlmann, 387ff.

47. Among the few successful proceedings was the case of the commandant of Buchenwald and Majdanek, Karl Koch, who after a lengthy investigation was finally sentenced to death by an SS court and executed in 1945. His accomplice, Hackmann, was likewise condemned to death, but was given a suspended sentence and transferred to a punishment brigade. On this, see the affidavit of Paulmann, July 11, 1946, Nbg. Dok. SS(A)-64, and the affidavit of Morgen, July 13, 1946, Nbg. Dok. SS(A)-65. In Sachsenhausen, the special investigating commission was tossed unceremoniously out of the camp. In the summer of 1942, when the WVHA tried to convert the camps to labor deployment, several commandants of the old school had to give up their posts. Loritz, who was commandant successively in Esterwegen, Dachau, and Sachsenhausen, was transferred to Norway as HSSPF (Higher SS and Police Leader) because of "excessive cruelty." The Flossenbürg commandant, Künstler, was stripped of his post because of excessive "carousing"; the Dachau commandant, Piorkowski, was removed because of corruption, and dismissed from the SS a year later. The investigation in Auschwitz led only to a few arrests among the lower ranks. The officers had sufficient time to remove their riches, and one night the barracks building with confiscated valuables went up in flames. On corruption in the camp SS, see Hilberg 1982, 611ff.; Langbein 1980a, 337ff.; Kogon, 309ff.; Segev, 175ff., 194ff.

10. Classes and Classifications

1. Poller, 28.

2. On the criteria of structural analysis, see inter alia, Kreckel; Hradil; Berger. On an early attempt at a stratificational analysis of the camp using conventional criteria, see Goldstein, Lukoff, and Strauss, 57ff.

3. Regarding the system of colors and the position of individual groups of prisoners, see Pingel, 85–117, 168–71; Wormser-Migot, 430–74; Kogon, 67–74; Kautsky, 149–87; Marsalek 1980, 294–305; Langbein 1980b, 103–206; see also Herbert 1985, 100ff., 264ff.

4. Michelet commented on Dachau: "The Germans had shaved 'the road' right down the middle of their [the Italians'] heads, and the heads of the Russians. This humiliating

haircut, dividing the top of the head into two sections, stressed the fact that someone was a prisoner, making the individual look quite ridiculous. Later on, thousands more came to our camp. They were all poor devils who had no grasp whatsoever of what was happening to them. They died like flies" (165–66).

5. See Hüser, 79ff.

6. Thus, for example, Kautsky, commenting on Polish "fascists": "The hatred of the Germans and Jews mingled here with contempt for all other nations—one's Slavic brothers as well as the 'rotten' West—combining into an outrageous incarnation of chauvinism, coupled with genuinely fascist brutality and corruption" (174). The Norwegian Odd Nansen noted in his diary from Sachsenhausen that "along with the Germans," it was among the Poles that there were "the worst foremen, the biggest bruisers, the most extreme braggarts, the coarsest 'comrades'" (264). Such remarks, representative of numerous other comments in the literature by former inmates, reflect a widespread attitude toward Polish prisoners.

7. The reports by critical prisoners are by no means free of this tendency. In expressly emphasizing exceptions, they seem to assume that the categories were basically valid. Here are two examples from Buchenwald: "It must be stressed that the badges offered no absolute guarantee of the quality and real category of the wearer. For example, again and again one came across a number of prisoners among the greens who were quite decent guys, yes, even good guys. On the other hand, there were plenty of reds who actually could easily have had a green triangle" (Kogon, 73).

> Among my criminal friends, I did meet some terrific people—and, strange as it may sound, I still have to say so—I even encountered individuals of high moral character, who behaved like good buddies, without any reservations, in any and all situations. But the greater majority of the criminals were an underhanded, filthy, unprincipled, and crafty lot, and the only way you could protect yourself from being hassled by them directly or indirectly was by isolating yourself— though that was a difficult proposition, very hard to achieve. (Poller, 150f.)

In a similar vein, see also Kautsky, 153.

8. See Bourdieu 1987, 735.

9. See Marsalek 1980, 101.

10. Siegert, 452.

11. Kogon, 114ff.

12. Only with the transition to a system of self-provision did the *KZ-Inspektion* gradually come around to permitting the receipt of parcels by mail, although this was graduated by categories. In the winter of 1941, "Aryan" prisoners could be sent their own underwear; according to a circular order from Himmler dated October 29, 1942 (Nbg. Dok. NO-1514), they also were permitted to receive food packages. Czechs, some Poles, Yugoslavs, Germans, and Austrians received a relatively large number of packages. All Soviet citizens, Spaniards, Jews, Italians, NN prisoners, and Hungarians were excluded from this privilege.

13. On the general concept of "social capital," see Bourdieu 1983, 190ff.

14. There is disagreement when it comes to the classification of various categories. A few qualifications and explanations: The criminal prisoners, who had the most power of any category, did not exhibit the group cohesion of the political resistance groups, but made up for this lack by the close ties they had to the SS. Their social capital was

thus comparable to that of the political prisoners, if not even greater. The "preventive detainees" (*SVs*) were on a rung lower down, because they only obtained power if the SS had no prisoners available in "temporary protective custody" (BVs), otherwise known as "professional criminals." Otherwise, they were subject to considerable annihilatory pressure, not offset by any kind of group cohesion. The rise of the Germans among the "asocials" after the internationalization of the camps, and the advancement of the Spaniards following the initial years of their murderous persecution, have been taken into consideration; this was also true of the Poles. If you take relations in Auschwitz or Majdanek as a basis, Poles would have to be listed in close proximity to the political prisoners, because they occupied numerous middle-level positions as prisoner-functionaries in those camps. Social relations among Gypsies were not based on shared political convictions or a common worldview, but rather on a common familial and ethnic background. In the case of the homosexuals, sexual relations with prisoner-functionaries could improve their situations significantly; as a category, however, they were ranked at the lower margin, not far from the Jews.

11. Self-Management and the Gradation of Power

1. Naujoks, 234ff.
2. Levi (1989) has pointed up the structural importance of this group of auxiliaries: "The hybrid class of the prisoner-functionary constitutes its armature and at the same time its most disquieting feature. It is a gray zone, poorly defined, where the two camps of masters and servants both diverge and converge" (42). The aim of the following remarks is to cast some light on this gray zone, without making any hasty moral judgments.
3. See Popitz 1968, 24ff.
4. The journalist Kupfer-Koberwitz, who was not connected to a political party, commented as follows: "I had the impression that in addition to the SS camp regime, there was also a regime run by the prisoners. Prisoners ruled over other prisoners. So people were locked up in a double sense: by the views of National Socialism and the SS that embodied this outlook, *and* as a prisoner of one's fellow prisoners. We were just as much at their mercy as at the mercy of the Gestapo, maybe even more so, because they were with you, all around, day in, day out" (77).
5. Historiographic descriptions of prisoner self-administration are contained in Adler 1960a; Langbein 1980b, 31–61; Pingel, 56ff., 102–17, 159–66; Kirstein, 72ff.; Kaienburg, 156ff.; the report by Naujoks, the senior camp prisoner in Sachsenhausen, is especially instructive.
6. Naujoks (231ff.) comments on the difficulties encountered in recruiting reliable block personnel and trying to prevent the formation of cliques in the barracks.
7. Experienced political prisoners were able to defend their power and cause problems for their criminal rivals by falsely reporting the numbers of prisoners present and accounted for. In this way, they could impress on the SS commandant's office, which urgently needed the correct statistics for the central *Inspektion*, that it was impossible to operate the camp without a *Schreibstube* run by red functionaries. See, for example, the affair surrounding the green senior camp prisoner and informer Kuhnke in Sachsenhausen (Pingel, 114ff.), or the case of Gorbach in Dachau. In the latter instance, political prisoner-functionaries succeeded in preventing the transfer of a sick prisoner,

Gorbach, by threatening a work stoppage in the labor statistics office in the camp (see Schnabel 1966, 65–66).

8. Kogon, 86–87; Pingel, 103–4.

9. See Drobisch 1978, 97–98. Semprun (1984, 191ff.) provides insight into the national hierarchy within this prisoner office and the constant conflict with the SS.

10. See Marsalek 1980, 317.

11. A camp police force was set up during the war. In Buchenwald, this police force, made up of German-speaking prisoners, took over the guarding of the storerooms and camp surveillance after dark. In Mauthausen, the prisoner police force was outfitted with white pointed helmets, armed with sabers, and deployed to guard the Soviet POWs.

12. It was consistent that during the war, the SS initially accepted "tried and tested" German criminals into its ranks, and beginning in the autumn of 1944, political prisoners as well. Concentration camp prisoners were trained for service at the front in the Dirlewanger unit, and were then deployed against partisans and in the quashing of the 1944 Warsaw uprising. One consequence of this forced conscription of "volunteers" was that from 1943 on, the ranks of green prisoner-functionaries were thinned out, and political prisoners and foreigners could move up to take their place. See Auerbach; Kogon, 342ff.; Langbein 1980b, 351ff.

13. The official "regulations" for the block chiefs in Buchenwald, for example, ran two and a half typewritten pages. Along with performing surveillance tasks, each *Blockältester* had to keep various records: an inspection book, a monitoring book, a block card file, and a pocket-sized booklet with data on the prisoners; this booklet was always supposed to be carried on his or her person. (See Pingel, 297.) This high degree of bureaucratization provided the SS with the ability to determine whenever there had been an infraction of the rules—and thus an occasion for imposing a punishment.

14. In the reports, prisoner personnel were naturally evaluated from a moral point of view, generally with reference to group affiliation or a person's individual character. This is an insufficient basis for a sociological analysis. In order to gain some understanding of options for action, such an analysis would have to begin with the social facts themselves, the structural arrangement in which the prisoner-functionaries were entangled.

15. Bettelheim (1960, 169ff.) equates the final stage of adjustment among the old veteran prisoners with the psychological defense mechanism of identification with the aggressor. On this, see also Freud, 85ff. It cannot be denied that prisoners were often nearly as vehement in their anti-Semitism as the SS, or that they were exceptionally brutal or attempted to conform their appearance to that of the SS by getting hold of old parts of SS uniforms and strutting around in shiny polished riding boots. However, their anti-Semitism was not necessarily the product of a change in values experienced while in the camp; their brutality might not have been acquired as prisoners there. These phenomena can be rooted in an unconscious identification, though they are not necessarily so. One should not underestimate the need to set oneself off socially from those below one in the pecking order, a mode of distinction vis-à-vis the powerless and helpless. However, servility and imitation (by no means synonymous with identification) are social relations, not mental events. Under conditions of mortal enmity, someone who wishes to escape miserable material conditions will, almost inevitably, align himself or herself with those in power. The greater distance one placed between oneself

and those below, the closer one moved to the center of power. Moreover, alignment with the SS was a strategy to escape the fate of the pariahs. Moore also overlooks this form of social mechanics when, following up Bettelheim's identification thesis, he asserts that some prisoners had accepted the "moral authority of their oppressors" (64).

16. This form of order was practiced not only within the SS, but also in commands given to prisoner-functionaries. It laid down the general direction that had to be taken without specifying individual actions, thus forcing the subordinate to take the initiative. A typical example stems from the early period of Auschwitz. The leader of the *Strafkompanie* had all the green supervisors fall in and then gave the following general order:

> "You have been appointed foremen in recognition of your good conduct. I don't have to spell out to you what your duty is. You've had enough time and opportunity during your stay in the camp to familiarize yourself with that. Those you will supervise are Jews. In my Kommando, all I want are Aryans, is that understood?"—"Yes, sir!" was the unanimous response. Then we went to the camp. The new big shots already carried the symbols of their power: wooden clubs. . . . That same evening, thirty-seven dead bodies were brought to the washroom." (Roszanski, quoted in Langbein 1980a, 170)

17. Almost everyone who had access to the gigantic depot called Kanada in Birkenau, where the possessions of the victims of gassing were deposited, could take what he or she wanted. "SS members and prisoners were dependent on each other here: the prisoner who was arranging to lift some items had to bribe the SS man in order to be sure he would not be checked. The SS man who wanted to appropriate something for his own use in Kanada needed to have prisoners, because he himself couldn't rummage through the mountains of goods and select something without being noticed" (Langbein 1980a, 161).

18. See Marsalek (1980, 60) on the practice in Mauthausen. Smugglers here got off with the punishment of thirty minutes suspended from the stake or a reduced flogging. Traitors were placed in detention, beaten to death, or assigned to the *Strafkompanie* and then, soon thereafter, "shot while attempting to escape."

19. The SS conciously created this dilemma for the prisoner-functionaries. Consider Himmler's speech at Sonthofen to generals of the Wehrmacht on June 21, 1944:

> Okay, so one man is the responsible supervisor, I mean to say chief, with power over thirty, forty, over a hundred other prisoners. Once he becomes a Kapo, he no longer sleeps together with them. It's his responsibility to see to it that they reach the performance target, that there are no acts of sabotage, that the men are clean, and their beds made according to regulations. . . . A fresh recruit in a military barracks can't be any neater and more thorough than what is expected here. And the Kapo has responsibility for this. So he has to push his men. The moment we're not satisfied with him, he's no longer a Kapo, and he goes back to sleep with his men. But he knows full well that he'll be murdered by them the first night. (IfZ, MA 315 fol. 3949–50).

20. Although it was strictly forbidden, a number of German criminal prisoner-functionaries used their positions to engage in homosexual relations with young Poles or prisoners with pink triangles. The criminals compensated them with jobs as barracks assistants or Kommando messengers. These "Pipel" (slang for penis) as those so chosen were termed in Auschwitz, had special privileges, but were also particularly endan-

gered. If they betrayed the sexual inclinations of their partners, they exposed both themselves and their partners. The price they paid for their material advantages was nearly total powerlessness.

21. A typical scene was the distribution of food by the Kapo.

All eyes are pinned on the Kapo's face. There are still two pots, so there'll be seconds. The Kapo enjoys this moment every day; it is his sacred right to exercise this power over other men. And he has paid for it with the ten long years he's spent in the camp. Gesturing with the ladle, he points out those who are to get second helpings. He never makes a mistake. Only prisoners who are better workers, the stronger men, the healthier guys—only they receive seconds. A sick, a weak prisoner has no right to a second bowl of nettle soup. Not a single drop must be wasted. Not wasted on people who are going to go up the chimney anyhow. Because of their function, the foremen are allocated two bowls of potato soup with meat, taken from down deep in the pot." (Borowski, 92f.)

Kielar reported a similar scene:

Lunch was distributed by head Kapo Jupp, who was tall and scrawny and shouted a lot. Of the Jews standing in line for lunch, he had to clonk at least every second guy on the head with the ladle. He divvied up the portions so that something extra was left over for a few who had been favored by fate, and especially for the prisoner-functionaries. I also got something extra, though a smaller portion. The Jews were given the soup pots to lick clean. Emaciated, famished, they grabbed the pots, pushing each other aside. Jupp naturally used this opportunity to beat the jostling prisoners—to the general amusement of the SS men, who were watching the scene unfold. (135)

22. "Our task of encouraging prisoner-functionaries to adopt a friendly attitude could only be successful if we took tough action in the event of infractions, without respect of person. No matter who it was, anyone who became a tool of the SS was our enemy. It was necessary to struggle against him severely, uncompromisingly" (Naujoks, 232).

23. See Kogon, 336ff.; Adler 1960a, 223ff.

24. Freund reported from Buchenwald:

A defense squad was organized that was prepared to seize Kapos who had assaulted prisoners, subjecting them to a beating at some remote spot. Slowly but surely, the ground was cut from under the feet of the greens. Deaths were attributed to the greens, in quick succession, so that after a few months, the camp leadership suddenly transferred the greens one night to empty barracks and isolated them completely from the other prisoners. A closed transport then took all of them to the stone quarry at Mauthausen. (104–5)

See also Kautsky, 236.

25. The transfer of criminal prisoner-functionaries usually had a negative impact on the camp that admitted them. Those sent from Buchenwald enjoyed a free hand in the stone quarries of Mauthausen and in Majdanek. Those who had compromised themselves in the Mauthausen main camp found a new field of activity a few kilometers away in Gusen. There was a similar situation in Auschwitz: green prisoner-functionaries were removed from the main camp, but then could operate all the more freely in Birkenau.

26. Antelme reported as follows:

Our Kapos didn't beat us because there'd been some disruption of discipline. On the contrary:
our Kapos did everything they could to question the discipline we wished to see enforced,
since it would have eliminated the justification for their existence, rendering them superfluous.
In any case, it would not have allowed them to lord it over us as the demigods of the Kommando. More than anything else, they had to club us in order to live the way they wished, to
have the position they desired. We had to be totally and completely despicable. That was crucial
for them—vital. Thus, every proposal regarding organization was systematically rejected by the
Kapos and the senior camp prisoner, because any will in us for collective organization had to
be extinguished, we had to be degraded. After that, disrespect and flogging could reign supreme.
(Antelme, 178)

12. The Aristocracy

1. Antelme, 218–19.
2. On the distinction between class (*Klasse*) and estate (*Stand*), see Weber (177ff.);
it is, of course, a distinction that should be applied in this context *cum grano salis*.
3. One example from Dachau is representative of many:

Our man who's responsible for receiving the new arrivals, the German Willy Bader—the little
boss of room 2, who met us the night we arrived in the camp—was an extraordinary person. He
had considerable standing in the camp, and the man was definitely admired, something quite
unusual in such an environment. . . . Willy was a veteran Communist activist, and it's easy to
imagine what personal qualities he must have had in order to assert himself in such pandemonium, given that he was so short, it was almost a joke—the guy wasn't even four feet six inches
tall. His registration number was a low one, number 9; that not only instilled fear based on
his long past in the camp, but a mute respect as well. He'd already spent more than ten years in
this prison world. He'd laid the camp's foundation stones out in the swamps, soaked with the
sweat and blood of Hitler's first victims. . . . There he stood, a person who'd survived the
unimaginable, like Lazarus risen from the grave. In his small dreamy eyes, he bore forever the
frightening vision of the indescribable. (Michelet, 70–71)

4. Canetti, 284–85.
5. Zywulska describes this group from the perspective of a newcomer:

They'd come with one of the first transports and constructed the camp with their own hands—
where all there had been before was mire, ditches, and a few barracks. They were the
ones who'd laid down the streets, built the washrooms and toilets. Of the fifty thousand prisoners in that transport, only a few dozen were left. And they, of course, had gotten various
special functions. They already felt at home in the camp, and looked down condescendingly
on the new arrivals. What could we know about their suffering? Certainly nothing—at least
not yet. (184)

6. See Levi 1993:

At Auschwitz, in 1944, of the old Jewish prisoners . . . "*kleine Nummer,*" low numbers less
than 150,000, only a few hundred had survived; not one was an ordinary Häftling, vegetating
in the ordinary Kommandos, and subsisting on the normal ration. There remained only the
doctors, tailors, shoemakers, musicians, cooks, young attractive homosexuals, friends or com-
patriots of some authority in the camp; or they were particularly pitiless, vigorous and inhuman

individuals, installed . . . in the posts of Kapos, *Blockältester*, etc.; or finally, those who, without fulfilling particular functions, had always succeeded through their astuteness and energy in successfully organizing, gaining in this way, besides material advantages and reputation, the indulgence and esteem of the powerful people in the camp. (89)

On the Jewish prisoner "aristocracy" in Auschwitz, cf. also the differentiated presentation in Langbein 1980a, 197–206.

7. See Bettelheim 1960, 170–71.

8. See Goffman 1961, 62–63.

9. On the connection between killing and self-elevation, see Canetti, 260–61.

10. Consider two situations, one from the main camp at Auschwitz and one from the quarantine camp in Birkenau: "He's having a conversation with a couple of other green Kapos. Just told 'em he knows a new way you can kill a guy with just one hand. And to demonstrate the hold and movement, he calls over a Jew who happens to be walking by . . . grabs him by the neck and then breaks it with one hand. So the guy is lying there, dead" (Langbein 1949, 71).

After morning roll call, we're treated to a show. The block has assembled in formation. The arena is the area between blocks 18 and 19. The tiger, a towering block chief from a neighboring barracks. His paw is notorious. If he gets ready to throw a punch, he puts on leather gloves first, see, 'cause of the effect. The noise it makes. I've only seen one guy who wasn't sent reeling after getting bopped by this lanky block chief. And that really wasn't worth it. The man with the hard wallop was enraged by this failure. His prestige had suffered. He never worked without an audience. (Mannheimer, 109)

11. Cf. Veblen, 79ff.

12. To mention just three glaring examples: in 1942–43, the first camp scribe of Mauthausen, a con man from Vienna by the name of Leitzinger, got his meals almost every day straight from the SS canteen. He was shaved every day, and given a haircut every Sunday morning. The barber had to come in and then crawl on his knees from the room entrance to his master's throne. At morning roll call, he wore tailor-made stripped trousers, a blue sports jacket that resembled a uniform, and white gloves. Keller, the senior camp prisoner, was nicknamed by the prisoners "King Kong" because of his size, 110 kilos [242 lbs.–Trans.]. In Ebensee, where he was transferred at the end of 1943, he had a room of his own with a couch and chairs, radio, a cooking plate, servants, and even his own pig-fattening unit. His deputy, Dähler, had a girlfriend in the town whom he used to visit regularly, with the knowledge of the SS. (Marsalek 1980, 60–61.)

13. Bakels describes a typical scene involving the Luxemburgers, who enjoyed a privileged position in Natzweiler because of the many packages they received in the mail:

That evening a bunch of packages arrived for the Luxemburgers, and we could smell the aroma of the roast from far away through the curtain of falling snow. Almost automatically, I followed the scent. It looked like some sort of restaurant inside, a café, and music blared from the bright windows and out over the surface of the snow. I wasn't the only guy climbing up the stairs to the barracks entrance. A few shadows were already standing there, hands in their pockets, shifting from one foot to the other, or stretching their arms in the direction of the noise and the smell of the roast. I climbed up one more step and could see the striped capitalists; they were running back and forth with their pots and packages and plates in the evening light. I was standing up on the top step when two Luxemburgers appeared in the doorway to get a breath of fresh air and have a cigarette, after all they'd had to eat. The other shadows pushed ahead right in front of me. The laughter and conversation changed to shouting and cursing. I was shoved backward and stumbled down the granite steps into the snow. (209)

14. Such festive occasions were certainly not the general rule. They depended on the goods available, the personal freedoms enjoyed by the prisoner-functionaries, and the size of the camp. For a summary view of the top prisoner-functionaries in Auschwitz, see Langbein (1980a, 178ff.)

15. Cf. Bataille 1975.

16. See Goffman 1961, 93ff.

17. In the main camp, the orchestra had its concert hall beneath the brothel. The kitchen Kapo was the conductor. The orchestra in the women's camp, headed by Alma Rosé (see Fenelon), became quite well known. On the orchestra in the men's camp at Birkenau, see also the report by Laks and Coudy. On the following, cf. Langbein 1980a, 150ff.; Naujoks, 287ff.; Kogon, 152.

18. See Borowski, 186ff. On sports in Auschwitz, see Langbein 1980a, 155–56; on Mauthausen, see Marsalek 1980, 52, 62; on Buchenwald, see Kogon, 152.

19. Borowski describes a boxing match in Auschwitz:

We were let right in without any problem, even though the barracks was already jam-packed. They'd set up a ring in the large waiting room. Overhead floodlights, the referee was there (by the way, a Polish Olympics ref), the boxers were internationally famous. But only Aryans— Jews weren't allowed to take part. And then the people—those same guys who, day after day, punch in the teeth of the other men, guys who sometimes have no teeth left themselves. Yeah, and they're screaming and yelling for Czortek, for Walter from Hamburg, or some punk kid or other who had been trained in the camp for a big-time bout. They still talk today about number 77, a guy who punched around the Germans any way he wanted; he'd take revenge in the ring for everything that was done to the other men outside. The hall was heavy with dense cigarette smoke, and the boxers started slugging away at each other for all they were worth. They weren't professionals, but went at it with all the more energy and gusto. Staschek says: "That guy Walter, just look at him. Out in the Kommando, he can kill a *Muselmann* with one blow whenever he feels like it, and in here—he goes three rounds and nothin'. Even took a heavy right to his kisser. Guess there's just too many out in the audience watching." (152)

20. Lundholm (58ff.) reports that in Ravensbrück, she was made the "court jester" of a female German criminal because she knew how to entertain her every evening, telling sentimental stories. The prominent prisoner had an affair with a former SS man and regularly selected women for the camp brothels. She was finally lynched by a group of forced prostitutes.

21. Kielar describes his job as a scribe for a Kommando, something a German Kapo had arranged: "Since there was almost no work for a clerk, I copied down the lists of the men in the Kommando again and again—just so I wouldn't be doing nothing, and to avoid having to pick up a spade. As soon as I saw the Kommando leader approaching, the 'owl,' I pretended to be very busy. I went from prisoner to prisoner, checked their

numbers, wrote them down carefully in my notebook—only God knows how many times—and made a big show of the thing, as if my job was indispensable" (140).

22. See Veblen, 74.

23. On social closure as a method whereby social collectives set themselves off from others, see Weber (23–24, 202) and Parkin.

13. Mass, Exchange, Dissociation

1. Bettelheim 1960, 231.

2. Special difficulties arise when one attempts to describe the social world of ordinary prisoners. As a rule, they did not have a vantage point that permitted them to see the entire camp in a broad perspective. They were the majority in the camp, the minority among the survivors. For that reason, written testimony from the mass blocks is far more rare, and its horizon of experience more narrow, than the reports of former prisoner-functionaries.

3. See Adler 1964; Arendt 1986; Bettelheim 1960.

4. On the structure of social seriality, see Sartre, 278ff.; Sofsky 1983, 247ff.

5. For that reason, the customary sociology of the masses cannot be applied to relations in the camps. Its central foci, such as suggestion, imitation, impulsiveness, and leadership, have little significance for camp society. See Moscovici; Smelser; Pross and Buß. At best, certain pointers *ex negativo* can be extracted from the differentiated mass typology developed by Canetti, who also refers to "slow," "faltering," and "closed" masses.

6. See Schütz and Luckmann, 75ff.

7. See Améry 1971: "The victims were not only made into a 'series' by the oppressor. Since they constantly smelled, saw, and touched each other, they were deindividualized physically, and rendered an opaque mass of flesh. . . . We were . . . nothing but an aversion to one other. Necessarily, one felt sick of oneself, a feeling of self-weariness, since everyone sensed he was nothing for his fellow sufferer but a person who took away his bread, air to breathe, space to move in" (223–24).

8. Reciprocal facelessness is described by Antelme in connection with a situation in which the prisoners jumped to grab a mirror they had accidentally stumbled across:

> Since in our relations with the SS, a face was not only unnecessary, but could become undesirable, even dangerous, we all tried to deny our own face. In this, we were in accord with the SS. . . . Even in the relations of the prisoners among themselves, the face was burdened by this nonpresence, had almost become this nonpresence. Given the same stripes, the same shaven head, the progressive emaciation, the identical life rhythms, what an individual noticed about the others was basically just a face: one that was largely collective and anonymous. For that reason, there was this kind of second hunger that drove us all to find ourselves again through the magic of the mirror. . . . But you had to give up the mirror, pass it on to the next prisoner, who was already greedily waiting to take it. You stood in line for this piece of solitude. And while you held it in your hand, your loneliness, the others were badgering you, pestering. (71–72)

9. Levi (1989) has pointed to the lethal consequences of this communication barrier: "In short, you find yourself in a void, and you understand at your expense that communication generates information and that without information you cannot live. The

greater part of the prisoners who did not understand German—that is, almost all the Italians—died during the first ten to fifteen days after their arrival: at first glance, from hunger, cold, fatigue, and disease; but after a more attentive examination, due to insufficient information" (93).

10. In Auschwitz, most of the prisoners spoke Polish or Yiddish; from 1944 on, Hungarian became the second language in the camp. In Mauthausen, the Poles were the largest group, followed by the Russians, Jewish Hungarians, and French; in Neuengamme, the Russians and Poles together made up about half of the inmates.

11. Cf. Oschlies; Jagoda, Klodzinski, and Maslowski, 1987c; Levi 1989, 93ff.

12. See Goffman 1961, 56.

13. Serial coalitions (Sofsky and Paris, 195) are one of the most important forms of sociation in prisons as well. Here too, one should not overestimate the degree of cohesion and solidarity. On this, see the studies by Clemmer; Fischer; Hoppensack; Steinhagen.

14. On the general structure of friendship, see Tenbruck; Wiese, 463ff.; Kon, 85ff. On cooperation and friendship in the camps, see among others: Bakels, 246–47; Bettelheim 1960, 231ff.; Buber-Neumann, 187–88; Goldstein, Lukoff, and Strauss, 42ff.; Jagoda, Klodzinski, and Maslowski, 1987a, 37ff.

15. On illegal bartering, see among others Antelme, 217; Bakels, 248–49; Kielar, 226ff., 344ff.; Kogon, 143ff.; Levi 1993, 93ff.; Fröbe et al., 239ff.; Ryn and Klodzinski, 1987b.

16. See Marsalek 1980, 363.

17. Fleury put it thus:

> In the gigantic herd that we formed, there was no lack of specialists adept at stealing. They operated at all times of the day and night, in groups or individually. We (the French) called them "gangsters." They were interested in everything, but they clearly had a decided preference for cooking utensils, spoons, and strong solid shoes, since these items—which they then sold at the "market" that was held every evening out on the *Appellplatz*—permitted them to obtain ample amounts of bread, potatoes and cigarettes for themselves. Sometimes very violent fights broke out between the thieves and their victims, but the thieves always maintained the upper hand. Cigarettes were in particular demand, because they were a kind of money that circulated throughout the entire camp hierarchy, including the SS. . . . The "gangsters" knew that, and carried out attack after attack in order to get hold of this first-rate money. Nothing was able to hinder them from practicing their despicable profession. (Quoted in Fröbe et al., 241)

18. Vermehren arrives at the following overall judgment:

> Moral depravity in the camps had reached frightening proportions. . . . In his hunger, the prisoner stole from his fellow the little he had, satisfying that hunger temporarily. But it was not extinguished; it was just passed on, continuing to gnaw. Informers were everywhere, and since no one could be sure about the next guy, everyone began to take steps for his own security at the expense of the others. In order to escape punishment, they betrayed one another. This did not eliminate flogging, but just meant that it was meted out to the more defenseless among them. They hated each other, because one person reduced the living space of the next; they sold one another for the sake of some meager external advantage. Brutal indifference reigned in the camp like a sickness. (103–4)

14. Work and Slavery

1. Langhoff, 201–2.
2. For an anthropological concept of labor, see Löffler and Sofsky, 438ff.
3. See also Arendt 1986, 444ff.
4. See Foucault, 307ff.
5. Thus, Adler (1964, 212) speaks of "state slavery." Kaminski (114–87) has been the most forceful recent proponent of this thesis, attempting to demonstrate parallels with Soviet "slave labor camps." As instructive as these findings are regarding individual aspects, they fail to grasp the radical transformation of the nature of labor within a system of absolute power. The counterarguments that Kaminski cites are all more convincing than the reasons supporting the thesis of the slave camp. Despite important insights and observations, Kirstein (129ff.) also fails to see the fundamental difference between slavery and the concentration camp system.
6. Thus, on January 25, 1942, five days after the Wannsee Conference, where the decision on plans for the Final Solution was made, Himmler informed Glücks that Jewish workers would soon be arriving: "Since we cannot expect Russian prisoners of war in the near future, I will be sending a large number of the Jews who are being emigrated from Germany into the camps. Get ready in the next few weeks to admit one hundred thousand Jewish males and up to fifty thousand Jewish females into the concentration camps. In the coming weeks, large economic orders will be presented to the concentration camps" (BA Koblenz NS 19/1920). This order formed the basis for the selection of Jews "fit for labor" on the ramp at Auschwitz, though that did not begin as a regular practice until six months later.
7. On April 30, 1942, Pohl ordered all commandants and factory managers to concentrate on labor deployment as their main task:"The camp commandant has sole responsibility for the deployment of workers. This deployment must be exhausting in the true sense of the word—in order to attain the highest degree of performance" (Nbg. Dok. R-129). That same day, he wrote to Himmler:

> The detention of prisoners solely for security-related, didactic, or preventive reasons is no longer a principal concern. Emphasis has now shifted toward the economic aspects. The mobilization of all prisoner labor, initially for the war effort (boosting of armaments production) and later for tasks in the construction of [postwar] peace, is assuming ever greater importance. This recognition leads to necessary measures requiring a gradual transformation of the concentration camps from their earlier one-sided political form into an organizational form in keeping with the economic tasks" (Pohl to Himmler, April 30, 1942, Nbg. Dok. R-129)

8. Circular decree of Glücks to all head SS camp doctors, December 28, 1942, Nbg. Dok. PS-2171:

> The best doctor in a concentration camp is not the one who believes he must be conspicuous by his use of uncalled-for severity. The best doctor is the one who maintains the capacity of inmates to work at the highest possible level by means of supervision and exchange at the individual work sites. Now, more than before, camp doctors must keep tabs on the diet of the prisoners. . . . Moreover, doctors must see to it that wherever possible, working conditions are improved at individual work sites. For this purpose, it is necessary for camp doctors to gain a direct firsthand impression of conditions in the workplace.

Several days later, on January 20, 1943, Glücks followed this up with a circular decree to camp commandants (Nbg. Dok. NO-1523): "I hereby make all camp commandants and directors of camp administration personally responsible for maintaining the working capacity of the prisoners." In April 1942, they were still talking about "exhausting" the prisoners' labor; now the order of the day was its maintenance at any cost.

9. Circular decree of Glücks to all commandants, December 8, 1943, Nbg. Dok. NO-1544:

> I have noticed that the small-size prisoner Kommandos in particular are doing little or no work. The subordinate leader and sentries stand around at the work site, hardly taking any notice of the prisoners. One subordinate commander, taken to task for this, maintained that it was forbidden to push the prisoners to work harder. Naturally, that is pure rubbish. Each and every subordinate leader and guard must make sure that prisoners are busy at work. Of course, it is forbidden to beat, strike, or even touch the prisoners. Urging them on to work harder must be done only by verbal means. It makes no difference whether guards do this in German or a foreign language. The prisoner knows what he is supposed to do. I request that Kommando leaders be reminded every Monday about this self-evident duty of the guards.

This order documents just how far removed the *Inspektion* in Oranienburg was from the violent realities in the camps.

10. See circular decree of Himmler to Heydrich, Glücks, and all camp commandants, December 5, 1941, Nbg. Dok. NO-385. In the second half of 1942, some eighteen hundred prisoners were undergoing training as stonemasons, an extremely small minority; see Kaienburg, 141.

11. See Kaminski, 168–69.

12. See Herbert (1987, 227ff.); see also Kaienburg (313–41), who convincingly shows that there was no effective economization of prisoner labor nor any relaxation in the level of terror.

13. According to statistics of Health Office DIII, December 22, 1943 (Nbg. Dok. NO-1010), 57,503 prisoners died in the second half of 1942 out of a total of approximately 96,770 prisoners—in other words, about 60 percent. The mortality rate did not begin to decline until the spring of 1943, dropping from 10 percent in December 1942 to 2.8 percent in April 1943. But due to the sharp rise in the total number of prisoners, the absolute figures for the dead dropped far less than these percentages might suggest. Although relative mortality declined, another 58,008 prisoners died in the period from January to August 1943.

14. The discussion of "extermination by work" (*Vernichtung durch Arbeit*) often confuses the relation between means and ends with that between cause and effect. Whenever labor was a cause of the death of an individual, it is accurate to speak of annihilation by work, even if this was not always the intended policy of all authorities involved. To that extent, the debate remains restricted categorically to the limited framework of an intentional explanation. However, it is important to bear in mind that for the SS, labor deployment was always only a "temporary solution." As long as the prisoners were still alive, their labor should be exploited. The program of "extermination by work" was express policy for the category of prisoners in "preventive detention" (*SV* prisoners) handed over by the justice authorities to the SS. See memo of Thierack re: conversation with Himmler, September 18, 1942, Nbg. Dok. PS-654.

15. See Pingel, 132; Kogon, 143.

16. The controversy over the primacy either of economy or of politics suffers from a reliance on conventional conceptions of power and economy. It fails to grasp the transformation of the political economy that took place in the camps. The camp economy had as little to do with the rationality of capitalist accumulation as with the customary forms of political rule.

17. On the concept and historical morphology of slavery, see, among others, Davis, 29–61; Finley; Brockmeyer, 3–73.

15. The Beneficiaries

1. Antelme, 196.

2. The cui bono criterion (see Blau and Scott, 42ff.) is used here to trace changes in labor deployment and the rivalry between various offices.

3. On the history of SS enterprises, see Billig; Georg; Pingel, 64–68; Kaienburg, 70–137, 250–62.

4. See Georg, 108; Kaienburg, 140–41, 232.

5. Pingel, 66.

6. Monthly report of office chief W I to staff of section W, Attention: Hohberg, June 12, 1942, Nbg. Dok. NO-1049; Kaienburg, 253.

7. See Georg, 61. In Lublin, the DAW took over the workshops of the labor camp on Lipova Street. It had been set up in December 1939 by the SS and Police Leader Globocnik. Initially, 1,200 Jewish skilled workers were incarcerated there; later, as a result of exchange, it housed 2,500 Polish POWs of Jewish extraction. In 1942, it began operating a box factory on the grounds of the airport near Chelmska Street, and a sawmill in Pulawy. In the autumn of 1943, there were some 5,500 inmates of the Majdanek camp deployed in these three factories. When all Jews were shot on November 3, 1943, "bloody Wednesday," the DAW was forced to cut down on production (see Marszalek, 59–60, 115ff.). A job with DAW was thus no protection against mass annihilation. In order to get the plants running again, 250 skilled workers were transferred from Dachau, Buchenwald, and Sachsenhausen to Lublin as core personnel in the beginning of 1944 (see Georg, 98).

8. On the textile plants in Ravensbrück, see Georg, 66–69; Zörner et al., 67–73; Zumpe.

9. Along with the clothing factories of the Waffen-SS in Dachau and Ravensbrück, Texled covered roughly 20 percent of the needs of the Waffen-SS, an army numbering more than nine hundred thousand men. At the beginning of 1944, a factory was put into operation in which the field clothing of Waffen-SS troops was washed, repaired, and ironed. This was an extremely dirty job because the blood-drenched parts of soldiers' uniforms had, as a rule, only been inadequately disinfected.

10. On the tailoring workshop, see Buber-Neumann, 256–66, as well as the testimony by Vaillant-Couturier before the Nuremburg Tribunal on January 28, 1946 (IMT, vol. 6, 249–50).

11. On the special staffs and the Dora-Mittelbau camp complex, see Fröbe et al., 28–43; Bornemann and Broszat; Bornemann; Dieckmann; Pachaly and Pelny.

12. According to statistics of the WVHA for Göring dated February 21, 1944 (Nbg.

Dok. PS-1584), some 36,000 prisoners were deployed in the aviation industry at this time; 3,434 were at BMW (Dachau-Allach), 2,695 at Messerschmitt (Dachau-Augsburg), 2,065 at Heinkel (Mauthausen-Schwechat), and 5,939 at the Heinkel plant in Sachsenhausen.

13. See Marsalek 1980, 98ff.; Ziegler, 195ff.

14. Hitler apparently viewed the shifting of armaments production into subterranean facilities as more than just a crisis measure required by the war. He demanded: "Under no circumstances should the measures introduced be implemented as something transitional. Rather, they must mark the beginning of a large-scale and final relocation of the entire complex of German industrial plants underground, since only in this manner can we create the prerequisites over the long term for maintaining production facilities for a war" (Führer Conference, March 5, 1944, quoted in Milward, 128).

15. Kammler is supposed to have given his construction staffs in Dora the slogan: "Don't worry about victims. The job must be done, and in the shortest time possible" (quoted in Bornemann and Broszat, 165); see also Herbert 1990, 174–75.

16. See Bornemann and Broszat, 168, 197–98.; Pachaly and Pelny, 106–7.

17. On the following, see Pingel, 123–51; Broszat, 108–20; Langbein 1986. Herbert (1987) sheds light on the connections between the deployment of concentration camp inmates and broader labor market policy; see also Herbert 1990, 172ff.

18. See Hilberg 1982, 621.

19. Schieber to Speer, May 7, 1944, Nbg. Dok. Speer-6; see also Pingel, 280–81.

20. Pohl to Himmler, April 5, 1944, Nbg. Dok. NO-020. In his Sonthofen speech to Wehrmacht generals on June 21, 1944, Himmler mentioned the figure of forty million person-hours of labor reportedly put in by concentration camp inmates. That would correspond to a total of 160,000 prisoners working as forced laborers. The discrepancy between the figures of the SS and those of the Armaments Ministry probably arises because the ministry only counted the prisoners actually deployed in industrial production. Following a different procedure, the SS counted all laborers who had been placed at the disposal of the branch, especially for work in construction and cleanup operations.

21. See Herbert 1987, 231; Herbert 1990, 175.

22. These figures are based on the data assembled by Schwarz (143–99). In the main, Schwarz relies on the lists in the *Bundesgesetzblatt* for 1967 (*BGBl* I 1967, 233–65), 1977 (*BGBl* I 1977, 1786–1852), and 1982 (*BGBl* I 1982, 1571–79), the catalogs of the International Tracing Service of the Red Cross for 1969 and 1979, and the *Informator Encyklopedyczny* (Warsaw, 1979) issued by the Main Commission for the Investigation of Nazi Crimes in Poland. Schwarz lists a total of 1,202 external subcamps. Of these, it is possible to reconstruct the duration of existence for 987. It can be demonstrated that 566 (57 percent) were not set up until after July 1, 1944. Thus, not until the turbulence of the war's final phase was there a concomitant rapid local differentiation of the concentration camp system.

23. Only in recent years has there been intensive historical research on the *Außenkommandos* and their strength and type of deployment. See Ferencz; affidavit of Sommer, October 4, 1946, Nbg. Dok. NI-1065; Prisoner Deployment for Purposes of the Aviation Industry by the WVHA, February 21, 1944, Nbg. Dok. PS-1584. On the Buna plant in Auschwitz, see Hilberg 1982, 623–29; on Krupp in Essen, see Herbert 1986 and 1985, 190–221; on BMW-Allach, see Zofka; on the camps in Hannover, see

Fröbe et al.; on the camp complex in Natzweiler, see Vorländer et al.; Kirstein; on Kaufering and Mühldorf, see Raim 1992.

24. See Kogon, 291.

25. Marsalek 1980, 87, 97–98.

26. Ibid., 95–96, 108.

16. Work Situations

1. Rohmer, quoted in Ernst and Jensen, 76–77.

2. It is not possible to cite exact data on the quantitative distribution of various forms of work. The listing by Schwarz (146–99) provides an approximate picture, but employs the undifferentiated collective category "industry." Labor deployment in industry usually did not mean work in industrial production, but rather in cleanup operations or construction. The extent of labor in mechanized production was limited, and should not be overestimated. Of 970 external camps, 465 (48 percent) can be classified as "industrial"; 297 Kommandos (31 percent) were put to work constructing roads, tunnels, or antitank ditches, 98 (10 percent) performed "services" for the SS or National Socialist offices, with 54 of these coming from the camp of Dachau alone. Forty-two external Kommandos (4.3 percent) were deployed in agriculture and forestry. This list does not include the Kommandos of the main camps that were deployed in stone quarries, workshops, and industrial plants located near the camps.

3. On the phenomenological situational analysis of pathogenic labor, see Löffler and Sofsky, 138ff.

4. Ibid., 167–68, 521–22.

5. See Ziegler, 46; Kogon, 118ff.; Marsalek 1980, 94, and the reports in Billig, 232ff.

6. See Weiß-Rüthel:

> Everything trembled here from the rumble and roar of work. The old kilns were dismantled at breakneck speed, the frames of enormous machines were lifted by prisoners from the camps without the aid of cranes or winches. . . . Everything was done at double-time tempo, everybody had to run, carrying something or not. Jews pulled a heavy roller weighing many tons over a clay roadbed. Like a living conveyor belt, eight hundred Czech students rushed down wooden footbridges into the hull of a barge, snatching from its depths the cement packed in paper bags. The gray-white, corrosive powder ran down their sweat-covered bodies, ate into the skin, the lungs. . . . Squad leaders shouted, striking the running prisoners who were not fast enough for them with heavy wooden clubs. Prisoners collapsed under the weight of iron girders, were dragged to their feet, and slogged on, moaning as they went. . . . And despite all this, there was within this hell another separate hell, the *Strafkolonne*. . . . Jews were done in there, "finished off," as the expression went in camp jargon. . . . Out in a tenacious moor that mercilessly swallowed up anyone who entered it, these doomed men were deployed on drainage operations, and kept on the job until they either plunged to their death voluntarily—after being driven out of their mind by the blows of their foreman—or stumbled accidentally into the moor's clutches. . . . In the shortest amount of time, these miserable souls worked themselves to death, shoving a heavily laden iron wheelbarrow at double time, struggling while its narrow wheel quickly sank down to the hub in the morass. (64–65)

See also Naujoks, 110ff.; Kaienburg, 93ff.

7. See Gondzik, quoted in Ernst and Jensen, 32–33; Bauche et al., 169ff.; Billig, 228ff.; Kaienburg, 195ff., 262ff., 415ff. Meier 1946 describes transport operations at the clinker factory:

> Most of the work involved was exhausting drudgery. For example, you just needed to be part of the transport detail deployed in moving sand, cement, mortar, roof tiles, machine parts, and the like to the clinker factory or around the grounds of the plant. The Kapo in charge, who was usually a criminal, had virtually unlimited power, and he made sure the pace was at a gallop—or as we used to say, "on the double" [*im Karacho*]. If someone had spent four to six weeks in this Kommando working from 7 A.M. to 6:30 P.M., constantly on his legs, he was in such a deteriorated physical condition that he could no longer perform the assigned work of the squad. And this was considered one of the "better" work squads. (68)

8. See Ziegler, 208ff.

9. See Bleton.

10. See Wysocki 1986, 55–56, and the report of the Yugoslav prisoner Stane Tusar, September 6, 1963 (Forschungsstelle für die Geschichte des Nationalsozialismus in Hamburg, Hans Schwarz papers).

11. See Zofka, 72.

12. Marsalek 1980, 92.

13. Kuder, in quoted Ernst and Jensen, 102–3; on the concentration camp in the Limmer neighborhood of Hannover, see also Fröbe et al., 299–329.

14. See Löffler and Sofsky, 240ff., 275–76; see also the already classic analysis by Popitz et al., 157–58.

15. Cf. Löffler and Sofsky, 283–84.

16. Ibid., 244–45.

17. A poem, "Kulen, Kulen," by the prisoner Heinz Henschke aptly captures the significance and tedium of this heavy menial labor of the "moor soldiers" (quoted in Suhr, 83): "Diggin', diggin', / early, late, just a-diggin' every day; / early and late, just diggin'. / Diggin', diggin', / it's hard, it's heavy, just a-diggin' every day. / Diggin' hard and heavy. / Diggin', diggin', always just gotta dig, / they make ya dig. / Dig, dig, year after year, / every day, nothin' but diggin'. / Year after year, / nothin' but diggin'!" [There is also a famous antifascist song of the *Moorsoldaten* that begins: We are the moor soldiers, marching with our spades, to the field.—Trans.]

18. This was the case, for example, on the plantation grounds in Dachau, where many clerics were deployed to plant herbs and tea leaves. "Neither beasts of burden nor motors were used. Human hands, prisoners' hands, had to work the stony soil year after year. The prisoners were ordered out onto the large fields working in rows of two or three hundred men. Equipped with spades, they turned over the black, gravelly soil, driven on by the SS men, Kapos, and supervisors. It wasn't permitted to have a breather, or to sit up straight. 'Get a move on, OK, hustle it! Get moving, men, shake your ass!' And the blows from clubs made the work a kind of slavery" (Heß, quoted in Schnabel 1966, 141). See also Kogon, 113–14; Sigel.

19. See, for example, Schnabel 1966, 138; Kogon, 111; Buber-Neumann, 188; Suhr, 90.

20. In Sachsenhausen, during the first winter of the war, up to five hundred prisoners were forced to stand jam-packed together in a dormitory all day long until the Komman-

dos had returned in the evening. See Naujoks, 166–67. "The Sachsenhausen camp was, strictly speaking, not just a labor camp. Whoever didn't work was assigned to the so-called *Stehkommando*. Then he had to stand for several hours in the morning and afternoon in a room that was packed to overflowing, nobody knows why. It was an idea whose mother was harassment, and whose father was an idiot" (Skowron, quoted in Kaminski, 104).

21. Ackermann (in Sachsenhausen Komitee West-Berlin et al.) describes an exemplary situation from the experience of a Kommando deployed in the Sachsenhausen clinker factory to unload bricks:

We prisoners, who were just a small number, were supposed to stand in a long extended chain stretching from the boat to the truck, catch the bricks with our naked hands, then toss them on to the next person in the chain. In less than an hour, my hands were lacerated, cut open, they really hurt. Despite this, the boat was supposed to be unloaded quickly. So there were repeatedly sentries who made us work faster and faster. So that you had to catch the next brick before you'd even managed to pass on the one you were still holding. Since some bricks fell to the ground, the SS punished the alleged "saboteurs" by striking them with clubs or rifle butts in the lower back or the knees. On top of this, they threatened to report them to the camp leader. (29)

22. See Kupfer-Koberwitz:

Pieronie ordered us to stand between the tracks, about two and a half meters apart. On command we all had to bend down at the same time and grab the tracks. On his order, we then lifted them up and hauled them off. It worked, though you could see that every man was trying his hardest, expending his last ounce of energy. If just one guy had let go, all the others would have been hurt. So each man gritted his teeth and pitched in. We did the seemingly impossible, and lugged the heavy tracks for some thirty meters. Naturally, Pieronie was cussing us out in the worst way. But he didn't strike anybody, because he was afraid the man hit might drop the tracks. Later on, I took part in many similar relocations of tracks, and I saw a number of prisoners lose two or three fingers, crushed in the process. (323)

23. See Kogon, 117; Kaminski, 155–56.

24. Kielar describes a fairly typical scene from an Auschwitz construction Kommando near the village of Monowitz, where Polish prisoners had received food from the civilian population and then bribed the SS with it: "The SS men were uninterested in the work of the prisoners. They went to their sentry posts and laid down for a pleasant snooze. Naturally, the prisoners took advantage of this, pretended to be working, and looked around to see whether they could manage to find something to eat here. . . . The SS men generally kept their word. They performed their duty to guard us by sleeping in the bushes or the barn. They'd only stir and show some signs of life when the Kommando leader paid us a visit" (144–45).

25. See, for example, Fröbe et al., 80ff., on the link between the bonus system and the Kapo system in the Stöcken neighborhood of Hannover.

26. The pattern of the perceptions held by German civilians in Buna-Monowitz is described by Levi (1993) with a shift in perspective that is rare in the literature by prisoners:

In fact, we are the untouchables to the civilians.... They hear us speak in many different languages, which they do not understand and which sound to them as grotesque as animal noises; they see us reduced to ignoble slavery, without hair, without honour and without names, beaten every day, more abject every day, and they never see in our eyes a light of rebellion, or of peace, or of faith. They know us as thieves and untrustworthy, muddy, ragged and starving, and mistaking the effect for the cause, they judge us worthy of our abasement. Who could tell one of our faces from the other? For them we are "Kazett," a singular neuter word. (120–21)

On civilians in Auschwitz, see also Langbein 1980a, 502–22.

27. A special, "cushy" job in the international society of prisoners was that of interpreter. This socially intermediate position offered substantial opportunities for role-playing. The interpreter could function as an accomplice of the Germans, an intermediary for his or her fellow prisoners, or even their advocate (cf., for example, Antelme, 176). Writing on the basis of his experience in Labor Camp III in Kaufering, Ervin-Deutsch describes how an older Hungarian farmer, who ultimately advanced to the position of block leader, succeeded in using the language barrier for the benefit of the prisoners:

He preferred to deal with "organizational problems," inundating us at the top of his voice with his advice. He ran around pompously; now and then, he had a conversation with the supervisor of Organisation Todt and with the guards. In this way, he wished to land himself a nice little job.... Now Uncle Darvas no longer had to work at all. He assisted the man from Organisation Todt when people were divided into groups. He ran between the small groups pretending to be important, shouting, brandishing a small stick. Despite this, he tried to encourage the men in a warm-hearted way: "Damn it! ... Holy mother of God! Get to work there. Faster, faster! Don't worry if I squeal like a stuck pig. But when I shout, then that blasted work leader doesn't stick his nose everywhere, see, so it's better if I shout. Doesn't hurt anybody. Now when I start shouting, you guys just act as if you're working. Move around. If he's standing far away, you don't have to load anything on your shovel.... If I start hollering, it means that he's watching us again—which means that you guys have to work." (105–6)

28. See Langbein 1980b, 320–34. For a general treatment of the covert labor struggle, see Hoffmann.

29. See Bornemann and Broszat, 189–90; Pachaly and Pelny, 137ff.

17. The *Muselmann*

1. Levi 1993, 90.

2. "Finally, you confuse the living and the dead. Basically, the difference is minimal anyhow. We're skeletons that are still moving; and they're skeletons that are already immobile. But there's even a third category: the ones who lie stretched out, unable to move, still breathing slightly. People wait for them to die and make room for others" (Lévy-Hass, 48). Further, note Elie Wiesel's recent remarks (1995, 26) on the occasion of the fiftieth anniversary of the liberation of Auschwitz: "The 'Muselmänner'—those resigned, extinguished souls who had suffered so much evil as to drift to a waking death. Turning their backs on life and the living, they felt no further terror or pain. They were dead but didn't know it."

3. See Arendt 1981, 164ff.

4. In many reports by prisoners, the *Muselmann* is only mentioned in passing. Although he was the social figure who typified mass dying in the camps, it appears that the disregard and indifference with which he was treated in the camps are reflected in numerous prisoner reports that ignore his presence. Exceptions are Langbein (1980a, 11–28) and the documentation assembled by Ryn and Klodzinski (1987a) on the basis of an investigation conducted among former prisoners.

5. See Kogon, 400. The origin of the term *Muselmann* is not known. The expression was in common use especially in Auschwitz, from where it spread to other camps as well. Its meaning is by no means clear and unambiguous. It apparently was an allusion to the supposed fatalism of Muslims. Another explanation associates the typical movements of *Muselmänner*, the swaying motions of the upper part of the body, with Islamic prayer rituals (see Marsalek 1980, 356). In Majdanek, the word was unknown. The living dead there were termed "donkeys"; in Dachau they were "cretins," in Stutthof "cripples," in Mauthausen "swimmers," in Neuengamme "camels," in Buchenwald "tired sheikhs," and in the women's camp known as Ravensbrück, *Muselweiber* (female Muslims) or "trinkets." Common to all these designations is the clearly negative connotation. These are scornful, mocking labels that express rejection and disdain.

6. See, for example, Baeyer and Baeyer-Katte, 196ff.

7. See Ryn and Klodzinski (1987a):

It is the extraordinary living conditions in the camp, and most particularly its unique psycho-social atmosphere, that shaped the special nature and specific character of the disease of radical starvation in the concentration camps. That ambience was marked by an unusually heavy concentration and intensification of biological and psychological traumata, which induced total physical exhaustion and eventually led to death. As we know, the intensity of these traumata was so powerful that in many instances, prisoners died without any direct physical or biological cause: death could occur due to psychological hyperstress. (92)

8. See Dreitzel, 299–300. The *Muselmann* no longer had any of the options that total loss of contact ordinarily still leaves the individual. He was not able to offer overt resistance, nor could he submit totally and completely to the expectations forced on him. He was no longer capable of action of any kind.

9. See Cohen, 70ff.

10. "The *Muselmann* awakened pity in none, and no one showed him any human warmth. Fellow prisoners, whose own lives were threatened, paid him no attention. The *Muselmänner* were nothing but an annoyance for the prisoner-functionaries, and they were just useless refuse for the SS. Both got rid of the *Muselmänner*, each in their own way" (Adamczyk, quoted in Ryn and Klodzinski, 1987a, 127).

11. As Mostowski put it:

The SS man went past slowly, and looked in the direction of the *Muselmann* who was coming straight at him. All of us squinted to the left to see what would happen. And this creature bereft of will and thought, slouching along in his clattering wooden clogs, walked right into the SS man. The SS man shouted and struck him over the head with his riding whip. The *Muselmann* stopped, not quite sure what was happening. When he'd been given a second and third blow with the whip for not having removed his cap, he shit in his pants (he had diarrhea). When the SS man saw the black spot that was spreading around the wooden clogs of the *Muselmann*, he was beside himself with rage. He pounced on him, kicking him in the abdomen, and after he lay there on the ground in his own excrement, he kicked the man's head and thorax. The *Muselmann* did not resist. After the first kick, he doubled over in pain. A few more kicks, and he was dead." (Quoted in Ryn and Klodzinski, 1987a, 128–29)

12. See Fuchs, 203ff.

13. On the concept of the double mass, see Canetti, 73–79.

18. Epidemics

1. Bakels, 304–5.

2. See Kimmel, 384ff.; Siegert 1979, 444, 475; Johe 1970, 33; Kaienburg, 177ff.; Marsalek 1980, 172ff.; Marszalek, 123ff.; Langbein 1965, 583–90; Langbein 1980a, 235ff.; *Auschwitz*, 97ff.; Szymanski, Szymanska, and Snieszko, 202ff.; Zámečnik.

3. See Foucault, 251ff.; Ruffié and Sournia.

4. The respective designations in National Socialist racial discourse: *Auswurf der Menschheit, Träger artfremden Blutes, Erbkranke, Gemeinschaftsfremde, Volksschädlinge* [—Trans.].

5. See also Hilberg 1982, 693–94.

6. On this, see the reports from Auschwitz collected by Jagoda, Klodzinski, and Maslowski (1987d) using a written questionnaire.

7. Commenting on the "family camp" in Auschwitz where the deportees from Theresienstadt were housed, Elias (1988) noted: "Every prisoner was careful not to admit that he was sick. Therefore, he stood bravely for roll call and, supported by friends, dragged himself to work. Everything possible and impossible was done to keep the sick in the housing barracks in order to protect them from 'hospitalization.' Hardly anyone taken to sick bay ever came out again alive" (148).

8. Naujoks (280ff.) describes how in the autumn of 1941, the *Schreibstube* had to organize a prophylactic delousing operation in the Sachsenhausen barracks itself, against the opposition of the camp management. Prisoner self-management imposed bans on leaving the blocks, formed its own "delousing" squad, and took measures for the disinfection of all woolen blankets and for fresh underwear. Although lice were discovered on more than three thousand prisoners, the camp leaders threatened punishment for this "unauthorized behavior," but then decided not to go ahead with sanctions. When an epidemic broke out a few weeks later anyhow, the camp was placed under quarantine, and was subsequently disinfected by a civilian firm.

9. Lettich comments on block 7 in the men's camp at Birkenau:

When you opened the door, your first spontaneous reaction was to step back and hold your nose, because the air was so disgusting, acrid, stifling, impossible to breathe. There was screaming and moaning everywhere. The sick lay on wooden boards, eight and ten to a bunk, where there was barely room for five men crowded closely together. So most of them had to sit up. All manner of illness, all possible sorts of injury were represented in this jail for the sick: typhoid fever, pneumonia, cachexia, edema, broken arms and legs, skull fractures, all jumbled together. How could the doctors have treated these poor creatures, even if they had had the opportunity for that, without medicines and only paper for bandages? It was impossible. Sometimes you got ten or fifteen tablets for eight hundred or nine hundred sick patients. And what was the use of

providing medical care and applying bandages anyhow, if twice a week attendants had to load
the sick onto trucks that drove up to transport them to the gas chambers? Superfluous human
matériel, just taking up room, was liquidated totally and completely by the German method.
(Quoted in Langbein 1980a, 238–39)

In other concentration camps not equipped with gas chambers, these jails for the sick,
such as *Revier* IV in Neuengamme or the Boelcke barracks in Dora-Mittelbau, were
similar "waiting rooms for death."

10. Kielar comments on the prisoner medical attendant M. Panszcyk, a former art
student, who was involved in administering injections of phenol in block 20 in the main
camp at Auschwitz:

He was a man with unfulfilled ambitions who had finally achieved what he had longed for:
power. He strutted like a peacock, serious, self-important, conceited. . . . He wished to become
a master over life and death. After all, that was something. So he soon found a proper activity
for himself. Although it had nothing to do with his artistic interests or the cardinal principles of
humanity, he could now decide on life and death just as he chose. His pathological megaloma-
nia gave free rein to the most base sadistic predispositions. This was cleverly exploited by the
SS doctors: they provided him with a phenol syringe with which he was allowed to shorten the
lives of those who had to die anyhow. (73)

See also Langbein 1980a, 214ff.

11. See, for example, the description by Michelet (210–51) of the final months in
Dachau, when an epidemic of typhoid fever bifurcated camp space: the entire eastern
row of blocks became a camp for the dying, separated only by the broad central street
from the west side of the camp, the realm of the living.

19. Terror Punishment

1. Gorondowski, 132.

2. The literature generally speaks summarily of "punishments" in the camp. However, that obscures the difference between comparatively regulated punishment procedures and arbitrary acts of excess. The transformation of penalties into *Terrorstrafe* is
not even a theme. Thus, the impression arises that the catalog of norms valid in the
camp entailed nothing but a gradual stiffening of customary military systems of norms
and sanctions, a turning of the screw. But a key structural feature of camp power is the
link between normativeness and arbitrary will—they certainly are not mutually exclusive: terror can, in a certain sense, be established and initiated as a norm. See also the
illuminating remarks in Pohlmann (387ff.) and Kirstein (85ff.).

3. See Spittler, 23.

4. For more detail, see Paris and Sofsky.

5. Kogon, 124.

6. Even to inquire about regulations was to provoke the SS and its accomplices.
Jaworksi reports from Auschwitz:

I looked for regulations that had some validity for us in the camp. I thought they were written
down somewhere as a set of rules, available for general information. Unfortunately, I couldn't
find them. Suddenly I happened to see the block clerk, and so I turned to him: "Excuse me, sir,

are there any regulations for prisoners in this camp? I'd like to familiarize myself with them, so as to avoid trouble." He looked at me as if I were crazy, punched me in the face and said: "There's your regulations, Mr. Commissioner!" This explanation cost me two teeth. (Quoted in *Auschwitz*, 103)

7. See Bettelheim 1960, 209ff. However, Bettelheim is mistaken: to disappear in anonymity did not entail a loss of individuality. To avoid becoming conspicuous was not a task for the personality: it was a highly active achievement in the art of self-protection.

8. In Mauthausen, prisoners called out the code number "eighteen"—an expression from the card game skat—to one another whenever an SS man or Kapo approached. The code word for "all clear" was "twenty." As a rule, the prisoners communicated with gestures that were generally understandable in the international society of the camp, such as a forefinger raised to closed lips.

9. An undated list for internal SS use prepared during the war mentions no fewer than forty-seven crimes punishable by official flogging (see Dachau Archives, no. 7151). A few examples: ten strokes of the cane were given for "negligence at work and undisciplined behavior," twenty for "absence from the work place" and stealing of food, fifteen for "insolence toward a member of the SS" or "cutting up a woolen blanket"; the "theft of a potato" was punishable by five strokes on the whipping block.

10. On December 2, 1942, Himmler instructed the commandants, via Liebehenschel, the chief of Department I, to use "corporal punishment in the future only as a final resort" and to submit punishment orders for authorization (Nbg. Dok. NO-1515). Several weeks later, on January 20, 1943, he issued an order to the commandants via Glücks for the "most careful personal scrutiny" of all requests for corporal punishment (Nbg. Dok. NO-1521). Shortly after the incorporation of the Oranienburg *Inspektion der Konzentrationslager* into the WVHA, however, corporal punishment was stiffened once again. In a communication to all camp commandants, dated April 4, 1942 (Nbg. Dok. PS-2199), Liebehenschel passed along Himmler's instruction "that in his orders for administering corporal punishment (for both male and female prisoners in protective custody and detention), if the word *verschärft* [more severe] has been added, the punishment should be carried out on the naked buttocks," a regulation that was a common, long-standing practice in the camps in any case.

11. There was a certain reduction in the use of corporal punishment in the period between 1942 and 1944 only where previous commandants were replaced by SS leaders directly from section D, who endeavored to strengthen internal control and supervision in the camps.

12. See *Auschwitz*, 106ff.; Naujoks, 179ff.; Komitee der antifaschistischen Widerstandskämpfer der DDR, 54ff.; Zörner et al., 93; Ziegler, 60ff. A preliminary stage prior to the institutionalized *Strafkompanie* was penal labor under similar working conditions, but without segregated housing and isolation from fellow prisoners; see Richardi, 143ff.

13. Note also the practice of suspending prisoners on stakes or trees, generally at semipublic locations, such as in the yard of the camp prison. The prisoners' hands were tied behind their backs and they were then suspended by them from stakes, tearing sinews and dislocating wrist and arm joints. The punishment lasted up to two hours. Those who survived were generally left permanently crippled or with severe injuries.

The prisoners were unable to work for a certain period. For that reason, Himmler banned the practice in 1943 in the course of the campaign for labor deployment.

14. See *Auschwitz*, 103ff.; Kogon, 128ff.; Richardi, 129ff.; Rovan, 176ff.; Suhr, 102; Wiechert, 78–79; Höß, 56–57. On corporal punishment more generally, see Hentig 1954, 380ff.; Hentig 1955, 365–82.

15. See Broszat: "The purpose was consciously to document and drill in the notion that corporal punishment had been removed from the arbitrary will of the individual guard and was, so to speak, a proper form of punishment. By using several SS men to carry out the flogging, the mistreatment was to be rendered impersonal and anonymous. Right from the start, each member of the guard force was supposed to become accustomed to this procedure, which he might be ordered to participate in at any time" (51).

16. See, for example, Marsalek 1980, 250. [The reference to the bird is from a well-known folk song, "Kommt ein Vogel geflogen"; the allusion is to the colloquial German expression "the (jail)bird has flown the coop" (*der Vogel ist ausgeflogen*)—Trans.]

17. See Canetti: "Those orders . . . that are serious about death, have set their sights on it and really lead to death, leave the fewest traces in the recipient" (379). On the rare cases of open resistance to providing such executioners' services, see Langbein 1980b, 225–26.

18. On the history of this death penalty, see Dülmen, 133–34; Hentig 1954, 206–53; Leder, 102–19, 200–209.

19. The most famous, even legendary, incident of this kind was the execution of the Jewish messenger and interpreter Mala Zimetbaum in Birkenau. She had escaped with the Pole Edek Galinski in June 1944, disguised in SS uniforms. After capture at the Slovakian border, both were brought back to Auschwitz for execution. However, Zimetbaum succeeded in slashing her wrists with a razor blade before the entire assembled women's camp, and then spraying her blood in the face of an SS man—a dramatic act of martyrdom to which the SS reacted with a barbaric orgy of beating. At the general roll-call assembly in the men's camp, Galinski tried to hang himself—in order, as he had promised before his escape, to avoid falling live into the hands of the hangman. However, the executioner loosened the noose again and started the procedure from the beginning. At the final moment, there was a rare salute. "The silent crowd of thousands of prisoners slowly disappeared into the falling darkness. There was a deathly quiet. A group of SS men was moving back in the direction of the camp gate. Suddenly, unexpectedly, a command in Polish resounded from the side of the square where block 4 was located: 'Caps off!' . . . The entire camp showed the dead man their last respects" (Kielar, 341). See also Birenbaum, 148; Kagan, quoted in Adler, Langbein, and Lingens-Reiner, 209ff.; Langbein 1980a, 298–99; Levi 1989, 155–56.

20. Cf. Foucault, 44–90.

20. Violent Excesses

1. Kautsky, 100.

2. Levi (1989) speaks correctly about "useless violence, as an end in itself, with the sole purpose of inflicting pain" (106). The concept of "act of excess" as used here thus designates a specific mode of violence. It is secondary whether these acts were ordered, covered, condoned, or sanctioned by SS superiors. The decisive feature of excessive force is not the absence of a command, but its gratuitousness, as an "end in itself."

3. See Popitz 1986, 76.

4. The criminological work of Jäger (1982, 1989) contains important comments. However, he limits the concept of an "act of excess" to individual acts not based on a specific order. Lurking here in the background is the problem of the supposed "necessity to obey orders" (*Befehlsnotstand*). Jäger correctly points to factors of group dynamics operative in the reduction of inhibitions. By contrast, his analysis gives less prominence to organizational structures, and particularly to the interactive dynamics involved and the manifold methods of excess. For that reason, greater emphasis will be given to these dimensions here.

5. Gehlen, 25–26.

6. See more generally Berger and Luckmann, 77–78.

7. Cf. the jury verdict of the district court in Bonn (8 Ks 1/58), February 6, 1959, against block leader Schubert and Sorge, the rapport leader and leader of labor service, known among the prisoners as "Iron Gustav." Sorge was given a life sentence for each of sixty-seven murders, Schubert for each of forty-six murders; each man was also given an additional sentence of fifteen years for attempted murder, homicide, and accessory to murder. See Dam and Giordano, 331–486.

8. Cf. Kogon, 219ff.; *Auschwitz*, 105ff.; Langbein in Adler, Langbein, and Lingens-Reiner, 159ff.; Ziegler, 64; Henkys, 50ff.

9. On the history of torture techniques, see Helbing; Keller.

10. Améry 1977, 63–64.

11. The defense based on *Befehlsnotstand*, a common argument in many trials, is thus quite misleading as well. The perpetrator of acts of excess did what he did not because he was obliged to, but because he was permitted to. Excess is always action that is subject to social influences, but these influences do not abrogate its character as action. Its ultimate reason does not lie in compulsion, but rather in the absolute freedom of the perpetrator—a salient feature that a sociological analysis must also take into account.

12. See Kogon, 115, 119.

13. See Henkys, 53. For his "meritorious service" as organizer of the mass annihilation in Auschwitz, Otto Moll, together with Camp Commandant Höß, was awarded the War Cross with swords. In the Dachau trial in 1946, he was sentenced to death and hanged.

14. On boredom as a source of cruelty, see Fromm (279ff.). However, he places stress on character structure, failing to consider the frame of destructiveness.

15. See Bahrdt, 53.

16. See also Duster, 80ff.

17. See Henkys, 54; Marsalek 1980, 209; Jäger 1982, 37–38.

18. See Marszalek, 138ff.; *Auschwitz*, 110ff., 116; Kimmel, 405–6.

19. See Canetti, 50ff., 130ff.

20. Langbein 1980b, 298ff.; Marsalek 1980, 255ff. The Mühlviertel, where the market town of Mauthausen is located, is a geographical area north of Linz in the state of Upper Austria.

21. Quoted in Marsalek 1980, 261–62.

22. "It enraged him to be thrown into inner turmoil by the prisoner, to be projected into a conflict between the wish to do his duty and the feeling that it was wrong to mistreat. This conflict made him angry. By growing more cruel he tried to deny the conflict, and at the same time to discharge his anger. The more such a prisoner managed

to touch the SS, the angrier he got, and the more his anger exploded in violent abuse"
(Bettelheim 1960, 229).

23. Popitz 1986, 95.

24. Cf. Arendt 1986, 455–56; Jäger 1982, 312–13; Jäger 1989, 170–71.

25. Bernard and Renger, 94–95.

26. See Naujoks, 182–83; Komitee der antifaschistischen Widerstandskämpfer der
DDR, 53.

27. Siegert 1986, 75.

28. Ziegler, 37–38, 58.

29. Kogon, 233–34; Rabitsch, 65; Marsalek 1980, 84, 221–22.

30. See Kogon, 115–16.

21. Selection

1. Mannheimer, 101–2.

2. On the following, see Grode; Klee, 345–55; Kogon et al., 65–80; Lifton, 134–44.

3. See Section D to commandants, March 26, 1942, Nbg. Dok. PS-1151-P.

4. Two examples by way of illustration: on a registration form, the diagnosis listed
is "fanatic hatred of Germans + asocial psychopath." The main symptoms: "dyed-in-
the-wool Communist, unworthy to serve in the armed forces, sentenced for high treason
to six years in prison." On another form: "stateless, rabble-rousing Jew, anti-German;
in camp, insolent and lazy." Quoted in Klee, 346, 348.

5. See, for example, Naujoks, 247ff.

6. The total number of victims cannot be reconstructed. Estimates run at least as high
as 15,000. In 1942, at least 2,593 were transferred to the Hartheim installation. From
August 1941 to the summer of 1942, at least 1,386—possibly even as many as 4,000—
were removed from Mauthausen, and another 2,980 prisoners were removed in 1944.
On July 28, 1941, 575 prisoners were transferred from Auschwitz to Sonnenstein; in the
summer of 1941, 450 were sent from Buchenwald, followed in March 1942 by at least
another 400 prisoners. At the beginning of June 1941, 269 prisoners were transferred
from Sachsenhausen. Some 1,200 were selected out in the women's camp at Ravensbrück in the winter of 1941–42. See Grode, 86–87, 116ff., 201–2; Kimmel, 388; Marsalek 1980, 156–57; Kogon et al., 78ff.; Komitee der antifaschistischen Widerstandskämpfer der DDR, 149.

7. To that extent, the organizational function of selection far exceeds the hygienic
rationality of the SS doctors noted by Lifton (180). What Lifton terms the "Auschwitz
ecology" was basically true of every concentration camp, even the satellite camps: the
active creation of an "equilibrium between extermination and work productivity."

8. Cf. Marszalek, 144ff. "Donkey" (*Gamel*) was the slang term in Majdanek for a
Muselmann.

9. Selections in the women's camp are described by, among others, Zywulska, 210–
11; Birenbaum, 114ff.; on Ravensbrück, see the affidavit of Nedvedova, September 6,
1946, Nbg. Dok. NO-875.

10. This report by Z. Rebilas (in Ryn and Klodzinksi, 1987b, 310) is among the few
in which prisoners attempt to communicate what they felt during the selection.

11. On the following, see Zámečnik, 135–36; Siegert 1979, 473; Kogon, 282; Marsalek 1980, 175–76; *Auschwitz*, 117–18; Klodzinski; Lifton, 186–92, 254–68.

12. See Klodzinksi:

> Killing by phenol injection was an absolute secret of the prisoner hospital. It was forbidden to talk about it. Whoever informed the patients committed a crime that could cost his life. The personnel of the prisoner hospital saw no reason to tell those who were doomed about the fate that awaited them, since they regarded it as unavoidable, irrevocable. On the contrary, the personnel quite consciously did everything they could to leave the victim in the belief that going behind the curtain and the injection administered there were part of a normal medical procedure.... Within the group of those condemned to death, any circumstance that could have pointed to imminent death was ... interpreted in just the opposite way. When it came to concepts such as hospital, doctor, medical attendant, injections, medical operation, all quite familiar notions over many years, everyone thought of the struggle to save life—not of murder. (279)

13. In general, *Revier* personnel were in no position to alter anything in the actual practice of selection. Hermann Langbein, the personal scribe of Wirths, the camp doctor in Auschwitz, was the sole prisoner who had some success: he managed to persuade his superior to have phenol murders halted. Wirths had been ordered to restrict the spread of typhus in the camp. However, the attempt to confine the disease could only prove successful if those who were infected actually came to the *Revier* and were isolated there. Yet because it was well known in the camp that the infirmary meant possible death, many prisoners preferred to remain in the camp, and thus infected the others. The only way out, as Langbein suggested, was to discontinue the practice of "death by injection." Wirths demanded written proof of the existence of this lethal procedure, which he claimed to know nothing about. When he was given such evidence, he transferred the main culprits: the doctor, Entress, and the SS medic, Klehr. Regular phenol injections were largely restricted, and there was an evident decline in mortality in Auschwitz and Birkenau during the course of the year. On this in detail, see Langbein 1980a, 48–52.

14. In order to prevent this, SS doctors in Auschwitz occasionally reversed the deceptive maneuver and carried out "negative selection"—that is, they selected out those who should *not* be sent to the gas chamber. "Whoever had hid before the selection was thus automatically committed to the hands of death, because his prisoner number was on the list for the block, and was called out when the trucks arrived" (ibid., 241). See also Lifton, 191.

15. See Foucault, 239ff.

16. Canetti, 340ff.

17. See *Auschwitz*, 133ff.; Lifton, 189.

18. See Czech 1989, 882, 920; Vaupel, 82ff. In the autumn of 1944, several transports with hundreds of exhausted prisoners were sent back to Auschwitz from the Bavarian camp complexes Mühldorf and Kaufering, which operated as *Außenkommandos* of Dachau. Along with the SS, members of Organisation Todt were also responsible for the selections. "To a certain extent, the camps at Kaufering and Mühldorf can also be regarded as satellites of Auschwitz: their prisoners did not come from Dachau, but in large part from Auschwitz, and also returned there again if they fell ill or became unfit for work" (Raim 1992, 237).

19. See Vorländer et al., 210–11. On the conditions in Vaihingen, see also Bakels, 278–323.

20. On individual transports, see also Kolb 1985, 32–33, 42–43. To clarify: I refer here not to the evacuation transports at the war's end, at which no selections were carried out, but rather to transports of the sick. It is well known that Bergen-Belsen, especially the women's camp there, was not only meant for sick and feeble prisoners, but was also the final stop for many death transports.

21. On the following, see Rückerl, 168ff., 210ff., 223–24; Hilberg 1982, 612, 656–57.

22. See Kogon et al., 238, as well as Wetzel, 127ff.; Fleischer, 273; Hirschfeld, 165.

23. See Herbert 1987, 232; Hilberg 1982, 631–32.

24. These calculations are based on figures from Czech 1989, 241–938.

25. Ibid., 576ff.

26. After the Warsaw ghetto uprising (April–May 1943), the only building left intact in the ghetto was the Gestapo prison. On August 15, 1943, this prison was formally converted to a concentration camp. In July 1943, three hundred prisoners had been transferred to Warsaw from Buchenwald. Some twenty-five hundred male and female prisoners from the Warsaw camp, along with a thousand Polish workers, were deployed in pulling down and removing 2.6 million cubic meters of rubble, bricks, and masonry, and leveling destroyed buildings in order to transform the former site of the ghetto into a park. On May 1, 1944, the Warsaw concentration camp became a subcamp attached to the Majdanek main camp. From August 24, 1944 on, prisoners were "evacuated" to Dachau, Flossenbürg, and Stutthof; cf. Schwarz, 199.

27. R. Vrba, a former block scribe in Birkenau, who successfully escaped in April 1944, refers to the dilemma-ridden consequences of resistance in the camp:

> If the camp needed, say, thirty thousand prisoners, and five thousand died, they were replaced by a fresh batch taken from the Jewish transports. If only a thousand died, a thousand were replaced. And a larger number were gassed. Thus, improvements in living conditions inside the concentration camp increased the number of deaths in the gas chambers, and decreased the death rate among the prisoners. It was clear to me that an improvement of conditions in the concentration camp had no influence on the process of annihilation. Consequently, my view of the resistance movement and its task was that improving conditions was only a first step. The resistance movement had to realize that the most important goal was to terminate the process of mass annihilation, to shut down the machinery of death. . . . But it was clear to me that the purpose of any act of resistance in a concentration camp such as Auschwitz could not be the same as in Mauthausen or Dachau. While the policy of resistance in these camps made it possible for political prisoners to survive, that same noble policy in Auschwitz perfected and oiled the machinery of mass annihilation. (Quoted in Lanzmann, 202–3)

28. See Czech 1989, 699–700; *Auschwitz*, 31ff.

29. Czech 1989, 894ff.

30. In his Kraków notes of November 1946, Höß (162–63) also describes the conflict of interest. The criterion of fitness for work also allowed camp management to legitimate to the *Inspektion* in Oranienburg the high number of prisoners gassed. On January 27, 1943, Office DII of the WVHA, responsible for worker allocation, ordered that the commandant's office "immediately register" some 5,000 Jews on their way from Theresienstadt to Auschwitz, because they were needed by the construction department in Auschwitz and I. G. Farben. Weeks later, the commandant's office justified the low number of prisoners formally admitted by mustering figures: of the 5,022 prisoners,

4,092 had been "housed separately," i.e., sent to the gas chamber, since the men were "too frail," and most of the females were still children. It was no different at the beginning of March 1943, when the WVHA reminded the commandant's office that the Jewish skilled workers who had arrived from Berlin were there to cover the needs of I. G. Farben, and should be assigned to the Farben Buna plant immediately, without being kept in quarantine. However, of the 10,412 Jews, only 2,390 were chosen; 7,432 were gassed. See Czech 1989, 429ff.; Hilberg 1982, 620–21.

31. See Lifton, 150.

32. Lifton quotes from an interview with an SS doctor:

> There were numerous discussions: Should one gas [many] or should one [gas fewer]? Where is the limit to be set? That is, if you take more old people into the camps, then there are more diseased people, and that, for many reasons, is the worse problem if they are in the working camp ... where there is only so much possibility [for keeping limited numbers of people alive]. ... Then the camp leadership comes ... and says, "You're sending us people we can't do anything with. They'll only croak." ... You understand that about these purely technical issues there were heated and intense discussions. (176–77)

33. See Langbein 1980a, 420.

34. Lifton, 394.

35. The following description refers to the first ramp located between the main camp and Birkenau. The branch line was not finished until 1944; it ran right into the middle of Birkenau, and shortened the distance to the crematorium. The scene is described from the viewpoint of the SS by Höß, 163; see also affidavit of Broad, October 20, 1947, Nbg. Dok. NI-11984. For the perspective of the new arrivals, see, among others, Frankl, 28–29; Levi 1993, 19ff.; Ménaché, quoted in Adler, Langbein, and Lingens-Reiner, 59–60; Wiesel 1985, 38ff. One of the most precise descriptions is contained in Borowski, 110ff. He describes the scene from the angle of prisoners deployed for ramp duty—that is, from the perspective of a third party.

36. See Levi 1993: "We had expected something more apocalyptic: they seemed simple police agents. It was disconcerting and disarming" (19).

22. The Death Factory

1. Müller, 151.

2. In Mauthausen, Sachsenhausen, Stutthof, Neuengamme, Natzweiler, and Ravensbrück as well, prisoners were murdered in gas chambers (see Kogon et al., 245–80). In addition, the SS set up a mobile gassing van running back and forth between Mauthausen and the nearby subcamp, Gusen. However, the concept of "death factory" used here is focused more on the element of *constant, routinized slaughter* than on the technical facilities involved. Even the *Genickschuß* installations in Buchenwald and Sachsenhausen, where thousands of Soviet POWs were liquidated under the guise of a medical examination, were not death factories in the strict sense. These were organizational precursors with elements of death factories: death on an assembly line and the systematic deception of the victims. They could perhaps be termed local "death workshops," involving a low level of organizational integration and without prisoner laborers to do the dirty work.

3. See Kogon et al., 110–45; Rückerl, 259ff.; Dawidowicz, 175–76.

4. Benz, 1991, 17; Hilberg 1982, 604; Arndt and Scheffler; Scheffler, 145ff.; Langbein 1980a, 70ff.; Golczewski, 462ff., 495; see also Piper, 89ff. The number murdered in the gas chambers at Auschwitz is less than the total number of Auschwitz victims. Piper estimates that the total was 1.1 million. Of the approximately 400,000 persons admitted to the camp, some 200,000 perished. Many were taken during selections and sent to the gas chamber. However, it cannot be established how many died as a result of shootings, phenol injections, exhaustion, or other violent excesses. For that reason, the figure here necessarily remains a very rough minimal estimate.

5. See Kogon et al., 146–93; Hilberg 1982, 592ff.; Rückerl; Donat; Glazar; Schwarz, 210ff.

6. For more detail, see Grode, 179ff.; Kogon et al., 148ff.

7. In terms of social origin, this personnel came from quite stable, albeit modest, family circumstances. Their fathers were workers, independent artisans, or minor officials. Almost all had completed an apprenticeship in a trade or business, though some had been unemployed for a time before 1933. They were all somewhat older men who had been conscripted to serve with T4. When they were sent to the extermination camps, most were between thirty and forty years old. Detailed data on the biographies of the twenty-seven men later accused can be found in Rückerl, 295ff.

8. See Scheffler, 147–48; Marszalek, 136ff.; Kogon et al., 241ff.

9. See Hilberg 1982, 596; *Auschwitz*, 118ff.; Czech 1989, 447, 455, 459, 528, 533.

10. For a description of the process of annihilation, see *Auschwitz*, 118–35; Hilberg 1982, 649–62; Rückerl, 135–45, 166–76, 217–26; Höß, 127–32; affidavit of Gerstein, April 26, 1945, Nbg. Dok. PS-1553; affidavit of Broad, December 14, 1945, Nbg. Dok. NI-11397; affidavit of Broad, November 20, 1947, Nbg. Dok. NI-11984; Kogon et al., 204ff., 224ff.; Glazar; Müller; Nyiszli, quoted in Adler, Langbein, and Lingens-Reiner; Lanzmann.

11. Such a situation is described by Müller:

The persuasive speeches of the SS leaders had an effect. The initial mistrust and suspicion yielded to hope, perhaps even a sense of certainty that everything would turn out all right. Hössler had recognized the situation and also let himself be questioned. In order to provide the large-scale deceptive maneuver with a veneer of total honesty, he put on a perfect theatrical performance to the now guileless audience. "You, over there in the corner," he called out, pointing to a small man. "What's your profession?" "Tailor" was the quick-fire response, as if shot from a pistol. "Men's tailor or ladies'?" Hössler asked. "Both," the man replied confidently. "Excellent!" Hössler seemed to be elated. "You're just the kind of people we need in our shops. When you finish showering, then report to me directly. And you over there, what's your line?" He had directed this question to an attractive, somewhat older woman standing right up front. "I'm a nurse, sir," was her response. "Well, then you're lucky, we badly need nurses in our infirmary, and if there are any other nurses here, report to me after you have bathed." "We need artisans of all kinds," Grabner now chimed in. "Plumbers, electricians, auto mechanics, welders, bricklayers, and concrete mixers should all report. But we also need unskilled laborers too. Everyone'll get work and good wages." Then Grabner closed with the words: "And now, get undressed. Hurry up, so the soup won't get cold." (61–62)

12. On the following, see Müller, 52ff., 118ff., 132ff.

13. In the reports from Treblinka, mention is made of an enormous dog, part St. Bernard, that answered to the name of "Barry." His master, commandant Karl Franz, would incite the animal with the command "Hey man, grab that dog!" to attack prisoners and tear their lower bodies limb from limb. See Rückerl, 234ff. The head of the Auschwitz crematoria, Otto Moll, a man of unparalleled imagination, had a preference for setting his German shepherd loose on young, attractive Jewish women.

14. Rückerl, 191.

15. Ibid., 169–74, 185–94; on the organization of work in Treblinka, see ibid., 210ff.

16. Cf. *Auschwitz*, 123ff.; Levi 1989, 50ff.; Langbein 1980a, 221–34; Bendel; Nyiszli, quoted in Adler, Langbein, and Lingens-Reiner; Müller; Pozner, 55–62, 169–73, as well as the manuscripts written by members of the Sonderkommando and discovered after the war near the crematoria and the recently published interviews with survivors of the Sonderkommando contained in "Inmitten des grauenvollen Verbrechens."

17. Nyiszli, quoted in Adler, Langbein, and Lingens-Reiner, 67–68.

18. Müller, 156ff.

19. Ibid., 222–23.

20. Cf. Czech 1989, 827.

21. This apathy sometimes was mingled with feelings of hope and revenge. That is evident from remarks by a member of the Birkenau Sonderkommando cited by Zywulska:

> Naturally I could have run and thrown myself onto the fence, because you can always do that. But I want to live. And what if the miracle happens we're all waiting for? Maybe we'll be liberated, today or tomorrow. Then I'll have my revenge, then I'll tell the world what happened here—inside there. . . . Because as far as the work's concerned, well, you can get used to that, if you don't go crazy right off the first day. You think maybe that those guys who're busy working in the munitions factories, you think their work is any more noble? Or the ones here, in "Kanada," who sort out and ship all the stuff for them? We're all working under orders, and we all work for them. Our work's just more unpleasant. I don't want to live just for the sake of living, but to have my revenge. They sent my whole family to the gas. . . . You think there's nothing but brutal people in the Sonderkommando. Let me assure you, these are people just like anyone else—only a lot more unhappy. (318–19)

22. Kielar, 344–45.

23. A former member of the Sonderkommando in Treblinka said:

> No more transports arrived, and the whole camp was empty. And then suddenly, when there was hunger everywhere, and it was gettin' worse and worse, and in the worst starvation, well, suddenly *Oberscharführer* [SS sergeant] Franz comes over. He stops there in front of us and says: "Okay, men, tommorow the transports are going to start rolling in again!" We didn't say anything. We just looked at one another the whole time, and each of us was thinking: "Tommorow the hunger's gonna be over and done, a thing of the past." . . . The transports came from a special camp in Saloniki. . . . They were wealthy people, and the transports brought a lot of stuff, too. Then something arose that was awful, sure, awful for the others just like for me. A feeling of powerlessness, impotence, a sense of shame and disgrace. Because . . . well, we pounced on all that stuff. . . . We were the factory workers in Treblinka . . . and we were dependent on the whole process of fabrication . . . which means, the process of killing in Treblinka. (R. Glazar, quoted in Lanzmann, 196–97)

24. See Glazar; Kohn; Langbein 1980b, 306–11; Steiner; Wiernik; Willenberg; Golczewski, 478.

25. See Langbein 1980b, 311–19; Novitch; Pechersky; Rashke; Rückerl, 194ff.

26. Czech 1989, 898ff.; Garlinksi, 324ff.; Gutman, quoted in Adler, Langbein, and Lingens-Reiner; Langbein 1980b, 229–34; Müller, 232ff., 246–59.

27. Gutman, quoted in Adler, Langbein, and Lingens-Reiner, 216.

28. Report of the Soviet Commission on War Crimes, May 6, 1945, Nbg. Dok. USSR-008.

Bibliography

IN ORDER to make the bibliography more accessible for the English-speaking audience, works that were originally published in English are also listed, within brackets, in their original English-language edition. English translations of some works originally published in German or other languages are also indicated in brackets. Footnotes and references in the text, however, refer to the German-language edition when that edition was the one used by the author.

Adler, H. G. 1960a. "Selbstverwaltung und Widerstand in den Konzentrationslagern der SS." *VfZ* 8:221–36.

———. 1960b. *Theresienstadt 1941–1945. Das Antlitz einer Zwangsgemeinschaft.* Tübingen.

———. 1964. "Gedanken zu einer Soziologie des Konzentrationslagers." In Adler, *Die Erfahrung der Ohnmacht. Beiträge zur Soziologie unserer Zeit*, 210–26. Frankfurt am Main.

———. 1974. *Der verwaltete Mensch. Studien zur Deportation der Juden aus Deutschland.* Tübingen.

Adler, H. G., H. Langbein, and E. Lingens-Reiner, eds. 1984. *Auschwitz. Zeugnisse und Berichte.* Frankfurt am Main.

Adorno, T. W. 1955. *Prismen. Kulturkritik und Gesellschaft.* Frankfurt am Main.

———. 1977a. "Erziehung nach Auschwitz." In *Gesammelte Schriften*, vol. 10, part 2, 674–90. Frankfurt am Main.

———. 1977b. "Was bedeutet: Aufarbeitung der Vergangenheit?" In *Gesammelte Schriften*, vol. 10, part 2, 555–72. Frankfurt am Main.

Améry, J. 1971. *Widersprüche.* Stuttgart.

———. 1977. *Jenseits von Schuld und Sühne.* Stuttgart.

Antelme, R. 1987. *Das Menschengeschlecht.* Munich.

Apitz, B. 1986. *Nackt unter Wölfen.* Frankfurt am Main.

Arendt, H. 1964. *Eichmann in Jerusalem.* Munich. [Originally published as *Eichmann in Jerusalem: A Report on the Banality of Evil* (New York, 1936).]

———. 1981. *Vita activa oder vom tätigen Leben.* Munich.

———. 1986. *The Origins of Totalitarianism.* London.

———. 1987. *Macht und Gewalt.* Munich. [Originally published as *On Violence* (New York), 1970).]

———. 1989. *Nach Auschwitz. Essays und Kommentare I.* Berlin.

Arndt, I. 1970. "Das Frauenkonzentrationslager Ravensbrück." In *Studien zur Geschichte der Konzentrationslager*, 93–129.

Arndt, I., and W. Scheffler. 1976. "Organisierter Massenmord an Juden in nationalsozialistischen Vernichtungslagern." *VfZ* 24:105–35.

Aronson, S. 1971. *Reinhard Heydrich und die Frühgeschichte von Gestapo und SD.* Stuttgart.

Auerbach, H. 1962. "Die Einheit Dirlewanger." *VfZ* 10:250–63.

Auschwitz. Geschichte und Wirklichkeit des Vernichtungslagers. 1980. Reinbek.

Baeyer, W. von and W. Baeyer-Katte. 1973. *Angst.* Frankfurt am Main.

Bahrdt, H. P. 1984. *Schlüsselbegriffe der Soziologie.* Munich.

Bakels, F. B. 1982. *Nacht und Nebel. Der Bericht eines holländischen Christen aus deutschen Gefängnissen und Konzentrationslagern.* Frankfurt am Main.

Bastian, G. 1965. "22. März. 1933—Der Tag der Errichtung des Konzentrationslagers Dachau." *Mitteilungsblatt der Lager-Gemeinschaft Dachau,* April.

Bataille, G. 1975. *Das theoretische Werk.* Vol. 1: *Die Aufhebung der Ökonomie.* Munich.

———. 1978. *Die psychologische Struktur der Faschismus. Die Souveränität.* Munich.

Bauche, U., et al., eds. 1986. *Arbeit und Vernichtung. Das KZ Neuengamme 1938–1945.* Hamburg.

Bendel, P. 1946. *Témoignages sur Auschwitz.* Paris.

Benz, W. 1987. "Die Abwehr der Vergangenheit. Ein Problem nur für Historiker und Moralisten?" In Diner, *Ist der Nationalsozialismus Geschichte?*

———, ed. 1991. *Dimension des Völkermords. Die Zahl der jüdischen Opfer des Nationalsozialismus.* Munich.

Berben, P. 1968. *Histoire du camp de concentration Dachau, 1933–1945.* Brussels.

Berger, P. A. 1987. "Klassen und Klassifikationen. Zur 'neuen Unübersichtlichkeit' in der soziologischen Ungleichheitsdiskussion." *KZfSS* 39:59–85.

Berger, P. L., and T. Luckmann. 1969. *Die gesellschaftliche Konstruktion der Wirklichkeit. Eine Theorie der Wissenssoziologie.* Frankfurt am Main. [Originally published as *The Social Construction of Reality* (London, 1967).]

Bergmann, W. 1983. "Das Problem der Zeit in der Soziologie." *KZfSS* 35:462–504.

Bernard, R., and D. Renger. 1984. *Neue Bremm. Ein KZ in Saarbrücken.* Frankfurt am Main.

Bettelheim, B. 1960. *The Informed Heart: Autonomy in a Mass Age.* Glencoe, Ill.

———. 1979. *Surviving and Other Essays.* New York.

Billig, J. 1973. *Les camps de concentration dans l'économie du Reich Hitlerien.* Paris.

Birenbaum, H. 1989. *Die Hoffnung stirbt zuletzt.* Hagen.

Blau, P. M., and W. R. Scott. 1962. *Formal Organization.* San Francisco.

Bleton, P. 1987. *Das Leben ist schön. Überlebensstrategien eines Häftlings im KZ Porta.* Bielefeld.

Boberach, H. 1983. "Die Überführung von Soldaten des Heeres und der Luftwaffe in die SS-Totenkopfverbände zur Bewachung von Konzentrationslagern 1944." *Militärgeschichtliche Mitteilungen* 2, no. 83:185–90.

Bornemann, M. 1971. *Geheimprojekt Mittelbau. Die Geschichte der V-Waffen-Werke.* Munich.

Bornemann, M., and M. Broszat. 1970. "Das KL Dora-Mittelbau." In *Studien zur Geschichte der Konzentrationslager,* 155–98.

Borowski, T. 1982. *Bei uns in Auschwitz. Erzählungen.* Munich.

Bourdieu, P. 1983. "Ökonomisches Kapital, kulturelles Kapital, soziales Kapital." In Kreckel, *Soziale Ungleichheiten,* 183–98.

———. 1987. *Die feinen Unterschiede. Kritik der gesellschaftlichen Urteilskraft.* Frankfurt am Main. [Published in English as *Distinction: A Social Critique of the Judgement of Taste* (London, 1985).]

Brandhuber, J. 1961. "Die sowjetischen Kriegsgefangenen im KL Auschwitz." *HvA* 4: 5–82.

Brandt, H. 1985. *Ein Traum, der nicht entführbar ist. Mein Weg zwischen Ost und West.* Frankfurt am Main.

Bringmann, F. 1981. *KZ Neuengamme. Berichte, Erinnerungen, Dokumente.* Frankfurt am Main.

Brockmeyer, N. 1987. *Antike Sklaverei.* Darmstadt.

Broszat, M. 1967. "Nationalsozialistische Konzentrationslager." In Buchheim et al., *Anatomie des SS-Staates,* 2:11–136.

Broszat, M., and E. Fröhlich, eds. 1979. *Bayern in der NS-Zeit.* 2 vols. Munich.

Buber-Neumann, M. 1949. *Als Gefangene bei Stalin und Hitler.* Munich.

Buchheim, H. 1967a. "Befehl und Gehorsam." In Buchheim et al., *Anatomie des SS-Staates,* 1:215–318.

———. 1967b. "Die SS—das Herrschaftsinstrument." In Buchheim et al., *Anatomie des SS-Staates,* 1:11–212.

Buchheim, H., et al. 1967. *Anatomie des SS-Staates.* 2 vols. Munich. [Published in English as *Anatomy of the SS State* (New York, 1968).]

Burger, A. 1985. *Des Teufels Werkstatt. Im Fälscherkommando des KZ Sachsenhausen.* Berlin.

Busch, R. 1987. "Zur Geschichte der KZ-Außenlager an der Porta Westfalica." In Bleton, *Das Leben ist schön,* 6–14.

Canetti, E. 1984. *Masse und Macht.* Hamburg. [Published in English as *Crowds and Power* (London, 1962).]

Carlebach, E., et al. 1984. *Buchenwald, Ein Konzentrationslager. Bericht der ehemaligen KZ-Häftlinge.* Frankfurt am Main.

Carls, H. 1946. *Dachau. Erinnerungen eines katholischen Geistlichen aus der Zeit seiner Gefangenschaft 1941–1945.* Cologne.

Chalk, E., and K. Jonassohn. 1990. *The History and Sociology of Genocide: Analyses and Case Studies.* New Haven.

Cicourel, A. V. 1973. *Cognitive Sociology: Language and Meaning in Social Interaction.* Harmondsworth, England.

Claussen, D. 1987. *Grenzen der Aufklärung. Zur gesellschaftlichen Geschichte des modernen Antisemitismus.* Frankfurt am Main.

Clemmer, D. 1958. *The Prison Community.* New York.

Cohen, E. A. 1953. *Human Behavior in the Concentration Camp.* New York.

Comité National pur l'érection et la conservation d'un mémorial de la déportation au Struthof, ed. 1982. *KZ Lager Natzweiler-Struthof.* Nancy.

Conquest, R. 1978. *Kolyma: The Arctic Death Camps.* Oxford.

———. 1988. *Ernte des Todes. Stalins Holocaust in der Ukraine 1929–1933.* Munich. [Originally published as *The Harvest of Sorrow: Soviet Collectivization and the Terror-Famine* (New York, 1986).]

Czech, D. 1970. "Deportation und Vernichtung der griechischen Juden im KL Auschwitz." *HvA* 11:5–38.

———. 1989. *Kalendarium der Ereignisse im Konzentrationslager Auschwitz-Birkenau 1939–1945.* Reinbek.

Dam, H. G. von, and R. Giordano, eds. 1962. *KZ-Verbrechen vor deutschen Gerichten.* Frankfurt am Main.

Davis, D. B. 1966. *The Problem of Slavery in Western Culture*. Ithaca, N.Y.

Dawidowicz, L. S. 1987. *The War against the Jews, 1933–45*. London.

Demant, E. 1979. *Auschwitz—Direkt von der Rampe weg. . . .* Reinbek.

Dicks, H. V. 1972. *Licensed Mass Murder: A Socio-Psychological Study of Some SS Killers*. London.

Dieckmann, G. 1968. "Existenzbedingungen und Widerstand im KZ Dora-Mittelbau unter dem Aspekt der funktionellen Einbeziehung der SS in das System der faschistischen Kriegswirtschaft." Ph.D. diss. Berlin.

Diner, D., ed. 1987. *Ist der Nationalsozialismus Geschichte? Zu Historisierung und Historikerstreit*. Frankfurt am Main.

———. 1988. *Zivilisationsbruch. Denken nach Auschwitz*. Frankfurt am Main.

Distel, B. 1985. "Der 29. April 1945. Die Befreiung des Konzentrationslagers Dachau." *DH* 1:3–11.

Dlugoborski, W., ed. 1981. *Zweiter Weltkrieg*. Göttingen.

Donat, A., ed. 1979. *The Death Camp Treblinka: A Documentation*. New York.

Dreitzel, H. P. 1972. *Die gesellschaftlichen Leiden und das Leiden an der Gesellschaft*. Stuttgart.

Drobisch, K. 1978. *Widerstand in Buchenwald*. Frankfurt am Main.

———. 1987. "Frauenkonzentrationslager Lichtenburg." *DH* 3:101–15.

Dülmen, R. von. 1988. *Theater des Schreckens. Gerichtspraxis und Strafrituale in der frühen Neuzeit*. Munich.

Durkheim, E. 1960. *Les formes élémentaires de la vie religieuse*. Paris.

Duster, T. 1973. "Bedingungen für Massenmord ohne Schuldgefühl." In Steinert, *Symbolische Interaktion*, 76–87.

Edvardson, C. 1986. *Gebranntes Kind sucht das Feuer*. Munich.

Eiber, L., ed. 1985. *Verfolgung—Ausbeutung—Vernichtung. Lebens- und Arbeitsbedingungen der Häftlinge in deutschen Konzentrationslagern*. Hannover.

Elias, N. 1984. *Über die Zeit. Arbeiten zur Wissenssoziologie II*. Frankfurt am Main.

———. 1988. *Die Hoffnung erhielt mich am Leben. Mein Weg von Theresienstadt und Auschwitz nach Israel*. Munich.

———. 1989. *Studien über die Deutschen. Machtkämpfe und Habitusentwicklung im 19. und 20. Jahrhundert*. Frankfurt am Main.

Ernst, C., and U. Jensen. 1989. *Als letztes starb die Hoffnung. Berichte von Überlebenden aus dem KZ Neuengamme*. Hamburg.

Ervin-Deutsch, L. 1986. "Nachschicht im Arbeitslager III in Kaufering." *DH* 2: 79–122.

Fassina, P. G. 1962. "Problèmes de l'étude du Camp Bergen-Belsen." *Revue d'histoire de la Deuxième Guerre mondiale* 12:3–43.

Fein, H. 1990. "Genocide: A Sociological Perspective." *Current Sociology* 38, no. 1.

Fenelon, E. 1980. *Das Mädchenorchester von Auschwitz*. Frankfurt am Main.

Ferencz, B. B. 1981. *Lohn des Grauens. Die verweigerte Entschädigung für jüdische Zwangsarbeiter. Ein Kapitel deutscher Nachkriegsgeschichte*. Frankfurt am Main. [Originally published as *Less than Slaves: Jewish Forced Labor and the Quest for Compensation* (Cambridge, Mass., 1979).]

Finckh, P. 1983. "Namenlos—vergessen—verdrängt: Das KZ Oberer Kuhberg Ulm." In Garbe, *Die vergessenen KZs?* 93–96.

Finley, M. L. 1985. *Die Sklaverei in der Antike*. Frankfurt am Main. [Originally published as *Ancient Slavery and Modern Ideology* (New York, 1980).]

Fischer, G. 1973. *Soziale Phänomene in einer Strafanstalt. Eine empirische Studie auf Basis soziometrischer Untersuchungen in den Gemeinschaftszellen*. Hamburg.

Fleischer, H. 1991. "Griechenland." In Benz, *Dimension des Völkermords*, 241–74.

Foucault, M. 1977. *Überwachen und Strafen. Die Geburt des Gefängnisses*. Frankfurt am Main. [Published in English as *Discipline and Punish* (New York, 1979).]

Frankl, V. E. 1982. *. . . trotzdem Ja zum Leben sagen. Ein Psychologe erlebt das KZ.* Munich.

Freud, A. 1977. *Das Ich und die Abwehrmechanismen*. Munich.

Freund, J. 1945. *O Buchenwald*. Klagenfurt, Austria.

Friedländer, S. 1987. "Vom Antisemitismus zur Ausrottung." In Jäckel and Rohwer, *Der Mord an den Juden im Zweiten Weltkrieg*, 18–60.

Fröbe, R., et al. 1985. *Konzentrationslager in Hannover. KZ-Arbeit und Rüstungsindustrie in der Spätphase des Zweiten Weltkrieges*. Hildesheim.

Fromm, E. 1977. *Anatomie der menschlichen Destruktivität*. Reinbek. [Originally published as *The Anatomy of Human Destructiveness* (New York, 1973).]

Fuchs, W. 1973. *Todesbilder in der modernen Gesellschaft*. Frankfurt am Main.

Garbe, D., ed. 1983. *Die vergessenen KZs? Gedenkstätten für die Opfer des NS-Terrors in der Bundesrepublik*. Bornheim-Merten.

Garfinkel, H. 1956. "Conditions of Successful Degradation Ceremonies." *American Journal of Sociology* 61:420–24.

Garlinksi, J. 1975. *Fighting Auschwitz*. Greenwich, Conn.

Geertz, C. 1987. *Dichte Beschreibung. Beiträge zum Verstehen kultureller Systeme*. Frankfurt am Main. [Originally published in part as *The Interpretation of Cultures: Selected Essays* (New York, 1973).]

Gehlen, A. 1977. *Urmensch und Spätkultur. Philosophische Ergebnisse und Aussagen*. Frankfurt am Main.

Gennep, A. von. 1986. *Übergangsriten*. Frankfurt am Main.

Georg, E. 1963. *Die wirtschaftlichen Unternehmungen der SS*. Stuttgart.

Giddens, A. 1984. *The Constitution of Society: Outline of the Theory of Structuration*. Cambridge, England.

Gilbert, M. 1962. *Endlösung. Die Vertreibung und Vernichtung der Juden. Ein Atlas*. Reinbek.

Glazar, R. 1989. "Treblinka—Die Falle mit dem grünen Zaun." *DH* 5:253–76.

Goffman, E. 1961. *Asylums: Essays on the Social Situation of Mental Patients and Other Inmates*. Garden City, N.Y.

———. 1971. *The Presentation of the Self in Everyday Life*. Harmondsworth, England.

———. 1974a. *Frame Analysis: An Essay on the Organization of Experience*. Cambridge, Mass.

———. 1974b. *Das Individuum im öffentlichen Austausch*. Frankfurt am Main. [Originally published as *Relations in Public: Microstudies of the Public Order* (New York, 1971).]

Golczewski, E. 1991. "Polen." In Benz, *Dimension des Völkermords*, 411–98.

Goldstein, J., I. E. Lukoff, and H. A. Strauss. 1991. *Individuelles und kollektives Verhalten in Nazi-Konzentrationslagern. Soziologische und psychologische Studien zu Berichten ungarisch-jüdischer Überlebender*. Frankfurt am Main.

Gorondowski, S. 1986. "Bericht über Mauthausen." *DH* 2:123–32.

Gostner, E. N.d. *1000 Tage im KZ. Ein Erlebnisbericht aus den KL Dachau, Mauthausen und Gusen.* Innsbruck, Austria.

Greif, G. 1995. *"Wir weinten trauenlos. . . ."* Cologne.

Grode, W. 1987. *Die Sonderbehandlung "14f13" in den Konzentrationslagern des Dritten Reichs. Ein Beitrag zur Dynamik faschistischer Vernichtungspolitik.* Frankfurt am Main.

Grosser, A. 1990. *Ermordung der Menschheit. Der Genozid im Gedächtnis der Völker.* Munich.

Grünwiedl, M. 1934. *Dachauer Gefangene erzählen.* Munich.

Gurvitch, G. 1964. *The Spectrum of Social Time.* Dordrecht, the Netherlands.

Haardt, W. D. 1983. "Was denn, hier—in Moringen?" In Garbe, *Die vergessenen KZs?* 97–108.

Halbwachs, M. 1985. *Das kollektive Gedächtnis.* Frankfurt am Main.

Hall, E. T. 1959. *The Silent Language.* Greenwich, Conn.

Hammerich, K., and M. Klein, eds. 1978. *Materialien zur Soziologie des Alltags.* Sonderheft 20, *KZfSS*, 177–219.

Harff, B., and T. R. Gurr. 1988. "Toward Empirical Theory of Genocides and Politicides: Identification and Measurement of Cases since 1945." *International Studies Quarterly* 32, no. 3.

Haug, W. 1986. *Politische Verfolgung. Ein Beitrag zur Soziologie der Herrschaft und der politischen Gewalt.* Grüsch, Switzerland.

Haulot, A. 1985. "Lagertagebuch Januar 1943–Juni 1945." *DH* 1:129–203.

Helbing, F. 1983. *Die Tortur. Geschichte der Folter in Kriminalverfahren aller Zeiten und Völker.* Aalen.

Henkys, R. 1964. *Die nationalsozialistischen Gewaltverbrechen. Geschichte und Gericht.* Stuttgart.

Hennig, E., 1983. *Hessen unterm Hakenkreuz. Studien zur Durchsetzung der NSDAP in Hessen.* Frankfurt am Main.

Hentig, H. von. 1954. *Die Strafe.* Vol. 1: *Frühformen und kulturgeschichtliche Zusammenhänge.* Berlin.

———. 1955. *Die Strafe.* Vol. 2: *Die modernen Erscheinungsformen.* Berlin.

Herbert, U. 1985. *Fremdarbeiter. Politik und Praxis des "Ausländer-Einsatzes" in der Kriegswirtschaft des Dritten Reiches.* Berlin. [Published in English as *Hitler's Foreign Workers: Enforced Foreign Labor under the Third Reich* (Cambridge, 1997).]

———. 1986. "Von Auschwitz nach Essen. Die Geschichte des KZ-Außenlagers Humboldtstraße." *DH* 2:13–34.

———. 1987. "Arbeit und Vernichtung. Ökonomisches Interesse und Primat der 'Weltanschauung' im Nationalsozialismus." In Diner, *Ist der Nationalsozialismus Geschichte?* 198–236.

———. 1990. *A History of Foreign Labor in Germany, 1880–1980.* Ann Arbor, Mich.

Heydenburg, M. R. 1990. "Der Alptraum der Ordnung. Die Mentalität der Wachmannschaften in den nationalsozialistischen Konzentrationslagern." Master's thesis. University of Göttingen.

Hilberg, R. 1982. *Die Vernichtung der europäischen Juden. Die Geschichte des Holocaust.* Berlin. [Originally published as *The Destruction of the European Jews* (Chicago, 1961).]

―――. 1987. *Sonderzüge nach Auschwitz*. Frankfurt am Main. [Originally published as *The Role of the German Railroads in the Destruction of the Jews* (Chicago?, 1976).]

Hirschfeld, G. 1991. "Niederlande." In Benz, *Dimension des Völkermords*, 137–66.

Historikerstreit. 1987. *Eine Dokumentation der Kontroverse um die Einzigartigkeit der nationalsozialistischen Judenvernichtung*. Munich.

Höhne, H. 1984. *Der Orden unter dem Totenkopf. Die Geschichte der SS*. Munich.

Höß, R. 1983. *Kommandant in Auschwitz*. Ed. M. Broszat. Munich. [Published in English as *Commandant of Auschwitz* (London, 1959).]

Hoffmann, R. W. 1981. *Arbeitskampf im Arbeitsalltag. Formen, Perspektiven und gewerkschaftspolitische Probleme des verdeckten industriellen Konflikts*. Frankfurt am Main.

Hopp, J., and G. Petersen. 1987. *Die Hölle in der Idylle. Das Außenkommando Alt Garge des KZ Neuengamme*. Hamburg.

Hoppensack, H. C. 1976. *Über die Strafanstalt und ihre Wirkung auf Einstellung und Verhalten von Gefangenen*. Göttingen.

Hradil, S. 1987. *Sozialstrukturanalyse in einer fortgeschrittenen Gesellschaft*. Opladen.

Hrdlicka, M. R. 1991. *Alltag im KZ. Das Lager Sachsenhausen bei Berlin*. Opladen.

Hüser, K. 1982. *Wewelsburg 1933–1945. Kult- und Terrorstätte der SS. Eine Dokumentation*. Paderborn.

"Inmitten des grauenvollen Verbrechens" 1972. "Handschriften von Mitgliedern des Sonderkommandos." *HvA*, Sonderheft 1.

Internationales Buchenwald-Komitee, ed. 1961. *Buchenwald. Mahnung und Verpflichtung*. Berlin.

Iwaszko, T. 1964. "Häftlingsfluchten aus dem KL Auschwitz." *HvA* 7:3–58.

―――. 1967. "Das Nebenlager Laurahütte." *HvA* 10:87–101.

Jäckel, E., and J. Rohwer, eds. 1987. *Der Mord an den Juden im Zweiten Weltkrieg. Entschlußbildung und Verwirklichung*. Frankfurt am Main.

Jäger, H. 1982. *Verbrechen unter totalitärer Herrschaft. Studien zur nationalsozialistischen Gewaltkriminalität*. Frankfurt am Main.

―――. 1989. *Makrokriminalität. Studien zur Kriminologie kollektiver Gewalt*. Frankfurt am Main.

Jagoda, Z., S. Klodzinski, and J. Maslowski. 1987a. "Das Überleben im Lager aus der Sicht ehemaliger Häftlinge von Auschwitz-Birkenau." *AH* 1:13–51. Weinheim-Basel.

―――. 1987b. "Opfer und Peiniger." *AH* 1:53–87. Weinheim-Basel.

―――. 1987c. "'Bauernfuß, goldzupa, himmelautostrada'. Zum Krematoriumsesperanto, der Sprache polnischer KZ-Häftlinge." *AH* 2:241–60. Weinheim-Basel.

―――. 1987d. "Selbsthilfe und 'Volksmedizin' im Konzentrationslager." *AH* 2: 149–87. Weinheim-Basel.

Jahn, E. 1990. "Zur Phänomenologie der Massenvernichtung. Kolyma, Auschwitz, Hiroshima und der potentielle nukleare Holocaust." *Leviathan* 18:7–38.

Johe, W. 1970. "Das KL Neuengamme." In *Studien zur Geschichte der Konzentrationslager*, 29–49.

Johe, W. 1981. *Neuengamme. Zur Geschichte des Konzentrationslagers in Hamburg*. Hamburg.

Kaienburg, H. 1991. *"Vernichtung durch Arbeit". Der Fall Neuengamme. Die Wirtschaftsbestrebungen der SS und ihre Auswirkungen auf die Existenzbedingungen der KZ-Gefangenen.* Bonn.

Kaiser, P. M. 1975. "Monopolprofit und Massenmord im Faschismus. Zur ökonomischen Funktion der Konzentrations- und Vernichtungslager im faschistischen Deutschland." *Blätter für deutsche und internationale Politik* 5:552–77.

Kaminski, A. J. 1982. *Konzentrationslager 1896 bis heute. Eine Analyse.* Stuttgart.

Kárný, M. 1986. "Waffen-SS und Konzentrationslager." *Jahrbuch für Geschichte* 33:231–62.

————. 1987. "'Vernichtung durch Arbeit'. Sterblichkeit in den Konzentrationslagern." *Beiträge zur nationalsozialistischen Gesundheits- und Sozialpolitik.* Vol. 5: *Sozialpolitik und Judenvernichtung*, 133–58. Berlin.

Kautsky, B. 1948. *Teufel und Verdammte. Erfahrungen und Erkenntnisse aus sieben Jahren Konzentrationslager.* Vienna.

Keller, G. 1981. *Die Psychologie der Folter.* Frankfurt am Main.

Kielar, W. 1982. *Anus Mundi. Fünf Jahre Auschwitz.* Frankfurt am Main.

Kimmel, G. 1979. "Das Konzentrationslager Dachau. Eine Studie zu den nationalsozialistischen Gewaltverbrechen." In Broszat and Fröhlich, *Bayern in der NS-Zeit*, 2:349–414.

Kirstein, W. 1992. *Das Konzentrationslager als Institution totalen Terrors. Das Beispiel des KL Natzweiler.* Pfaffenweiler.

Klawe, W. 1987. *"Im übrigen herrscht Zucht und Ordnung. . .". Zur Geschichte des Konzentrationslagers Wittmoor.* Hamburg.

Klee, E. 1983. *"Euthanasie" im NS-Staat. Die "Vernichtung unwerten Lebens".* Frankfurt am Main.

Klodzinksi, S. 1987. "Phenol." *AH* 1: Weinheim-Basel, 277–80.

Kogon, E. 1974. *Der SS-Staat. Das System der deutschen Konzentrationslager.* 13th ed. Munich. [Published in English as *The Theory and Practice of Hell: The Concentration Camps and the System Behind Them* (New York, 1950).]

Kogon, E., et al., eds. 1986. *Nationalsozialistische Massentötungen durch Giftgas.* Frankfurt am Main.

Kohn, S. 1945. *Opstand in Treblinka.* Amsterdam.

Kolb, E. 1962. *Bergen-Belsen. Geschichte des "Aufenthaltslagers" 1943–1945.* Hannover.

————. 1985. *Bergen-Belsen 1943–1945.* Göttingen.

Komitee der antifaschistischen Widerstands Kämpfer der DDR, ed. 1982. *Sachsenhausen.* Frankfurt am Main.

Kon, I. S. 1979. *Freundschaft.* Reinbek.

Konau, E. 1977. *Raum und soziales Handeln. Studien zu einer vernachlässigten Dimension soziologischer Theoriebildung.* Stuttgart.

Konieczny, A. 1989. "Das Konzentrationslager Groß-Rosen." *DH* 5:15–27.

Konzentrationslager. 1988. *Dokument F 321 für den Internationalen Militärgerichtshof Nürnberg*, Frankfurt am Main.

Kosthorst, E., and B. Walter. 1985. *Konzentrations- und Strafgefangenenlager im Emsland 1933–1945. Zum Verhältnis von NS-Regime und Justiz. Darstellung und Dokumentation.* Düsseldorf.

Krause-Vilmar, D. 1983. "Das Konzentrationslager Breitenau 1933–1934." In Hennig, *Hessen unterm Hakenkreuz*, 469–89.

Kreckel, R., ed. 1983. *Soziale Ungleichheiten*. Sonderheft 2, *Soziale Welt*. Göttingen.

Kruse, L. 1975) "Crowding—Dichte und Enge aus sozialpsychologischer Sicht." *Zeitschrift für Sozialpsychologie*. 6:2–30.

———. 1980. *Privatheit als Problem und Gegenstand der Psychologie*. Bern.

Kruse, L., and C. F. Graumann. 1978. "Sozialpsychologie des Raumes und der Bewegung." In Hammerich and Klein, *Materialien zur Soziologie des Alltags*, 177–219.

Kupfer-Koberwitz, E. 1957. *Die Mächtigen und die Hilflosen. Als Häftling in Dachau*. Stuttgart.

Kuss, H. 1989. "Aussonderung, Konzentration, Vernichtung. Zur Geschichte der nationalsozialistischen Konzentrationslager und der Vernichtung des europäischen Judentums. Ergebnisse und Fragen der zeitgeschichtlichen Forschung seit 1981." *Neue Politische Literatur* 34:375–408.

KZ-Museum Dachau. 1978. *Katalog des KZ-Museums Dachau*. Munich.

Laks, S., and R. Coudy. 1948. *Musique d'un autre monde*. Paris.

Langbein, H. 1949. *Die Stärkeren—ein Bericht*. Vienna.

———. 1965. *Der Auschwitz-Prozeß. Eine Dokumentation*. Vienna.

———. 1980a. *Menschen in Auschwitz*. Frankfurt am Main.

———. 1980b. *. . . nicht wie die Schafe zur Schlachtbank. Widerstand in den nationalsozialistischen Konzentrationslagern*. Frankfurt am Main.

———. 1986. "Arbeit im KZ-System." *DH* 2:3–12.

Langhoff, W. 1935. *Die Moorsoldaten, 13 Monate Konzentrationslager*. Zürich.

Lanzmann, C. 1986. *Shoah*. Düsseldorf.

Laqueur, W. 1983. *Bergen-Belsen-Tagebuch 1944/45*. Hannover.

Lautmann, R., W. Grikschat, and E. Schmidt. 1977. "Der rosa Winkel in den nationalsozialistischen Konzentrationslagern." In Lautmann, ed., *Seminar: Gesellschaft und Homosexualität*, 325–65. Frankfurt am Main.

Lechner, S. 1988. *Das KZ Oberer Kuhberg und die NS-Zeit in der Region Ulm/Neu-Ulm*. Stuttgart.

Leder, K. B. 1986. *Die Todesstrafe. Ursprung, Geschichte, Opfer*. Munich.

Levi, P. 1989. *The Drowned and the Saved*. New York. [Originally published as *Sommersi e i salvati* (Turin, 1986).]

———. 1993. *Survival in Auschwitz*. New York. [Originally published as *Se questo e un uomo* (Turin, 1958).]

Lévy-Hass, H. 1979. *Vielleicht war das alles erst der Anfang. Tagebuch aus dem KZ Bergen-Belsen*. Berlin.

Lichtenstein, H. 1979. *Majdanek. Reportage eines Prozesses*. Frankfurt am Main.

Lifton, R. J. 1986. *The Nazi Doctors: Medical Killing and the Psychology of Genocide*. New York.

Lingens-Reiner, E. 1966. *Eine Frau im Konzentrationslager*. Vienna.

Löffler, R., and W. Sofsky. 1986. *Macht, Arbeit und Humanität. Zur Pathologie organisierter Arbeitssituationen*. Göttingen.

Löwenthal, L. 1988. "Individuum und Terror." In Diner, *Zivilisationsbruch*, 15–25.

Longerich, P., ed. 1989. *Die Ermordung der europäischen Juden*. Munich.

Lundholm, A. 1988. *Das Höllentor. Bericht einer Überlebenden*. Reinbek.

Lyman, S. M., and M. B. Scott. 1970. *A Sociology of the Absurd*. New York.

Mannheimer, M. 1985. "Theresienstadt—Auschwitz—Warschau—Dachau. Erinnerungen." *DH* 1:88–128.

Marsalek, H. 1980. *Die Geschichte des Konzentrationslagers Mauthausen*. Vienna.

———. 1987. *Konzentrationslager Gusen*. Vienna.

Marszalek, J. 1982. *Majdanek. Geschichte und Wirklichkeit des Vernichtungslagers*. Reinbek.

Matejka, V. 1984. *Widerstand ist alles. Notizen eines Unorthodoxen*. Vienna.

Matussek, P. 1971. *Die Konzentrationslagerhaft und ihre Folgen*. Berlin.

Meier, C. 1987. *Vierzig Jahre nach Auschwitz. Deutsche Geschichtserinnerung heute*. Munich.

Meier, H. C. 1946. *So war es. Das Leben im Konzentrationslager Neuengamme*. Hamburg.

Michelet, E. 1960. *Die Freiheitsstraße, Dachau 1943–1945*. Stuttgart.

Milward, A. S. 1966. *Die deutsche Kriegswirtschaft 1939–1945*. Stuttgart. [Originally published as *The German Economy at War* (New York, 1965).]

Mitscherlich, A., and E. Mielke, eds. 1978. *Medizin ohne Menschlichkeit. Dokumente des Nürnberger Ärzteprozesses*. Frankfurt am Main.

Moore, B. 1978. *Injustice: The Social Bases of Obedience and Revolt*. New York.

Moscovici, S. 1986. *Das Zeitalter der Massen*. Frankfurt am Main.

Müller, F. 1979. *Sonderbehandlung. Drei Jahre in den Krematorien und Gaskammern von Auschwitz*. Munich.

Müller-Münch, I. 1982. *Die Frauen von Majdanek. Vom zerstörten Leben der Opfer und der Mörderinnen*. Reinbek.

Nansen, O. 1949. *Von Tag zu Tag—ein Tagebuch*. Hamburg.

Naujoks, H. 1987. *Mein Leben im KZ Sachsenhausen 1936–1942. Erinnerungen des ehemaligen Lagerältesten*. Cologne.

Novitch, M. 1980. *Sobibor: Martyrdom and Revolt*. New York.

Oschlies, W. 1986. "Lagerszpracha. Zu Theorie und Empirie einer KZ-spezifischen Soziolinguistik." *Zeitgeschichte* 13:1–27.

Pachaly, E., and K. Pelny. 1990. *KZ Mittelbau-Dora. Zum antifaschistischen Widerstandskampf im KZ Dora 1943–1945*. Berlin.

Paczula, T. 1987. "Organisation und Verwaltung des ersten Häftlingskrankenbaus in Auschwitz." *AH* 1:Weinheim-Basel, 159–65.

Paris, R., and W. Sofsky. 1987. "Drohungen. Über eine Methode der Interaktionsmacht." *KZfSS* 39:15–39.

Parkin, F. 1983. "Strategien sozialer Schließung und Klassenbildung." In Kreckel, *Soziale Ungleichheiten*, 121–35.

Pawelczynska, A. 1981. "Differenzierung der Häftlingsgemeinschaft und Überlebenschancen im KZ Auschwitz." In Dlugoborski, *Zweiter Weltkrieg*, 171–83.

Pawlak, Z. 1979. *Ich habe überlebt—Ein Häftling berichtet über Majdanek*. Hamburg.

Pechersky, A. 1968. "Revolt in Sobibor." In Suhl, *They Fought Back*.

Pingel, E. 1978. *Häftlinge unter SS-Herrschaft. Widerstand, Selbstbehauptung und Vernichtung in Konzentrationslagern*. Hamburg.

Piper, F. 1991. "Estimating the Number of Deportees to and Victims of the Auschwitz-Birkenau Camp." *Yad Vashem Studies* 21:49–103.

Pisar, S. 1979. *Das Blut der Hoffnung*. Reinbek.

Pohlmann, F. 1992. *Ideologie und Terror im Nationalsozialismus.* Pfaffenweiler.

Pollak, M. 1988. *Die Grenze des Sagbaren. Lebensgeschichten von KZ-Überlebenden als Augenzeugenberichte und Identitätsarbeit.* Frankfurt am Main.

Poller, W. 1946. *Arztschreiber in Buchenwald.* Hamburg.

Popitz, H. 1968. *Prozesse der Machtbildung.* Tübingen.

———. 1986. *Phänomene der Macht.* Tübingen.

Popitz, H., et al. 1957. *Technik und Industriearbeit.* Tübingen.

Postel-Vinay, A. 1987. "Eine junge Französin im Krieg." *DH* 3:77–100.

Pozner, V. 1982. *Abstieg in die Hölle. Zeugnisse über Auschwitz.* Berlin.

Pross, H., and E. Buß. 1984. *Soziologie der Masse.* Heidelberg.

Puchert, B. 1963. "Aus der Praxis der IG Farben in Auschwitz-Monowitz." *Jahrbuch für Wirtschaftsgeschichte* 2:203–11.

Rabitsch, G. 1970. "Das KL Mauthausen." In *Studien zur Geschichte der Konzentrationslager,* 50–92.

Raim, E. 1989. "Unternehmen Ringeltaube. Dachaus Außenlagerkomplex Kaufering." *DH* 5:193–213.

———. 1992. *Die Dachauer KZ-Außenkommandos Kaufering und Mühldorf. Rüstungsbauten und Zwangsarbeit im letzten Kriegsjahr 1944/45.* Landsberg.

Rammstedt, O. 1975. "Alltagsbewußtsein von Zeit." *KZfSS* 27:47–63.

Rashke, R. 1982. *Escape from Sobibor.* Boston.

Richardi, H. G. 1983. *Schule der Gewalt. Die Anfänge des Konzentrationslagers Dachau 1933–1934. Ein dokumentarischer Bericht.* Munich.

Rose, R., and R. Weiss. 1991. *Sinti und Roma im "Dritten Reich". Das Programm der Vernichtung durch Arbeit.* Göttingen.

Rosenberg, H. 1985. *Jahre des Schreckens ... und ich blieb übrig, daß ich Dir's ansage.* Göttingen.

Rosh, L., and E. Jäckel. 1990. *"Der Tod ist ein Meister aus Deutschland". Deportation und Ermordung der Juden. Kollaboration und Verweigerung in Europa.* Hamburg.

Rousset, D. 1946. *L'univers concentrationnaire.* Paris.

Rovan, J. 1989. *Geschichten aus Dachau.* Stuttgart.

Rückerl, A. 1977. *NS-Vernichtungslager.* Munich.

Ruffié, J., and J. C. Sournia. 1987. *Die Seuchen in der Geschichte der Menschheit.* Stuttgart.

Rummel, R. 1990. *Lethal Politics: Soviet Genocide and Mass Murder since 1917.* New Brunswick, N.J.

Ryn, Z., and S. Klodzinski. 1987a. "An der Grenze zwischen Leben und Tod. Eine Studie über die Erscheinung des 'Muselmanns' im Konzentrationslager." *AH* 1: Weinheim-Basel, 89–154.

———. 1987b. "Tod und Sterben im Konzentrationslager." *AH* 1: Weinheim-Basel, 281–328.

Sachsenhausen Komitee West-Berlin, et al. 1984. *Niemand und nichts vergessen. Ehemalige Häftlinge aus verschiedenen Ländern berichten über das KZ Sachsenhausen.* Berlin.

Sartre, J.-P. 1967. *Kritik der dialektischen Vernunft.* Reinbek. [Published in English as *The Critique of Dialectical Reason* (London, 1976).]

Schätzle, J. 1974. *Stationen zur Hölle. Konzentrationslager in Baden und Württemberg 1933–1945.* Frankfurt am Main.

Scheffler, W. 1987. "Chelmno, Sobibór, Belzec und Majdanek." In Jäckel and Rohwer, *Der Mord an den Juden im Zweiten Weltkrieg*, 145–51.

Schmied, G. 1985. *Soziale Zeit. Umfang, "Geschwindigkeit" und Evolution*. Berlin.

Schnabel, R. 1957. *Macht ohne Moral. Eine Dokumentation über die SS*, Frankfurt am Main.

———. 1966. *Die Frommen in der Hölle. Geistliche in Dachau*. Frankfurt am Main.

Schütz, A., and T. Luckmann. 1975. *Strukturen der Lebenswelt*. Neuwied. [Originally published as *The Structures of the Life-World* (London, 1974).]

Schwarz, G. 1990. *Die nationalsozialistischen Lager*. Frankfurt am Main.

Segev, T. 1992. *Die Soldaten des Bösen. Zur Geschichte der KZ-Kommandanten*. Reinbek.

Semprun, J. 1981. *Die große Reise*. Frankfurt am Main.

———. 1984. *Was für ein schöner Sonntag*. Frankfurt am Main.

Sereny, G. 1974. *Am Abgrund*. Frankfurt am Main. [Originally published as *Into that Darkness: from Mercy Killing to Mass Murder* (New York, 1974).]

Siegert, T. 1979. "Das Konzentrationslager Flossenbürg. Ein Lager für sogenannte Asoziale und Kriminelle." In Broszat and Fröhlich, *Bayern in der NS-Zeit*, 2:429–94.

Siegert, T. 1986. *Dreißigtausend Tote mahnen! Die Geschichte des Konzentrationslagers Flossenbürg und seiner hundert Außenlager von 1938 bis 1945*. Weiden.

Sigel, R. 1988. "Heilkräuterkulturen im KZ. Die Plantage in Dachau." *DH* 4:164–73.

Simmel, G. 1968. *Soziologie*. Berlin.

Smelser, N. 1972. *Theorie des kollektiven Verhaltens*. Cologne. [Originally published as *Theory of Collective Behavior* (New York, 1963).]

Sofsky, W. 1983. *Die Ordnung sozialer Situationen*. Opladen.

———. 1988. "Vom Verschwinden des Grauens. Eine Reise durch Deutschland." *Neue Rundschau* 4:19–40.

———. 1990. "Absolute Macht. Zur Soziologie des Konzentrationslagers." *Leviathan* 18:518–35.

Sofsky, W., and R. Paris. 1991. *Figurationen sozialer Macht. Autorität, Stellvertretung, Koalition*. Opladen.

Solzhenitsyn, A. 1975. *The Gulag Archipelago*. New York.

Spittler, G. 1967. *Norm und Sanktion. Untersuchungen zum Sanktionsmechanismus*. Olten, Switzerland.

Stein, G. W. 1967. *Geschichte der Waffen-SS*. Düsseldorf.

Steiner, J. F. 1979. *Treblinka*. New York.

Steinert, H., ed. 1973. *Symbolische Interaktion*. Stuttgart.

Steinhagen, H. 1976. *Die informelle Sozialstruktur einer Gefangenengemeinschaft*. Göttingen.

Stokes, L. 1979. "Das Eutiner Schutzhaftlager 1933. Zur Geschichte eines 'wilden' Konzentrationslagers." *VfZ* (4):570–625.

Stokols, D. 1972. "On the Distinction between Density and Crowding." *Psychological Review* 79:275–77.

Streim, A. 1989. "Konzentrationslager auf dem Gebiet der Sowjetunion." *DH* 5: 174–87.

Streit, C. 1978. *Keine Kameraden. Die Wehrmacht und die sowjetischen Kriegsgefangenen 1941 bis 1945*. Stuttgart.

Studien zur Geschichte der Konzentrationslager. 1970. Stuttgart.

Stuldreher, C. L. 1989. "Deutsche Konzentrationslager in den Niederlanden. Amersfoort, Westerbork, Herzogenbusch." *DH* 5:141–73.

Suhl, Y., 1968. *They Fought Back.* New York.

Suhr, E. 1985. *Die Emslandlager. Die politische und wirtschaftliche Bedeutung der emsländischen Konzentrations- und Strafgefangenenlager 1933–1945.* Bremen.

Suter, D. 1983. *Rechtsauflösung durch Angst und Schrecken. Zur Dynamik des Terrors im totalitären System.* Berlin.

Sydnor, C. W. 1977. *Soldiers of Destruction: The SS Death's Head Division, 1933–1945.* Princeton.

Szymanski, T., D. Szymanska, and T. Snieszko. 1980. "Das 'Spital' im Zigeuner-Familienlager in Auschwitz-Birkenau." *AH* 1: Weinheim-Basel, 199–208.

Tenbruck, F. 1964. "Freundschaft. Ein Beitrag zu einer Soziologie der persönlichen Beziehung." *KZfSS* 16:431–56.

Timpke, H. 1970. "Das KL Fuhlsbüttel." In *Studien zur Geschichte der Konzentrationslager*, 11–28.

Tuchel, J. 1991. *Konzentrationslager. Organisationsgeschichte und Funktion der "Inspektion der Konzentrationslager", 1934–1938.* Boppard.

Turner, V. 1969. *The Ritual Process: Structure and Anti-Structure.* Chicago.

Vaupel, D. 1984. *Das Außenkommando Hessisch-Lichtenau des Konzentrationslagers Buchenwald 1944–1945.* Kassel.

Veblen, T. 1986. *Theorie der feinen Leute. Eine ökonomische Untersuchung der Institutionen*, Frankfurt am Main. [Originally published as *Theory of the Leisure Class* (New York, 1899).]

Vermehren, I. 1946. *Reise durch den letzten Akt.* Hamburg.

Vogt, H. 1983. *KZ Moringen—Männerlager, Frauenlager, Jugendschutzlager. Eine Dokumentation.* Göttingen.

Vorländer, H., et al. 1978. *Nationalsozialistische Konzentrationslager im Dienst der totalen Kriegsführung—Sieben württembergische Außenkommandos des KZ Natzweiler/Elsaß.* Stuttgart.

Vrba, R., and A. Bestic. 1964. *Ich kann nicht vergeben.* Munich. [Originally published as *I Cannot Forgive* (New York, 1964).]

Weber, M. 1972. *Wirtschaft und Gesellschaft.* Tübingen.

Wegner, B. 1982. *Hitlers politische Soldaten. Die Waffen-SS 1933–1945.* Paderborn.

Wehler, H. U. 1988. *Entsorgung der deutschen Vergangenheit? Ein polemischer Essay zum "Historikerstreit".* Munich.

Weinmann, M., ed. 1990. *Das nationalsozialistische Lagersystem (CCP).* Frankfurt am Main.

Weiß, H. 1985. "Dachau und die internationale Öffentlichkeit. Reaktionen auf die Befreiung des Lagers." *DH* 1:12–38.

Weiß-Rüthel, A. 1949. *Nacht und Nebel. Ein Sachsenhausen-Buch.* Berlin.

Wetzel, J. 1991. "Frankreich und Belgien." In Benz, *Dimension des Völkermords*, 105–36.

Wiechert, E. 1980. *Der Totenwald.* Frankfurt am Main.

Wiernik, J. 1979. "One Year in Treblinka." In Donat, *Death Camp Treblinka*, 147–88.

Wiese, L. von. 1933. *System der allgemeinen Soziologie.* Munich.

Wiesel, E. 1985. *Night/Dawn/Day.* New York.

———. 1995. "Stay Together, Always." *Newsweek*, January 16, 1995.

Willenberg, S. 1961. "Revolt in Treblinka." *Yad Vashem Bulletin* (Jerusalem) 8–9.

Wollenberg, J. 1982. "Vom Auswandererlager zum KZ. Zur Geschichte des Bremer Konzentrationslagers Missler." *Beiträge zur Sozialgeschichte Bremens* 1, no. 5: 85–150.

Wormser-Migot, O. 1968. *Le système concentrationnaire Nazi (1933–1945)*. Paris.

Wysocki, G. 1982. *Zwangsarbeit im Stahlkonzern. Salzgitter und die Reichswerke "Hermann Göring" 1937–1945*. Brunswick.

———. 1986. "Häftlingsarbeit in der Rüstungsproduktion. Das Konzentrationslager Drütte bei den Hermann-Göring-Werken in Watenstedt-Salzgitter." *DH* 2:35–67.

Zámečnik, S. 1988. "Erinnerungen an das 'Revier' im Konzentrationslager Dachau." *DH* 4:128–43.

Zerubavel, E. 1976. "Timetables and Scheduling: On the Social Organization of Time." *Sociological Inquiry* 46:87–94.

Ziegler, J. 1986. *Mitten unter uns. Natzweiler-Struthof: Spuren eines Konzentrationslagers*. Hamburg.

Zimmermann, M. 1990. "From Discrimination to the 'Family Camp' at Auschwitz. National Socialist Persecution of the Gypsies." *Dachau Review* 2:87–113.

Zörner, G., et al. 1982. *Frauen-KZ Ravensbrück*. Frankfurt am Main.

Zofka, Z. 1986. "Allach—Sklaven für BMW. Zur Geschichte eines Außenlagers des KZ Dachau." *DH* 2:68–78.

Zumpe, L. 1969. "Die Textilbetriebe der SS im Konzentrationslager Ravensbrück." *Jahrbuch für Wirtschaftsgeschichte* 1:11–40.

Zywulska, K. 1988. *Tanz, Mädchen . . . Vom Warschauer Ghetto nach Auschwitz*. Munich.